"Think like a philosopher, pray like a priest, create like an artist, strategize like a corporate executive, and fight like a samurai!"

— Michael A. Johnson, on the role of the Principal

D0503330

7

Preface

This book represents a compilation of the lesson plan objectives' notes from my Teacher to Assistant Principal (AP) and AP to Principal courses that I taught as Superintendent of Community School District 29 in Queens, New York (CSD29Q). It also serves as the working textbook from many years of being a principal and superintendent. During my time as superintendent, I was appointing, mentoring, professionally developing, supervising, evaluating/rating, and unfortunately, in some cases, removing school principals from their positions. This book is about defining the best practices of an effective school-based leader (SBL), the principal. And although the ideas and strategies presented can be applied and adapted to any school level, I am specifically focusing on the work and mission of the high school principal. Through my experience as a teacher, principal, and superintendent, I have learned that the principal's position represents one of the most important determining factors of a school's success. For sure, there is no one single member of a school's staff who can exert the amount of influence and power to push a school in one direction or another. Because of the unique culminating and concluding role a high school plays in the K-12 educational system, the high school principal-ship carries with it a unique and complicated job description. Now, SBLs at the pre-K to early childhood, elementary, and middle school levels carry with them their own organizational challenges, but high school represents the "last stop" on the K-12 education journey. High school is our last shot to correct and/or fill any skill or knowledge gap the young person will need to survive in the world to realize a positive and productive adult life. While the leadership lessons presented here are focused on high schools, they can be easily translated and transferred to the equally important leadership challenges and work that is required in the leadership for pre-K through middle school.

The 30 chapters in this book represent the critical areas of concern that constitute the daily life of a high school principal. At every moment, with every decision and action taken, multiple and overlapping issues that relate to these 30 topic areas are in serious play. A principal's mastery and effectiveness are essentially measured by his or her ability to demonstrate a high level of knowledge and skills competency in these areas of leadership.

An executive VP of a well-known multinational corporation who was participating in the NYC Department of Education's then "Principal for a Day" program spent a day partnering with me as the honorary principal of Science Skills Center High School (SSCHS) in Brooklyn, New York. We debriefed in my office at the end of the day, at which time he commented, "I am just blown away. I will never think of public high schools in the same way. I just don't know how you do it. You are called on to play so many different roles, with so many different people, in the course of a single day's work. This more than matches the intensity and pressures faced by any of our top executives."

And my response to him was, "Actually, sir, this was a rather uneventful and quiet day!"

I had a similar experience at Phelps Architecture, Construction and Engineering High School in Washington, D.C. A District of Columbia Public Schools (DCPS) official who had a prominent military leadership background, former U.S. Army General Anthony Tata, remarked to me after visiting Phelps: "You remind me of the most effective and successful commanders I saw in the war—those battlefield leaders who both followed the rules but also creatively 'amended' the rules when the conditions required an approach that the central command could not see because of their distance from the heat and reality of the battle."

These two insightful views, unfortunately, are often the exceptions to the general misconceptions about the nature and role of the principalship. We have been told for so many years that public schools should adopt the organizational cultural practices that are found in the private industry arena, or the military. And for sure, as I point out in this book, the most effective principals will design a leadership approach that draws from the organizational practices of both the profit and nonprofit sectors, the military, marketing, sports, the creative and performing arts, social and industrial psychology, science and engineering research, etc. But with this book, I am also asserting that the unique mission and work of public education provides us with an opportunity to present our contribution to the conversation and studies of executive management leadership; after all, the overwhelming majority of the most influential and successful leaders in the world had to be influenced and made successful at some point in a school.

In my many years in educational leadership, I have learned there is one consistent and universal truism about the role of the public school principal: *Just about everybody, both inside and outside of the school building, will know more about your job and how to do it better than you can!* The truth is that most people, including many professional educators, don't have a clue about the real challenges, specification of duties, knowledge, and skills requirements associated with the principal's position. This book seeks to uncover and make sense of a profession that impacts the lives of so many citizens of every nation in the world.

For many years, I worked hard to explain these job requirements, utilizing an easily understandable linguistic format for people to understand. This was often done for parents and teachers who serve on School Principal Selection Committees. This book could serve as a standards and rubrics guide to inform these committees on what to look for when selecting a new principal. After having served on many of these committees, I can honestly say that there is a critical need to help parents, teachers, and communities to get the best information in order to answer two essential questions: (1) What are the attributes of an effective principal? (2) Who would be the most effective principal for their school?

Public schools have been under a strange attack over the last two decades. I say *strange* because of the fact that, for a cultural institution whose very reason for being is learning, there has been a hostile takeover by folks who say that knowing, learning, and experience are not skills that are required to teach, lead a school, or run a school district. Poor children and children of color (as is always true historically in the U.S.) have borne the brunt of this ill-informed idea. We find that children who are in the most need of expert, knowledgeable, and experienced teachers and school-based educational leaders are overexposed to ill-equipped and untrained, noncertified educators. There is a false belief that the knowledge and skills required to be a school principal can be easily transferrable from other fields (e.g., fast-food restaurant management). This misguided error ignores the importance of the professional expertise and training required for the principal's position, but it also ignores the critical importance of public schooling itself. The consequences of educational policymakers recklessly experimenting and playing games with children who are in the greatest need of a good and effective educational experience has also led to the diminishing respect for the profession and all of its practitioners, not just principals.

Tragically, for the majority of schools on the receiving end of this "school reform experiment" approach, it has meant permanent intellectual and spiritual damage to their children, thus harming their chances for a positive and productive adult life. This book aims to establish that supervision and leadership in any legitimate profession requires knowledge of the art and science of that profession, in our case pedagogy, and that specific school leadership-management skills and techniques, along with formal licensing and certification, are essential requirements for anyone aspiring to the principalship.

For the principal who is presently in place, my objective is to present a system of standards and accompanying rubrics that would help him or her to understand the real attributes of a good principal as well as a good and effective school. I am also asserting through this book that "good" and "effective" are processes and journeys, not destinations—the point being that the most important contrast and comparison you should think about as a principal is how each year your school competes with its own previous school year.

This book is a knowledge and skills mastery check-off guide for teachers and APs aspiring to become school building principals. And, perhaps most importantly for the sake of students (and your emotional well-being), it provides insight on whether the principalship is truly the educational role to which these teachers and APs are truly called.

Both my principal and superintendent's experience has unfortunately taught me that some communities—along with their civic, religious, and political leaders—do not have access to the information that would help them to define, recognize, understand, and, ultimately, defend an effective school principal. Defining, knowing, and defending a good school is even more complex and difficult. This book—utilizing as little education jargon as possible— attempts to close that information gap between "entitled" and "unentitled" communities/parents concerning the attributes of an effective principal and the profile of a good school.

Finally, one of the objectives of this book is to help present or future parents of a high school student to at least know and understand the fundamental workings of a high school. If a school and its principal are effective, then that means on a daily basis the principal is often operating outside of the district's political "shenanigans," the rules and regulations, and the limited systemic expectations of the school system. As I learned as a superintendent, parents and a well-informed community can play an important role in protecting and keeping a good principal. A great deal of what parents should know about their child's school and principal being effective is obscured in the language and bureaucratic fogginess of public education rituals and practices. With this book, I want to lift the cloud that prevents parents from fully understanding where their child is spending this important life-determining high school daily experience.

What this book is and is not

Although this book contains a great deal of my personal and professional autobiographical life story, it is not an autobiography.

I want to link many of the ideas in this book to real people, places, educational situations, problems, challenges, and events that actually occurred in school districts and buildings. Throughout the book, I offer real examples from my experiences as a principal and supervisor (superintendent) of principals; these sample incidents bring to light the many public education school leadership hits and misses. But more importantly, I provide examples of the best practices displayed by the successful principals I have met in my career. I also want to bring to the public's attention the chronic and hidden underperformance of schools that are thought to be high-performing. With this book, I hope to invite a more creative and thoughtful evaluation system that would measure a school and its principal's own capacity against their own performance.

A great deal of the reason for a school leadership evaluation deficiency failure is that we have not really invested in our executive school-based leadership personnel. We utilize a model of the principalship that is neither relevant, appropriate, nor effective for the modern public school setting and, of course, its children. A school's long-term academic success should be neither accidental nor arbitrary. Schools should also not mislead the many parental and public stakeholders with inconsistent achievement production. In fact, a steady academic achievement state can be greatly realized through an intelligent, strategic, brave, and audacious school building leader!

— MAJ/2018

Dedication

Education is our ever-present helper and hope for a better tomorrow.

To all of the great principals, who work so tirelessly and unselfishly to make this world a better place by providing the best opportunity for the future custodians of our Mother, planet Earth, ensuring that they be skilled, ethical, and moral members of the human family.

To the poor and disenfranchised children of our nation—regardless of race, religion, place of birth, financial resources and zip code—who deserve and need the best educational resources and instruction available as well as the most effective models of school building leadership.

To Pauline Johnson, whose strategic, brilliant, educationally centered, spiritual, and moral stewardship guided an often-confused, "at-risk" Brooklyn boy who loved reading books and school into a life of educational service. Your life was the foundational model for this book.

To Bernice Gloria Ingraham, who—with solo heroic bravery—successfully raised 5 boys in the difficult streets of Harlem while she continued to enhance herself and served as a wonderful life model for me and them.

To James Christopher Johnson, who very much embodied the full meaning of this book and my work. His undiscovered and underutilized genius and talent represents the most important challenge of our nation: What to do with a smart and talented student of color.

To Christina Paulette Westbrook, who, in a time that was too brief, renewed my faith and strength to live and write this book in creative exile.

To Mom and Pop Walker, whose never-faltering kindness and spirituality healed me and offered sanctuary through every difficult trail, trial, and tribulation.

To Dr. Mark Walker, who has never (since our teen years) failed to encourage and inspire the best in me.

To Dr. Monica Sweeny, my good friend and cheerleader on this project.

There were many people and places that nurtured and pushed my vison and practice of high school leadership, and eventually school district leadership: New Visions For Public Schools, CCNY, Empire State College-SUNY, Bank Street College, Teachers College-Inquiry Program, Eli Ginzberg and the Revson Fellowship Program, Adelaide L. Sanford, Gerald Deas, Asa G. Hilliard, Frank Macchiarola, John Henrik Clarke, O. Roger Anderson, Rene Arcilla, Dorothy Burnham, Gene Geisert, Robbie McClintock, Celeste Morris, Jonas Soltis, Al Vann, Milfred Fierce, J. Jerome Harris, Lonnetta Gaines, Richard Tarpinian, Jitu K. Weusi, Frank Mickens, Rudy Crew, Ray Cortines, Harold Levy, Naomi Barber, Joyce Coppin, Don Roth, Steve Prenner, Lorraine Monroe, Frank Pignatelli, John Ferrandino, Pat Haith, Jacqueline Charity, and Linda Powell Pruitt.

To all of my former students: You convinced me even when my faith was tired and weak; you took on my challenge of seeking high academic achievement and made it your own. To be excellent was not to be "like somebody else;" it was to be who you were, who you were born to be; it was you meeting your own standards of excellence.

To all of my former colleagues and professional friends who shared my love of education and appreciated its power to transform the world by transforming and expanding the minds of each child that we served.

Acknowledgments

Every good work is the product of discouraging disappointment that is transformed into a positive, productive effort. To answer the question once posed by my nephew, Steven Ingraham, *what did I learn from my professional life experience*, I learned that the quality of the school-based leadership was a critical component in a school's success. This book project was a multi-year work of reflection, love, joy, sadness, hope, and an expectation that my professional experience in education could help others to be more effective school building leaders. I have also learned disappointingly over the years that there are large information gaps among different social, economic, and racial communities in this nation concerning what a good and effective school looks like.

I could not have pulled this off without the encouragement, support, and assistance of several people. First, a sincere thank you to my wonderful editor, Latoya Smith, who was talented enough to relegate a great deal of my pedagogical version of "War and Peace" to the "cutting room floor" and, most importantly, for focusing the book and editing out the sections that were really the chapters of the next book(s). To Abiola Sholanke, whose editing skills focused and sharpened my message. A big thank you to publicist Maitefa Angaza, who helped me to identify the amazingly critical audience to reach for the book. During the time of writing this book, my sister, Gloria Ingraham, became very ill and eventually passed away. I thank my nephew, Richard Ingraham, for kindly picking up my part of caring for her; he wanted me to complete this book, and he never once complained.

My appreciation to all of my former students, especially Chryssey Schloss-Allen, Latoya D. Ashe, Shonelle Hall, and Teneka Hardy—who, despite their now adult and professional responsibilities, allowed me to weekly access their memories and views from a high school student's prospective. They were under the illusion that I was just reminiscing with them, but it's an old man's trick; I was really drawing on their vast mental archives. The former students and colleagues of SSC-Inc., SSCHS, and Phelps ACE High School, who even in their comments on social media, inspired parts of the book; they really helped me to remember a great deal of our many accomplishments, projects, and activities that I had forgotten.

Chapter 1:
The Ethics of the Principalship

What is needed in professional education is a prime ethical directive.

Let us fast-forward to the twenty-second science fictional century, when student cadets attending the Starfleet Officers Academy are grappling with the challenges of following as they travel to other planets, Starfleet's Prime Directive:

"As the right of each sentient species to live in accordance with its normal cultural evolution is considered sacred, no Starfleet personnel may interfere with the normal and healthy development of alien life and culture. Such interference includes introducing superior knowledge, strength, or technology to a world whose society is incapable of handling such advantages wisely. Starfleet personnel may not violate this Prime Directive, even to save their lives and/or their ship, unless they are acting to right an earlier violation or an accidental contamination of said culture. This directive takes precedence over any and all other considerations, and carries with it the highest moral obligation."

— *Genta, Giancarlo (2007). Lonely Minds in the Universe: The Search for Extraterrestrial Intelligence. Springer. p. 208.*

As a lifelong fan of *Star Trek*, I could not help but notice the most important "prime directive" affirmed by every Starfleet officer begins with the rights of "sentient species" outside of themselves: to have the right "to live" in a natural progressive evolutionary peace. Further, this right is not conditional, transitory, or based on convenience. It is, in fact, sacred. Imagine an organization so rich with purpose; a mission so necessary and important; a leadership so focused, dedicated, and sincere about the service and duty it is performing, that nothing—including personal danger, life, and sacrifice—can supersede its primary ethical responsibility! I also imagine that there is a great trust and hope that a society places in those members of such an organization. And I envision that these fictional brave and dedicated warrior-officers were strictly guided by a series of ethical directives, which, in many ways, will define the very essence and meaning of their work but will also, in a real sense, define who they are. However, we need not travel to a science-fictional or future time in outer space just to discover such a force for our own present time.

As a present or aspiring School-Based Leader (SBL), we could look into our own present time for examples of how one could operate under a professional code of ethics. What kind of modern-day and real places, missions, and objectives would offer us examples of a scared code of ethical principles? Perhaps, we could observe a U.S. Navy submarine crew, a hospital trauma unit, a team of firefighters, or even some of those professionals who have chosen to work and lead in a public education system! And interestingly, all of the beforementioned professionals could not achieve their sacred objectives without having successfully completed some form of a K-12 educational experience.

As members of a higher-order thinking and reflecting species, we all have a natural inclination to learn. But how can we effectively learn if we are not effectively taught? For many good reasons, our planet's human species is born with a contemplative composite of creativity—an infinite brain nurtured (and seeking to be continually nurtured) with a sense of inquisitiveness, imagination, inventiveness, innovation, and exploration. We are inclined from birth to investigate, test, evaluate, interpret, understand, and become knowledgeable about the world we inhabit. Learning is a necessary instinct, as it is connected to the survival of the individual and, in a larger sense, to the species itself. Awareness and perception skills are connected to the skill of communication. Even a baby of any species must learn how to communicate its needs and fears to the adult members of its species. Awareness, perception, and communication skills will become lifelong activities. Effective learning is a survival skill, and a child's ability to acquire that learning has become synonymous with healthy growth and maturation. There is also the evolutionary responsibility on the part of the young to learn, and the adult members of our species are to teach and prepare the youth to replace the adult members of the species.

There is, on the other side of the child/adult replacement equation, the natural wish on the part of the elders to teach and prepare the young to assume their roles as humanity's caretakers. With this in mind, why wouldn't this awesome responsibility, on the part of the adult members of society, not inspire a profoundly serious set of professional educational ethical directives? If we truly feel that the care, protection, and well-being of our planet and its inhabitants are dependent on the capabilities and knowledge of our young people, then why does the education of all children not rise to the importance that would earn them a binding ethical commitment from their elders who are specifically charged to educate them? Now, I am not talking about the standard school district list of laudatory slogans like, "all children can learn," "we believe in excellence," "it takes a village...," etc. As well-meaning as these positive cheering points may be, they fall victim to their general and overused natures. I am less interested in promotional slogans and very much interested in making the case for a series of prime educational ethical directives, which cannot be sacrificed in any way. These are the foundational and uncompromising beliefs that would essentially define our education profession. Further, these sacred principles of practice would define and guide all of our other official, regulatory, and contractual directives connected to the public education of our young. They would in essence take precedence over all other systemic-organizational considerations, and practicing them would represent for us "the highest moral obligation."

Without a clear ethical code of behavior and professional practice, the voices and actions of professional educators will always be subject to the doubts of the public as to who we are and why we have chosen to engage in this great work. The absence of a non-negotiable and uncompromising set of ethical principles invites any and all (both the pedagogically uninformed and unqualified) to weigh in and, in many cases, make policies that drive and determine the practices of our profession. But we should not be upset with all of the external interference, for the professional ethical standards that should guide our work must start within ourselves.

Educators: What is our professional ethical code of behavior and practice?

A profession that cannot profess a series of unalterable and uncompromising professional ethical codes is, in my view, not really a profession. If we could not trust our legal attorneys to advocate in our best interest, our medical professionals to not harm us and maintain patient confidentiality, or architects and engineers to assure us that our buildings are not in danger of collapsing upon our heads, then they would not be considered professionals in their respective fields.

Why don't we provide our students with our highest and best efforts? Where is professional education's ethical evaluative system that is erected to ensure that the public good comes before the personal and financial well-being of adults? But, also importantly, where are the standards that serve to maintain the respect and credibility of the collective members of the education profession? A good start would be simply to make sure that the best and most experienced practitioners are servicing our weakest and most in-need students. Further, make sure that a child's zip code won't determine the quality of educational enrichment, art, music, and STEM (science, technology, engineering, and mathematics) resources they receive as well as their access to gifted, talented, rich, and exciting educational experiences. A professional educational code of ethics would also speak to the expected outcome of that professional work effort. What are the expected competencies we want to see in young people who have been under our care for twelve to thirteen years? What should they know, and what will they know how to do? More importantly, what type of operational culture, level of skills, and expertise will be needed by those professionals we ask to work in such an organization? Academic performance tracks with free lunch forms (Title I), which track with being in or near poverty, so we know that under-resourced schools can't compete with schools that are not only better-financed but that also have parents who supplement the school's budgetary allocation as well as fund their children's out-of-school informal education experiences. When you add teacher expertise, experience, and certification, along with effective school building leadership to the equation, poor kids don't have a chance. For those disentitled students—who, over the course of many consecutive years, are exposed to a series of low expectations, and ineffective instruction and principalship—these conditions are not a professional ethical promise for success; rather, they represent the prison pipeline, the unskilled, and underemployed train from academic failure.

In too many of the worse (for students) places in public education, "adult employment interest" will conflict and win against the best interest of the students. For example: the professional ethical problem of getting the best practitioners and most experienced teachers in front of those students who are in the greatest need of those teachers. But because of legislative statutes and contractual labor agreements, this does not happen. These same statutes and contractual labor agreements also supersede the principal's ability to hire and keep the best teachers and/or those teachers who are the best fit for the school's mission. Teachers are more easily separated from public school employment for committing a serious crime than for poor and ineffective teaching. All of these "politically driven" decisions represent the core ethical values that we really practice, and I think the public gets that! It is not what we say we believe about children, but what we actually do to those children, that speaks loudly to our ethical value system! At this point, some are going to assert that one goal of public schooling is to serve the interests of both staff and students well. And in so many ways, they are right. One attribute of "good schools" is their ability to create a school environment that balances having a supportive and professionally satisfied staff along with being able to successfully educate children. Helping to establish those highly effective teaching and learning conditions becomes a professional ethical imperative for the principal. But even in those highly effective schools, the school staff members cannot remove themselves from holding the successful education of students as their highest purpose. And, so, the question remains, why don't we educators have an uncompromisingly high and rigorous standard of ethical behaviors that is required by all members of a profession? And, further, in failing to adopt these professional ethical principles, does it suggest that education does not rise to the level of a profession? I would suggest that education is in essence a profession (one of the greatest) that is presently diminished and held captive by internal and external political forces that prevent the emergence, discussion, and establishment of a system of uncompromising ethical standards. If there is any hope of turning education away from its inadequate and mediocre results—and into the intellectual growing profession it is destined to be—we must adopt a serious set of strong, resolute ethical codes and principles that are designed, monitored, evaluated, and ultimately sanctioned by the members of the profession itself. Part of the reason for this chapter is to help every principal clearly define on which professional ethical hills he or she will choose to fight.

What ethical principles should professional educators believe, stand, and fight for?

What are the professional ethical standards of professional educators that members of the public can recognize, understand, verbalize, and evaluate? And at what cost (financial, personal) are we, the professionals and society at large, willing to invest to achieve that reality? Adopting such an ethical code would require that we replace, not tweak, our present politically guided educational system with one that is truly focused on the best interest of the children.

23

And it would further require that education professionals and society both decide that all of the nation's children—not a select few—have equal value and worth. Without that primary affirmation of purpose, that fundamental ethical principle cannot be established. However, let's be honest here. The SBL or teacher who engages in this practice is asking for trouble because the political culture of public education is organized around the idea of producing (a few) winners and (a lot of) losers, with the poor and students of color making up most of the losing group. This means that you have a choice to make. You are either with the hopes and aspirations of students, their parents, and their communities, or you are against them. The other big ethical challenge for the SBL is that students arrive to the school door across a wide spectrum of learning readiness. The challenge is, what are you willing to do to make the school success accessible to that wide spectrum of students?

Waiting for the perfect child and parents

Now, some inside of the profession would claim, openly or quietly, that we can only effectively educate a child who has the right parental/home structure. They would go on to say (or think and wisely not say) that we cannot educate them if they are poor, if their parents are not college-educated, if their parents don't care (in the way we define and recognize caring), if they live in high socio-economic stressed communities, if the parents don't speak English well. And, yes, if those children are Black or Brown since, if we are to be honest, in our society skin color seems to denote natural limits and ceilings to learning. And if this is our present belief system in public education, perhaps, then, the primary ethical code could, at the very least, be honest. Tell parents, taxpayers, and the many stakeholders the truth from the beginning. And that truth would be that we cannot effectively educate a child, unless they arrive to Kindergarten possessing a preferred list of qualities and unless the parents have equipped their children with all of the formal and informal educational attributes and skills that make them school-ready.

Any professional educators who claim that they cannot do their jobs effectively unless "society" first gets its act together—meaning, we have zero unemployment, no poverty or hunger, adequate housing, and no poor communities—are not professional educators. I don't see society getting its act together any time soon, so what do we do until then? The "we can't do anything until society is fixed" is an ethical stance, and where one stands (for or against) on

24

that statement speaks to your fundamental ethical position on public education.

The origins of people's ethical positions could often be traced to their own personal K-12 educational experiences. I believe that if all individual principals (or teachers) wish to understand why and where they stand ethically on what can/must be done, then they must first examine the biographical path they traveled to arrive at their present positions.

A professional educational leader's ethical code of standards begins in our own childhood.

As a youngster, I stood outside my Brooklyn, New York house and watched as the terrible flaming-orange arms of the fire sought to gather everything we owned. I was safe outside, fortunately, due to my Boy Scouts training that taught me to first not panic as I escaped by crawling along the floor to the door. Touching and determining if it was safe and then dashing down the stairs and escaping to the safety of the cold Brooklyn winter. I am embarrassed today to look back and remember that my thoughts (after seeing that everyone was out safely) were totally focused on the reality that my books, like the house, would not be able to withstand the power of the fire. I would later compare and contrast this moment while sitting in a high school English class, where I read the novel *Fahrenheit 451*. Fire, like the fear of tyrants, is the natural enemy of books and knowledge. And, yet, there I was on the sidewalk not thinking about my clothes, furniture, and all the things that fill a house, but instead I was thinking primarily about my books! My thoughts were powerfully interrupted as I focused on the very organized, purposeful, and diligent actions of the NYC firefighters. I was totally captured by how, on this cold night, they were engulfed in water that was quickly turning them into walking icicles. I was amazed to see how they went inside of a burning house from which I was so desperately trying to escape. I appreciated, but did not fully understand, that the firefighters were operating under some kind of ethical oath. This oath compelled them to risk their lives for my books, my house, and a family that was not their own. That night I added "firefighter" to the now long, and forever expanding, list of professional persons I wished to become in a single adult lifetime. For there was something about witnessing acts of bravery that would compel people to risk their lives to save the lives of strangers.

Firefighting became one of my life-goal metaphors for how I wanted to live when I became an adult.

As an adult professional educator, I often looked back on that day as a measure of my commitment to do my best to serve children for whom I have no family connection. What became clear to me as an adolescent, and even clearer as an adult, is that there is something about living by a difficult and challenging code of ethical honor—a code that eventually truly defines what your life and living is all about.

Who were you before you became a professional educator?

A good start to uncovering your "ethical roots" is to write a short informal autobiography, focusing on the rituals, practices, habits, and the religious and cultural beliefs of your upbringing and family. Take a serious look at what has created you and made you into the person you are today. Our thoughts on ethics and morality are influenced by those events that we encountered in our formative early childhood and adolescent days. All leaders, including those who work in schools, are in some way influenced by their upbringing. This is really interesting for principals because you will need to take some extra time in reflecting on your own school experience as professional educators; observing yourself in your K-12 settings, but now through the eyes of a trained educator, is an interesting experience. Seeing yourself in school (across many grades) and as a product of a particular era will provide you with an amazing insight into what you believe about schools as well as how you will act on those beliefs.

My own professional ethics-building experience

I realized that being a first-generation 1950s' Caribbean-American had a tremendous impact on the molding of my present worldview. For example, there is this structural foundational belief in the minds of many emigrants regardless of race, ethnicity, or nation of origin to stay focused on the reasons for uprooting oneself and traveling to a different country. There was a rugged individual-collectivism that was practiced by the 1950s' Black Caribbean community in NYC that so powerfully influenced me. It was not that they were ignorant to issues of race in the U.S., it is just that their response to racism was to bring a laser-like focus on how they could create the best outcome in a challenging situation. And most importantly, it was about how to create an environment where their children could make a generational improvement in quality of life over their own situation. Essentially, this meant not focusing on outside factors but combining their resources when necessary to positively improve their own lives and the lives of their children—the central theme of enduring present sacrifice and suffering in the cause of generational progress. This idea of taking responsibility and control of one's destiny and not waiting to be controlled by external factors has, and will always be, a cornerstone of my educational ethical foundation.

But just think of the amount of strength, pioneering spirit, courage, and faith that it takes for people to leave the safety, familiarity, and comfort of their native country. To pick up and leave family and friends, and then travel for the opportunity of a better life for you and your children. This, for me, was a major lesson of life. When your parents and family elders grow up in a nation where school is not free, their attitude and expectations of your responsibility in a free educational system is clear and dramatic. This is the attitude that motivated that generation of 1950s Caribbean emigrants to fear charity, laziness, a lack of frugality, and a fierce hatred of mediocrity. Life looks very different when failure is not an option, and you feel that any problem can be overcome by your own efforts. If you are poor, you work more hours or get more jobs. If you don't have a lot of money, spend less. And for a person to not take advantage of education, well, that was a sin.

The role of religion and faith in the development of my professional ethical belief system

Religiosity and faith in God had a tremendous influence on how I formulated my educational ethical belief system. To deny this great influence on my life would be to deny a large part of who I am. I fully understand that as a public administrator, I must show tolerance, respect, and reverence for all faith traditions. But part of accomplishing that goal is to be fully aware of your own religious worldview and how it influences your professional views. My Caribbean Episcopalian Bed-Stuy Brooklyn church played such a major part of my life growing up that, even as a teenager, I wanted to go to church and did not need any encouragement. I attended "K-Young Adult" Sunday school, served as an acolyte, and was a Cub and Boy Scout. In high school, I had even considered the priesthood as a vocation. I truly believed in certain tenets of the faith and applied them to my role as an educator. To me, education is the fundamental solution to all problems in the world! And based on these principles and my solid religious background, I came up with a set of commandments:

- Ignorance is a sin and can lead to a sinful life.

- Not fully utilizing one's gifts and talents is a sin.

- God sees every human action no matter how small; no sin (or good deed) goes unseen!

- The rewards of the world are temporary, illusionary, distracting, ultimately shallow, and unsatisfying; they are the destructive opposite and the eternal enemy of all that is good.

- Suffering, denial, discipline, and loss build character and a more perfect spiritual personality. To win in a world controlled by Satan is to, in fact, lose.

- The sacrifice of one's life, particularly for those who are not friends or family, in the war against evil is a sacred gift: a compassionate and ultimate act of empathy and commitment to some cause greater than one's self.

- Every person (whether student or educator) is born with a purpose—a special, unique calling—and when that purpose goes undiscovered and undeveloped, that person is destined to create a "disturbance" in the peace and well-being of humankind and the planet. Education and schools are the finders and developers of individual callings!

- We humans cannot contemplate the mind and purpose of God. There are things that will happen in this life that may even be senseless such that only God understands the reason for them happening. "And we know that all things work together for good to them that love God, to them who are the called according to his purpose." (Romans 8:28 KJV)

Try as I may to deny it, but a great deal of my professional educational ethical code is a reflection of that 1950s' Anglican Church acolyte kid's faith-based view of the world, the faithful young church and Sunday school attendee who was taught and believed that the symbol of the Cross explained and clarified all of life's purpose and meaning. I wanted to save people and do good works, even if it meant I would need to make great sacrifices, even if it cost me everything.

High professional ethical standards produce high professional practice and performance standards.

As a principal, I was fortunate enough to take a group of students on a tour of an active U.S. Navy nuclear submarine. I was immediately struck by the sense of mission, discipline, and purpose on the part of the entire crew. The level of commitment to expertise and excellence sought by all assigned to the ship was impressive. For when you are deeply submerged in the middle of an environment that is unfriendly to humans (or any species that lacks gills, for that matter) while eating, sleeping, and working next to a nuclear reactor, a bunch of torpedoes, and sea-to-surface missiles, the idea that such a system could tolerate incompetence seemed like an extremely dangerous idea. The purpose of a nuclear submarine demands that the organization set clear, high standards of excellence and expertise. I was informed by a naval officer of the strenuous, complex, and challenging screening process that was connected to being selected for service on a submarine. Further, the amount of cross training with multiple job assignments was amazing. Walking around the submarine, I wondered what public education would look like if we took such a serious approach to our work. On that day, I felt both pride in those submariners and a sadness I did not share with the staff and students on the trip. I would often feel this sense of sadness whenever I encountered any group of professionals who were pursuing excellence in the way of principles and practices. There was a mixture of admiration and disappointment. Something terribly important was missing from my chosen professional field—a publicly professed commitment to abandon all of the restrictive expressions of mediocrity and take up the charge of an uncompromised mission to properly prepare children to effectively live, thrive, and properly manage the future. These moments would always force a sense that what we do as professional educators is critical for the lives and well-being of not only individual children but also the safety and well-being of the nation.

Honor and respect begin at home.

We educators must honor and respect our own profession first if we hope to receive the honor and respect we want from the society we serve. That missing code of ethics is ironically one of the primary reasons that the education profession is not held in the high regard and esteem for which it is due. If the public perceives us as just nonessential bureaucratic civil service employees, focused on a paycheck and not children, then we are in constant trouble of being disrespected. It is no wonder that the public and other stakeholders harbor such a collective sense of caution. Elected officials want to make policy decisions, often not even bothering to consult us. The problem is that society knows what it sees, and they don't see us honoring a series of professional sacred ethical codes. It is not enough to say that we work hard; the real hard work we don't take on is to have an uncompromising mission—a sense of direction, purpose, and sacrifice. The public, at large, spends huge amounts of money on public education, only to see us produce mediocre results. And our only response to our lack of success is that we insult that same public by blaming society for not sending us the "best" students. The present practice and having a built-in organizational excuse system of why we can't effectively educate all children suggests to the public that we are not serious about our work. Real "high-risk organizational" professionals like our firepersons or submariners don't make excuses for poor or inadequate practices. They don't fail to adjust to adverse and challenging conditions. They don't say that they can only succeed under perfect conditions or when the people they serve are model citizens. Instead, they make sincere and serious changes in their practices to produce a positive outcome. They are compelled to make those changes, not because those changes are comfortable but because if they don't a person or persons will be seriously injured or die and the mission will fail. We professional educators, on the other hand, have actually grown comfortable with a large amount of our work efforts failing.

Ms. or Mr. Principal, what is your professional ethical profile?

With school-based leadership ethics, personal history defines what matters most to us. Principals who do not think that their personal histories influence their ethical, personnel, and policy decisions are deluding themselves, and worst, they are confusing and deceiving their school communities. It is like those professional educators who claim not to see race, ethnicity, color, or religion. This assertion is both disingenuous and dangerous to the emotional and educational well-being of the students under their charge. Instead, we need to acknowledge that these feelings exist and push them out of private settings and into a more monitored, positive, and productive professional development environment of our thinking. Use our past experiences, both positive and negative, to help us think through our personal ideological inclinations so that we are better able to help the children under our charge. As a principal, it is important to know who you are and what you believe. Adversity, setbacks, and/or success and triumphs will surely bring your true personality to the surface and reveal your most deeply held values. And since a series of large and small adversities can happen in any given school day, it then suggests that "values clarification" should be a high priority for that school building administrator. Every principal must ask and answer the question, what do I really believe, and dare not hide from the true answer, especially since most of these answers will eventually be made public anyway!

Unlike private meditative reflections on ethics, your administrative ethical decisions will always be on display in the public arena for all to see and feel. As a principal, you will continually be forced to make difficult ethical decisions. Thus, every day, and throughout the day, you should be asking yourself the following questions as a guide that will lead you to the best possible answer for every critical situation:

- Why did I choose to go into (and remain) in education?

- Who am I biographically in this particular situation?

- How would I feel if this were my child?

- Who, both internal and external to the school, benefits the most from this decision?

- How do I save the maximum number of children?

- In this particular case, what is really in the child's best interest?

- What are the consequences of a decision to make no decision at all, in essence, deciding to leave a situation unresolved?

- How do I harm the least number of children?

- To what extent is the decision fair, captures the nuances of the situation, and is balanced?

- Who, and what, am I seeking to protect with this decision?

- Is this decision about concrete positive change or just the appearance of change?

- How does this decision help or hurt children in the school?

- Which group, or cohort of students, is harmed the most (or least) by this decision?

- Does this decision give some students an unfair advantage? If so, how much? And over which students?

- Am I trying with this decision to save children or my job?

- This decision (fill in the blank with a letter) _____ the school's primary mission.

    A. *Enhances, reinforces, makes clear, strengthens, adds to, builds on...*

    B. *Subtracts, obscures, weakens, diminishes, contradicts...*

    C. *Challenges, strains, calls into question, is/is not addressed by...*

    D. *Parts of, some, or all of the above... (the landing zone for most of your decisions)*

These are ethical questions that should continually be on a principal's mind when making day-to-day decisions. They are taken home every night for daily reflection and will gather in your head each morning as you journey to the school with your preparatory thoughts of the challenges you are about to face. They are also guaranteed to meet you once you step inside the school doors. These questions will faithfully follow you throughout the school day. Normally, the first part of my day is a morning prayer as I make my rounds in the empty school building. This prayer is not just an expression of my personal professional mission, it is also a recognition and confession of the many challenges I face each day. The number of events that can take place in a school day—all of the rules and regulations that are not part of my design—must, in some way, be brought under my influence or control. The second part of my prayer is more specific and includes names, faces, and situations.

At the end of each day, keeping a clear mind, knowing the outcome I am hoping to achieve, and asking myself the above list of ethical questions all allow me the ability to be satisfied knowing that I've made the best possible decisions, armed with the best information, the best reflection, and the best of intentions. Don't bother worrying, for you will need all the sleep you can get to be able to repeat this process the next day, and with a new set of challenges!

The ethics of providing intellectual safety zones for children of color and why this principle is so important to me

Highly academic-achieving Black and Latino kids can sometimes feel isolated and alone. These students need intellectual sanctuaries where they can feel free to practice their art as well as find others like themselves, coaches, encouragement, safety, and support. This safe place is particularly important for Black and Latino boys, who might spend an entire school day hiding their smartness by often engaging in deflecting and distracting self-destructive behavior.

In high school, the majority of my schoolmates were White. And because everyone in my classes seemed to fall achievement-wise into some sort of bell curve, it never occurred to me that smartness was something that was assigned by race. I saw some White kids who were smart, some who were average, and some who were not so smart at all. I also noticed that students of all races seemed to show their levels of talents in different academic areas. I think the powerful high academic achievement insulation environments of my elementary school, middle school, and high school experiences did not force me to be confronted with the idea that intellectualism, curiosity, or academic achievement were some kind of race betrayal. And when you combine my school experience/expectations with my home experience/expectations, you can see the beginning stages of an ethical life belief system that will serve as a great source of my ethical view of education. I loved books, reading, and learning, so as a professional educator I always wanted to protect children who reminded me of myself. My personal experience has caused me to reject this artificial notion of an achievement gap for which, although it is not explicitly and honestly said, is believed to be in some way linked to biological deficiencies of Black Americans. My personal experience has forced me to push back against this notion and to affirm that academic achievement, STEM, and intellectualism is very much an expression of the Black collective personality, as any other cultural expression. It has been my lifelong professional assertion that this fatal negative narrative of grouping all Black students as struggling academically or broken and in need of fixing is an organic cultural assumption present in most public school systems, including those controlled by Black people. Sadly, it is not just a belief limited to White educators or White educational policymakers. It is oftentimes the belief of church members, neighbors, or family members. A smart Black kid with a love of books and learning, a gifted STEM (science, technology, engineering, art and mathematics) child could in some ways be a lonely stranger in their own Black community. This sense of isolation discourages many Black students from ever wanting to be and/or act smart if that smartness is interpreted as an act of committing racial betrayal. As a principal, I internalized and practiced the ethical position that I would always establish and defend intellectual sanctuaries for students of color. Principals must create smart safe zones in their schools and understand that taking that position may place you in conflict with a lot of folks, including Black folks. But it is one of the most important and necessary battles that a school leader must wage in behalf of students. Operationally, this means that the principal must provide students with academic/intellectual teams, activities, clubs, programs as well as recognition and awards events as much as the budget and academic staff will allow. This intellectual sanctuary will never emerge as a core principle of the school's culture unless the principal is personally committed to its necessity. An effective SBL must affirm a school culture that says it is not only okay to be Black and smart but that it is in fact the most desired state in life and that academic underachievement and failure are the true acts of racial betrayal.

Professional ethics must be exercised and practiced daily.

As school leaders, we are in an endless pursuit of excellence. There will always be a learning road for us to travel: more skills to learn and perfect as well as qualities to grow. Any journey is made easier by having a descriptive series of directional road signs to guide us along our intended route. When we reach a fork in the road, it is the ethical directional sign post anchored in our hearts that will move us in the best direction. An ethical practice, like any form of strength-building activity (e.g., Yoga or martial arts), must be consciously practiced every day. A daily ethical praxis requires some quiet time to exercise our thoughts.

As a principal, we spend most of the day on stage. We are constantly performing multiple tasks as principal, leader, teacher, friend, parent, counselor as well as acting as the symbolic embodiment of the school's mission. Everyone is looking at, and to you, to see how you respond in every serious moment; alone time is rare. As I stated, it is critical to take time at the beginning of the day for meditation and reflection. It is also important to engage in this practice alone in your office at the end of the day. After a brief review of the day with your top lieutenants, you should take notes of their observations. These notes will help you to see your perceptions and understandings of the day's events as well as your school's administration leadership team's critical analysis. This authentic assessment is important to the success of your post-debriefing ethical reflection. You should have such an honest relationship with your staff that they feel free to offer you a different or larger perspective of a particular event versus your preferred version of that event. After that meeting, soften the lights and get started. The point of this reflection is that you leave the school day at school versus taking the day's issues home with you. Failing to critically examine the day's ethical challenges in your office at the end of the day will place a great strain on your emotional and physical health—and, perhaps, place negative pressure on home family relationships. Remember, tomorrow is another day to get things right, another opportunity to improve and do better.

Once the principal has established a daily ethical code of practice and is reflecting on that practice, the real work begins. The standard ethical codes start with the common ethical responsibilities expected of any appointed principal, usually statutorily and contractually stated, but then goes much further. In the language of education, this is the individual principal's personal ethical standards. A set of rubrics should be developed that will allow for a clear definition of how and why a particular decision upholds, modifies, compromises, threatens, or abandons a particular ethical standard. This system of rubrics clarification will allow the elements of that ethical code to be instantly recognized by its applicable properties to, and in, each incident, decision, and event that takes place in the school day. There is a terrible price that a school leader pays for self-disillusionment and self-dishonesty. And that price is the equivalent of constructing a house utilizing defective and deficient building materials. The principal must be totally honest with him or herself concerning any decision or action that falls short, even slightly, of the stated professional ethical code of standards. You will find that you fail daily to meet the highest levels of your ethical standards, and that's the good news. First, because it means that you actually have, are concerned with, and are seeking to be governed by a practice of high professional ethical standards. Secondly, the principalship and your personal-ship, in particular, is a journey that is ever pursuing an excellent ethical practice, and you will fail often in this pursuit, but the pursuit itself is a sign of a healthy, positive, and productive leadership practice. Principals are not perfect ethicists, but instead they are learning on the job and from the job. But this school leadership journey is made much more meaningful and manageable when we use the navigational power of a strong code of ethical standards of practice. And these ethical principles reveal, define, and refine the core values that drive our practice. The higher the ethical standards, the harder it is to follow them, but, ultimately, they make us better and more effective principals and human beings. These ethical standards also cannot be disconnected from the foundational principles of our philosophy of education. It is impossible to separate the *why* we believe from the *what* we believe; and, so, let us now look at that process of translating a professional ethical system into a professional philosophical system.

Chapter 2:
The Educational Philosophy of the Principal

The key to discovering, unlocking, and deciphering our educational philosophy will be found in the core narratives of our personal stories.

As adults, we are often in a constant state of personal revelation, reconstruction, restoration, and the redemption of our childhood memories and earlier adult selves.

Neither a title nor position will allow me (even if I chose to try) to escape from my own existential American reality. I am Black and born in a nation where my skin color is a societal identifier and constant underestimation of who people believe I am and what I am capable of becoming. All of the personal and professional titles I could ever accumulate in life—man, American, teacher, principal, or superintendent—will always be filtered through the lens of my skin color. I don't like this reality, but it is what it is. And to borrow an assertion from one of my favorite authors, Ralph Ellison, I am both unmistakably visible and at the same time tragically and painfully invisible. It is like living in a constant bar-less prison where my dreams and hopes are under ever-present guard (dare I dream too big!). I am a citizen of a nation that seeks to proscribe my freedom and aspirations in a culture of second-class citizenship and low human potential expectations. By reasons of competency, conscience, and calling, I have decided to serve in the field of education, specifically to serve those students whose potential and personhoods are perhaps underestimated and surely as underappreciated as I am.

Education was my above and underground railroad in seeking freedom from a life of disrespect, disenfranchisement, and dismissal. It was the very Art of War and the heart of my war against a societal political culture of racial depersonalization. My primary weapon of personal and mass instruction was STEM, books, and learning. To truly be an effective SBL, one must immerse oneself into the reading and absorbing of seemingly unrelated (to educational administration) topics in history, philosophy, fictional literature, anthropology, theology, sculpture, painting, dance, dramatic plays, poetry, topical journals, and biographies as well as seek out examples of excellence to observe and study in every part of human endeavors. All of this rich and diverse intake of knowledge will all come together and make sense in the context of what a principal will face on a daily basis. This accumulation of seemingly disconnected information will serve as the principal's guiding philosophy of the work that is required to be done. And if it is true that knowledge is power, then those in position of leadership must be never-ending seekers and custodians of a wide spectrum of leadership development knowledge. That knowledge begins with a knowledge of yourself—who you are and what experiences, exposures, family traditions, and rituals contributed to the person you have become. You need to be open to learning and knowing things you had no idea were even related to the requirements for the principal position. Standing and observing with a determined honesty, both inside and outside of yourself, will give you a tremendous insight into your leadership weaknesses and strengths. Your biographical story is an important part of this ongoing lesson.

The perceptions of others can also be helpful and even necessary as long as you remember that everyone, well-meaning or not, will always bring the weight of their own biographical story to their observation and to the conversation they are having with you. Everyone has a story, and they, like you, are more or less on an existential journey in trying to decipher that life story's meaning.

The person inside of the principal; the child inside of the person

Continuing my autobiographical sketch, it is important to note that I was a child who, because of the color of my skin and the nation in which I was born, was marked at birth for destruction. And if not for the plan and protection of God, family support, strong ethical principles, and moral values, I probably would have met the unfortunate destructive fate of many of my neighborhood contemporaries. The adults in my neighborhood life were all critical life-experience mentors that guided my upbringing. I was extremely fortunate to have a wealth of elders who made every effort to direct and incline my life into a positive and productive direction. These wonderful people constantly convinced me that there was this great well of potential stored inside of me just waiting to cultivate some good and greatness in the world. These were the Black elders who witnessed, up close and personal, the cruel brutality of American segregation and discrimination. So, for them, I represented a kind of hope for the redemption and restoration of Black people in America. The elders of my youth framed my thinking on individual family and collective community's sacred parenting and leadership responsibilities. As a principal, I sought to follow the model of those loving and nurturing elders of my youth. And, so, to the greatest extent possible, I struggled to protect the children in my care from physical and emotional harm; to provide an atmosphere where education, intellectual stimulation, learning, and growth can take place; to promote the best ethical and moral work and living habits for the children to follow; to prepare the children to exceed their parents' present economic and educational conditions; to oppose those who don't have the best interest of the children as a core interest but have sole control over the emotional, educational, and intellectual well-being of the children; and to presuppose that along with food, clothing, shelter, and safety, a set of moral and ethical standards are also a central requirement of parenting and community life. Most importantly, none of the elders of my youth possessed great amounts of wealth, but they did possess, and sought to pass on, a wealth of good values. In fact, the influential elders of my childhood didn't need to be wealthy or even formally educated; all that was required was the exercise of their natural generational improvement instinct—a belief that the young children in their care should "do better than us!"

As a youngster, I swam in this sea of encouragement and confidence-building, and this gave me the courage to live an inventive, imaginative, creative, and intellectually inquisitive childhood. Was every adult a good role model in the 1950s? No. Did we have drug addicts? Yes. Did we have adults involved in some area of criminality? Yes. Although they were not always successful, these elders made the most valiant effort they could muster to see us safely through to a positive and productive adulthood. Our Brooklyn, N.Y., Crown Heights neighborhood was a giant sieve that unfortunately trapped and destroyed so many of the young men of my era. The big lie I no longer tell myself was that I was some kind of super-smart and super-talented kid while all of those young casualties (my friends and neighbors) lacked smartness and talent. The truth is that I had the opportunity to express my intellectual gifts and talents and they did not; it is that simple. I was born into a family that expected, nurtured, protected, and encouraged a type of intellectual, spiritual, and physical excellence. Life was something special and it was not to be put to the random chance of success through luck or some abstract and false concept of societal fairness. I believe that a child's chances for life success increase exponentially based on the number of adults at home, in the extended family, in the community, in informal educational institutions, community organizations, and religious institutions who are sincerely committed to that child's success.

I did not build it (my personal, professional, and life success) alone!

It was important as a professional educator that I dropped the attractive, but false, narrative of a life of personal exceptionalism; the true educator must see every child as exceptional and endowed by the Creator to engage in some unique and exceptional purpose. So much of life's personal outcomes are based on the individual's social encounters and influences. This has helped me to remain humble, knowing that if many of my "failed" friends had my family behind them, their lives might have turned out differently. Children need a great deal of positive, natural nurturing to survive and thrive in the challenging, and sometimes hostile, environment into which they may be born. But the ignored children of disenfranchisement need a double dose! And there's a great need not only for the presence of good parents but also the support and commitment of a collective community of good parents.

My school parents: The Ellis Island emigration effect in NYC public education

There was a 1950-60s' universal NYC cultural belief that public schools should serve as a vehicle for socio-economic, "class" advancement. This cultural belief would extend beyond K-12 public schools to the City University of New York (CUNY) college system. This idea was deeply rooted in the practical and symbolic meaning of two famous NYC landmarks: Ellis Island and the Statute of Liberty. There was this strong belief that NYC schools would give everyone a chance to overcome any unfair hand that was dealt by geography, family history, or society—that public education could successfully challenge and end any poverty narrative and break any family cycle of destitution.

In every sense, one's history or present condition did not, solely because of public education, necessarily determine that person's destiny. And throughout our public education experience, we NYC students were constantly propagandized and educated into believing and accepting the public school-powered "rags to riches" legendary narrative. There was always the story of someone from a poor or emigrant background who utilized the NYC public school system to drastically change the expected trajectory of their lives. We even heard those stories from our own teachers, whose parents may have come from the "old country" to America—poor, non-English speaking, and without a formal education—but now because of the NYC school system and CUNY, their children are standing before us as teachers and members of the middle class! This may sound corny to a non-New Yorker, but to us NYC kids, these stories were inspiring, exciting, and real. Most importantly, it gave us a sense that we, too, could use school to catapult ourselves into better life possibilities. For this first-generation American kid, these stories matched the Caribbean emigration "pull yourself up by your own bootstraps" stories I heard at home. So why would I think they were not true? Powerful and sacred myths that are believed don't need to be 100% accurate, they just need to be said over and over by a lot of voices of authority and influence, and then they begin to take on the power of trueness! And make no mistake, these childhood "principles of trueness" didn't simply disappear from my psyche just because I became an adult or a school principal. These early fundamental beliefs in the power of how public education served as a vehicle for human transformation, elevation, and empowerment established themselves as the foundations and pillars in the later evolvement of my philosophy of education.

Living and growing up in Crown Heights, Brooklyn, also helped me to see a diverse racial, ethnic, and cultural environment, where being working-class (and having to work hard as a member of that class), poverty, suffering, going without, struggling to make ends meet, etc., were seen in my world as universal afflictions and not just societal challenges that were limited to Black people. And, so, like my White classmates, we were all in school to prepare and provide ourselves with the skills that would allow us to live reasonable and decent lives as adults. We all knew that there was no great financial inheritance waiting for us once we reached adulthood. And, yes, as we were often told, school would be our ticket to a better life!

All I am trying to do here is to get the practicing and potential principal to self-examine his and her own biographies. For we are, in many ways, a compilation of all that has happened in our lives before this present moment.

In fact, how these biographical events are interpreted will have a great deal to do with those seen and unseen motivational ideas that define our educational philosophy. We represent, in part or whole, the affirmation, rejection, or translation of our own personal experiences. The self-evaluative journey through our own childhood shapes our understanding of "effective parenting," and our K-12 school experience will definitely craft and mold our vison of a school leadership that is driven by a fundamental philosophy of education.

A principal can avoid a great deal of pain, suffering, and disappointment if he or she takes the time to explore the ideas that help to frame his or her worldview. I look back now and realize that a great deal of bad decisions and mistakes I made as a principal occurred because I had not fully explored the historical and personal psychological forces from my childhood that framed my adult thinking. We must ask the questions: What part of your leadership style is being driven by your personal history? Are your expectations and "followership style" standards, in actuality, reflective of how you yourself wish to be supervised; also, how does that perception play out in the hiring, staff supervision, coaching/professional development, and evaluation process? Finally, is your vision for parent involvement and engagement a desire to see the type of parenting experience you had growing up?

An effective principal must be able to look at the school in a thoughtful and clinical way while at the same time being able to decenter and look at his or her leadership style utilizing the same level of authentic analysis. Answering the "who did we bring to the principalship" question is an essential part of that process. The other important reason for exploring your biography is to better understand yourself as an SBL in the fullness of your personality. We often emphasize the importance of the term "metacognition" (thinking about one's own thinking) in the education field. It would seem then that a developmental-metacognition review—particularly when it comes to our ideas concerning things like justice, equality, parental expectations, the purpose of education, learning style, "followship" style, and leadership style—would be of great value to any person who took on the important work of serving as a leader of a school.

The principal's biographical sketch essay is a critical component of the full philosophy of education (POE) statement.

Now that you have established the need and essential practical purpose of developing a biographical sketch that reveals the foundations of your beliefs system, you can now utilize that information to form the structural frame and daily operational working practices that successfully reflect the elements of both your philosophy of education (POE) and your philosophy of school leadership. As school leaders, we need to give our POE a higher level of attention and importance, for the POE represents the true actualization of our ethical principles—what we believe to be the purpose and meaning of schooling and the primary role of those who have chosen the school leadership path.

Your POE should evolve and change as you grow.

Stepping away from the important theoretical work presented in supervision and administration certification programs and into a school is a moment of professional enlightenment. You'll find quickly that the internal members of a school family as well as the external stakeholders for the school will refuse to conform to most of the theoretical models you've studied. The complexities of the human personality create a dynamic psychological experience that causes the school leader to continually rethink the primary principles of the POE. Due to both personal experience and professional growth, your POE should grow, evolve, change, and be a dynamic, ever-expanding, and ever higher-reaching document. Now, this is not a call to design a POE that does not commit to some concrete and definable affirmations for which the SBL is seriously committed. There is a need, however, to place the elements of your POE in the context of a real day-to-day school experience and, most importantly, to test the POE's effectiveness in responding to real people with real concerns, challenges, aspirations, and interests inside of a working school.

One of my end-of-the-school-year principal reviews was a critical review of my personal POE in light of the school year's victories, challenges, and setbacks. Although I never found myself deleting an item or section of my POE, I did very often find myself modifying some sections. The important point here is that the POE is a measure of your own personal and professional growth.

Your POE is also specifically designed to help with the development of your self-directed professional development and self-supervisory plan of action. The principal or SBL who hopes to be effective must create his or her own professional development plan (the details of which I will go into later) and then align his or her practice and production next to the standards of the POE.

This annual end-of-year-review of my work juxtaposed to my POE was one way of facing an honest, and sometimes harsh, assessment of my year as a school leader. But this practice also produced some uplifting and conformational information, meaning it revealed the many plans, projects, programs, and initiatives that reflected the best elements of my POE.

And, as with any self-reflective exercise, there are always the hidden dangers of blind spots, prejudicial and biased distortions, and the invention of story lines that are far removed from reality. It would be wise to share that personally designed end-of-year review assessment with your administrative leadership team, key staff members, and anyone else with whom you feel comfortable who might benefit from your educational vision for the school. As to the important exercise of sharing and having discussions concerning your reflections on your POE, sharing this information with your staff is of great importance. You do not know if you will suddenly have to leave the school due to promotion, retirement, illness, or death, so there is a great need for documentation of your philosophical vision for the school, even if your successor chooses to change all, or parts, of that vision. Title I school students and staff (and the school in general) are often the greatest victims of an incomplete and/or bad transition from one school leader to another. And, so, let us take some time discovering, developing, rethinking, or reshaping our present POE in light of a school-based leadership role.

Forming and being formed by your POE

This dynamic POE document should be built on several important learning objectives:

- It should define what public education is and, thus, what it is not. It must explain the education profession, the purpose of the profession, and who you are in the profession. The POE should also establish the societal, political, and economic intentions of the schooling experience as well as reveal which students you champion in the school system and how you plan to transform that advocacy into everyday practical practices. Public education is a political experience, so let's not pretend that it is not. A POE should be the foundation of that theoretical path that you have chosen to follow; it is the beginning of your journey to a specific objective, the designated path and directional signs that lead to the final objective and the end of the journey itself—that place where the philosophical underpinnings and explanations of the school's mission are established. The POE should identify the underlining reasons for all decisions, plans, strategies, policies, and programs you hope to see in a school. Everything that exists in your vision of schooling and school leadership should be present in the POE.

- The POE should be both aspirational as well as having a realistic operational capability. It should have the ability to be generally adaptable to every activity and place in the school while specifically addressing even the smallest expressions and seemingly innocuous aspects of a school's day-to-day work. That means phrases like, "it takes a village, all children can learn, etc.," are wonderfully poetic but ineffective as working parts of a POE.

- The POE establishes, explains, concretizes, and extends your personal and professional ethical principles.

- The POE will provide a better and more thoughtful hindsight when reflecting on your own personal educational experiences—a tool by which you can investigate the evolutionary process that has led to your present psychological and emotional state, values, and belief systems. It will give you a present insight into your day-to-day leadership questions and challenges. It will also utilize that insight to sift through the many, sometimes overwhelming (and often, more or less useful) rules, regulations, and mandates as well as the plethora of theoretical educational theories that saturate our profession. And it will give you foresight into making proactive decisions to challenges present and seen, and those that are waiting to be seen.

- The POE should provide you with an honest perception of yourself as the SBL as well as your hopes and aspirations as a human being and professional educator.

- The POE should reveal what is most or least important to you in this work; what you truly value; what your ultimate vision is for the school; how you want to supervise others; what the "endgame" is of this educational experience; what results you hope for; and how you want to be defined by students, staff, and the school community of stakeholders when you reach the end of your professional career.

- Your POE should serve as a guide for your daily personal practice and decision-making.

- In writing your POE, there should be a style/format that incorporates standards and rubrics: a type of guide or "how to" to transform your ethical vision of an effective school into practical school applications and procedures.

- Your POE should define both how educational problems are posed and how they are solved. The POE translates standard educational terms as it also filters the unofficial language used by educational professionals. This POE is in essence the undergirding set of valued principles that guide all of your principles of action and/or inaction as a practicing principal. The POE must expose that which is done but not said in public education and reveal that which is said about all children and in actuality only done for a privileged few.

- Your POE will serve as a daily moral-ethical exercise and workout guide. Not having a stated POE does not mean that an SBL does not have one. Failing to think about and seriously develop a POE means that the school leader will (by default) be led by a philosophy of confusion, emotionalism, and the absence of a thoughtful and strategic approach to the creation of an effective school. A good POE should clearly define and explain the role and responsibilities of every member of the school family (students, parents, teachers, non-instructional staff, supervisory staff, and the principal).

- A POE cannot be fully and honestly written without the inclusion of the principal's personal educational story. This knowledge is just as important as any pedagogical knowledge gained from the readings in supervision and administration certification programs. In this sense, our POE is very much a response to, the rejection of, or the reproduction of some or all of our own personal educational experiences. To make it personal means you must include your reflections on both the best and worst moments in your educational life. Were the schools you attended clean, safe, and supportive of your gifts and talents? What teacher ignited your imagination? When, and in what class, did a lesson lead you to challenge and perhaps even change your point of view? What acts of kindness, concern, and guidance did you receive from educators who might have seen things in you that you yourself did not necessarily see? Those moments in our own schooling should give you a profound insight into the best practices of K-12 education. Knowing, understanding, and reflecting on our own personal historical educational experience is a part of our forming an effective educational leadership philosophy.

- Remember, you can lift and merge sections of your POE for a public document, but the entire POE is not for public consumption.

Okay, now it is time to draft your true personal and confidential POE! Let's start with a list of guiding questions. And since this is not a public document, the responses should be truthful and honest.

Some Thought-Provoking Writing Prompts:

1. Why is education a universal, human, societal, and individual concern? Societies have over the centuries created some form of public education for what purpose?

2. How is public schooling specifically organized in the U.S.? And why is it organized in this particular way?

3. What is good and effective school leadership? What is the meaning and purpose of the principalship?

4. What are my primary personal and professional ethical concerns of the education profession?

5. In my hierarchy of professional care and concerns (e.g., job security, career aspirations, or finances), where do the students' abilities to learn rank?

6. What is my dominant/preferred learning style? How do I best take in information?

7. How do I personally prefer to be supervised? Why?

8. What were my favorite subjects in elementary school, middle school, and high school?

9. Did I feel emotionally, physically, and intellectually safe in each of my K-12 school experiences? If yes or no, where, when, how, and why?

10. Three present or historical educational leaders I admire the most are_____, _____, and _____. For the following reasons:

11. (Most important for middle and high school administrators) How has my subject/content area of specialization influenced my view of life, education, schooling, and school leadership?

12. Of all of my K-12 teachers, which individuals would I hire as teachers, and why?

13. Why and how did I choose to do my professional work, specifically in early childhood, elementary, middle, or high school settings?

14. Personalities, historical events, philosophies, and ideas outside the field of education that have greatly influenced my ideas concerning professional educational practices include...

15. How did the era, national geography, state, city, neighborhood, type of living conditions (e.g., large family, middle or working class, single-parent home, apartment, or private house) influence my thinking about education?

16. Political, anthropological, psychological, theological and philosophical theories that have influenced my views on education include...

17. The ten most pivotal life-changing events in my life were...

18. Who are my heroes, both in and outside of education? Why?

19. What are my professional educational working definitions of educational terms like: Effectiveness, Expectations, Excellence, and Efficacy?

20. Fill in the blank: Education must _____ the _____ of each student that is touched by it.

These 20 prompts provide an opportunity for the aspiring or present SBL to deeply explore those ideas that lie directly below our pronounced ideas.

They also allow us an opportunity to discover our unconscious belief system and clear up any conveniently and creatively constructed narratives about our home and educational life. I learned as a superintendent that a great deal of what can be (and should be) known about a principal can be gained in the learning about that principal's K-12 school and home upbringing. It was always one of the first questions I asked the person; it's fascinating to see eyes light up, even when those eyes are in the heads of adults as they reminisce about their own personal school days. And, so, let's look closely at our own first view of school as a student.

Your philosophy of education begins when you were a K-12 student.

Although I did not fully (pedagogically) understand why my K-12 schooling experience was good, I did understand that there was an intellectually stimulating and high expectations quality to it. In both my elementary and middle school experiences, I attended schools that were racially and ethnically diverse. My elementary school (common in that time) had numbered classes (1, 2, 3…8) where the lower the number, presumably the "smarter" the students in that class; I suspect those placements were based on reading ability. I was fortunate, thanks to my mother, to be an early strong reader entering elementary school. I was always placed in the more challenging elementary classes. In middle school, I was fortunate to attend a gifted and talented program. These early educational experiences presented a place where I was successful and recognized for academic success. I now know that my educational reality was not the standard educational reality for all, or even most children. But when you are a child and the reality you are exposed to is the only reality you know, then that is your reality. For the writing of the POE, this perception can be a powerful frame to your understanding of schooling. In high school, I became a child of school integration busing, which took me far away from my integrated neighborhood and friends. This experience exposed me to a wider segment of NYC's white citizenry. These students only lived with other white citizens. I now suspect that my particular high school was selected for this busing integration project because the school leadership and staff probably were judged as having the best potential of making it work politically and educationally. And make it work they did! My high school principal went on to become a superintendent—not an easy task in the highly competitive 1970s NYC educational school leadership community. Also, looking back, I think I can honestly say that I was exposed to some really excellent teachers and college advisors. My middle and high school experience established a standard that would eventually show up in my POE as well as in my school leadership practice. These ideas became the foundation in what I believe to be a major purpose of the POE, and that is to define what you truly believe a good and positive educational experience should look like. For example:

High expectations: This is the idea that school administrators, counselors, and instructors begin with the sincere belief that the students are fully capable of receiving and processing a high level of intellectually rigorous academic work. In many ways, this critical starting point is a central column of support for my entire philosophy of education.

High efficacy: High efficacious behavior was almost always in play, particularly in elementary and middle school, but also in high school. This meant that school administrators and teachers had a fundamental belief that the students they served possessed the ability to succeed; therefore, those professional educators searched for, and exhausted, all of their personal energy, professional knowledge, talents, gifts, skills, and intelligence to make those expectations a reality. This is essentially the shifting of the entire responsibility for learning away from the child's parents, neighborhood, race-ethnicity and economic status, and onto the teacher's skills and determination to succeed.

High evidence of rigorous work: The belief and operational practicing of high expectations and high efficacious behavior will naturally lead to the introduction of standards-based rigorous academic work. Students needed to be pushed to their personal best, and further a pedagogy based on rigor would also reveal to both educators and students those undiscovered and untapped skills and interests that lie dormant in children until they are strategically drawn out by an effective teaching and learning experience. Rigorous academic work has a related mind-expanding and personally revealing quality. Young people are quick to tell you what they like and don't like. But I have always believed that they are operating with incomplete information, and part of the learning process should be to expand those areas of unknown knowledge, exposing students to talents and interests they have but haven't yet discovered!

High environmental efficiency: The combination of high expectations, high evidence of efficacious behavior, and high levels of rigorous academic work demands a learning environment that will support these important effective teaching and learning activities. The school must practice and produce a school environment that does not squander time and, in fact, will manage and use time wisely. The school, in general, and the classroom have to be free of distractions and misbehaviors. Students were interested in a lot of different things, and those interests were safeguarded and protected. In my high school, I was able to explore through electives: creative writing, photography, poetry and fiction, art and sculpture without any fear. And, so, creating the maximum safe teaching and learning experience would eventually become a cornerstone of my POE and a primary concern of my principalship.

It did not go unnoticed as I reflected on my K-12 school experience that there was never a moment that I did not share my school and classroom with White schoolmates.

Creating and crafting the formal POE

First, it is substance over style as this is not a document for publication and distribution. You should begin this task when you have ample time and a quiet space to think and reflect.

Start with a rough draft, almost as if you are speaking freely to yourself. A physical or electronic journal can be used. I personally have found Dragon Naturally Speaking software to be useful. But either a pen or keyboard can be utilized to meet the individual's comfort level. I would not attempt to complete the document in one sitting, rather it can be done in sections. Consistency, rather than speed, is key, and as one of my high school English teachers taught me about rough drafts, "Don't get it right, get it written!" And, so:

- Start off with a serious and sacred dedication, a phrase, a quote, a poem that reflects and summarizes your overriding philosophical theme.

- Begin with this rationale for your philosophical perspective. The big "why" concerning your choice of profession; this is the opening to your true heart, the defining statement of who you are!

- It can be as long or short as you think it should be!

- The format can be in a narrative essay format, semi-autobiographical format, or a straight bullet point-driven document.

- Everything you need to know in life, you learned as a teacher. So, think of this effort as writing a lesson plan on School Leadership Life, complete with conceptual and behavioral objectives.

- Be as creative as you want to be (you make the rules!), and don't be afraid to introduce poetry, music lyrics, drawings, or any other technique that will help you to tell this important story.

- Tell the real and imagined summation of your professional life. This is what people will say you stood for and believed years after you have left the land of the living!

- Your POE should represent your "Declaration of Independence" from fear, ineffectiveness, mediocrity, and aimlessness as well as give meaning and purpose to the real work of school leadership, beyond the limited job description. This is what you truly believe this work is about!

- It is the crafting of a moral, ethical, and passionate call to action. It should reveal what is ultimately important to you. Reading and reviewing this document year after year will help to remind you why you went into education.

- This POE exercise should also help you, as the SBL, to interact with your own personal and leadership thoughts. What are you thinking about as you craft this document? What are your greatest fears? What are those things that bring you personal and professional satisfaction and joy? Who are you, really?

- Your POE should challenge you!

- A POE will unfortunately create some theoretical distances between you and some of your professional friends and colleagues. Remember, you don't need to convert your colleagues into seeing your point of view. My position has always been, "They can do what they do, and I will do what I do!"

- If this exercise is approached with truth and honesty, you might come to the conclusion that the role of an SBL is not for you. And for your sake, and the sake of the children, that is not a bad realization to receive.

- If this effort is approached authentically, it will unfortunately identify and predict all of your moments of suffering in this work. But it will also offer you a vision of all of your moments of joy and hope!

A philosophy of education should always be a work in progress and should be progressing toward a more effective professional and progressive practice.

Make it stand on a firm ethical foundation while, at the same time, adaptive and flexible in order to respond to the dynamic nature of public education. Somewhere between the third and fifth year in the principalship, you will cease saying, "I have seen it all!" Further, as a school building principal, you will be placed in many situations that don't easily lend themselves to statutes, rules, and regulations. The role of the principalship is to continually adapt and respond to new and different situations. Therefore, the POE is not a static and "dead document" that a school leader will attempt to follow verbatim. Schools are ultimately "human spaces," which means they are subject to the diversity, complexity, and unscheduled emotional actions and behaviors of human beings.

My POE

A note of caution to aspiring or practicing SBLs and principals: The POE that I am presenting here has been written at a stage in my life when I am no longer seeking any formal district/school-based position. Many of the ideas and concepts that I have put down on paper here were, and will always be, in my mind and definitely part of my practice. However, I would not put many of the thoughts documented below on a job application. In large part because public school systems are unfortunately inclined toward school (and district) leaders who will essentially follow the standard public education game plan. You should think very carefully about to whom you share and discuss this version of your POE. This is, after all, for your own personal professional development.

Here I offer the latest adaptive expression of several sections of my POE work in progress:

The United Nations Proclaimed in its Declaration of the Rights of Children:

"The Child shall in all circumstances be among the first to receive protection and relief."

And, "The child is entitled to receive education, which shall be free and compulsory, at least in the elementary stages. He shall be given an education which will promote his general culture and enable him, on a basis of equal opportunity, to develop his abilities, his individual judgment, and his sense of moral and social responsibility, and to become a useful member of society."

This proclamation in many ways represents the philosophical foundation of my practice. First, that the educational rights of American children are based on the fundamental human rights of all children; and that means all children in America! The singular purpose of schooling is the creation of an environment in which future generations can be nurtured in the development of intellectual, inquisitive, creative, analytical, behavioral, and physical skills. Public schools should serve as protecting and perfecting agencies on behalf of some of the most valued and vulnerable citizens of a society...its children! Schools are also the place to grow ethical and moral talents in such a way that students would utilize their skills for the good of themselves, their families, community, the nation, and the world. Further, a school district or school as a political entity can represent many things to many people. But to the children and their parents who are served by these entities, the educational experience is a one-time opportunity to fully realize their calling in life and then receive the tools to manifest and practice that unique and special calling in the world. Thus, as district trustees, managers, school-based administrators, teachers and support staff, our charge is to discover and enhance the natural inclination on the part of young people to uncover the mysteries of nature (along with their true learning natures), the exposure to thought-provoking ideas, the exploration of the yet to be explored, and as a result, also help them to uncover and develop their own unique gifts, talents, and contributions to human society.

Public education, in particular, has a unique opportunity to bring individuals together who represent diverse nationalities, religions, and socio-economic stations in life. Schools can model our best thoughts on the equality of access and exposure to the richness of our nation. That is, we can choose to make equity of resources and the equality of access to quality high standards and expectations, such that all children have a chance to become their best selves.

The power of public education is that a diverse community is brought together under the same roof and for the same purpose—learning. Millions of different parents, all sending their children to similar places, where they hope that their children can have a life that is qualitatively better than the lives they themselves presently enjoy. That is the sacred and unbreakable promise of public education to the parents of our society. But the underside of this story is a deep and pervasive cultural belief and practice that utilizes factors of race, ethnicity, gender, real and "manufactured" disability, religion and socio-economic (class) standing, not as a motivational tool of empowerment and learning, but rather as a means of denial and disqualification. Too many of our students in public education are only there to serve as throwaway political talking points and generators of cash to fund the educational well-being of other children. In fact, the schools of the poor and disenfranchised are designed to prepare a future income for their wealthy-enfranchised fellow students who attend "good" schools while the unfortunate attend "not so good" schools. This is accomplished through the poor, disenfranchised student's attendance at a planned and predictable school and district that is characterized by a systemic organizational culture of ineffectiveness and disinterest. A permanent class of under-achieving, failing, "pushed out into the world," unprepared, and under-skilled students is now the acceptable societal norm. The large poorly educated class of students will later as adults serve as the feeder system for a vast social pathology-fixing service industry. Their marginalized status means that many will work (if they are lucky to be employed) in wage-depressed jobs. And because of their lack of a bank of marketable skills and knowledge, combined with their ever-constant potential to fall into a chronic underemployment status, they then run the risk of being turned into "human feed" for a vast, ever hungry criminal injustice-prison system.

I declare independence from, and war on, such a system that is based on a pedagogy of domination and despair, along with the cruel suppression of a child's hope for the opportunity to be fully human in the future. I am compelled to stand as an educator who is in total opposition to that demeaning and destructive purpose and system of public schooling. I stand firmly and fight on the side of the dispossessed, disrespected, and disregarded children of our nation.

It is in the nation's best interest to expand the educational achievement enterprise to poor students and students of color. Not just as a matter of equality and morality but for reasons of national survival as well. We have a responsibility to fully utilize all of our natural strengths and resources for the good of ourselves and for the benefit of all of humanity. Fulfilling our national promise of providing the world with the model of educational justice and compassion requires courage. I believe our primary attribute as a country is to be in the position to gather the diverse collective, cultural intelligence of many different peoples, and place that intellectual advantage in the service of the nation. Again, it will take the courage and forward vision to get out of our present comfort zone of racial, ethnic, and economic class selfishness, but the reward for the nation is priceless. The political decision that some children are worthwhile while others are not, based mainly on criteria that is outside of the child's control, contains another great losing strategy. Ultimately, this national attitude of denying some children a promising future means that no children are truly honored and safe in our society. The truth is that we really don't do a good job with our highest-performing students because we compare their academic achievement status to students who are terribly underperforming and not to some higher academic standard and ideal. We could, by producing a larger number of "educationally whole" citizens, both lead in being the best cooperative, contributing, charitable, and peace-producing citizens of the world community of nations. But we cannot be moral leaders of the world education community when we choose to declare a war of educational neglect on large segments of our population. Parents and students should not be forced to play a life-determining lottery game of trying to land in an effective well-led school. Parental income and the parent's level of education can't be the deciding factor in a child's future. Poor schools and poor children can't serve as the dumping grounds for ineffective, inexperienced, and uncertified teachers and school leaders and then unfairly say that these children and schools are failures. We must also stop turning Black and Latino students into commodities, selling them to some opportunistic educational entrepreneur. Instead, we should force every public school to become seriously competitive and sincere in their efforts to fully educate their children. Parents are "voting with their feet," not because they are in either like or love with charter schools, but because they are desperately trying to save their children by getting them into a school that expresses some interest in their child's academic success.

History has taught us that the existence of segregated schools in this nation has meant that separate schools have never been educationally or financially equal. We must provide children with a good learning opportunity no matter what school they attend. We need a national rigorous core curriculum and

56

standards; a school environment where teaching and learning can actually take place; strong and effective school building administrators; adequate resources to close the very real parent-resource and education gap; a teaching staff that is expert and experienced; and an environment where all students are exposed to high levels of efficacy, expectations, and professional excellence. For sure, the child we as a society fail to educate will grow up angry and failing to realize their purpose in that society; he or she will lash out and seek to harm other members of society, whether or not those citizens were guilty for his or her failed educational experience.

Starting with what we have learned historically about pedagogy, it would seem that we have more than enough information about how to properly educate all children, regardless of the level of formal education and financial capability of their parents. We are a nation of great intellectual talent, inventiveness, creativity, wealth, and resources to achieve any goal that is humanly possible. The missing components that take us away from that commitment are the political and economic interest that supersede the interest and educational well-being of too many children in our educational systems.

The primary question is, should a small group of educational theorists be in charge of the educational outcomes for all students? And can we include the great volume of work by educators of color who have blessed us with their educational theoretical wisdom and/or school-based effective practices? These folks have worked hard to eliminate the barriers to Black and Latino student academic achievement, and they have produced a wealth of strategic steps that schools and school leaders can utilize to successfully scale those barriers that block students of color from successfully learning.

Also true is that Black and Latino civic and political leaders (and their White colleagues) should think about consulting more with the professional educators of color when questions arise concerning:

- Teacher or school leadership quality, tenure, placement, and professional development.
- Initiatives and policies put forward by school districts.
- Teacher recruitment and training.
- Strategies and programs for Black and Latino students who are on and above grade-level standards.
- A plan to educate and empower Black and Latino male students.
- Expanding and strengthening the STEM-CTE pipeline.
- School improvement, school redesign, school reform, and raising student academic achievement.
- The closing of real and artificial gaps.

- Affirming the culture and history of students.
- School disciplinary procedures and policies.
- Standardized testing.
- School safety and security.
- Charter schools and vouchers.
- School leadership training and development.
- Professional development.
- Gifted & Talented and other academically advanced programs.
- A common core curriculum.
- Teacher/student/school integration/diversity.

Without the theoretical and practical input of professional educators of color, many communities will be forced to deal with education policy decisions without the benefit of having access to information and assistance from an important and knowledgeable team of professional educators.

An important step in truly reforming public education would be to reclaim the true meaning and purpose of testing and assessment. However, for that to happen, parents and the public would need to feel a sense of trust in the professionalism of our work. We would need to convince them that we can honestly assess the quality of our own work and that which prevents us from producing high student academic achievement among all students.

There are some very useful reasons for testing individual students. Testing is an essential diagnostic tool that professional educators need in order to determine the necessary teaching methodologies necessary to support student learning. Testing and assessments need not always take the form of an exam. For example, a teacher utilizing questioning techniques to probe the level of students' comprehension during the course of a lesson is a critical assessment tool. As is the teacher asking students to utilize and apply a conceptual objective presented in the lesson in a demonstrated project performance-related way. Further, standardized testing removes the possibility that teachers can receive a "false-positive" feedback that can often be the case with teacher-designed exams. When standardized exams are aligned with learning standards, not only will administrators and teachers be able to properly assess student learning, the exam results will greatly inform the staff of the effectiveness of both instruction and the strategic quality of school leadership.

Principals should consistently be in the process of assessing student academic performance based on the curriculum content standards from the beginning, throughout, and at the end of the school year.

In addition to this, it is clear that the vast majority of schools don't have a strategic plan to address the educational needs of students of color who are on or above grade performance level, even when using the presently flawed standardized assessment systems. This creates a national environment where students become at risk of not receiving an appropriate (for their educational needs) and required high level of academically challenging and intellectually building classwork.

Finally, I truly believe that if a school is to effectively serve its student body, the key pivotal decision that must be made is the selection of that school's primary leader—the principal. For no other member of a school's staff can affect that school's capacity to be a high-achieving institution. Schools cannot effectively strive toward academic excellence if the school's leader is poorly prepared, pedagogically ignorant, lacking instructional knowledge, and strategically deficient.

Chapter 3:
The Principalship in Practice and Praxis: From Vision to SuperVision

My experience has taught me that a school can overcome a lot of negative things; however, it is very difficult for a school to thrive as a positive learning institution if an ineffective principal is in the leadership role.

Safety first!

"You can't," my former superintendent once said, "educate a child who is injured and at home, or who is in the hospital!" Creating a safe and secure school environment and providing parents with the assurance that their child is safe in your care is Priority #1! You can't lead scared. When an SBL fails to effectively lead, bad things happen. Some examples include:

- The annual, and in many cases, preventable series of serious injuries and deaths of high school varsity athletes due to poorly managed coaches.

- The large number of students who are chronically absent from school (for days or weeks) because of threats, or actual physical or verbal bullying. A student not in school is not learning!

- The student who told me once at a high school I visited, "I just 'hold it' until I get home, because the bathrooms are not safe!"

- A teacher in a math class at a school I visited asked a student to not call her a bitch again, as I sat observing in the back of the room. I became fixated on the word "again" and wondered how the school got to a place where calling a teacher a bitch was granted an "again" status.

- A student who hurls multiple curses at the teacher and is escorted by security to the dean's office. On his way out, he makes it clear that he will return and continue to display poor behavior. (He does indeed return to continue to disrupt the class!)

- Or the student who is killed while in the school's care.

I remember the story of a teen in Brooklyn back in September, 2013 who drowned on a class trip upstate after having been warned numerous times to leave the lake. The first question is, who is responsible for this child's death?

Poor home training or poor faculty training?

Even if they did not learn better at home, excuses cannot be used as a reason to not educate and protect children. And it definitely can't be used as a rationale to allow students to hurt themselves and other children! I would even go further and say that school is society's best and last chance to teach healthy emotional habits. School is the best place to teach life skills, for it is the place where young people spend a large amount of time. So, can we as educators proactively insert ourselves into whatever parental teaching effectiveness gap that exists in a student's head? That means treating the practice of school safety and security as an essential part of the school's theoretical and operational mission. It requires defined standards and measurable objectives, making it a major part of the SBL's organizational and procedural planning.

As a superintendent, I noticed that in almost every case of a student being seriously injured in a school, the situation always showed evidence of organizational, communication, procedural, teacher, and/or school leadership errors and missteps: the lack of clear preventative procedures, the absence of redundancy checking, not detecting procedural gaps, missing or not updated rules and regulations, unclear standards and expectations, and, finally, the fear of negative pushback.

As we think of the tragic drowning case, let's analyze some pertinent questions:

- Was there a list of school trip behavior procedures and protocols?

- Did the students receive a "pre-trip" briefing on those procedures; were they reminded of the school's expected behaviors?

- Did the trip coordinators employ a student buddy system for the duration of the trip? The idea that each student is responsible for the other at all times?

- Did the teachers and administrators have their own precaution policies? Was there a "code red" plan for a problematic student; or in the case of a trip of a great distance, for a staff person to accompany an unruly student back to a staff person waiting for him or her at a designated pick-up spot (e.g., airport)?

- Did the teachers in charge of the trip follow the procedural plan stated in the trip's parent permission slips? Is there a standard procedure whereby the trip staff can call a school administrator for permission to respond to any necessary change in the trip's procedures?

- Were there pre-trip behavioral standards that would disqualify a student from going on a trip?

- Did the school have a standard "Error on the side of student safety" override rule? (For example, even if swimming was one of the authorized activities for a trip, the teachers have the authority to cancel that activity if the water is too rough, an absent or overly distracted life guard, etc.)

- Did this particular student exhibit previous behaviors that would call for the staff to exercise extra supervision, or to ban him from the trip completely?

- What actions were taken/not taken after the first, second, or third warning was given to the child?

- Why were the students in the group in which the one student drowned so far away from the rest of the larger group? An authorized school staff person must have eyes on all students at all times.

- Why were the teachers not aware, or made aware, through professional development, of some fundamental principles of the psychological workings of the teenage mind?

- What role does the principal play in making sure all of the above is in place and understood before students set foot outside of the school building for any activity? You, the SBL, is responsible in this kind of situation.

The above and similar questions should form the framework for the development of the school's outside activities' policies and procedures.

There is nothing more dreadful than having to inform a parent(s) that their child is seriously injured or, even worse, dead while under your care. It very much falls on the school administration to make sure that staff is well versed in school and district safety policies and in the relevant and applicable civil law, regulations, and procedures. I am not an all-out fan of bureaucratic procedures, but most of these established laws and regulations make sense in terms of safety and security, and following them prevents tragedies from occurring. This may mean that a principal must risk being called out for being too strict or not wanting the children to have fun in order to keep students safe. But we cannot abdicate our professional responsibility of helping students to not hurt themselves or others because they (or their parents) think they don't like the policy. We must practice a morally ethical efficacy by not looking away as students place themselves in dangerous or deadly situations.

In every case, the degree of student compliance to an adult staff person's directive is measured in that child's response to a single authoritative request. This is why multiple requests for the same safety directive dangerously signals to a teenager that he or she has choices outside of an adult's decision. Further, psycho-linguistics is also in play in safety and discipline; the above drowning incident should inform us that a teenager voicing the phrase "okay" simply translates into "I hear you" but not necessarily that he or she understands or will even comply with your directive. The respect and authority of an adult staff member must first be established in the school building before taking students outside of the school's walls.

A safe teaching, working, and learning environment is non-negotiable!

You must create a safe learning environment if you expect students to progress academically. This allows teachers to effectively teach and students to have the space to safely learn. Add the factor that in high schools, a student who does not feel safe or who is being verbally or physically bullied will often decide not to show up for school! This is why principals must solve discipline problems on the front end or else these discipline issues will consume all of your school leadership time.

As you spend large amounts of your time addressing disciplinary issues, the quality of instruction deteriorates, which then creates an increase in disciplinary problems as the school rapidly descends toward greater school dysfunction and academic underachievement! Your first task as principal is to break that destructive educationally defeating cycle. You may need to expend a little more time in the initial establishment phase of developing a sound and effective discipline program. Or, you may need to invest a bit more annually in helping ninth-graders adapt to the school's behavioral expectations. But over time, the initial strategic planning, attention, and investment will pay off, and you will have more time to be an instructional leader. One of the best ingredients for a safe school atmosphere is a high level of quality instruction! Students will instinctively rebel against poorly planned and delivered lessons, particularly when they are accompanied by low expectations. The students also have an additional instinctual skill that will let them know when a teacher is unprepared and not fully committed to their success. The interesting thing about high schools is that students, specifically those who keep a constant eye on their GPA and standardized test scores, will complain to the principal if the teacher obviously does not have a lesson plan or if the lesson is poorly presented. That's actually the best-case scenario. Another type of response would be for the students to rebel and express their discontent during the class itself, and that rebellion could very much show up as misbehavior. Good instructional practices and good student behavior reaffirm each other. The successful principal makes sure that both are operationally functioning at a high level in the school at all times.

Many SBLs can only see a military-criminal justice response to school discipline problems, an approach that is doomed to fail. Seeking to establish a calm learning environment through brawn rather than brain will only create a disruptive response from students who don't see things your way. The principal must out-strategize the disruptive students in a school. You need a clear and descriptive set of expectations for bringing students into the well-behaving fold. This is as close as we get in education to a scientific law: *In any Title I school, no matter its academic performance level, the "miseducation detractors" are in fact a small minority of students while the vast majority of students come to school every day wanting to learn.* That fact is actually to the principal's advantage! The majority of students who really want to learn can become your allies in creating a positive learning environment in the school. You must put in the time creating that safe environment where quality instruction is the acceptable norm. If you fail to win over the majority who want to learn, you will be fighting a losing battle in the effort to establish a safe and productive school environment. There is, I believe, a cohort of students in every poorly organized school who are underperforming simply because of the school's disruptive environment. These students, if given the opportunity of attending a well-managed school, would pass both their classes and standardized exams.

Fear and a failure to plan, communicate, and execute a strategy are the greatest enemies of school safety and security success.

To construct this safe teaching and learning environment, know that fear is your worst enemy. Labor union rules/contracts/agreements may try to hold you to the strictest adherence of contractual workplace rules, which is the death bell for any school seeking to create a peaceful atmosphere. They may also push back against your campaign to improve the quality of instruction in all classrooms and further oppose your removal of chronically ineffective teachers who have not been able to positively respond to even your best professional development support. Ineffective instructors with classroom management problems absolutely contribute to a deterioration of their classroom and school's positive learning environment. On the positive side, if you create an atmosphere where teachers and staff are safe and respected by students, those teachers will support you, even as their union may hate your guts.

Then there are the "enabling" parents of students who are bullies, who chronically misbehave, and who are destructive to the classroom and school climate—all whose disruptive behaviors you must stop. These parents may complain to the superintendent, school board members, civic leaders, elected officials, etc., and these officials may even act in an unhelpful and unproductive way, for both the child and the school just to get these parents off their backs or to make a favorable impression. (Oddly, these same public officials will be the first to condemn you for leading an unsafe and academically underperforming school.) If the parents are politically connected in some way, they will of course feel that they have the ability to give you grief, preferably through one or several of the abovenamed political officials. My thoughts as an SBL went something like this: The principalship is a position that, because of the nature of the job, will in one way or another bring you political heat, so if you are going to take the heat, why not take it for leading a school where staff can safely work and children can effectively learn!

Failing to plan a safe school strategy is your next and second-greatest enemy.

Nothing that happens in a school, good or bad, is by accident. We are mistakenly led to believe that an effective school has a strategic plan to act effectively and that an "ineffective" school lacks a plan. *The truth is that an ineffective school is just as strategically planned to be ineffective as the effective school is about planning to be effective!* The misconception exists because the ineffective school's leadership and staff don't have meetings in which the agenda focuses on how they can be ineffective. The ineffective school might even have a bold and ambitious mission statement. But, no matter how bold, lofty, wonderful, and well-displayed these goals may be, without a concrete strategic plan of action, complete with objective and assessable tools of measurement and parodic evaluations, the wonderful words on the wall become just that. Wonderful words on the wall.

Organizational ineffectiveness is a product of ineffective thinking and planning. Academic failure, as I explain in the next chapter, becomes the true culture of the school, not because that is what the educators in the building hope for; rather, academic or discipline underperformance emerges because of the deficiency of strategic and thoughtful planning.

The SBL who hopes to have an effective, good learning environment must put a thoughtful plan in place that will counteract all of the anti-academic achievement elements that can undermine the success of a school. One thing you probably won't learn in your supervision and administration courses of study is that if you lead a school with a majority of Black and Latino students, you must put a plan (social and disciplinary) in place to protect, encourage, and enhance the well-being and school life of students who want to be smart. This is a critical tipping point issue. The more students who want to learn, the more they will achieve academically; thus, the academic achievement culture will grow exponentially.

It is critical that the SBL thoughtfully and strategically take on all elements of academically disruptive, anti-learning psychology in the school while at the same time strategically building a culture of pro-learning and pro-academic achievement to defend the school's positive learning culture. In schools that serve children of color and poor students, a positive culture of learning will be under constant attack because society has essentially abandoned these students, except to the point where their attendance means money. You must let them know, even if they push back against it, that the reason you want them in school is so they can learn; and, therefore, the learning environment must be protected. The consistency of that affirmation will over time sink into most students.

Any aspect of the school's environmental culture not organized by you will still get organized. Unfortunately, it may not get organized in a way that is good for children or for you. Get a plan, take a stand, and do the best and right thing for the children. But if you expect a school to be peaceful, work, and function well naturally without your and the staff's strategic intervention, then the plan is for dysfunction, chaos, violence, and, ultimately, academic failure.

Failing to effectively communicate your safe school strategic plan is the third enemy.

"Stop it, we don't do that here!"

A good, peaceful school strategic plan for productive learning is only as good as it is known and understood by all of the members of the school community. I have met (as superintendent) with many principals who had wonderful school safety plans buried in their brains or beautifully written on paper. As the SBL, you must be the chief spokesperson for the vision of the school. You must also be the chief promoter of every initiative that you and the staff have developed to make sure students are academically successful. As a principal, I strove to stay on message when faced with any situation (good or bad) in the school. A major part of communicating the mission plan is that all of your actions must reflect and reinforce the school's overarching mission statement. And even during those times when external rules, regulations, laws, and/or mandates contradict the school's mission plan, you must break or bend that order or rule. But even when you are following that not-so-good regulation or rule, it must be explained to the staff in the context of the school's transcendent mission. The key is to transform the school's vison into a set of schoolwide acknowledged and acceptable standards, such that things may from time to time get dim, but the visionary light is never totally extinguished and will always be present to guide all actions and decisions. Words are important in schools; words explain how the school chooses to define events, people, challenges, obstacles, and successes. They, therefore, also define how the school community will act and react in response to threatening (to the mission) external and internal events. One of the sweetest words I ever heard came from an upper-class person at my former school, Science Skills Center High School (SSCHS). The student was speaking to a pair of "play-fighting" first-year ninth-graders. "Stop it, we don't do that here!" said the upper-classwoman. I would hear that phrase spoken time and time again in relationship to many inappropriate behaviors, until the ninth-graders finally got it. I have also watched students pick up paper in the hallway and deliver it to the nearest garbage can, their actions speaking to the concept of working and learning in a clean environment. If we deconstruct that critical phrase "We don't do that here!" it will completely explain the important relationship between language and thinking—and, in this case, collective language and collective cultural thinking:

"We" suggests that the student speaking is not dividing and separating the school community into adults and students. *We* are one school community, with one mission, speaking with one undivided voice.

"Don't" speaks to our standards that are reflected in our behavior and pursuit of academic achievement. We *don't* do that particular behavior because we have come to a collective understanding that the behavior in question gets in the way of achieving our mission of being a total learning and academically achieving community.

"Do" the right and proper thing, for what we *do* here is focus our energy on the creative, constructive, positive, and productive. It does not mean that we don't have fun; it means that how we choose to have fun must fall into the category of safe, uplifting concern for the safety of others and creatively engage our physical and mental skills to work in a coordinative way. Finally, we are thoughtful and careful to not do things that, although seem fun in the beginning, have a high probability of producing a not-so-fun ending.

"That," which you are doing, is defined as past middle school behavior (sorry to my middle school colleagues). We, on the other hand, are on the last leg of our public school journey, which means we must in four years shed all childish silliness as we prepare to enter the adult world where the expectations, rules, penalties, and the "forgiveness-passes" that will be provided are limited. *That* behavior in which you are engaged will not work at a place of employment or college; no that will not work in the cruel and unforgiving adult world after high school.

"Here" this school is the place that believes in certain unique values and standards, and each of us is here to fulfill our own personal mission that is nec-

essarily consistent and connected to the school's mission. And, so, the primary *here* question is, why are you (we) here? And the fact that I, a fellow student, is even having this conversation with you should suggest that here, we do things a little (and/or a lot) different!

"We don't do that here!" completely explains how language must reflect the school's safety/security mission plan. It also defines "winning" for the principal, for when you hear yourself in other adults and students in the building, you realize that the school's mission is not just isolated inside of you. But even more importantly, when you hear the school's mission and purpose come un-coached or unsolicited out of the mouths of the students, that, my friend, is one of the best moments in a principal's life.

Failing to practice that strategy and plan consistently is the fourth enemy of a safe school.

One very important characteristic of a good and effective school discipline plan is consistency!

Perfection may be a wonderful abstract goal, but the consistent practice of good habits will make any individual SBL, or school, become better in practice. As the SBL, you must engage, promote, and practice all of the elements of a good school, even as your school struggles through occasional setbacks in realizing that objective. The key is to never give up, never give into institutional cynicism. No school, no matter how high-performing, acts at every moment in a perfect, or even effective, way. The key is to engage in authentic self-evaluation, and then take decisive and concrete steps to employ strategic plans that continuously improve the school's effectiveness status. The best rules when inconstantly applied is the same as or, in some cases, worse than having no rules at all. Everyone in the entire school family should be clear, even if they don't agree or like it, that action A will absolutely generate response B. And these "responses" are a constant in every aspect, event, and territory of the school's life: during the school day, after-school, on trips (remember our tragic student drowning incident), on teams, at athletic events, during assembly programs, in the cafeteria, etc. The fastest way for a principal to lose the respect (and therefore power of authority) from the staff, students, and parents is to not apply the discipline code forcefully and consistently—and in particular the stated consequences for student disrespect, bullying, classroom and in- and out-of-school misbehaviors. You can always substitute mercy for justice, when mercy is the justice that is required in a particular situation.

School safety and security is in the eyes of the beholder.

There is a tremendous difference in how schools perceive the safety and security needs of their students. In "good and effective schools," the student population is not viewed as people who must be contained rather than protected. Students in "good schools" are able to move around independently but responsibly—visiting the library, departmental offices, study centers, computer rooms, and classrooms not in session to talk to teachers, and the college/career office during their lunch periods, or just forming impromptu study groups on hallway floors. There is real art and sculpture displayed throughout the school. Security is seen as a force to guarantee student learning and safety, not just as a force to contain and arrest students. There are probably no metal detectors as the school is seen as a place you come to learn, not to hurt other people. There are very few bathroom visits by students during class time because students are highly competitive. Students also get to class on time because they don't want to miss important information. In those "good schools," the physical space is clean and inviting, and the smallest item in need of repair or replacement is done quickly. In any school, young people will adjust to the standards that adults in the building establish because teenagers are so amazingly flexible and open to change. They will adjust quickly to positive stimuli, and once they are on board, they will respond in the most positive and energetic ways. So, why not give them a chance to experience a clean and safe school environment; they might surprise you! Don't assume that by putting art throughout the building that they will destroy it. And they won't, especially when you explain that the presence of the art is a tribute and honor to their discipline and intellectual maturity. One of the most positive examples I saw of this principle was displayed by one of my former principals when I was superintendent of CSD 29 NYC. Principal Eleanor Andrews placed expensive African and African-American sculptures and artifacts on low tables throughout her elementary school. I watched as the students in pride warned other students to slow down, be careful, or watch where they were going so as not to disrupt the art exhibits.

There is a reason that *Lord of the Flies* has survived so long on our standard student reading list. Its message: Students may ask for the freedom and authority to run the school building, but in reality, they feel unsafe and lost when they are forced to assume that role. I always tell nervous principals I am coaching to never mind the pushback from students—and very often their parents. The students really want the school organized, managed, led, and directed by adults. And regardless of the level of resistance to their own best interest they may offer, they know—sometimes better than some adults—that to realize their life goals and dreams, they need a positive, peaceful, clean, and constructive learning environment. And you, the principal, must fight to create that safe and clean learning environment, even at the cost of engaging in some trying and stressful moments. The battle to create a positive and peaceful learning environment is probably one of the hills you want to die on, because living in an out-of-control, academically underperforming school is a fate worse than death!

Principals cannot be successful if they are afraid of instituting and enforcing high behavioral standards.

When I became a superintendent and traveled around the district talking to various staff persons and parents, somewhere in the top ten list of complaints from teachers was the inconsistent application of the school's discipline practices and procedures as well as the absence of concrete consequences for student misbehaviors. With the parents it was, "I told a school administrator that a student was (bothering, threating, bullying and/or picking on) my child and then no follow-up by the school…!" My walk-throughs of schools, superintendent suspension hearings, and parent complaints reaching my office would very much confirm that the many expressed concerns I heard were true. Students and staff can't thrive in a chaotic environment. Along with the human need for food, water, and shelter, there is a critical need for safety and security. The school building must be safe, clean, welcoming, protective, encouraging, and inspiring if there is any hope that teachers can teach and students can learn. Unfortunately, the dysfunction that exists in too many of our Title I schools has created an acceptable state of normalcy. You can't lead scared, particularly in high schools, where you can face students who may have spent their entire K-8 experience not being challenged to reach their attitudinal and behavioral best. A well-functioning, well-organized, and focused school experience may be a form of cultural shock for these students. I have spent a lot of my eleven years as a principal explaining to both students and parents that their understanding of what constitutes a school is different from my own. In many cases, they had no idea how a "real" school should operate. And, so, part of the unique struggle of my own high school principalship was to define the concept of "normal" and "acceptable," thus also defining the school's behavioral and disciplinary expectations and standards. In these group and individual conversations, the principal must establish a "philosophical beachhead" of standard cultural-linguistic expectations like:

- Coming to school every day on time!

- Coming to school every day, on time, and ready (prepared) to learn!

- Coming to school with books and learning materials and having done the homework!

- Coming to school dressed properly in accordance with the school's dress code.

- This school is not a democracy; the adults are ultimately the decision makers.

- You need not agree or understand a policy or procedure, but your lack of agreement and/or understanding does not exempt you from adhering to that policy and procedure.

- School is, and should be, hard.

- School is your (the student's) place of work; act like it academically, behave like it, and produce like it!

- Respect the classroom.

- You have a right to be safe and a right to learn to the best of your ability.

- Keep the building clean!

- Good and appropriate noise only!

- Cultural language, behavior, and attitudinal "code switching" must be used. This is a school! The "keeping it real" part of our mission is graduation.

- There are grave consequences for the destruction and misuse of any school property.

- There are grave consequences for threats (verbal or physical) and violence inflicted on another school family member.

- The school must be a place of peace and safety for everyone; fun must be expressed in a healthy way. There is a way to address conflict that does not involve fighting.

- Schools represent society's investment in you and your parents' hope for you; this school is not a place for you to hang out for four years!

- If you are poor, a student of color (and in particular a male student of color), school is your only viable pathway to a successful adult life. Everything else is either dependent on the decisions of others or a potentially dangerous activity or outcome.

- The work product of your place (school) of employment is academic work. The work should be high quality and reflect your best efforts.

- Get to every class on time and be prepared to work.

- A full spectrum of aesthetic intellectualism is practiced here: arts, music, literature, STEM, history, etc. Learning and knowing is a good thing.

- Being smart is good and okay here.

- Being smart and male is good and okay here.

- This school is the antidote to any societal discrimination and "unfairness." The enemy, therefore, is anyone who diminishes, degrades, disrupts, and denies the opportunity for students to learn at the highest level.

- The ISS room in this school is called ARC because our goal is to not have a punishment room but rather an Attitude Readjustment Center.

- This school is designed to break negative generational cycles, predictions, and traditions.

- This school exists to help students (and parents) to realize generational leaps of quality of life improvement.

- Young ladies are comfortable pursuing a STEM academic track here.

- Friendly academic competition for the highest grades is normal here.

- Successfully competing on standardized exams (SAT, ACT, AP, etc.) is expected here!

- Academic achievement and improvement, the honor roll, is honored, recognized, and rewarded here.

- Academic competitions and teams are normal here (chess, STEM, robotics, literary, debate, etc.).

- All learning should be led and complemented with a series of uplifting ethical and moral principles. The objective of skills acquisition is the realization and equipping of a call to service.

- The classroom is a place of serious work; socialize on the weekend or at lunchtime.

- Respect the work product of the teacher, and also respect the teacher and all members of the staff.

- Students have a right to question, protest, and challenge, in a responsible and productive way, any adult action.

- Students have a right to expect and receive the highest level of enriching academic instruction.

- Students have a right to expect high expectations from the school staff. The school staff will exercise its right to "push-pull" every student to their academic and behavioral best.

- Students should strive to pass every class with the highest grade possible. Failing classes is not acceptable, nor should it be the norm!

- Qualitative-Quantitative learning time. A peaceful, positive, and productive classroom experience is actually the standard expectation here.

- All classes (including non-standardized testing subjects) will provide the same level of rigorous academic work and expectations.

- We seriously practice and uphold the principle of Scholar-Athleticism, even when our standards are in conflict with the school district's standards. We seriously recognize that in the phrase Scholar-Athleticism, the word "Scholar" is not first by accident.

- The school will seek to discover (uncover), nourish, develop, and expand on the talents and gifts of all students. And this is whether they or their parents are aware of these attributes.

- The school reserves the right to influence and impact the student's out-of-school learning experiences and time.

- The school will step into and reduce the parent-information resource gap by providing students with in-school and out-of-school informal educational experiences.

- A total emphasis on academic achievement and moral character development in every non-course school activity, team, club, and program.

- Every student must develop a positive and productive post-high school plan (each student can change it if he or she so chooses) and then pursue an academic course of study that supports that objective.

- Every student must pursue a STEM Liberal Arts course of study that allows for the maximum ability to pursue many different career and college options/objectives.

- Perform every day with a post-high school objective in mind, starting with a successful graduation!

Many of the abovementioned qualities of a good and safe school environment may appear to be a no-brainer. However, the thoughtful principal must work every day with the idea of turning these qualities into permanent parts of the school's personality. These objectives will not emerge, and surely not be widely practiced, without a comprehensive plan that establishes and then institutionalizes them. Schools lacking such a plan will be pulled in the opposite direction, into an unsafe chaotic and confused state that pushes against academic achievement. As principal, you are probably (hopefully) required to submit a school safety plan to the district or superintendent. But you and your staff will find it necessary to augment and supplement that plan internally. There are some excellent sections of a standard school safety plan format, for example a school evacuation plan and site if the building cannot be occupied. However, for the complex requirements that are needed to keep a school and its occupants truly safe and secure—and, in particular, safe to teach and learn—you will need to go beyond the requirements of the standard school safety plan form.

You must strategically fight against official rules, regulations, laws, and political structures that not only get in the way of establishing an effectively safe school but also in many cases create and encourage the presence of unsafe schools. Each SBL must analyze his or her own particular political environment, his or her personal status in the system, and then make a *wise* decision as to what he or she can change or modify, what he or she must allow, must learn to live with, and perhaps do to counteract its negative consequences. This is a school-by-school, individual principal decision. I never advise principals to do some of the things I did as a principal. I did what I needed to do because I was committed to having a school where learning was the primary mission and activity. What can't be taught in administration and supervision certification programs are principal bravery and wisdom, which are different from thoughtless and reckless decision-making. Without quality school leaders, students who attend schools, particularly in high poverty areas, will lose their way and perhaps more importantly lose out on a future career promise. And just like it is foolish for schools to wish for parents and students you don't have, it is also foolish to think a school is going to automatically become safe and conducive to learning without effective school leadership. But a principal should know that every ticket to a safe and secure school has a price; so, the question is, what price are you willing to pay for safety and security? Before you answer that question, you may want to better your ability to understand the *Tone*, *Climate*, and *Culture* of the school. Let's explore these three important factors in the life and, unfortunately, sometimes academic performance death of a school.

Chapter 4:
Mastering, Managing, and Effectively Monitoring the *Tone*, *Climate*, and *Culture* of the School

School Tone: the "feel" of the school

Many people assume that all acquired knowledge is limited to information or numerical data gathered in some type of generally understood format. But, anthropologically and just below our conscious minds, we are capable of assessing people and situations as part of our natural "animal" defense mechanisms. And that is before we even speak to that person. Every day in every situation, we all engage in some type of body language display, analysis, and interpretation. Through our senses, humans are constantly evaluating a great deal of environmental information, much of it below the level of conscious and rational awareness. As professional educators, we know that learning is a continuous activity that takes place just as efficiently outside of school as inside the school—thus the power of the informal education system (i.e. public libraries, museums, dance, music, art classes on the weekend). What the effective SBL must do is to perfect a technique whereby you can read those information-rich indicators that tell when something is amiss about the school. That skill will require a type of decentering that will allow you to observe the school and yourself as if both of you were performing on a stage and at the same time sitting in the audience. It takes a combination of experience and honesty to assess what the school should be and the associated rubrics that will define those standards. In high schools, parents are usually not coming by the school to drop off flowers or cookies for the staff. They are more than likely coming to the school because of a problem. The standard tone-setting for a parent's visit is critical. I encouraged and professionally developed my security and office staff's performance objectives in order to set the best *Tone* so that the parent agitation can be lessened and not increased after encountering the front door security staff. Of course, this approach may not completely eliminate the possibility of a parent coming up to the school to tell somebody (usually the principal) off, but it can dramatically reduce the confrontational odds by a more thoughtful and professional security staff approach.

I define *Tone* as the un-surveyed and possibly uninformed feel of a school. One of the meetings you want to have in which you do a lot of listening and very little talking is with your students who have visited other schools—for meetings, competitions, or sporting events. Listen carefully to their observations and insights, which are not based in pedagogical knowledge or analytical data. I have found that teenagers are extremely honest, and their comments can be enlightening! First, because their observations are always cast in a compare-and-contrast format with their own school, listen to what their concerns and comments are about their school and the other school. Plus, I have found over the years that their conclusions about the *Tone* of schools they visited, in every case, was correct and matched my interpretation of that school. You can get the same effect when students from another school visit your hopefully effective school, and offer unscreened opinions of comparisons and contrasting elements of the two schools.

The first sign of a school's *Tone* is that feeling you get when you arrive to the school. The physical presentation of the school leading from the area outside surrounding the school, the neatness and cleanliness of the building as you walk in the front entrance area, the path to the main office, a visit to an office in the building—all of these areas are the school's announcement to all visitors about "who and what we are!" The attitude, approach, and practices of the security staff are telling. The way you are greeted and treated in the main office (within five to ten seconds of walking in) will announce if the school is either parent/visitor friendly or unfriendly. Also, the look and sound of the school is just as important. In fact, a school's *Tone* is so pronounced and loudly revealing that an experienced, knowledgeable, and insightful SBL can walk around an empty school building on the weekend and learn a great deal about that school's daily Monday-Friday practices! If you visit enough schools, as I did as superintendent, you will notice some predictable patterns of effectiveness and ineffectiveness. The *Tonal* factors you detect, in isolation, does not tell the entire story of a school, but it sure as heck will point you in the right direction! For example, I was once visiting a high school in a school district with which I was working as a consultant, and in the first ten minutes of my visit, I was standing in the hall with the principal and a member of the superintendent's staff. The bell rang and students exited their classes. The first thing I noticed was that something was wrong with the way the students were moving as well

80

as the volume of their voices. After the second late bell rang, there was still a large number of students who were in some stage of arriving to, but still not in, their classrooms. There seemed to be no sense of urgency to get to class. When some lingering students were asked to move to class by an AP, one student remarked, "I will go to class as soon as I finish what I am saying." (To keep my peace, I had to keep repeating the mantra, "This is not your school, this is not your school!") Those brief *Tonal* moments led me to hypothesize a great deal of possible performance outcomes about the school. And when I looked at the published academic, punctuality, and attendance performance data on that school, my *Tone*-driven hypothesis was confirmed.

As a principal becomes more proficient and thoughtful in their craft, they will be able to detect the Negative-Positive *Tonal* Modulations-Fluctuations in their own school, but that takes practice, time, and thoughtful praxis. To put it in the words of science education, properly perceiving the *Tone* of a school is a working hypothesis (a well-informed guess) of what is actually taking place with the academic performance of a school. But a good science educator would also say that you must be willing to test that hypothesis and be open to proving your hypothesis right or wrong. It can be dangerous to make a grand assumption about a school when one is exposed to a small area and in a short time period, so we should also be careful not to discount the need for actual data, more observation time, and critical analysis reports. The other important point here is that this *Tone*-based hypothesis rests on another hypothesis. And that is, a high-performing school and an underperforming school both exhibit their respective true qualities and personalities (*Culture*) in every aspect of the school's life. The entire school's real mission is revealed a thousand times during the course of a school day in small cumulative acts that may, in themselves, not seem to connect to academic achievement, but they absolutely do! In other words, qualities of a high-performing school will include students moving quickly to class, students themselves discouraging any interruptions to the start and flow of the lesson, or students exhibiting a sense of academic urgency (e.g., anxiety about GPA or standardized exams). They are not moving quickly to class for the benefit of adults (even if the adults support and encourage it); they are really doing it for themselves.

Now, I know that there is the danger of coming to conclusions too quickly, having gathered too little information. But for any person, in any type of leadership position, the practice of forming first impressions and intuition can at times be indispensable skills. These skills are the most useful when they are bolstered with experiential practice, professional knowledge as well as studies of human psychology, management, systems, operations information, emotional intelligence, and old-fashioned "mother wit!" Principals are forced to make many decisions every day on continually emerging problems and make those decisions quickly. These problems that require immediate decisions most often fall outside of the realm of regulations and statistics. Ultimately, we lead a complex institution that is composed of diverse and complex people, so no amount of technical tricks, smooth algorithms, fancy theories, and formulas can really help a principal when overnight reflection time is not an option. A sizing up of the *Tone* in a particular situation could be the best short-term information available. And most importantly, the *Tone* can serve as an early indicator of a larger, or perhaps, more dangerous problem that is waiting just down the road to meet you!

The Tone provides a good first glance at a school's true nature as well as its natural inclinations.

I remember in my first week as a superintendent, I was walking up the sidewalk to a middle school for my first visit. Students in one second-floor classroom had half of their bodies out of the windows as they threw objects, including books, onto the ground while yelling obscenities. It was a disturbing introduction of what the school was truly about. Indeed, ineffective schools scream their ineffectiveness like those students were screaming at me on that day. And every single act of ineffectiveness in a school is independently bad, but at the same time, each serves as a small interdependent example of all of the terrible wrongs in a school. Seeing those students hanging out of the windows as they hurled school property and invectives on someone who was visiting their school cannot be seen as an isolated act. The *Tone* being established by those students was a surface expression of the true nature of the school. The *Tone* may be small and incomplete, but it never lies! Every classroom in a school is also a representative sample of the school; for a school is truly only as strong as its weakest instructional practitioner. Explanation: Effective schools have a critical mass or threshold of good teachers who can compensate and correct the work of the few poor or average instructional practitioners. The opposite is true in an academically underperforming school where the number of ineffective instructional practitioners overwhelms and neutralizes the good work of the smaller number of effective and well-practiced teachers. But as

82

I entered the building, I observed many other *Tonal* elements, which would graphically explain the school's poor academic performance data:

- Large numbers of students arriving to school late. Thus,

- Large numbers of students missing most or all of their first-period classes.

- Those who were reasonably late (ten to fifteen minutes) went to class but then interrupted the flow of instruction and learning.

- During the changing of classes, the majority of students arrived to their classes late. "Late," meaning that they were not in their seats and ready to work by the time the second late bell rang.

- Too much hall traffic (bathroom visits) during class time. Most of these trips were not out of a biological necessity, rather students using their bathroom passes as a way to take a break from the class. Of course, the re-entering procedure by these students often caused further instructional interruptions, including the fact that information and directions that was provided by the teacher while they were out those five to ten minutes had to be explained and/or repeated.

- Too many classroom disruptions from learning in the classrooms. In most classes, students actively engaged in small, to medium, to many acts of off-task behaviors, including comedy/jokes, inappropriate commentary, peer teasing, mobile phone engagement, social talk, and in some cases just refusing to do the classwork.

- Black and Latino boys clustered in the back of the room of most classes.

- I noticed that in every class I visited, actual learning didn't start until we were seven to fifteen minutes into the period. There was a school-wide low number of minutes that were actually dedicated to various quality levels of instruction, which meant that even if some classes were able to get started ten minutes into the period, the quality and quantity of learning was questionable.

- In my notes, I have renamed the APs as ADs (Assistant Deans) because they spend all of their time dealing with discipline issues and no time as instructional leaders—they all walk around with loud walkie-talkies.

- A poorly organized (too many negative incidents) lunch period carried the loud and disruptive cafeteria "atmosphere behaviors" into the classes that followed with not-so-good results.

- A poorly organized and theory-less ISS and discipline program; there is no serious academic counseling or rehabilitative work taking place in ISS.

- A very unorganized and underutilized library program.

- An underappreciated and under-resourced creative, performing, and graphic arts program.

- A visionless, purposeless technology program. In fairness here, this school, like many of the schools in that district, were victims of massive computer fraud and had classrooms and computer rooms that housed missing or unusable computer equipment.

- The absence of rigorous academic work in the majority of classes, and in some classes no academic work at all. Several teachers were literally fighting ("stop that," "sit down," "leave her alone," "watch your language," etc.) to get to the end of the period.

- *Tonal* observations giving a good hint into the depth of the school's ineffectiveness. In one particular class, a young lady was sitting on a desk as she braided another young lady's hair who was sitting in a chair. This suggested to me that this type of behavior was not strange and in fact grew out of a long history of disrespect for what should have been happening in that classroom.

- Sectioned off and separate special education classes were simply holding pens where no real instruction took place. In one class, the teacher spoke to the class as I entered. "Class, this is our new superintendent, try to behave yourselves." She said this as if pleading with students to behave. One young man in the back of the room, I guess designating himself as the class spokesperson, proudly blurted out, "Fu*k you and Fu*k the new superintendent!"

- A poorly organized dismissal procedure, which meant that any unresolved student conflicts were resolved by the students themselves in the blocks that adjoined the school. I actually had to personally break up one fight. Thus, the reason for my receiving (prior to the visit) a long list of daily complaints into my office from the homeowners surrounding the school.

And later that evening, I compared my *Tonal* Notes with the school's actual performance data:

- High student absenteeism.

- High student lateness—their first-period course failure rate was unbelievably high.

- High teacher turnover.

- A "critical mass" (too many) of new teachers with one to two years of experience.

- High teacher absenteeism, which led to a burnout-sickout cycle. The teachers who had the best attendance were "punished" by being forced to cover so many classes of absentee teachers during their preparation periods. Naturally, these teachers themselves became ill from overwork and stress, further contributing to the absentee teacher problem. Only the most "desperate" teachers in the substitute teacher pool wanted to go to that school—desperate, meaning that these were the most competency-challenged teachers in the sub-pool. Of course, this did not help an already-compromised school environment. There was no schoolwide substitute plan of action, such that these subs could actually do a good job if they tried. Some teachers left really good plans and procedural guidelines, others left nothing, leaving the subs to invent a lesson on the spot—always a prelude to serious classroom misbehaviors.

- A critical mass of substitute teachers. When you employ too many subs on any one school day in a school that is already struggling with discipline issues, the level of discipline will automatically deteriorate badly. For the students in this school, the presence of a "sub" means "hunting season" is officially open! The students also see "sub time" as an opportunity for them to fulfill their need to explain to the substitute teacher the rules and procedures of the school and class; this never turns out well. And this is why a school seeking to be excellent will have: (1) Good teacher attendance. (2) A really good choice of substitute teachers who are professionally developed and prepared via an orientation and a substitute teacher's manual. (3) Or, because teacher daily attendance is so good, they can cover these few and rare classes with internal teachers who won't get burned out and who know the school and students well. (4) An excellent absent teacher plan such that the behavioral objectives of the school are seamlessly enforced, and that the learning continues on a challenging and rigorous level, even though the classroom teacher is absent (or must leave the class suddenly).

- The school's standardized exams performance data correlated with all of the visual and experiential *Tonal* data I collected when visiting the school.

Now, as bad as things looked and were at that school, all of the above negative issues were and are preventable and fixable in any school. But I'll save that for a later chapter. For now, I want to make the point that principals must be sensitive and alerted to the information a school and the school family members produce outside of published school data. Critical state and district statistical information about a school can often be gathered and provided at a time when it is least useful for the principal and staff. Principals need to expand the definition of data and information gathering beyond statistics. Some indicators that suggest that a school is either in, or rapidly heading toward, chronic academic underperformance may include: large numbers of students arriving to school or class late, a small percentage of class time actually being dedicated to effective teaching and learning, the overwhelming majority of parents who show up for Parent-Teacher night/day are for students who are performing well or exceeding academically, "Nerdism" and not academic underperformance are seen as the most undesirable state for a student by the student body, students are not concerned about grades or test scores, or there is low efficacious behavior among teachers. The purpose of the principal engaging in a lot of walking around the school and visiting classes daily is to take notes of these unexpressed occurrences and then place them into a collage-like portrait of the larger message of what the school is truly about. This primary analysis will automatically lead us to probe deeper into these observations to seek the origins of the occurrences that hinder the school from performing at its best. And for that deeper analysis, we need to examine those *Tonal* factors that reveal and are connected to the school's *Climatic* revelations.

School Climate: How the school is perceived by its different internal stakeholders

A school's *Climate* is what the school family members perceive the school to be. There was a principal once who thought he provided all of the positive organizational elements that support teaching staff and that are generally associated with teacher satisfaction, but their perception of that principal's leadership profile was a little different from his perception of his leadership performance profile. When voting for a union representative, they rejected a candidate who embodied the school's mission—a teacher who possessed great intelligence and pedagogical knowledge who sincerely cared about students for a person who was the absolute opposite of everything the school stood for. And, so, this is a serious warning to any principal to not lean heavily on his or her own perceptions, for one's perceptions might be tragically out of sync with the staff's perceptions of the school.

Reading the climate

The *Climatic* informational data can be best found in the casual comments that are a critical part of the school's daily dialogical experience. The SBL should be aware that a great deal of negative comments might escape your ear, but that does not minimize its existence or importance in how people see and go about their work. The principal may need to engage in the art of good listening. There is power in paying attention to even the smallest, seemingly casual, comments that reveal a deeper school cultural belief system. Here's a list of some *Climatic* perceptions or statements in a school that the principal may or may not hear:

- "I don't feel as a _____ that my work is important or recognized here."

- "How is what I do part of the school's mission?"

- Student or teacher: "I don't feel safe in this school!"

- "The principal mostly favors and supports _____ (fill in the blank: varsity sports, science, history, mathematics, technology, marching band, etc.)."

- "As a parent, I don't feel welcomed (or respected) in the school!"

- "The teacher/administration doesn't like and is picking on my child!"

- Staff Person: "The parents of the students in this school don't understand and appreciate the importance of education!"

- Teacher: "These students don't care about education and academic achievement!"

- Student: "Teachers don't care about students being successful in this school!"

- "Professional development in this school is useless and a waste of time."

- Student (and possibly teacher): "They (administrators) only pay attention to the 'bad' kids!"

- "They (administrators) only care about the 'smart' kids in this school!"

- "All that the administration cares about is standardized testing (scores)!"

- "Disciplinary rules mean nothing in this school!"

- Student/Teacher: "X student(s) are the teacher's/administration's pets; they get more and get away with more!"

- Teacher/Staff Person: "The principal or 'administration' is only out to get us!"

- "This building is filthy and poorly maintained, and this is how they feel about me!"

- "I am carrying my workload and somebody else's, too!"

- "The only time I hear from teachers in this school is when my child gets in trouble!"

- "Because of standardized tests, nobody in this school cares about art, dance, PE, music, the library, and other classes!"

- Any member of the school family (staff, students, administration, parents): "This is not a good school!"

Some good and positive examples:

- "We are on a mission here, and I feel my work is critical to accomplishing that mission!"

- "I feel that the school administrators are always open to hearing my side of the story."

- "As a _____ (guidance counselor, cafeteria supervisor, teacher, custodian, etc.), I feel supported in this school!"

- Parent: "The school is proactive when the first signs appear of my child underperforming in any behavioral and/or academic area."

- "Teachers care about us here!"

- "I teach a non-standardized testing course, but my resource request and concerns are seriously addressed by the school's administrators."

- Students and teachers: "I feel safe here!"

- "School administrators are very visible during the school day and make themselves available to the other members of the school family."

- Staff Efficacy: "I don't care what the parents do or don't do, I know what I am going to do!"

- "Teenage growing issues aside, the students in this school are essentially good!"

- Students: "We can learn in this school without classroom disruptions!"

- "There is always a consistent response and follow-up response to a disciplinary issue!"

- Staff Person: "I am proud to say that I work at _____ High School!"

- Student: "I am proud to say I attend _____ High School!"

- Parent: "I am proud my child attends _____ High School!"

- "This school is clean, well maintained, and an inspiring place to work and learn!"

- Any member of the school family (staff, students, administration, parents): "We may not be perfect, but this is a good school!"

These sample expressions are examples of the ways in which various school community members might perceive or experience the school. As a principal, you should know that complaints naturally make up the majority of expressions. And that is because people in general tend not to offer praise when something is working well or as it is intended to work. But all of these statements (good and bad) offer a kind of truth because it is how the school family members feel, regardless of the objective reality. You should also know that every principal's decision or policy pronouncement, no matter how large or small, will have its group of fans and detractors. It is rare to get anywhere near a 100% agreement for any decision, policy, plan, initiative, or procedure, but individual school family members, departmental, and job category perceptions are seriously important. I offer two examples:

The diverse dynamism of schools can often create real or imagined conflicting interest. A decision, rule, policy, regulation, initiative, plan, or project can be interpreted in different ways by the many different members of the school family. For example, I once saw how creating special education/regular education inclusion team-teaching classes created concern from many different school family stakeholders, and for different reasons. Special Education (SPED) teachers and Regular Ed teachers both had concerns about losing their previous independent working situations. They worried about how this "team-teaching thing" would actually work, particularly in a high school. And both were concerned about how these classes would translate for their formal observations and ratings. SPED parents felt that their children would not receive the appropriate services and support. The Regular Ed parents thought that the SPED students would disrupt, lower academic rigor, and/or slow the class down. All of these concerns and many others they raised were extremely valid and appropriate. It helped the eventual acceptance of the program by all involved because I sincerely listened and seriously responded to all of the many concerns. The important point here is that the *Power of Perception* cannot be ignored or underestimated. It is important for the principal to be able to distinguish between critically valid questions and concerns, no matter how poorly expressed, from negative opposition and/or undermining behaviors.

In high schools, there are always some forms of friendly competition between the content departments. This is understood and expected as these teachers are perhaps the most focused content area practitioners in the K-12 system; they view themselves and tend to socialize, bond, and advocate by departments. A school leadership challenge may arise over budgetary/resources allocation decisions. It is not uncommon for one academic department to feel that another academic department is receiving more financial attention. Great care must be given by the principal to both speak and act in the spirit of fairness and transparency. And "fairness" being defined as consistent with, and supportive of, the school's mission. The principle being upheld here is *strategic budgetary mission driven planning*—everyone getting what they need to succeed, though not everyone necessarily may receive the same thing. This is the only way for the principal to address the resource perception issues in schools. Principals can help to raise the quality of perceptions in the school by utilizing better communitive and explanatory methods, with a focus on the larger school mission. And as I explain later in detail, the principal can also help themselves here by putting in place a robust fundraising program, which will allow for additional school financial resources beyond the standard district budget allocation!

Now, although perceptions serve as the revelatory tool for determining the *Climate* of a school, this does not mean that those perceived realities are in fact aligned with the true reality. But, it can't be said too many times in terms of the rules of school *Climate* assessment that perception is a type of reality that is just as powerful and influential as the actual objective reality. In some cases, it can be even more dangerous when a critical level of bad perceptions are shared by a significant number of members of the school family.

Misinformation masquerading as information

A great deal of what emerges as negative perceptions in a school could be initially created by incomplete information, misinformation, and/or the misinterpretation of information. A false narrative could be passed informally from person to person right under the principal's nose! The effective SBL must be able to stay in front of these never-ending and recurring school rumors that can often steal the power and goodness of the truth. Further, rumors acting as agents of perceptions have their own power and deleterious effects given the wide spectrum of human motivational psychology (e.g., fear of loss, favor, resources, or status).

91

The Tone-Climate Continuum in practice

If the *Tone* best describes the fundamental, initial "surface" perceptions of one who is observing the day-to-day operational behaviors of a school, the *Climate* describes the more deeply felt and expressed perceptions of the internal school community, which, as we stated in the previous section, may or may not be grounded in objective reality. The *Climate* as it is expressed through perception is a view seen through the lens of subjectivity. But we also said that upon reaching a critical mass of individual negative perceptions, acting in an additive fashion will lead to a general negative school *Climate* that produces "blame-ism," mistrust, unhappiness, and eventually through diffusion, organizational dysfunction, ineffectiveness, and academic underperformance. But there is a connected continuum of beliefs and practices that link the *Tone* and *Climate*. The internal perceptions, opinions, and attitudes of the school family are unconsciously and obviously announced via the *Tone* of the school to visitors as well as to the school's internal stakeholders. An office staff that is not customer-friendly to parents or visitors will not be able to suddenly turn on the charm for the staff and students. The people who work, live, and learn every day in the school building will be fully aware and affected by the poor maintenance and cleaning standards of a school building custodial staff. And, so, the school's *Tone* is an emotional response to the school family's internal perceptions of the importance and sacredness of the school's mission. In a poorly led school, the entire school family will be aware that things are not working well for anyone. This general perception of underperformance, underachievement, and collective organizational low self-esteem (by staff, administrators, parents, and students) becomes self-nurturing and self-fulfilling to the extent that even when there is a success story, it is seen by the school family as an aberration.

Perception has the power to create perceptions.

On every level and at every moment, schools are engaged in some form of public relations work, both internally and externally. There is the management of communication (good and bad events), marketing the mission, creating and building the "school brand," advertising and image-building as part of the school recruitment and fundraising plan. The principal should have no doubts about the power and influence of the internal and external perceptions and how they deeply affect the people who work and study every day in the building. School family members could be either "talking up" or "talking down" their own school. And it is only natural for most school people to want to be associated with a winner, not a loser—even if they, by their own actions and behavior, are major contributors to that loser status!

In both high schools I led, it was common for staff members in every job category to bring their family members and friends to their workplace for which they were proud. In both schools, students brought their friends and family members to visit. And in both schools, I had a high rate of sibling and family member student applications for attending the school. Like it or not, people talk, and it is very common for people to talk about the place where they work. Those conversations serve as a type of people-to-people public relations exercise. I don't know how many times, as a principal, people have come up to me at a public event to tell me that a neighbor, friend, family member, church/temple/masjid member, co-worker, employee, etc., was connected to a child who attended my school and that the person had so many great things to say about the school. If the internal stakeholders feel good and speak well of the school, then that good dialogue will influence the external views of the school, which will generate positive feedback and praise, eventually strengthening the energy, commitment, dedication, and resolve of the school's internal family to maintain the school's positive image. I read somewhere that, "A good name is more desirable than great riches; to be esteemed is better than silver or gold." A school's good name and image can translate into greater resource support from the district and societal sources outside of the school. A positive perception of the school definitely helps with funding because people, foundations, corporations, government agencies, and departments like to support what they perceive to already be effective and successful. High information-resourced parents, who are actively or deeply engaged with the education of their children, will tend to seek out and cluster in a particular school and benefit from parent-to-parent informal education resource sharing communication. Public schools complain a lot about uninvolved parents and how charter schools are siphoning off the most active and involved parents. But what are these schools doing to improve the Community Perception Relations (CPR) of their own institutions? I have always said as a superintendent that public education, if it got out of its own way, could change the public's perception of our viability and capabilities. For example, SSCHS attracted an amazing number of students who were first- or second-generation Americans. Many of these parents, whether they hailed from a country in the Caribbean, India, China, Korea, Mexico, etc., often said to me that what attracted them to

SSCHS was that it was an American school that in many ways reminded them of the disciplined and intense attention to hard study and academic achievement they experienced in the nation of their birth. Ordinary citizens in Washington, D.C., often commented to me that Phelps ACE and my leadership style reminded them of how the "old" Phelps and the "old" Dunbar operated when Black D.C. students were recognized as having the highest academic standards nationally, not just in D.C.

The principal must know as you try to "read" and interpret the *Climate* of a school via the stated perceptions of the school family members that behind every perception is a real person who brings their own story perceptions to situations. And, yes, gender, personal history and experience, culture, ethnic and racial issues can misshape their perceptions. The personal histories and memories (false and real) of their own schooling experiences, which parents bring to your school along with their children, are tremendous determiners of how they will perceive and act in your school.

Principals must be able to effectively translate the spoken Climatic perceptions.

Very often, people in a school will tell the principal what they think the principal wants to hear. And because schools are driven by cultural-linguistic factors, translation methods must be employed by the SBL to get at what people really mean when they verbalize X or Y perception.

Are staff members saying what they mean and meaning what they say?

Educational professionals have a history of speaking in politically correct terms; these terms, purposely or not, can be misleading to those who are outside of the profession—but deadly and dangerous when we ourselves are misled by our own language. We are quick to say something like "children come first" and then in actual work/practice we place a long list of items ahead of children such as costs, job security/rights/tenure, politics, vendors, race, ethnicity, etc. But, at the very least, "children come first" sounds good and it helps us to look good even as we don't really believe or practice it. Further, the hidden (from the principal) language and vocabulary of the school family members—perhaps spoken in places like the gym locker room or the teacher's lounge or cafeteria—are powerful and influential because they often drive attitudes and work-learning styles. Some of this is driven by the wide diversity of the school family membership. People can be connected to a school in many different ways (student's academic status, academic department, food services, security, clerical, etc.). Their personal situation, classification-categorization, and needs determine their perception of what they bring to the school as well as what they hope to gain from the school. Schools mistakenly give off the impression that everyone inside of the school fully understands their jobs and the jobs of others. Here, I have expanded the idea of job description into a job analysis explanation. Very often, it is only the principal who fully understands all of the diverse job classifications as well as the diversity of student needs in a school and how they all fit together.

The SBL should also think of the school's mission as the overarching and all-encompassing job description/category. And what is the best way to generate more positive perception statements about the operational quality of the school. It is a critical mission of defining a unity of purpose message that is effectively transmitted by and throughout the school family to an internal and external audience. Different categories of employees in a school building can and are under a diverse series of rules and regulations, timetables, deadlines, reporting procedures, relationships to external agencies, labor contracts, different evaluation systems, etc. And, so, if a regular education teacher were to be asked about the work of a special education teacher and vice versa, their answers would reveal a great deal about how these two teachers view the work of the other, but their answers will also tell us how each of them views their own role in reaching the school's mission. If members of these two teaching job categories see each other as the enemy or the educational other, then their individual teaching objectives as well as the school's overall academic mission objectives become harder to achieve. High schools are also inclined strongly towered departmentalism, which can seriously influence how teachers in a particular academic department perceive the school as well as their school colleagues who work in other academic departments. At times, these departmentally driven perceptions can get in the way of the schoolwide academic mission! The key here is for the principal to market and sell the idea that we may have come to the school with and for different reasons and may even want to achieve different objectives. However, our best chance for realizing our own success is to see how that individual success is inextricably connected to our collective success as a school.

Rumors and perceptions

Negative rumors in a school that are the manifestations of bad perceptions have their own power and deleterious effects, given the wide spectrum of human motivational and reactant psychology (e.g., fear of: loss, change, obsolescence, favor, resources, or status). All of this is to say that the SBL must be aware of the results that can be produced by the transmission of false or real negative rumors that are nurtured in the soup of *Climatic* commentary. We will talk next about how a general school *Cultural* perspective can limit the damage, counteract, and even destroy a false, half-truth, or even fully true negative rumor.

Generally held negative perceptions can unfairly wound a school in areas where it is really making progress. They can also deceptively provide a false sense of success where there is none. Principals do themselves and the school a disservice when there are "cover-ups" or a lack of candor concerning the challenges that the school faces. Problems can't be solved until they are properly identified and strategically addressed. If teachers perceive that there is a leadership credibility gap between the stated school rules for classroom discipline and what actually is allowed to take place in the classrooms, or that varsity athletes and sports are the primary focus for the principal, etc., then it does not matter if the principal is promoting a schoolwide narrative that academic learning is the school's primary mission. When the objective reality supports the staff's perceptions, then those perceptions are the painful reality of the school. The principal does not have the power to stop all rumors. But he or she can manage these perception-driven rumors. First:

- Have a real (not rhetorical) "open door" policy.

- Actively move around the school as if on a daily listening tour.

- Give the staff person, parent, and student your full attention, as if while that person is talking he or she is the only one in the school.

- Be available and open; don't let your body language say "don't bring me any bad news!"

- Be open to hearing what you don't necessarily want to hear. Remember: It need not be said in the most desirable or politically correct way!

- Set up several processes by which students (and parents) can communicate with you on a confidential level. For me, it ranged from some

96

parents and students having my home or mobile phone number, to students pressing a note into my palm as I stood at the door for the daily welcome-to-school greeting sessions. You then must guard their anonymity or you will lose credibility and the critical access to important unofficial school information.

- Be humble and understanding. Of course, you have 100 serious things presently in some stage of play. But for that student wanting a class change or internship, or that teacher who would like some additional books, materials, or equipment for a class project, this moment with you could be one of the most important parts of their school day. So give their question, concern, or request your serous undivided attention!

- Constantly promote the school mission at every opportunity.

There were many situations of student-to-student conflicts, incidents of home/family physical/psychological abuse situations, threats of suicide, and a student planning to run away from home that the above techniques allowed me to proactively and successfully intervene in before a bad incident took place, got worse, or a tragedy occurred. But this approach to intelligence gathering also allowed me to get in front of, provide clarification and an alternative narrative, and ultimately squash a negative rumor before these rumors reached their dangerous stages. Knowing your powers of influencing *Climatic* perceptions is important, but also knowing where you have less or limited power to control individual and collective perception narratives is equally important. Endeavoring to hear what you need to hear to be an effective SBL, rather than what you want to hear, is the beginning of leadership-learning wisdom. And another reason that the *Leadership Knowledge/Information Acquisition Hierarchy* is: *Tone, Climate*, and, ultimately, *Culture* is the most revealing indicator of what is truly going on in the school! And just as the analysis of the school's *Tone* (feeling, sense, and a primary hypothesis) pointed us in the direction of the school's *Climate* (verbal-body language, expressed and sometimes unexpressed perceptions, and those dangerous negative rumors), we will now see how the proper reading and understanding of the school's *Climate* gets us closer to truly understanding the school's ultimate profile and personality, which is defined as its *Culture*.

The School's Culture: What the school truly is, not what the school family thinks or claims it to be

"What people say, what people do, and what they say they do are entirely different things."

— Margaret Mead

The *Culture* of a school is not necessarily reflected in the school's name or mission statement. In fact, if it is named after a famous person, the school's *Culture* may have no resemblance to the life and work of that famous person. Just think of the many schools around the nation named after people like Harriet Tubman, Malcolm X, Martin Luther King, or Booker T. Washington. And, yet, it is not uncommon for these schools to not share any philosophical, academic, operational, or aspirational qualities found in these great individuals. The school's *Culture* is not the beautifully poetic and inspiring words found on its walls, website, or in its promotional brochure. Rather, the school's *Culture* is the school's real institutional personality, its true self. This authentic profile is reflected in its (1) Quantifiable Data. For example, average daily attendance and punctuality; moving from one class to another punctuality rate; ninth grade pass/fail/promotion rate; the school's ability to bring students up to speed— that is, the number of students who enter the school below "grade level" and then who go on to have an on-time quality graduation; internal and external standardized test scores; quality learning time; course pass rates; GPA; college acceptances and scholarships acquired. The number, richness, and diversity of electives, advance and AP course offerings in the school. The attendance rates of teachers. The number of new teachers in a given year—determined by the percentage of one to two years of experienced teachers divided by the entire teaching staff. The number of certified teachers and the number of teachers who hold Master's degrees and Ph.Ds in their content areas, etc.

The second important indicator of a school's true Culture will also be revealed in its (2) Qualitative Data. Some examples are: the quality of cleanliness and maintenance of the building; the level of positive and productive "learning noise" in the building, as opposed to learning distracting noise; the amount of administration and staff efficacy that is employed; the amount of academic rigor that is practiced generally throughout the school; the role of standards and rubrics as a general academic and operational guide for teaching, learning, working, performance, and evaluation; who is promoted as the school's model student heroes (e.g., varsity athletes, academic scholars, or even scholar-athletes!); the presence of post-graduation enhancing special programs (e.g., internships, The International Baccalaureate, Cisco or Microsoft certifications, Project Lead The Way Pre-Engineering); academic teams and activities (chess, law and debate, robotics, student literary journal, music/dance/drama performance companies[1]), the number and investment in courses and programs that bring academically deficient students up to speed. The after-evenings/weekends/school breaks activity offerings. A one-for-one matching of girls' and boys' varsity sports offerings. Do girls feel safe and encouraged to pursue STEM courses, clubs, teams, and programs? Do the boys feel safe to be smart and take courses like dance, art, and poetry? How does the school treat SPED students and/or students with physical disabilities? How much attention does the school pay to its most vulnerable students? Students who are already engaged with the criminal justice system, those students who have one or both parents in prison, those students who live in extremely dangerous home or neighborhood environments, students who are homeless, etc.; how does the school deal with its emerging or declared LGBTQ students (who often "come out" in high school)? The kind of intellectually enriching special programs, competitions, trips, and activities provided by the school.

The school's true *Culture* cannot be hidden; it is, in essence, what it is. The school's *Culture* is the school's *true* mission statement; its priorities, its vision, what it aspires to be as an institution, its core academic and operational, ethical, and professional beliefs. The school's *Culture* can't be invented, faked, or artificially manufactured by cute posters, T-shirts, hats, or fancy pedagogically correct slogans and posters. The school's *Culture* is the most resistant of the three defining qualities (*Tone* and *Climate* being the other two) to the influences of the school building leader. However, by way of a sincere, thoughtful, and principled practice, the school principal can become the pivotal catalyst in the creation of a high academically achieving school *Culture*. But, you should know that the school's *Culture* (good or bad) cannot be built for the staff, but rather it must be built with the staff.

There are many powers that you, as the principal, have at your disposal in helping to create an effective school *Culture*. There are a lot of things in the area of *Tone* and *Climate* that are easily fixable by means of better communication or an effective policy decision. However, the school's *Culture* is not so easily manipulated. First, you can't supervise the school's *Culture*; you can't mandate or memo your way to the school having a *Culture* of academic and operational excellence. For the school's *Culture* is the direction in which it is naturally inclined to move; something like an organizational-operational compass, where at every moment of the day, in every place of the building, and in every situation in the school's life, this is how the school shows up, and the true *Culture* determines where it ends up! The *Culture* of the school is the true fall-back/fall-forward position that the school family will automatically and comfortably revert to and assume in good and bad times. Which means that the school family will feel uncomfortable and resist—no matter how good and positive—any imposition on the school's *Cultural* value that is not an authentic part of the school's natural *Cultural* self. And this natural school *Cultural* state will inform and determine budgeting, staffing, extracurricular activities, curriculum-instructional initiatives, projects, programs, discipline procedures, staff-administration professional development, attendance/punctuality, etc. A school *Culture* that is based on academic underperformance and ineffectiveness is in a psychological-anthropological sense, a "perfect" state of being. "This is who we are, and we can do (and deserve) no better." These are the schools (and districts) that even when you give them nice things as a superintendent, their core collective belief in their collective unworthiness means that they must reject, undermine, and, ultimately, destroy those nice things.

The *Culture* is the overpowering shared unconscious belief of what the school and all who work and learn there are really about. Anyone in the school seeking to change the *Culture* will appear as outcasts. This is why effective teachers in ineffective schools will often choose to isolate themselves. If the SBL is seeking to create a positive, encompassing, and empowering school *Culture* for all students, then it must be thoughtfully and strategically planted, nurtured, and grown in the sustaining and renewing power of daily practice; but the planting, nurturing, and growth must be deeply embedded into the hearts and minds of the school family, not just in the principal's heart and mind.

If rigorous classwork, a quality teaching and learning environment, and high student academic achievement is truly a primary objective, then the school's *Culture* will demand that those goals be the driving force behind any and all organizational decisions, large and small. Things like excellence, high standards, effective and efficacious behaviors, must go beyond catchy phrases and into the daily routines of the school's practices. In short, a positive school *Culture* is not just what it says, it is what it does. For the principal, it is important to know that a school, with or without your input, will have a *Culture*. A school without a school *Culture* is an impossibility! Now the question is, what will the *Culture* of your school be?

The school's Culture is a shared philosophical and psychological vision.

As the principal, you have probably come to the dramatic realization that you can't teach every class; be in every part of the building; go on every student trip and excursion; coach every team; be the faculty adviser for every club; or supervise every activity, program, competition, initiative, etc. And, so, unless there is a shared high standard for the collective *Cultural* understanding and agreement by the school family of what constitutes excellence, the school will naturally decline toward ineffectiveness. But even constructing an ineffective school *Culture* takes work and consistency. Yes, strange as it may seem, to establish an ineffective school takes hard work, and the consistent practice of maintaining ineffective strategic planning. Or not having a strategic school improvement plan at all, which produces the same bad results. On the surface, that hypothesis may sound counterintuitive, but if we accept that no school can be cultureless, then even an ineffective school *Culture*, no matter how unintentional, must be practiced and reinforced daily for it to work—or in terms of children, not work.

Building a school Culture of resistance, resilience, restoration, and affirmation

The only question that remains for the practicing principal is, what is the *Culture* of your school? Most people who compare an ineffective school to an effective school don't always fully appreciate what is in play here. The primary difference is that effective schools work hard at being good, and they consciously strive to achieve the school's mission; this takes place in every part of the school's environment. The ineffective school (and the people who staff it) work very hard; it's just that their hard work is without a proper strategic direction that would produce the desired academic success for students.

The cultural language of schools

Effective schools have a cultural-linguistic vocabulary that is dramatically different in both a quantitative and qualitative sense from an ineffective school. But my experience has taught me that those effective schools that specifically serve large numbers of students who are challenged with societal, political, social, and economic roadblocks have their own unique collective cultural language of empowered expressions. Some of these expressions include:

- "Academic Achievement is what we are all about!" Knowing that learning is what is most important here as well as the work it will take to move toward perfection.

- "Speaking and Acting with Bravery and Boldness!" If a school is to be successful with its students—in particular, a school that serves children of the poor and those members of our society who face severe socio-economic challenges—there is a necessary boldness and bravery of heart and spirit that is required.

- "Commit to a Culture of Compassionate Competitiveness!" Competition—as in friendly, not ugly—between students and academic departments helps them to realize and produce their personal best.

- "The Determination and Will to Get Things Done and to Get Them Done Right!" In their hearts, the school leaders and teachers want the school to be successful! One of the things I have learned from my experience with Career Technical Education (CTE) programs is the positive emotional effect on students when they successfully complete a project. Perhaps a good start for any school staff and leadership team is to practice a culture of simply doing what you claim you want to do for students!

The connectional shift from Tone and Climate to Culture

The primary analytical shift from *Tone* to *Climate* into *Culture* is the de-emphasis on what is being said and a greater emphasis on what is actually being done. The actions after the words are spoken is the school's authentic *Culture*. Some of public education's standard phrases must be followed up by concrete actions that operationally confirm, rather than betray, those assertions. The truth of a school means moving beyond slogans and into behaviors, daily practices, organizational habits, rituals, official (and unofficial) policies and procedures. What (and who) does that school really respect and honor? What values are non-negotiable and worth fighting for? What principles do they hold sacred? What does the school do when it finds itself in a moment of setback or failure? Does the school despair and play the blame game? Does it take time to recognize and celebrate success? And does the staff analyze this success as a way to help them plan for the next level of victory as a way to expand the victory to larger cohorts of students? The school cultural belief is present even in the midst of celebration; the idea that what is most important is that we create a school environmental culture where educational victories are the natural expectation, not the exception!

A school Culture of group protection

What does a safety and discipline *Culture* look like in an effective school? Does it maintain the core values and balance of justice and mercy? What are the acceptable standards for appropriate behavior; the organizational response to the breaking of these standards; the consistency of consequences; and the rewards (incentives) for students who behave and perform well academically? What are the positive avenues for student descent, protest, and the appealing of an action taken by an administrator or staff person? Is there an in-school suspension program (ISS)? What part does it play in the academic mission of the school? Is it just focused on punitive punishment? Or does it practice the "Three R's" and its primary purposes: Reconstruction, Restoration, and Re-connection to the shared *Cultural* values of the school?

The evidence of Cultural immersion

The school's mission is embedded into everything the school does. Every activity that takes place in the school—no matter how much fun—is also an opportunity for students to learn civility, character development, citizenship, good ethical behavior, concern for others, team work, intellectual empowerment, and the rubrics of adult world expectations. Positive values and habits must be a primary learning objective of every club, team, organization, and activity in or outside of the school.

103

The staff's collective Cultural affirmation of the dignity and humanity of students, their parents, and the communities where they live

Unfortunately, we live in a society that in its present state is organized to deny, diminish, and sometimes denigrate the human personalities of selected disenfranchised people. The school must engage in a practice of *Cultural* resistance to societal stereotypes, a school *Culture* that goes to war against the false ideas that only certain racial, ethnic, or gender groups can excel at STEM; some people are born not being good at mathematics; poor people and people of color don't care about their children; or one's history defines and confines his/her future story. The effective school not only erects a *Cultural* defense against such negative theories and practices, but it goes further to affirm the history, culture, and worthiness of students and parents. There is the belief that students will become good at what they practice, and if only given a limited set of choices, they will become good and interested in only those limited choices. There is a collective staff commitment to not make excuses for why students can't learn and then translate that commitment into concrete actions so that children will learn—a school *Culture* of inclusion, respect, and recognition that honors all of the diverse members of the school family and the unique gift they bring to enrich the promise of the school to enrich the world.

A place of Cultural communication and listening

Staff, parents, and students have access to the building administrators. And there are multiple ways in which the SBL team makes itself available to the other members of the school family. With an "open door" policy that operates in words and deeds, a student or staff person should be able to stop by the principal's office or stop him or her in the hall to ask questions or discuss concerns that arise. In those moments, the principal is not the principal of the school, but only the principal for that one person. That, of course, requires the positive practice of the SBL team not locking themselves away in an office, but rather spending huge amounts of time during the school day moving around the school building, leading by listening to school family members' concerns and being present in the many places the school family members are gathered. If parents visit the school, they should not need an appointment to meet with a school administrator. Administrator/parent-teacher/student meetings should not be limited to formal parent-teacher conference days. The SBL team spends time visiting and meeting with the various staff persons where they work. The principal makes student home visits.

This is a school *Culture* that says to the disenfranchised poor students that, "This time in your life, this school in particular, and education/academic achievement in general are your ladders to a better, more rewarding, fulfilling, and meaningful adult life. Seize it! Don't waste it!"

A school Culture of high expectations

A school where the adults collectively say, "You will thank me later for working you so hard and holding you to high standards!" Every effective school I have visited practiced this belief. There can be no selling out students academically for the sake of comfort or unprincipled peace. The school must be a safe and supportive model of the real world. But even more important is a complementary school efficacious *Culture* that says, "I will do all that is within my strength and talent to make you, the student, successful!"

A collective sense of school Cultural awareness

There is a conscious awareness on the part of the staff and students (not just the administrators) of what is and what is not the school's core cultural beliefs and practice. Everyone recognizes when the school's mission culture is being properly demonstrated, enhanced, and when that school culture is being challenged, threatened, or diminished.

In Summary: Effective school building leadership means effectively managing the Tone, Climate, and Culture of the school.

I believe that a school will naturally incline and decline toward mediocrity and ineffectiveness, unless the principal in cooperation with the staff decides otherwise. The presence or absence of a school *Culture* is not an option; the only question is, what will be the quality and character of that school's *Cul-*

105

ture. The quality of that school's *Culture* is congruent to the degree to which that staff identifies with the students and their struggle for admission and full membership into that class of citizens who are able to realize their full potential. A school *Culture* lacking in confidence—one which does not believe in the ability and internal power of the school to educate its children—will yield to the external political powers that promote poor and inadequate education. A school leadership *Culture* of fear dooms most of its students to failure or underperformance, no matter how competent the teaching and support staff. The science of school *Culture* demands that most of the staff will more than likely match or lower themselves to the expectations level of the school leader (principal); those staff persons who are competent, committed, and still in the pursuit of excellence will be isolated, castigated, and eventually will leave. My superintendent experience suggests to me that schools are resilient enough to survive most things; an incompetent principal is not one of them, as are:

- A school culture that does not empower, but enslaves.

- A school culture that does not enable, but cripples.

- A school culture that fails to enrich a student's spirit, but impoverishes and imprisons that spirit.

- A school culture that does not embrace efficacy, but encourages academic failure.

- A school culture that does not expand learning opportunities and possibilities, but kills student dreams.

- A school culture that does not seek to live its positive mission statement every day, but lives a lie.

- A school culture that does not lift hope, but destroys all possibility of hope.

Also of critical importance to know are the following tenets:

- A school culture will either address student deficiencies or reinforce those deficiencies.

- A school culture will either direct students into or away from the "school-to-prison pipeline."

- A school culture in which the staff does not "leave it all on the field" will betray children.

- A school culture must master/maximize learning time or else be mastered by lost learning time.

- A school culture in which the adults are not in charge means "chance" and "randomness" is in charge.

- A school culture that does not give its students the tools to competently compete in life destroys their life chances.

- A school culture of low expectations will surely realize those expectations.

- A school culture waiting for perfect students to arrive will ill serve the students who do show up.

- A school culture waiting for perfect parents will disrespect and disregard the parents they have.

- A school culture that does not let students in on the "hidden rules" of life sets them up to be victimized by those rules.

- A school culture that does not hold schoolwide academic rigor as sacred will educate a few and lose many.

- A school culture that says, "The only way out of poverty is professional sports," is impoverishing the dreams of their students.

- A school culture that does not have a "stay until the end plan" is a push-out drop-out factory.

- A school culture that is committed to academic achievement "incrementalism" will sadly, with some skill, achieve it.

- A school culture committed to bold and significant academic achievement will, by sheer will, achieve it.

- A school culture that is not driven by a professional ethical "prime directive" is just a place of adult employment.

- A school culture that does not continually challenge to renew itself fails over time as conditions and events change.

- A school culture that is not in pursuit of excellent practices is destined to practice mediocrity.

- A school culture that is not led by a compassionate, committed, knowledgeable, and strategically smart principal will, at best, realize small pockets of individual staff members' success. But the school generally will never rise above the level of competence than the level of competence practiced by its principal.

Chapter 5:
A "Good School" Showcases a School Culture of High Academic Achievement, in Practice and Performance

Leading a successful public school carries a great risk to the principal who is primarily a "careerist" first and an educator second. But the greatest reward for your efforts is when you save those students who have no powerful political voice to champion their cause; you, the principal, must become that champion voice. There are many resources that can be used to determine the "success" of a school such as newspaper coverage and statistics, magazine articles, and/or local politician "letter grades," but the main problem with these external evaluative measuring tools is that they assume all schools start from the same place and with identical students. The truth is that if these "evaluators" actually exposed the true "underperforming" aspects of all schools and the reasons for the tremendous inequities between schools—and more importantly, how the game is rigged for some schools to always lose and others to win—then perhaps some good would come out of these efforts. If the various measuring methods were being performed with the best of intentions of: how do we best educate all children? Perhaps then you would see a dramatic shift in the way the underperforming schools are budgeted, staffed, and led. Public education as we presently know it would no longer exist. The underperforming schools' staffing would be the best practiced and experienced in the profession. And these pedagogues would have the latest and best of educational support materials, equipment, and resources available. Every struggling school building would essentially be a full-time, social/medical services center. The school would operate seven days a week, twelve hours a day. The school systems would adopt the "treat every child who came to us as if they were an orphan" approach, made famous by former NYC Chancellor Frank Macchiarola—essentially closing the parent resource gap and providing care and support for students, such that every student in the school would have access to the same informal educational opportunities as their more entitled and privileged age mates. I could list more radical changes that would be needed for these students and schools to compete fairly with other schools, but I think you get the idea.

As a principal, you can't wait for the above conditions to arrive; too many people, not just newspapers and magazines, are invested in having a public education system that can designate schools as either the best or the worst. Imagine that non-pedagogues and unpracticed observers evaluating schools, and so what could possibly go wrong—well everything! Having received a K-12 education can't be the single standard required for being able to thoroughly and correctly assess the quality of schools.

However, hope is on the way. For I believe that there is a critical way to look at schools and, in particular, school principals' competencies to gain better insight into how they are really serving students. I also believe that if we change the measuring algorithms, we might find that some schools that are presently designated as high performers are in fact terribly underperforming and vice versa. Now wouldn't that be an interesting list!

Principals, school staff, parents, and the students who are depending on them can't wait for radical systemic policy initiatives that would ensure better educational outcomes for students, regardless of their school affiliation. Further, present and prospective high school parents need a process by which they can determine if a school is indeed operating at its best and in the best interest of its children. As a principal, I have counseled thousands of high schoolers to pay less attention to those annual "best college" lists and more attention to what is the best college for "you." A big university may look interesting and even exciting; but perhaps one could do better financially and/or actually increase the odds of graduating by attending a more attentive and nurturing smaller college or be exposed to the mentoring, caring, and societal service atmosphere found on an HBCU campus. Yes, "best" can be in the eyes of the beholder, meaning what is in the best interest of the individual student's personality.

Understanding why a school is a "High Reliability Organization (HRO)"

While studying on a Revson Fellowship at Teachers College, Columbia University, I discovered an interesting concept in one of my required readings.

This discovery came from a book titled *Managing the Unexpected* by Weick and Sutcliffe. In this book, the authors seek to describe and deconstruct the personality and the characteristics of "High Reliability Organizations (HROs)." When these organizations fail in operational practice or in the pursuit of their primary mission, there is a high probability that some type of catastrophic event will occur. In these cases, a failure is not just an inconvenience, rather it can result in a serious injury, tragedy, or the loss of one or many lives. It is important to understand how these HROs manage the unexpected. Weick and Sutcliffe state it thusly:

> "We attribute the success of HROs in managing the unexpected to their determined efforts to act mindfully. By this we mean that they organize themselves in such a way that they are better able to notice the unexpected in the making and halt its development. If they have difficulty halting the development of the unexpected, they focus on containing it. And if some of the unexpected breaks through the containment, they focus on resilience and restoration of system functioning."

As mentioned earlier in the book, I had my own experience with an HRO when I took a group of Phelps ACE students aboard a U.S. Navy Nuclear Submarine (USNNS). Because of the severity of the job and close working/ living space required, a specific type of personality was needed for the position: a highly competitive and most sought-after (in the best meaning of the phrase) "emotionally balanced individual." The submariners would also need to be able to work (literally and figuratively) under great pressure and have the ability to multitask. I also noticed that submariners eat, sleep, relax, and work extremely close to a nuclear reactor, powerful and deadly Tomahawk missiles and torpedoes. A critical nuclear accident aboard a submarine leaves very little escape options for the submariners inside the vessel. Finally, all this work is taking place deep under water, an environment not designed for the human respiratory system. Walking around the sub, it became clear that a simple mistake, lack of focus, or just "sloppy work" could lead to a catastrophe. In short, if the people who work in submarines are not at the top of their games, bad things can happen; people can die. So, this USNNS HRO must recruit the very best in their ranks. I'm sure you're asking, why bring up this school trip to a U.S. submarine and what does the concept of an HRO have to do with defining a good school? I understand that public schools are not military organizations, but neither are hospitals, and still I think that both fit the definition of HROs because when they fail, serious harm and/or death occurs.

I can think of no other organization that is more challenged each year by the unexpected than a public high school. Each new school year, we take on an entire cohort of new students, many of whom are either ending or working themselves somewhere through the middle of that biologically programed period of utter confusion and conflict called adolescence. The K-8 education program too often sends academically weak (read: unprepared to do high school work) students. Meanwhile, no returning from summer break tenth through twelfth grade students are the same as when they left regarding their individual developmental psyche. Each year brings many personal changes for both staff and students, some happy and helpful, others painful and not so helpful. The addition of new staff persons, teachers teaching courses for the first time, and the ever-changing external political, financial, statutory, and regulatory changes introduce important new variables into the problem of having a successful school year. Schools, if nothing else, are incubators of unexpectedness, which is why it takes an HRO management approach to produce successful outcomes in them.

My point here is that schools share an important characteristic with our previously mentioned submarine and other HROs. And that is because a great deal of our work falls into the realm of the unexpected. I have spent eleven years in the principal's seat, and I can honestly say that I can't think of any two days that were alike. If you want something to change in a school from the ordinary to the out of ordinary or to the extraordinary, just wait five minutes! A severe asthma or sickle cell anemia attack, a child that has been put out by a parent or ran away from home, the cafeteria supervisor calls you (true story) two hours before the first lunch period to inform you that she no longer has hot water (and based on health department codes, can't serve lunch)—these events can happen separately, sequentially, or all at once. And, so, a great deal of school time is spent managing the unexpected, which is why smart strategic planning is an indispensable tool of the principalship. *For the record: As I called for the district's emergency plumbers, I directed the cafeteria supervisor to pull out every large pot they had and start boiling water, because not serving lunch to the students was not an option. The first lunch period went forward without a hitch. The students (as should happen) had no idea of the crisis, and by the second lunch period, the plumbers had our hot water working!*

But the HRO = Possible Catastrophic Event equation is also something we have in common with other HROs. When we fail, people die. Now the death may not be dramatically instantaneous, although a child drowning on a school trip and a drop-out who engages in or is the victim of a shooting will both end in a physical and/or psychological death. Most of the "deaths" that are produced by educational failure can be emotional and physical, both subtle and complex. It can be the death of the imagination, spirit, or of someone's future. It is the young person whose gifts and talents go undiscovered and undeveloped, who now spends a lifetime experiencing a type of internal death. The young people who leave our high schools before graduation or who graduate with what is essentially a useless diploma.

What if we saw our public schools as HROs and treated them as if they were incubators for the future planetary caretakers? For sure, there are some fortunate children in this nation for whom their school has definitely been designated an HRO. These effective schools have taken on the primary task of preparing young people to fully participate in their own and the nation's future. Unfortunately, that reality does not apply to large numbers of our nation's children. These No (or low) Reliability Organizations (NROs) will ultimately come back to haunt the very nation that has established them as we continue to make major shifts in the racial/ethnic demographics in the U.S. Developing nations will continue to build the internal capacity to absorb their own professionals and thus export less of them to the U.S. Therefore, we will need to depend more and more on our own citizens for economic growth and, in some cases, for national security reasons. But before that intellectual capital crisis happens, millions of students, their parents, and communities will be doomed to generational degeneration. If there is any hope of saving large numbers of children and in turn saving ourselves as a nation, it will mean transforming public school NROs into HROs. The alternative is a nation unprepared to meet the challenges of the future. And, so, what does a "good" school that acts like an HRO look like?

Good schools are not by accident. Before they are good schools, they began to act like a good school.

A good school must be a highly ethical organization.

Characteristics: The foundation on which a good school builds its operational practices is a sound ethical belief system. The Educational Prime Directive is in full force here. No union or labor agreement, central office, external political considerations will take precedence over the primary interest and well-ending educational result for students. When a conflict arises between the interest of an adult and the interests of students, the interest of the students should come first. It also means that the staff is wedded to a set of values and principles that grow out of their profound understanding of the unique role they play in society. They are the guardians and actualizing agents of human development. Each child, without prejudice, is a unique gift to the present and future world, and the primary task of this good school is to identify, invest time and effort, inspire, and induce each child's gifts and talents to rise to the surface, and be fully realized in the world. This school staff believes in the inherent rich goodness of its students and their own ability to make good on their ethical beliefs and practices. What this school says it believes, it believes, and what this school believes, it does.

A good school must be highly knowledgeable of pedagogy.

Over the last few years, professional expertise has fallen on hard times in the field of public education. We have unfortunately entered the age of amateurism serving as the face of school change, improvement, or "reform." And also unfortunate is that the bulk of this amateurism movement has been visited on poor children and children of color. The good school honors, in both the ranks of school leaders and teachers, the acquisition of formal pedagogical training, content knowledge, experience (time), and professional expertise. But it is also important for these schools to be open to innovation, the latest best practices, and continuing professional development. There is a good balance between the known and what they need to know. A characteristic of a low-underperforming school is high teacher turnover, such that an experienced culture of effective methodology can't take root and grow. This is also accompanied and further harmed by a negative "tipping-point" of new teachers. That negative tipping-point is when the number of new (1-3 years of teaching experience) teachers working in a school far exceeds the capacity of the school administrators and the effective veteran teachers to properly mentor them.

A good school must be a highly efficient organization.

Characteristics: A good school is first extremely efficient with one of the most important of school resources. Time on task! There is a general sense that in every school the teaching and learning experiences are fully maxed out during the course of a school day. This is a false assumption. The standards for classroom behaviors that negatively impact the learning environment varies greatly from school to school (and classes inside of schools). In a highly efficient school instructional disruptions are antithetical to the school's culture: There is zero tolerance for the disturbance of classroom learning. There are many students present each day and arriving to school on time. There is very little learning time wasted, as learning and activities that support learning are continually ongoing and present in the home and other out-of-school activities. Students move to and between classes quickly, and there is little movement out of classrooms during classroom instructional time. Distracting noises (e.g., PA announcements and classroom interruptions) are not part of this school's operational culture. There is a productive use of student and staff "non-assigned" time; students go to tutoring sessions during lunch periods, study individually or form study groups; students will use their free time during and after school to visit places like the college/career center. Every space in the school is in essence and practice, a classroom. There is an expectation of preparedness among the staff and students; they maintain a constant state of ready to teach and ready to learn. The instructional support team and program are uniquely situated to save time and not waste efforts, such that teachers are able to invest the greatest amount of time in the service of instruction. The school leadership organizational style is structured to detect early, address quickly, and solve thoroughly any potential threats to the teaching and learning experience.

A good school must be a highly effective organization.

Characteristics: Because the school is effective at getting students to pass classes at a high percentage rate (HPR), the school is able to offer a large number of elective and advanced courses. An effective HPR also puts students in the most advantageous situations to do well on standardized exams (by expanding vocabulary, responsive writing, and general knowledge competency) as well as explore possible future career options by taking electives and advanced classes. The school is able to save and positively redirect financial resources when students are not forced into credit-recovery situations. In fact, there is a possible algorithm that would reveal that the number of credit-recovery courses offered strongly determines the number of advanced and elective courses offered in a school. The school culture is effective in convincing both students and staff to make a maximum effort to realize the mission. The school's success is translated into the success of individual members of the school family.

A good school must be a highly efficacious organization.

Characteristics: The staff of this good school are convinced that—through their skills, efforts, determination, and individual and collective talents—they are able to make students academically successful. They are not naïve and understand the enormous socio-economic challenges many students bring with them when they arrive to school each day. They are also aware of the huge educational gaps and deficiencies students bring from home or a prior formal school learning experience. They see their roles as stepping into the gaps and through the power of their knowledge and actions, closing those gaps. The good school staff looks at the time the student spends in school, in terms of education, as the most important and influential time of the child's learning day! This good school seeks to break down the artificial wall that exists between formal and informal education. The staff at this school seeks to teach students the essential positive and productive life habits employed by all of those who are successful in our society. The model student and model parents are the students and parents they have, not the ones they may have imagined when preparing to enter the profession. The staff in this school, regardless of job classification, believes that of the many variables that go into making a student successful, their role is the key influencer of a student's success. In this school, student failure is interpreted through the question, where did we fail this student? This school staff believes that everything that happens within the school is the single-most important life-changing event in the child's life. This school practices the "orphan approach" to serving children, meaning working as if the child has no parent and therefore stepping in to close the parent resource gap, or you enhance and magnify whatever positive contributions parents are making to the child's education. This staff also believes that they have the individual and collective team capacity to make the school experience work for students for whom it was not intended to work; they are the true practitioners of the best practices of "in loco parentis" (in the place of a parent).

A good school must be a highly equanimous organization.

Characteristics: Even a good school must operate and exist in the dynamic environment of public schooling. However, what separates an "effective" from a "less effective" school is when a threat to learning shows up, the staff respond with a calm and stabilizing internal environmental change that insolates, protects, and does not betray the school's mission—they are totally focused on the school's mission! These schools seem to have a central calming, philosophical centering posture for which they are always inclined, even when things are not going well or when a serious, negative event occurs. This effective staff is not easily distracted by all of the external public education noise; they stay focused on the meaning and practice of the school's mission.

A good school must be a "high expectations" organization.

Characteristics: The good thing about school academic achievement is that a great deal of it is predictable. Students, for the most part, are emotionally and intellectually flexible, and naturally will either over- or underperform academically based on what the school staff requires of them. The role of any good coach is to get more out of those being coached than what they realized they had. A central role of schooling is to help the student to discover and develop a learning capacity, talent, and gift of which they themselves were not aware. Every student should leave a school having discovered some wonderful activity in which they can excel. Whether it is in creative writing, art, dance, STEM, or playing a musical instrument—something should happen in school to produce a state of exceptionality for each student. Despite their many protestations, students want to please us (adults) and receive praise from us. They will also, contradictorily, ask for less pressure to perform well, even as they resent not being held to high standards. Students also resent teachers engaging in an unprepared or poorly prepared lesson, which is why they unfortunately always bring their own "lesson plans" to such a class setting, usually involving disruptive behavior. As educators, we can almost guarantee academic failure if we employ a culture of low expectations. It is my belief that, with some very few exceptions, students are not able to rise above the expectations of a teacher. And if a student is exposed to multiple years of teacher low expectations, the damage could be irreversible. A good school will not only practice a general culture of high expectations, they will also individualize those high expectations of those students who exceed the teacher's (or school's) expecta-tions. That means institutionalizing clubs, activities, programs, competitions, teams, advanced courses, electives, AP classes, etc., that continually challenge students to reach for, and obtain, the next level of learning achievement.

A good school must be a high esprit de corps organization.

Characteristics: A good school is a good place to work. And part of hav-ing a good place to work is the presence of a sense of unity and camaraderie among the staff. What can give meaning to work is a shared understanding of what that work means to students, our nation, and the world—not to mention, what that work means for the people engaged in that work. A good school will nourish its goodness through the common cultural understanding that what they do is important, therefore, they are important. This culture of a unified purpose and a common interest is founded on a collective belief that the school mission is a shared journey and goal. The principal can help to foster this envi-ronment by making sure that the serious individual challenges and concerns of the school staff members are adequately addressed. The work can and should be hard. But the unnecessary and artificial obstacles like inappropriate student behavior and the lack of supplies and resources need not make the work harder than it is. If the individual members of the staff perceive that only their work/ product and not their personal/professional worth and personality is important, then they will see their supervisors in a negative way. A shared mission with companionship is one of the most sought-out places in any challenging effort, and that is because it transforms the meaningless acts of work into works of love and, eventually, a love for the work.

A good school must be a highly energetic organization.

Characteristics: As a superintendent, I have observed the difference in *Tone*, the energy level of high-performing schools versus low-performing schools. Now, both types of schools can look busy, but a secondary difference is also the purpose toward which that extra energy is devoted. When we fail to look at schools holistically and only look at test scores and other quantifiable data, we miss out on the qualitative data that is so important in every school. A school's profile is much deeper than numbers, for behind those numbers are

118

the good or bad practices, principles, procedures, and unique school organizational cultural traits and personality. In good schools, there seems to always be something going on that intellectually and emotionally enriches the school family. Even fun activities are linked to some form of intellectual growth and knowledge acquisition. There is a very large and diverse number of activities that allows all of the members of the student body to locate a space to discover and develop their individual talents. Students and faculty in these schools also invest a great deal of after-school and weekend time into the many projects, programs, and activities the school fosters. Again, time comes into play here; in effective schools, students have places to be and things to do, and they are moving quickly toward these engagements. When I visit schools, one of the first things I look at is the body language of the staff and students (*Tone*); so much can be learned by observing the amount of energetic movement happening. The school should do an interest survey of both staff and students. First, you will be shocked when you realize the amount of talent you have on your staff, as they may have diverse hobby interests. These individuals can be the inspiration advisors for school clubs. You will see that students discover interests and passions about something simply by joining a club. Teenagers will swear, without any supporting information or experience, that they "don't like X activity," that is until you get them involved with that activity. The more diverse activities, contests, out-of-school exposures, programs, and competitions in a school, the more energetic and enjoyable the place becomes. Students need reasons beyond a diploma in order to get excited about coming to school every day.

A good school must be a highly extensible organization.

Characteristics: This quality of a good school reflects its desire to never be satisfied by remaining in an easy place: a school that is always seeking to reach that challenging but achievable positive place. The school pushes itself ever-forward without reaching a breaking point. There are no abstract unachievable goals; rather the school is achieving the maximum best of that which is practical and possible. This is a school that will continually avoid its safe comfort zone while maintaining its core positive values and mission, constantly reinventing itself in order to retain those core values and mission in the midst of an ever-changing environment. It is the institution that is in the greatest competition with its own history and past victories; each year's victories become the next year's baseline from which the next year's goals are established. It is the courage to go beyond its real and imagined limitations. The constant search and save mission of identifying that ever present "at-risk" student. I feel confident and comfortable saying that a school that simply does only what it did last year, even if that which they did was successful, will cause students to fail and fall behind academically in that present year. The highly extensible school will take strategically smart, calculated, but responsible risk.

A good school must be a highly empathetic organization.

Characteristics: The staff sees no barrier between themselves, the students, the parents, and the communities in which the students and parents live. The staff can identify the challenges that the students face on their educational journey, not necessarily because they lived it but because of their level of human concern and professional ethical convictions. The perceived shortcomings and self-destructive cultural practices the students and their parents may engage in are not the source for dismissive humor, scorn, condescension, or the rationale for disregard and disrespect. This is a school that believes in the fundamental concept that some children in our society succeed in school because they bring more "parental support capital," not because they are smarter. This is a school that seeks to educate all of its students but also feels no shame in leveling the playing field by identifying and operationalizing support for the traditionally ignored members of our society.

This school also posits empathy as part of its schoolwide learning curriculum. Students are taught to feel a sense of concern and sensitivity toward other students, staff, and all humanity. Students (both rich and poor) are investing a great deal in their education, and they have a personal and civic responsibility to create good and productive lives for themselves. The purpose of education is to acquire the knowledge, skills, and techniques to help others; our education should empower us to serve, not cause others to suffer. How we treat people who are in some way less fortunate than us says more about us than it says about them. We identify with the suffering and incompleteness of others because, as humans, we all face some type of challenge and/or inadequacy; some personal shortcomings are more obvious than others, but we are all human beings seeking to create a meaningful life through education. All people are fundamentally the same, and they all want the same things: to live in peace, to grow intellectually, to express their talents and gifts, and to create meaning and purpose in their lives. So, treat people like you would like to be treated yourself. However, understand that that can't happen if you don't first love yourself!

A good school must be a highly entrepreneurial organization.

Characteristics: A good school will have a rich prospectus and offerings of intellectually stimulating out-of-classroom projects, programs, clubs, varsity team offerings, and other activities that reveal and enhance students' talents. There is also the huge cost these effective schools cover by raising non-district allocated budgetary funds in order to pay for a rich and diverse list of non-required academic course offerings (e.g., Robotics Team, AP art or biology). There is no way that a school can meet the cost of having a dynamic and intellectually enriching out-of-required course activities through a standard district budget allocation. Therefore, the principal must take on the role of school entrepreneurial leader. That means that, along with teaching and learning, fundraising and resource acquisition must be part of the principal's repertoire. The school will also need to form a 501c3 foundation, partnerships, industry-specific advisory boards, and "Friends of the" chess team; drama club; fencing team; law and debate team/ club; STEM or CTE programs; Science Competition Research Program; art, music, and dance programs; etc. The school must close the parental financial resource gap by offering all students the opportunity to attend professional cultural performances, plays, cultural institutions, lectures, educational events, college tours, etc.; all of these activities require additional finance-raising on the part of the principal. But this necessary funding must be obtained, especially if the students in a Title I school hope to compete with other students in schools that may have a rich endowment (yes, some high schools have alumni endowments!) or affluent parents who can raise the necessary supplementary education enhancement funds. The "unofficial" non-allocation budget gap between rich and poor schools is one of the best-kept open secrets in public education. The access to additional funding provides students from "rich schools" with an unfair academic, social, and intellectual advantage. Therefore, the principal who does not work at a "rich and advantaged" school must put together a comprehensive fundraising and resources acquisition plan and program, or else you doom your students to a permanent educational disadvantage; yes, that shows up on standardized exams!

A good school must employ a highly enriched, culturally linguistic approach to supporting student success.

In order to do this, a school must explore, define, and in some cases redefine the following words:

"Risk" and "At-Risk"	"Friends"	"Fun"
"Wining"	"Testing"	"Commitment"
"Nerd"	"Time"	"Honesty"
"Success"	"Parent Involvement"	"Habits"
"Progress"	"Parent Engagement"	"Perseverance"
"Support"	"Study"	"Rigorous"
"Smart"	"Fairness"	"Discipline"
"Respect"	"Code-Switching"	"Consequences"
"Accountability"	"Follow-Up"	"Rubric"
"Responsibility"	"Justice"	"Expectations"
"Failing"	"Appropriate"	"Standards"
"Leadership"	"Closure"	"Scaffolding"
"Enemy"	"Safe"	

All of these (Climatic) words and terms have significant school culture meanings when employed by the school family (students, parents, and staff) members. And most important to know is that these words draw their meaning and significance from the school's overarching mission. A good school understands the importance of words and definitions and how they came to define things in the way that they do; they also understand that the words and practices of high student academic achievement must be in alignment.

A good school must be a highly empowering organization.

Characteristics: Schools should serve as transformative places where the people who work and learn in them are changed by encountering that school's environmental culture. It is a fundamental law—a school that lacks institutional confidence in its own power to successfully educate its students also can't empower those students to have confidence when facing the outside world. I have used the term "school family" throughout the book; this is not by accident. The adults and young people that make up a good school's internal population (and the parents) is in every sense a family. Each person rises or falls based on the behavior, achievement, and positive production of a fellow family member. Many administrators and teachers probably don't want to admit this, but professionally we are a proud and competitive group. As a principal, I have attended meetings with my APs and teachers and observed the pride on their faces and in their body language when they interacted with their colleagues from other high schools. When staff development activities bring teachers and support staff from other schools, they talked about how lucky my staff was to work in such a school. When students and staff start to get younger siblings, cousins, and other family members applying for admission to the school, it says something about that school. Feeling good in and about the place you study or work is an extremely important attribute of an effective school. Schools that can't get out of their own underperforming way, where the leadership and staff as well as the parents are cynical, un-invested and not proud of the school, means these schools are also hard places to work, in large part because too many people (students and staff) in the building would rather be someplace else. The people who either learn or work at a school must ultimately feel empowered by that experience. If one of the objectives of the educational encounter is to empower both the teacher and the taught, then schools must establish a schoolwide learning objective of producing personal and institutional empowerment as a natural and normal exercise of the school's cultural and operational practices. For in the final analysis, it's about the school-based leadership, the academic rigor and richness, instructional expertise and integrity as well as the quality of the teaching and learning environment; these contributing elements serve as the key organizational tools and indicators of individual and the collective school family's sense of empowerment.

A good school must be a highly heuristic organization.

Characteristics: This is a school that is continually learning from itself about itself in order to improve itself. One of those beforementioned cultural expressions is the word *assessment*. All one needs to do is to put the word "standardized" in front of it and we are off to the ideological battle races. Many stakeholders, both inside and outside of schools, have staked a claim to the meaning, purpose, value, and the appropriate applications of the word assessment or testing. But what do the words like "standardized," "assessment," and "testing" mean to you as a professional educator? And, further, what do they mean to your school family and your school's academic mission? A good school is highly effective in its approach to engaging standardized assessments. I think that it is safe to say that standardized testing isn't going away any time soon. And, so, the question is, how should the school utilize standardized assessment tools? There is no argument that information in the form of quantitative and qualitative data is an essential tool for the effective leader of an effective school. It is critical, however, that these two data-collection paths be correctly placed in the service of academic and school culture improvement. Presently, most public schools are being forced to administer assessments and collect data in the wrong way and for the wrong reasons. At the same time, many of those standardized evaluation activities can be of great educational value, exposing important educational needs and/or organizational and teaching methodological weaknesses inside the school. Good and effective schools use standardized assessments and are not used by them for purposes other than to improve the quality of teaching and learning.

We see that a "good" school produces many recognizable characteristics that can be both qualitatively and quantitatively measured and evaluated. Giving both qualitative and quantitative data equal weight is much more challenging and of course requires the presence of experienced, skilled, and professional "best school leadership practitioners" to come up with the best rubrics for evaluating a school. The present "best" evaluations allow for too many opportunities for schools to "game the system." For example, a high school can add an additional AP class, admit more students of color, and then claim "diversity victory" when in fact the school has no intention of having those students take the AP exam; and if they do, many of the scores will be a 1 or 2, which does not demonstrate proficiency let alone mastery, and more than likely end up being inadmissible for college credit. Truly expanding AP means engaging in the really hard work of developing a four-year AP plan that strategically expands AP participation by identifying and working with the on-grade level ninth-grade cohort students who without a school-wide strategic AP plan, will never get to the place where they will be able to take and succeed in AP courses. This plan will included a "strengthening sequence" in their pre-AP academic courses through a rigorous standards-based curriculum. But this won't happen without the imagination, vision, and professional knowledge of the school's leader. One of the best indicators (and important evaluation) of a good high school leader is that he or she will start with the desired goal (in this case AP course taking) and then work backwards, starting in the ninth grade to build course-passing ability, academic rigor, resilience, good test-taking skills, and intellectual capacity in making the student "AP ready" by the time the student reaches the eleventh and twelfth grades.

We will see in the next chapter how a school wishing to function at its best must be led by a principal having the best leadership skills and intentions. Effective school supervision requires a SuperVision that continuously, with strategic thought and purpose, and in a comparing and contrasting way, looks simultaneously at the school's mission, its potential-capacity, and the school's actual operational practices (*Culture*). Without that SuperVision skill rudder, a school will drift aimlessly toward student academic underperformance.

Chapter 6:
The SuperVision Required to Effectively Manage All Functional Spaces In (and Outside of) the School Building

The entire school building, along with the area surrounding the exterior of the building, any attached yard, or athletic field, are by definition and designation teaching and learning spaces. Every foot of the abovementioned space is always, in a negative or positive way, representing and upholding the school's true organizational mission. The principal must think of the cafeteria, auditorium, locker rooms, hallways, front entrance station, stairways, main office, etc., as teaching and learning classrooms. Therefore, all of these "classrooms," like all learning school spaces, require a (school leadership) lesson plan. And like any good lesson plan, these lessons must contain the following essential elements:

- Conceptual and Behavioral Standards. (What is it that we want students to know, and what do we want them to be able do in relationship to the knowledge they have acquired?)

- Rubrics That Define and Explain Those Standards. (What is the process that will allow students to evaluate their own responses to the standards when an adult is not directly coaching them?)

- A Methodological Approach and Plan of Action to Teach Those Standards.

- An Assessment/Evaluation System that Provides Achievement Status Feedback to Both the Teacher and Student. (How close or far away are we from the student mastering the standards?)

- A Proactive Corrective Process to Address any Factor that Could/ Would Adversely Affect the Goal of Students Meeting the Standards.

The effective Principal and Assistant Principal's offices

The school building administrator's office should be seen as a multi-functional workspace. More importantly, these offices should be avoided during the school day, with the exception of necessary meetings that must take place inside them. The principal and APs should spend as little time as possible during the school day in their offices! Further, the administrator's office must also serve the function of a classroom when meeting with a student or parent and a professional development room when meeting with a staff person. And, so, just like any other classroom in the building, the school administrator's office must have a strategic lesson plan for effective operation. In other words, what are the learning and performance objectives that you want to accomplish whenever your office is used as a work or meeting space? What message do you want to send by the organization and decorative style of your office? Decorations and architecture, of course, are a matter of personal taste, but your office should reflect and model the school's *Tone, Climate,* and *Cultural* educational mission.

I had a resource/research library in my office as well as art and sculptures that reflected the school's diverse population. My office/conference room libraries contained a full spectrum of pedagogical, social science, instructional methodology, textbooks, history, fictional and nonfictional works, along with a wide variety of magazines and journals. It was important that I also had copies of the latest federal, state, local, and district statutes, laws, and regulations along with binders of all of the latest versions of the school-related specific job classification contracts and agreements. And because I had over 100-plus awards, plaques, and citations from various public and private organizations, I hung those items up—not for braggadocios reasons but rather to make a point to students that hard work can, and will, be recognized. Finally, I always made sure to reserve a bulletin board to post students' work. There is a low appreciation for the developmental psychology of teenagers. We assume that they have no interest in adult recognition and praise, but that is far from the truth. It is true that teenagers are naturally seeking a greater sense of independence and recognition from their peers, but they still maintain a parent-childlike need to receive the adulation and recognition from adults. I have found over the years that teenage students were thrilled when, as a principal, I posted that A+ essay from an English or history class, that 100 exam score from a science or mathematics class, a drawing from an art class, or those many letters students wrote promising to raise their

GPA scores! Prominently post students' work in your office and watch the response!

For administrative purposes, visualization was important for me, so I always posted critical path charts (maintained by my secretary) of weekly, monthly, and annual events and due dates as well as when I needed to start a project. This visual presentation allowed me to properly prepare for the successful completion of a task or project while avoiding conflicts.

Again, this is a personal preference decision, but as a principal I made it a habit of allowing students to eat their lunch in my conference room. This has to be understood in the larger context of a school culture whereby students often ate lunch outside of the cafeteria while attending tutoring sessions in a classroom. Further, this allowed the quieter and more introverted students to have a peaceful lunchtime setting. This practice, along with the lunchtime tutorials, helped with that traditional lunch period challenge faced by every high school principal of a medium-to-large school: to offer the fewest number of lunch periods while creating lunch rooms with the smallest number of (easily manageable) students. Finally, this offered the necessary opportunity for me to engage in authentic and edifying (primarily for me!) conversations with students.

In terms of the principal's office second shift, which starts after the end-of-day student dismissal, the organization and structure of your office falls again on personal taste and interest. I was fortunate to always have corporate partners or "friends" in the district storage facility who were able to provide me with nice, comfortable, and functional office furniture. I always had a music system that played relaxing music as I worked into the evening on all of the required paperwork that I refused to do during the school day. The principalship is hard, so you should make every effort to get yourself through that second shift in a comfortable and relaxing environment. I also had a soft desk lamp that allowed me to turn off the bright overhead office lights. With a refrigerator and microwave for snacks, a coffee/tea maker for mellow herbal tea, I was ready to start my second shift! As a principal, you should invest in creating the right aesthetics and atmosphere in your office, for it is the only peaceful place in the school that is solely dedicated to you.

Learning standards for the building, general classrooms, special instructional & non-instructional, work and gathering spaces

It is critically important for the principal to engage his or her SuperVision outside of his or her office! Know that secondhand information, no matter how well-intended, has been touched (filtered) by a human, making it inherently inferior to direct observation. The principal must spend as much time as possible walking the building, visiting classrooms, along with constantly checking all of the teaching and learning spaces (translation: every part of the entire building) in the school. Let's be clear here. Every space (not just the traditional classrooms) in the school—including the auditorium, lunchroom, stairways, hallways and bathrooms—are just as important as teaching and learning spaces. For the school administrator who hopes to be effective and successful, this understanding is the beginning of knowledge; not understanding this concept is the beginning of you becoming a failed school building leader.

This important understanding on the part of the principal to continually and personally see the school in full and active operation is, in my view, one of the most important parts of the job that is not stated in the official job description or employment contract. Not only did I invest a lot of time walking and observing the school building during the day, I also engaged in the daily practice of touring empty spaces/classrooms and unutilized spaces. Finally, something I learned as a principal: a great deal of information can be gathered about a school's culture when the school is not in operational session. It is amazing what a perceptive principal can see in the school building when they are free of the constant distractions of all of the normal school day atmosphere. For example, the quality and quantity of posted student work/product, classroom bulletin boards, the classroom architecture, or how desks are organized, the presence or absence of workstations, what is written or not written on the teacher's white board can tell you so much about what is important in that classroom. In those quiet moments, you will be able to see those things that support or hinder the school's mission. A principal must have a creative vision that allows you to see the school building critically and analytically in different times and stages of operation (or out of operation). The key to a principal having an effective SuperVision is to interpret all things observed. In almost every case I remember as a superintendent, when a principal found him or herself in some kind of serious trouble, the principal either saw or was made aware of a situation in its developmental stages but did not act on it. SuperVision means being able to look for trouble; or dangerous, negative, and tragic outcomes; and/or those things that help the establishment and performance of the school's mission.

So, what is the principal's SuperVision looking for?

- *"Would I want this for my child?"* Part of my SuperVision activity was to always and continually ask this question: Specifically, would you want your child (or any child) to utilize, be exposed to, or study in this particular space or classroom? That question should motivate a school leader every day as you take your daily tour of the school. If you are not constantly asking that question then, perhaps, there are a few other questions that are foremost in your mind like: how can you keep everyone happy by not making a difficult but necessary decision; how can you enhance or advance your career at the expense of your integrity and the school's academic success; or, how can you reach an unprincipled accommodation with the societal forces who have no serious interest or commitment to educating the children in your school? A true practitioner of professional SuperVision will also be forced to carry the burden of honestly confronting what you see to its logical fixing and correcting conclusion. Pretending not to see is a way of avoiding your commitment to the ethical and philosophical standards you claim to champion.

- *"Are there early stages of a bad outcome present here?"* There are many important questions that a principal must constantly ask, the type of questions that if not asked can sometimes get principals, particularly new SBLs, into serious trouble. You must be able to ask the question, are there any potential safety and security issues involved in what you see? The art of SuperVision is to see the evolving, emerging, and potentiality of a dangerous situation in its beginning stages. The average school administrator can probably respond well to a bad or negative incident given he or she has been properly developed and provided with a good incident response script to follow. But the best school-based leaders with the best SuperVision skills are really good at the (1) early detection of the problem; (2) the quick and effective eliminating response to the problem; and (3) the thoughtful acts of closure, follow-up, and ongoing monitoring of the results. These are the principals that district superintendents, the directors of guidance, directors of special education, directors of operation, and the legal department love! And that is because of their ability to see where a particular event could lead, even as it exists in its most simple and primary stages.

The good news (and the reason for this book!) is that this SuperVision skill and ability to visualize trouble coming is not an inherent gift. It is not an easy competency, but it can be taught and professionally developed in both aspiring and present school-based leaders. But this priceless ability to interpret what is seen with a strategic purpose requires an intellectual openness on the part of the principal, which will allow him or her to visually project that crisis that is not yet clearly visible. It is that ability to come up with several possible, hypothetical negative or dangerous outcomes based on information gathered from sometimes small and seemingly simple and innocent events. For example, every year in school districts all over our nation, you will find high schools that have a crisis with their senior yearbooks; it can result in a range of negative outcomes from student mental anguish, school administrators being disciplined, to a school (or school district) having to spend a huge amount of money to replace the entire printed senior yearbooks or paying some out-of-court penalties for defamation charges. Especially for cash-strapped districts, this is money (and time) that could be better spent on educational objectives. And yet, these events are preventable; in every case I have read about, the problem resulted from a leadership fail on the part of the principal, who did not properly supervise the teacher advisor, who in turn did not properly supervise the senior yearbook club student committee members. Nationally and annually, when bad things happen in schools and to a student or staff person, some percentage of events could be classified as acts of nature, for example, structural damage after a storm or fire caused by some electrical mishap. However, the majority of accidents and incidents that occur on a daily basis in a school are in fact preventable. As a superintendent, I saw that in almost every instance of a bad occurrence, there was also a failure in leadership. It was a case of the principal not properly assessing situations beforehand; not responding properly even after being warned by students, staff, or parents; and then not properly handling the said situation. How many times have I heard as a superintendent, "But I had them shake hands in my office?" And now you are shocked that they fought at the bus stop! And, so, the necessary complementary tools of a principal's SuperVision is the ability to have *super listening* skills along with *super inquiry* skills that will allow you to ask the right questions, of the right people, at the right times.

All big problems and incidents that occur in a school are connected to a lot of smaller indicators. These negative incidents don't happen magically; they come into tragic realization because of the absence of a strategic leadership awareness on the part of the principal to develop a safe and academically conducive, proactive, building-management plan. That Plan of Pro-action means engaging a SuperVisionary approach when walking around your school. Hopefully, you don't lag too far behind the learning curve, for you will quickly come to understand that in the daily life of a school, there are certain people (and their behaviors), places, times, situations, and things that hold the potential early stages of trouble, and as a principal you ignore them at your own professional peril!

Unrecognized bad acts have the power to create and support other bad acts. Students skipping class, gathering in bathrooms, or not getting to class on time are not just academic problems, they also provide a safety and security problem, allowing students to spend a considerable amount of time outside of the eyes of adults. No matter how adult-like high school students appear, any unsupervised time is risky. Any space not supervised by an adult in a school increases the possibility for problems, which is why principals and other school administrators must engage daily in unscheduled and unplanned walk-throughs. By deciding from time to time, in a moment's notice, to visit a floor's bathrooms, you have effectively closed the time window where bad things can happen. When I had my custodians sweep the hallways and check to see if bathrooms were fully stocked and cleaned after each class period's end, not only did this go a great length in making the school clean, but it also put extra adult eyes in play during class times. Principals must think of safety and security as a comprehensive effort that will need the support of all job classifications and departments to work effectively. Finally, it is critical for the principal to establish a school culture that assures school family members that you will be responsive when they inform you of a potentially serious situation, even when it is in its early stages. Failing to do this will send a terrible message to your staff. It is no accident that as a superintendent, one of the most common complaints I received from students, teachers, and parents was the absence of an effective response and follow-up by the principal. When principals fail to act on the intelligence they gather themselves or receive through the efforts of others, this is a sure recipe for a leadership malpractice disaster. Thus, an important part of the effectiveness of a SuperVision is for the principal to have *super follow-up and closing* skills to make sure that the real or potential threat to safety, security, and ultimately the school's mission has been completely neutralized, corrected, and eliminated so that the immediate and future similar situations don't ever occur again.

The strategic purpose of the principal's formal and informal visits to classrooms

Every school year (at the beginning of the year), you along with the APs, department chairpersons, and the school instructional coach must design a hierarchy of need and attention plan (not published) for visiting and providing support in the classrooms of first-year, one-to-three-year teachers, struggling teachers, and teachers showing signs of burnout. You can, and should, constantly revisit this plan to allow for increasing or decreasing the frequency of visits and the quantity of time spent on professional development activities for each individual or cohort of teachers.

The principal should utilize his or her SuperVision skills to get the full picture by way of short, informal visits to classes and other learning spaces in the building. Each classroom—every hall, the gym, cafeteria, locker room, bathroom, and ISS room—must in its own demonstrative way reflect the school's cultural mission of effectiveness, or else it will undermine that mission!

It is not enough to just see something good or bad, you must figure out what can be done about it. The principal must also resist the common urge to only work with the weak members of the teaching staff, thus denying the strong practitioners in the building with the professional development, feedback, and support they need in order to move toward mastery and excellence. There is always the danger that they can fall into an ineffective comfort zone if they are not properly and professionally supervised and challenged. Remember, your best and most effective staff persons (and don't forget your APs!) are still in need of a critical friend/coach who will provide them with valuable professional growth feedback.

I think that a school administrator must make every effort to convince members of the entire school family that they are in fact worthy and deserving of a professional life-enhancing environment. Most will spend between six to ten hours a day in that environment, so they should feel that the school's administrative leadership honors and respects their presence.

Now, consider these bulleted notes:

- A clean and well-maintained building is a central teaching and learning experience for the school family. Students will take their lead as to how they will treat a building based on the quality of maintenance of that building. Students will respond (negatively or positively) to the level of effort and concern they see the adults place in making the school look like a serious, professional space. Torn posters, papers on floors, broken lights or windows, broken closets, outdated fliers and announcements, or no real bulletin board posting of useful information suggests that what is done in the school is not important; therefore, they and their education is not important. This is crucial because students may be living in a home situation in which there is a shortage and/or deficiency of order and structure, good organizational plans (schedules), purposeful and practical rituals, and predictability. A physically well-organized school and classroom can greatly contribute to a school producing a strong, "calming" effect on those (and other) students. Further, some students with both diagnosed and undiagnosed disabilities can be greatly distracted from concentration and learning in disorderly, cluttered, and visually overstimulating environments. An effective teacher's orderly and well-organized classroom is an antidote to disorderly and disorganized thinking on the part of students, which is especially important for ninth-graders.

- Does this space enhance or endanger the academic program? As principal, I approached both formal and informal classroom visits with the preconception that there are at least two teachers in every classroom: the actual teacher of record and the classroom itself. The classroom as teacher means its aesthetics, inspirational and learning messages, cleanliness, condition, and organization are all teaching the students a lesson for which they are internalizing as they would any good lesson. The classroom environment is not a passive and inconsequential entity. The environmental state of a classroom will either enhance or undermine the work of the teacher's lesson. The principal should ask: (1) How would I feel sitting in this classroom as a student? (2) What is this classroom teaching (or not teaching) the students? (3) Do the aesthetics, architecture, pedagogical learning stations, and presentation boards of this classroom reflect the school's mission? (4) What does the state of this classroom say about the quality of my (the principal's) coaching leadership?

- What else am I looking for? How is time used and managed in this classroom? When and at what point in the period does the actual content instruction learning begin? And during the course of the lesson, how is the teacher able to effectively deal with any type of time-wasting distractions and interruptions? Further, to what extent have the students been taught to effectively be good and efficient time managers of their own learning? No matter how high performing a school is, the time efficiency-management differential from class to class will help or hurt the level of schoolwide academic achievement. This is where a school administrator who has the benefit of visiting different classes can be helpful to that teacher who may be unaware of how much time he or she is failing to effectively manage. With many new teachers, it could be just a matter of becoming aware of some of the standard best practices for improving classroom organization practices and teacher-student routines that don't lead to the loss of lesson time.

Your notes are also important as a way of self-evaluating your own approach to exercising your SuperVision. It should never be a random and unfocused exercise. Taking notes will help you to correctly remember later if—or when—you are suddenly pulled into an emergency response mode at any moment of the school day. Understandably, a principal walking around with a writing pad may cause some concern with the staff in general. A great deal of bad pedagogy and bad school leadership practices have entered and established themselves into the culture of public education. Effective principals today have a difficult task of convincing teachers and staff members that your job is not to get them fired. And that is why it is important to explain to all members of the staff, preferably at the opening staff meeting of the year, that nothing should be inferred by your taking notes as you walk around the school; this action is to help your memory and to help you to be the chief: safety officer, custodian/maintenance officer, student support services officer, and staff professional development officer of the building! This is important: The school *Climate-Culture* concept here is that you want to comfortably and convincingly help the staff to understand and appreciate that your "active" presence is to support them on their path to becoming master practitioners, not to "get" them! The principal does not succeed if a member of the staff fails.

Chapter 7:
An Effective Guidance/Counseling/ Career-College Center (GC-CCC) Department

This area of a school, particularly in Title I schools, can in many ways come to represent the heart of the school. And I use the word "heart" here to symbolize that a major part of the serious work of the guidance department is, at its core meaning and practice, the heart-healing station of the school. The guidance department is the central place in the school where the following activities on behalf of students take place daily: emotional support and care, life-education counseling and career guidance, protection and student advocacy—all of which will represent the department's primary mission efforts and daily activities. This is especially true for schools servicing students who are living in group homes; who are homeless; who are in some way under the supervision of the criminal justice system; students who themselves are parents; or those students whose parents face serious challenges emotionally, physically, and financially. The GC-CCC champions the causes of people society has often forgotten and ignored, those for whom schooling represents the one and only path to break the cyclical poverty narrative that so plagues so many communities in our nation. If these students have any chance of realizing a positive and productive adult life, they must be serviced by a strong and effective GC-CCC department.

It bothered me greatly, both as a principal and superintendent, to see principals who either did not know or did not care about the important attention that must be paid to the GC-CCC area of a school. I have heard a lot of excuses and rationales for cutting staff in these departments, mostly placing the blame on district budget cuts. But these GC-CCC departments are essential to a school's core function, and their work has a direct impact on learning and academic achievement. Therefore, just as with any other department in the school, the principal must have a good working knowledge and understanding of the GC-CCC's operational objectives and mission and, more importantly, how they work in cooperation and partnership with the goals and objectives of the academic departments. School superintendents should also direct a significant part of their discretionary funding to help strengthen these GC-CCC departments in schools, particularly in those high schools with large numbers of Title I/ESL/ELL/homeless students.

An important part of being an effective school building leader is to recognize the critical need for a robust and fully staffed GC-CCC program, which means there is the need to be competent and strategic in the area of school budgeting. It also means that the principal must be entrepreneurial in being able to raise funds and counseling resources outside of the school's formal allocation (I discuss the need for establishing a school 501c3 foundation later in the book). The principal must also think creatively about ways to make the budget allocation go further. For example, one of the most effective and quickest ways of saving money is to reduce the number of students who are forced to retake classes; ironically, the central part to that plan is having a strong and proactive GC-CCC department. The GC-CCC department takes on an even greater role in high schools because the students are on a time/credit/required courses/standardized exams list of graduation requirements, bench marks, and deadlines. A good GC-CCC team could serve as an early warning system that could play a major role in helping to reduce the number of students who fail classes and/or standardized exams that are required for graduation. This important process of high academic achievement/course passing rates leads to more available funds and the ability to invest those funds in projects, programs, and activities that support greater academic achievement as well as GC-CCC-related activities. This formula helps high-performing schools to remain that way and struggling schools to maintain their academic underachievement status. The vicious cycle of high and steady student academic failure, eating up funds that could be used to drive down academic failure, is essentially the school "eating" its own mission. The work of the GC-CCC can serve as a powerful intervention force to break that cycle; for much of the academic failure by students in high-poverty (Title I) high schools—especially by boys—will have little to do with their intellectual capacity and more to do with their incapacity to confront and defeat the many societal hurdles constructed to ensure that their education and lives lead to failure.

A key factor here for the SBL is to know the needs and requirements of the student population in your school and then to understand the level of counseling support services your particular students need. But all schools—high performing, medium performing, and low performing—must incorporate an appropriate GC-CCC program that would address the counseling needs of those students. An important measure of any school, regardless of academic performance level, is its strategic plan for how it will identify and support its most vulnerable students, the newly arrived to the U.S. students, ESL/ELL students and parents, the lost, lonely and confused, those who are struggling academically, students who are mildly or greatly disabled, those without good parental support, those students who themselves are parents, etc. The school-based leadership team and the GC-CCC team must draft an action plan that links the societal/emotional needs of students to the graduation requirements and the school's mission. They must design a plan of action that identifies the different counseling needs of various cohorts of students as well as organizational/operational responses to the many different challenges those students will encounter on their path to graduation.

Who are those seriously "at risk" student cohorts and what are the challenges they face?

First on the list annually are students transitioning from middle school to high school. I have always thought of the entire ninth-grade cohort as an "at-risk" group. I always gave special and early strategic attention to those students who arrived to high school after spending three years in a school cultural environment that was different from our school. It is, after all, better to take a counseling prevention/interventionist approach early before these students begin to struggle academically and even fail classes. And, so, I always asked the ninth-grade assigned guidance counselor in cooperation with the team of ninth-grade teachers to develop an early warning "watch and take action" list. In this way, we don't want to reach the end of the first marking period with the student having failed one or more classes. Getting ninth-graders off to a good start is one of the most important indicators and predictors for student success in high school and creates an advantageous situation in which those students can accumulate the maximum credits required for graduation. One of the problematic conditions that increases the dropout rate is students spending a lot of time in high school and not earning credits. Having students start off by passing all of their ninth-grade courses is a good way of keeping them interested and focused on graduation. After all, they can actually see themselves moving positively toward that goal. And the opposite is also true of students who don't successfully earn the number of credits that would allow them to become a tenth-grader see their path to graduation as being extremely difficult. Based on my personal professional observation, it seemed to me that by the end of ninth grade, student optimism, in reference to graduation, either increased or decreased based on the amount of credits earned in their freshman year. *And, so, it is important to simply note that placing all prior K-8 academic deficiencies aside, the high school contribution to the high school dropout process starts in the first semester of the student's first year in high school!* Thus, here would be the need for a thoughtful, aggressive, and proactive GC-CCC team and plan that would increase the number of bona fide (with earned credits) tenth-graders. This action would not only raise the graduation rate but also represent a positive addition to the school's budget (remember course repeaters cost money), which allows the school to do more important things with that additional funding, like hiring a sufficient number of school counselors.

Now, let us dig much deeper into the GC-CCC plan of action, without which significant numbers of students will fail to be academically successful and, ultimately, graduate:

- Ninth-graders who are severely unprepared in content skills and knowledge levels (based on K-8 academic performance and standardized test scores); these academic deficiencies are so serious that they would prevent these students from being able to successfully engage in high school-level academic work. This could mean functioning far below the skills required to read and process high school textbooks and other documents, missing significant and foundational arithmetic concepts and algorithms that would allow the students to succeed in a first-year high school algebra class.

- Students entering in the country for the first time. Also including students who, because of particular situations in their former countries, may arrive with significant gaps in school years.

- All students with IEPs.

- Students with chronic (long-term) medical, dental, and/or psychological issues (e.g., diabetes, sickle cell anemia, asthma, severe allergies).

- Students transitioning from homeschooling, private, or religious schools.

- Students' families who have dramatically altered and pushed forward their start-of-school year start date (this is a big problem in many ur-

140

ban schools and schools that service families that travel out of the country during the summer). They could also return late from a school/holiday/semester break or unfortunately be forced to attend a family member's funeral in another country.

- Students (transferring) in the tenth or eleventh grades who may have credit and other graduation requirement gaps. Also, the new school structure, rules, and culture can sometimes be a challenge. These students also need help to socially integrate into the school student family.

- Students who come from middle schools that we know have a history of not adequately preparing students academically or emotionally to be successful in high school.

- Students who did not attend the Summer Bridge Academy (SBA) or did not complete the summer pre-ninth grade work package and assigned readings.

- Students who are in need of additional academic/behavioral support based on their performance and the diagnostic testing in the SBA.

- Students flagged in the SBA or early in the school year who might have vision, dental, hearing or other medical problems that could adversely affect learning.

- Students who bring challenging home-living situations to the school such as being on probation, living in a group home, being raised by elder grandparents or other senior family members, or living in foster care.

- Students (particularly males) for whom the choice of the school is the parent and not the child, and they are angry and hostile about attending a "strict" (and "less fun") high school.

- Students who have histories of chronic lateness and/or absenteeism.

- Students who fail sections of the first semester Mathematics Diagnostics Exam[2].

- Students who have been challenged with discipline and behavioral control issues in the K-8 experience.

- Any and all arrivals from middle schools who lack the organization skills required to manage high school course work. The #1 academic achievement pitfall for many high school freshmen is their inability to organize their academic responsibilities. This becomes doubly difficult in schools that require a lot of projects and research papers, which is why a yearlong planner/calendar should be given to every ninth-grader, along with a workshop (use a PE or HE class period) taught by a member of the GC-CCC team as to how to actually use the planner. Giving every student a yearlong planner costs money, but this is money well spent as it will increase the number of academically successful ninth-graders by making sure they get and remain organized.

- Any and all students who need help in adjusting to the high school teacher's focus on content rather than individual student nurturing. Now, this is a hard one because many of my high school teacher friends hear this the wrong way. I'm not talking about the sincere caring and commitment capabilities of high school teachers, but it is true that the structure of high schools lends itself to a teaching and learning environment that encourages a greater level of student independence and personal responsibility than the K-8 world. Incoming high school students will simply need to make the adjustment that they are entering a system that is structured to provide less hand-holding on the part of teachers. This suggests a further and greater need for an effective GC-CCC team that would help students to successfully make that transition.

- Ninth-grade students who appear to be challenged by the academic expectations and standards, pace, size, speed, and organization of high school.

The guidance team must meet before the start of the school year, along with the Special Ed supervisor and the entire SBL team, and review every incoming student's individual health, behavior, and academic records before students are programed or scheduled into classes. I know this can be a tedious (and perhaps even costly) activity, but it is an important one. And if the district does not provide the funds centrally, it is important that the principal find the budgetary capacity to bring in the grade-level guidance counselors a little early before the start of the school year to meticulously review the records of incoming and transferring students. Students can't be reduced to a number; the SBL and the guidance team must attach a personality, a name, and most importantly, a need

142

and a support plan to every student. Remember, the high school game is often lost in the first semester if/when incoming students start to fail subjects. This places unnecessary pressure on the students, staff, and school to then "recover" credits. As I stated earlier, schools are unpredictable and dynamic places, so the best way to deal with multiple crises and interruptions is to plan in order to reduce the number of potential problems before the start of the school year. This allows the school to better deal with problems that will naturally arise every day. It is always a good school leadership strategy to go after and remove the clearly predictable problems early, which gives the school administrators more time to address the unpredictable issues when they pop up. A sure sign of an ineffective school is that it can never seem to get out of crisis mode; and, of course, the first casualty of being in a permanent state of crisis-fixing is the degradation in quality of the instructional program, which then creates more crises. It's important that the counseling and guidance department take the lead in strengthening these pre-vent-proactive efforts. One reason is that they are uniquely trained and sensitive to see potential challenges students may encounter when they start a new school experience. Students will arrive with a full spectrum of expectations of what high school life will be—some realistic and some not so realistic. To the extent that the guidance team can provide a proactive guidance bridge gives students the best possibilities to succeed. Giving incoming students a strong foundational start in high school will mean less intervention and corrective guidance as they move up in grades. And just like it is true in every academic department in the school, the principal must make the case that it is always better to do a little extra work on the front end, which limits a lot of heavy and emotionally hard work on the back end. The GC-CCC team must understand that every time a student fails a class, the odds increase for failing additional classes, absenteeism, behavioral problems, "super-seniorship," and, ultimately, dropping out of school.

With that good GC-CCC preliminary analytical work and planning out of the way, students who need additional academic support are placed in classes where they can receive it. Students who have been identified as seriously aca-demically deficient should be enrolled in tutorials on the first week of school (put on their official schedules), not a few weeks later when they are struggling and in danger of failing the class. The chronically late people (based either on their middle school records or their present difficulty in getting to school on time) should be assigned to attend a special meeting and workshop entitled, "How to get to school on time!" They are also informed during the session that until they prove themselves responsible, they will be required to sign in every day in the guidance office. The students who in middle school had a high number of unaccountable absences are warned that they would join the "wake-up call club" if they are absent one time for "not a good reason." All students have been given planners along with a warning of the many long-term projects to come. The students are made aware of where to go when they need information, help, and support, or just to talk to someone. The academic program is explained including all subject area weekly exams. Terms like study, homework, respect, bullying, etc., are defined and explained. The individual and group counseling sessions are set up. The IEP-mandated counseling is scheduled so as not to interrupt the child's academic program. The team-teaching Special Ed/Regular Ed classes are organized. Student handbooks and a presentation on school expectations, rules, and regulations has been completed.

And, so, with all of this great proactive-guidance in place, what could possibly go wrong? Well, sadly, a lot of things! In greater part because during the course of a school year, the children are maturing (and changing demonstrably), also the lives that the children live both inside and outside of school are also dramatically changing each year, and each grade level contains its own list of qualifying "must-do's" as the students move toward their senior year. A school must employ a steady, but flexible, guidance counseling program that can produce an environment of stability because this makes students comfortable to know what to do and where to go when problem X shows up in their lives. And, yet, the GC-CCC department is creatively agile enough to be able to effectively respond to these changes in the lives of the children it serves.

Continuing with the first-year students, a further challenge is that students don't come to a school for the first time and fall into neat psychological packages. We can develop some good working hypothesizes, but the truth is that there is just no way to perfectly predict an individual child's response to the high school experience. I have seen middle school "hell raisers" or poor academic performers get struck by "maturity lightning" and suddenly become transformed into high-performing students. On the other hand, I have seen students whose middle school records suggest that they should be first-round picks to be top high school academic performers who go on to bomb academically! Often this is because they really encounter stiff academic competition for the first time, or they discover the beauty of the opposite sex! The GC-CCC's close observation, assessment, and evaluation of a student's capacity to perform well in high school must continue throughout the first year of that new student's life. The guidance counseling team should spend the first weeks of school in intense meeting sessions with students as they observe their attitudes, behaviors, and academic performance. The GC-CCC team must also establish some "getting to know this student" dialogues with teachers in search of potential problems. Establishing good communication structures between the GC-CCC and teachers—and, in particular, the teachers of ninth-grade students—is a critical component in realizing the school's academic achievement mission. Therefore, the principal, APs, and department chairpersons must play an essential role in facilitating this communication-partnership system.

Effectively organizing the GC-CCC department's work assignments

There are several theories on how to organize the staffing assignments of the GC-CCC department. The decision should ultimately reflect the particular needs of individual schools. My approach is to organize the GC-CCC staffing along the lines of specialization and concentration as follows: a dedicated ninth-, tenth-, and eleventh-grade counselor, and a twelfth-grade counselor who will work with the career-college advisor. At each grade level, the principal must be involved in assisting and supporting those counselors with their assignment of getting students to fulfill each of those grade-level objectives. In addition, there is a need, especially in Title I schools for a full-time clinical psychologist and/or social worker.

What are these grade-level assigned counselors doing?

Required courses, credits, exams, study habits and techniques, organization and planning, personal problem-solving, negotiation and mediation techniques, parent-guardian conferences, support for the IEP (Individualized Education Program) team, managing and mediating the relationship between teacher and student, addressing issues of peer conflicts, and advocating on behalf of students with the dean and school administrators. They are primarily focused on getting the student successfully to the next grade and, ultimately, to graduation. Every grade-level counselor must have a list of learning objectives that helps both parent and student to become knowledgeable and fluent in the format and language of the high school promotional process via the transcript. This is important in high schools, for it is that critical moment when the guidance counselors seek to shift the parents and students away from the

K-8 mindset of how students are promoted to the next grade as opposed to how high school students are promoted using the Carnegie Unit system. No parent or student should reach the end of a school year believing that just because said student spent a calendar year in the school that he or she will automatically be designated a tenth-, eleventh-, or twelfth-grader in the next school year.

Each grade-level guidance counselor should develop a grade cohort appropriate list of tasks accompanied with dates by which those things (course and exam passing requirement) must be accomplished before a student is allowed to move to the next grade. These GC-CCC operational standards serve the primary purpose of making sure that no student will fall through the guidance counseling net. Knowing the specific check-off tasks for each grade level offers the students the optimal advantage for a successful high school and post-high school experience. These GC-CCC grade-level operational standards also even the playing field for those students who can't take advantage of parental academic guidance, parental education, financial ability, and the family's access to adults who can provide mentoring/career/college information and assistance to the student. The GC-CCC team should also meet with students by grade to provide them with those "soft" and successful life skills standards that are required to excel in both high school and adult life, for example:

What happens after I...

Time organization and management.

Strategic personal goal-setting/planning.

How to manage the supervisor (teacher, professor, etc.) relationship.

Positive self-confidence.

What does it mean to act and be professional?

Patience and gratification deferring.

Budgeting and financial literacy.

Good punctuality and attendance.

Discipline and focus.

Interviewing techniques.

How to protest or complain productively.

Living an honest and honorable life of integrity.

How social media can hurt my present and future!

Taking personal responsibility for your life.

Good verbal and body language skills.

Cultural behavioral and linguistic "code switching."

Everything that comes into your head does not need to be said.

All of these standards should serve as a core rubric for the supervision and evaluation of the members of the GC-CCC team. Although these members are passing students on to the next grade's guidance counselor, there is a document that will allow for a consistency of the counseling departmental goals and objectives. These objectives will follow students through their entire high school experience.

The Graduation Critical Path Chart (GCPC)

The GCPC is a four-year electronic plan by which students can get on, stay on, and continually check on their pace, progress, and proficiency in reaching graduation and their post-high school objectives. It is a calendar-structured path chart that establishes the courses to be taken (including everything from required courses, electives to advance, and AP courses); standardized exams that must be taken and passed; internships to apply for; school clubs, teams, and activities to join; and the must-do's in a weekly, monthly, semester, (year-round) annual scheduled format. This four-year plan is developed with the help of the ninth-grade guidance counselor and should start with the end career, college/professional school, and profession and then work backwards to the present ninth grade. This critical path plan should contain the following types of goal items:

- Ninth-grade sign-up for PSAT/Pre-ACT on…

- Take the PSAT/Pre-ACT on…

- Daily vocabulary-building practice: so many words a day…

- SAT/ACT/AP vocabulary words per week/month/year.

- My daily words/pages read schedule for the Readers to Leaders (*explained in the ELA department chapter*) program.

- What electives, advanced classes, AP courses lead me to my career-college goal?

- I want a STEM college major that requires calculus; what math courses are needed each year to get to calculus by the twelfth grade?

- What service/volunteer activities do I need to add to my senior portfolio over the next four years in order to enhance my chances of realizing my future career plans?

- What summer jobs and internships are aligned to support my future college and career aspirations?

I know it is not easy to get ninth-graders (or any teenagers) to plan ahead, particularly four years ahead; and it is also true that organizational and planning skills are probably among the greatest enemies of the average ninth-grader. But we must make the effort by informing students that there are no throwaway grade levels in high school; every high school marking period, semester and grade level counts, and what is specifically counted in each of those levels is the successful completion of a list of tasks and goals that are required for that grade level.

The GCPC (signed by parent and student) provides both child and parent with a road map that, if followed successfully, guarantees graduation in the most efficient period of time. The GCPC is not written in stone, and so the child and parent can revisit, modify, add, or delete electives and activities as the student's interest and career/college goals change; but the core general high school graduation requirements in the GCPC should remain the same. That core requirement is that every student will at least have the requisite transcript that will allow him or her to be college able and ready, if he or she so chooses that post-high school route. I believe requiring every first-year high school student to design a GCPC (a document that the student signs by name) will support a greater appreciation and understating of what is expected of that student and will also lead to much improved graduation rates.

Designing the Graduation Critical Path Chart (GCPC)

If the student plans to bypass college and enter a career, or to delay college attendance for a year or so, then a solid, adaptable, and creative plan via the GCPC must be developed. If the student plans to enter a CTE (Career Technical Education--a full chapter later in the book) certification program or a construction trades apprenticeship training program/school after graduation, again, an appropriate GCPC plan must be created. Students should be required to pick some kind of reasonable and productive post-high school plan of action; just getting them out the door with a diploma is professionally unethical. The grade-level guidance counselor must in cooperation with the College/Career Counselor (CCC) help those students who either plan to delay or completely avoid college organize their in- and out-of-school studies and learning activities with the same time and attention that is given to those students who plan to go straight to college. If the school offers pre-apprenticeship and CTE certification courses (e.g., Cisco, EMT, or Microsoft) then the guidance counselor is going to need to help those students organize a GCPC that will allow them to earn a college-ready high school diploma as well as prepare them to pass a certification exam and/or position themselves to gain admission to an industry, governmental, or corporation training program, or a skills trade apprenticeship program. Internships as well as after-school and summer scheduling are critical for these students. For those who plan to delay college for a year, the guidance counselor again in cooperation with the CCC must simultaneously apply the standard departmental efforts to realize the college admissions scholarships objectives while helping the students design a rich and meaningful out-of-college year plan. This could include things like the students writing a book, traveling/journaling/photographing, volunteering, participating in a yearlong internship, engaging in creative or performing arts mentoring and study, or gaining employment that can hopefully enhance their future college/career plans.

If the end goal for the student is to enroll in college right after high school graduation, then start at the end and build the GCPC planning backwards so as to cover every full-calendar year of the student's time in that school. With the help of the grade-level guidance counselor (who is in communication with the CCC), the students can identify which classes they need to take to realize a particular (type of) college and/or college/career major. Most students mistakenly believe that the college search process begins somewhere during the junior or senior year of high school. Actually, it begins in the ninth grade, when students are developing good writing, vocabulary, and presentation skills and also building a strong GPA, which is the primary measuring criterion for college admissions and scholarships. This admissions process continues in the tenth through twelfth grades as students build their transcripts as well as the elements of the student's senior portfolio. The transcript and the senior portfolio (actually constructed over four years) represents the chief marketing and promotional tools that will determine the quality of a student's post-high school life. Within the context of the GCPC, they answer questions including: What internships, school activities, teams and clubs match and enhance the student's college/career goals? How can the student make the most effective use of school breaks and the summer vacation to better enhance his or her senior portfolio? What electives, advanced courses, and/or AP courses best support the student's future college/career aspirations? What acts of volunteerism and service should the student perform that can be linked to his or her future college/career goals? What kind of image or profile does the student want to create for him or herself in this school (an important factor for winning internships and later receiving those important letters of recommendations from teachers and administrators)?

The GCPC should define the objectives for each of the four years the student is in the school. The chart should have a space for designating a "yes or no" space for indicating started, in progress, and completed, along with a task due date. For example, an excerpt from the ninth grade GCPC:

1. I am in a new school. What image do I want to establish? What is my plan for making a good and positive first and lasting impression? How can I start making the case for great teacher recommendations, internships, school scholarships and awards, special school trips, activities and programs? When my name "comes up" with the administration and staff, what is it that I want said about me?

2. Set up a meeting with my guidance counselor ASAP in the first semester of the first year of high school. (*The principal or GC-CCC departmental chairperson should help to facilitate these meetings; if you must, pay the guidance counselor to stay after school for the first couple of weeks of school. These initial meetings should be reasonably brief and focused on getting the student started on the GCPC. Over the course of the year, the guidance counselor can have longer meetings.*)

3. Complete first draft of the GCPC no later than the midterm of the first marking period.

4. The full four-year sequence of classes, including the prerequisite courses required for my college/career goals, have been incorporated into my GCPC. Checking to see if I am in the correct ninth-grade classes.

5. I have thoroughly read the student handbook and the course syl-

labus for each class, and I have incorporated all long-term projects and assignment deadlines into my physical and electronic calendar.

6. Thinking about scholarships early. "My future career/college plans will cost money. I don't want to burden my family (*parents like that part!*). I also don't want to leave college saddled with a huge amount of debt. So, what is my highest grade point average (GPA) plan?" (*As the principal you want to get students involved early in the "race to the top" of class rankings; it will absolutely help later with scholarships and college admissions.*)

7. I have put all school exams (e.g., course midterms-finals) and standardized exams (e.g., Pre-ACT or PSAT 10, city, state exams) dates into my book and electronic calendar. (*The school should fund this plan and policy for all ninth-graders to sign up and take the Pre-ACT and PSAT 10 exams in the ninth grade.*)

8. Master the SAT/ACT vocabulary and "turnkey" words and phrases in a year. Create SAT/ACT flashcards with the words and phrases on one side of the card, and the definitions and meanings on the other side of the card.

9. I have created a Dedicated College/Career File (DCCF) on a "jump drive" backed up on a computer hard drive, where I will keep my GCPC and a copy of my end-of-each-semester upgraded transcript. Start building my senior portfolio, which means all scanned documents (awards and recognitions, honor roll appointment, letters of commendations/recommendation, etc.) to be included in my senior portfolio. It is also where I will eventually keep college/career information, college/career contact information, my biographical sketch, resume, personal goals and objective statement, and all post-high school graduation information resources. No unrelated to college/career information should go in this file.

10. I have a plan to get to school and to all of my classes on time,

every day. If I miss a class for any reason, my plan for acquiring the information that was taught is _____.

11. I have a well-organized school/class documents and teacher handouts folder system with designated (separate) note-taking books for each of my classes.

12. I have a standard (*provided in the student handbook and the ninth-grade ELA class*) note-taking system that includes dates, standards, objectives, and topics of a lesson.

13. I have a plan and place to record homework assignments. I also will utilize my calendar to record, short- and long-term projects start as well as due dates (electric and/or paper).

14. I have a folder for each subject/class in which I could place all homework, assignments, and exams that the teacher has graded and returned to me.

15. Utilize the goals of the GCPC to pick manageable out-side-of-classroom activities in which to participate (e.g., team, club, or school service society). *(Part of the transcript and port-folio goals of the GCPC is to give students a broad and diverse presentation of skills and talents. You don't want a career/col-lege senior portfolio that only says, "just went to school and took required courses!")*

16. Don't fail classes because failing any class is never helpful! If seats are not assigned in every class, try to sit in the front row of the classroom. (Or, as close to the front as possible!) Let the teacher teach, keep it professional! Work hard, stay focused, and do my best!

17. I have a place for, and a way of recording, all of my grades on homework turned in, special projects and assignments, scores on all classroom exams and tests. *(This action has literally won higher grade appeals for students. It is also an essential tool of*

those students who, starting with the ninth grade, keep a monitoring eye on their class standings in the four-year GPA competition.)

18. I have all of the materials and supplies I need for all of my classes.

19. Sign-up date actions (before the final deadlines) for the Pre-ACT or PSAT 10 exams and any other special projects/programs/activities (e.g., internships, special school seminars and presentations, college tour/visits).

20. Establish a quiet and conducive home study space and schedule (e.g., two hours homework and two hours study). Or, if a home study space is not possible, seek an alternative (e.g., the school or the public library after school).

21. I have a plan to gain access to an Internet-linked computer and printer (outside of school). Or, a plan as to how I will use the school's computers.

22. As soon as it is available *(districts vary as to when in the first year, this actually takes effect)*, I will get a copy of my transcript and learn how to read and interpret all of its codes.

23. Hold off on forming serious friendships until the end of the first marking period; just be observant and choose wisely. Select friends who are moving in a positive and productive direction.

24. Helped by the GCPC, develop a list of a new skill, hobby, and talent annual learning plan *(keyboarding, photography, sculpture, stamp collecting, dance, golf, coding, etc.)*. I will enhance existing talents and expand each year into new areas of talent and knowledge. Try something completely new like learning how to play GO or golf.

25. Introduce myself to the CCC and the College/Career Center and become familiar with its workings, procedures, and resources.

(As a principal, CCCs have all told me over the years that they love when ninth-graders take an early interest in their post-high school lives!) And become familiar with the career college-going process, the information and opportunities posted on the CCC's bulletin board, and all of the available resources of the college/career center. Let my principal, guidance counselor, and CCC know that I am interested in acquiring a summer internship.

26. What are my plans and goals for after-school time, weekends, all of the school year breaks, and the summer vacation that will help me to realize my career/college objectives? Purchase a writing journal for daily musings, thoughtful reflections, and the recording of places and events. *(These notes from your personal journal can help with your autobiography that is required for the GCPC and essays when you return to school.)*

27. At the end of ninth grade: Review my transcript and meet with my guidance counselor to review my scheduled tenth-grade classes. What is my class (GPA) ranking?

28. Reconnect, renew, and/or establish quality out-of-school activities and involvements, for example, faith-based institution, organized sports, scouting, music/martial arts/dance classes, volunteerism, tutoring, community service project. *(Doing good and meaningful works while building the portfolio, resume, and biography!)*

29. Check the GC-CCC bulletin boards and see the guidance counselor or school administrator in the spring about a summer job or Summer Youth Employment Program (SYEP) assignment that is greatly inclined toward learning a meaningful skill, mentoring, and a source for good letters of recommendations.

30. *Before the ninth (or any) grade student leaves for the summer break, he or she should ask,* "Am I scheduled for the correct tenth-grade classes? Is my proposed tenth-grade class/course schedule consistent with the goals of my GCPC? Do I need to

make some adjustments to my GCPC due to a change in my vision, interest, opportunity, or new information I acquired? What are the GCPC career/college goal suggestions for how I should utilize my summer?"

In summary: The role and purpose of the Graduation Critical Path Chart (GCPC) is to increase the odds for every student to realize and obtain a successful graduation and post-high school goals and objectives life.

This document will serve as a guide and monitor for the GC-CCC department, students, parents, administrators and staff, as we seek to effectively and successfully move students through the high school process and toward graduation. It is also a critical tool for helping the school to increase the number of successful high school graduates as well as help students to design a good post-graduation plan. This process also constitutes the strategies employed by parents (or a friend or family member of the parents) who know and understand the "tricks and techniques" of how to successfully navigate the high school process. Success should not be left for parents and students to try to randomly guess and figure out on their own. All parents can want the best and most productive high school educational experience for their child, but not all parents will have access to the information (and this book) that will help them to organize that success. An important job of the GC-CCC team is to effectively close that parent information-resources gap. Also, be aware, principal, that in some school situations you may be accused of doing too much with this GCPP program. You may even come under criticism for hindering students from freely and independently finding their way through high school. But we know that for many of the at-risk student population (including high academic achievers), a laissez-faire school guidance approach would spell disaster for these students. Besides, we know that a version of the GCPP is practiced and utilized unofficially by information-rich parents and by the parents who are professional educators. Your (ethical) objective here is to open up the process to all students, regardless of the amount of outside-of-school "guidance counseling" services they are receiving!

Building an effective high school College Career Center

The school's College/Career Counselor (CCC) should be a specialized annually reappointed position in the school. I know some schools rotate the position, but that is not how I see these counselors at their most effective best. Being well versed on the dates and deadlines of the college scholarship/career and application process requires experience and focused expertise. Further, it is important that the same person at a school be able to develop a list ("rolodex") and relationship with key contacts (people, agencies, military, colleges, internships, scholarship sources, and human resources at companies with employment opportunities). Experienced CCCs will also be able to better troubleshoot challenging situations of which they have come to know over time, for example, working with homeless students, students or parents who are undocumented residents in the country, and students with disabilities; or, they can also properly advise students based on the feedback and experiences of previous graduates. Although there is no absolute "wall of work" that exists in the counseling and guidance department, based on the nature of the work, all of the counselors must often work together as a team to solve a particular problem. But I do believe that specialization, experience, and expertise in particular areas is required to have a successful department, and the unique tasks required of the CCC calls for focused and specialized knowledge. For reasons of emergency backup and professional development, the principal should make sure that all guidance counselors, especially the eleventh- and twelfth-grade counselor, have sufficient time to acquire a critical working knowledge of the important tasks, objectives, and deadlines of the CCC.

The CCC's strategic approach to the college admissions/ scholarship acquisition process

High schools, particularly those that serve Title I students, should not allow students to stumble through the college admissions/scholarships acquisition process based on the incorrect notion that they are now "adults." Secondly, and equally important, is that the CCC must provide support to offset the advantages of some students who will have family support who are well versed and active in the college-going process.

- The principal, guidance counselors, and the CCC should organize a series of early grade-level parent-student meetings as well as attaching them to the regular monthly parent meetings to discuss the college-going process. Outline at those meetings which courses, exams taken and passed, and which need to be achieved in order to realize a particular major; in- and out-of-school requirements for the development of a good senior portfolio; and check off items (GCPC) of things they should have in place and accomplished by the end of each particular grade. This information can also be part of a written parent information packet (in multiple languages), distributed at every parent meeting and parent visit and gathering at the school, e-mailed, sent home with students, mailed, and posted on the school's website.

- Plan a short parent workshop on reading and understanding the high school transcript. Explain the high school definition of "promotion to the next grade" as well as the district's and school's (if more is required) graduation requirements. This meeting is probably the best place to share with the parents the reason that the high school graduation is the only legal graduation ceremony in the K-12 school system. The principal and the CCC should remove any idea from the parents' heads that graduation will be an emotional decision; the law and statutes (distribute them) are clear, so calling up the superintendent, school board member, or elected official won't help since you will essentially be asking them to break the law. That "wake-up" segment alone will improve behavior and academic performance in the school the next day; besides, *all* parents are eager to attend their child's graduation!

- The CCC or any guidance counselor should lead a Reading and Interpreting My Transcript workshop for all new students. This information should be constantly promoted for all grades so that there will be no sad and tragic misunderstandings in the eleventh or twelfth grades when, unfortunately, some students come to fully realize and understand the true meaning of the term "graduation requirements."

- The CCC should hold weekly before, after, or lunchtime check-in meetings with individuals and groups of seniors, juniors, and then sophomores.

- The school must develop a plan to help those students (or their parents) who don't have the "proper" U.S. residency documentation but who wish to attend college. The earlier this information is known to the CCC, the better. A large part of helping these students is trust on the part of the student and parent for the school. Schools often find out the family's residency status when some type of governmental form is not signed and returned or when the student is eligible for a study abroad program and does not sign up. The earlier the family shares their residency status with the principal, the more options are available to the school. The SBL/GC-CCC teams should never engage in any illegal action, even if it means helping a worthy child and family. This is another place where a collaborative partnership with a related CBO and a law firm can be extremely healthy. These students are not necessarily in a hopeless situation, although of late (since 2016) the situation is much more challenging for schools to solve. In the past, I have been able to see many positive outcomes in these situations. In school districts with large numbers of students whose parents or the students themselves lack the legal residency documentation, it means that the principal and the GC-CCC team should have a counseling plan in place to start helping these students before they reach the twelfth grade.

- The school/CCC advisor should sponsor a panel discussion program for students and parents, featuring college admissions officers. At these sessions, the panelists should be asked to present the "do's and don'ts" of the process as they also enlighten the audience to the models of excellence in applications and essays as well as those that were not so excellent. This session will help reinforce many of the initiatives promoted by the school for which the students (and parents) may be skeptical such as a service-volunteering graduation requirement or why the school engages students in a broad spectrum of in- and out-of-school intellectual learning experiential activities (e.g., cultural institutions trips, internships, summer academies).

- The school/CCC should sponsor biweekly local and out-of-state college tours. These tours also help to cement positive relationships with the CCC and the college admissions officers. I have found that many colleges have well-organized and excellent educational and fun experiences. Colleges are also interested in diversity on the campus, so they are extremely eager and supportive of accommodating schools that represent the full spectrum of U.S. student population. Students should see a wide variety of colleges so that they can begin to develop their personal concepts for their ideal college atmosphere. Being able to visit different academic departments is also important, as something the students see or hear may stimulate a career interest. The students are also able to get a sense of what it means to live a college life: the pluses and minuses of either living on a campus or life as a commuting student while living at home. Further, students are exposed to the real cost of college and the kind of resources they will need over a four-year period. All students should be given a summer assignment to individually participate in a local or national college tour. Finally, seeing and feeling a goal up close makes that goal much more real and possible to achieve; college tours help to focus students' interests!

- The school/CCC should have a four-year (year-round) plan for those students who wish to attend a specialized college and/or program that has a highly competitive and very selective admissions process. Course selection, including electives, possible study or classes outside of the high school setting, focused after-school, weekend, and summer internships may be required. Special mentoring activities and letters of recommendations would be an important part of this process. Some of these college programs also require some type of an audition, extensive background review, interview process, and a presentation or a portfolio. I am speaking of colleges like the military academies and colleges (or college programs) that specialize in architecture, culinary, creative-performing arts, or the fashion industry.

- The school in cooperation with the CCC team should establish a school policy and organizational structure that would allow for *every* student in the school to be eligible (transcript ready) at the time of graduation to be able to attend either a two- or four-year college, if that is their choice. The school and CCC team should also plan to address those students who wish to either delay college for a year or those attending a two-year college with the plan to transfer to a four-year college. The CCC should also address the needs of students who are parents or who, for family personal reasons, must work full time and at the same time attend college (which is what I did). Very often, even well-meaning educators will read a lack of interest in college from a student as a well-thought-out decision, including the possible excellent decision for a student to delay college for a year. Everyone does not see college attendance as the right career path for them, which is fine. If not college, then the CCC should help the student to

159

draft a post-high school (CTE, civil service, etc.) career plan. Part of the professional competency of the CCC is to be aware of future employment and career trends, so as to advise students properly about careers they may be interested in, or to think about little known, new "evolving" careers that might interest the students if they knew about them. The vision of the CCC is grounded in the present but is also aware of future possibilities and societal changes. We need to prepare students to envision themselves five, ten, and twenty years into the future; what skills and competencies will they need over a long career period of time and possibly across many different careers? While respecting the "no interest in attending college" attitude and approach, we must also make sure that strategy is accompanied with a solid and sensible post-graduation career plan—one that is not just a display of a fear of college, a response to negative peer pressure, or the student displaying a fear of success. Talking and listening respectfully, not condescendingly, about their decision for not wanting to attend college is important in helping them plan out the best career path for them to pursue. However, the principal, SBL, and CCC must closely monitor both the college preparedness and the college-going activities of even the most academically capable Black and Latino boys. It is not uncommon for some of them to engage in self-sabotaging and self-destructive behaviors like not turning in the requisite documents, applications, purposefully misinforming or not informing parents of their responsibilities in the college application process. They may attempt to avoid the college grade-level meetings and workshops by missing deadlines and avoiding the College Career Center itself. With this group, the concept of "at risk" must expand its meaning to a student "at risk" of not diligently performing all of his college-going responsibilities. The key here is not to force all students to attend college after graduation; rather it is to separate those students who are legitimately pursuing a non-college career/life plan from those students who are just avoiding the college-going process for reasons other than a personal "choice" (e.g., just afraid of stepping into college and out of their comfort zone).

- The CCC should be a central resource organizer of an annual school event titled *College Week* where students and faculty are encouraged to wear college clothing and other college paraphernalia as the school-based college/career fair takes place that same week.

- The CCC should also organize school trips that would allow the juniors and seniors to attend local area college fairs. (Primarily focus on eleventh- and twelfth-graders, but space allows inclusion of the tenth- and ninth-graders as an academic reward trip.) One of the great enticement tools for convincing and getting colleges to visit my school was based on the students' well-prepared presentations at a college fair. Based on our student's excellent questions, we were able to get many individual college recruiters to visit for a day in our College Career Center.

- Having single college recruiters come and set up in your college center is extremely important for several reasons:

  o Students are able to ask more detailed questions of the college recruiter, thus, gaining a better understanding of the visiting college in general and in particular the academic department for which they are interested. They are also able to explore the full financial aid and tuition support aspects of the college.

  o The recruiters (now having the time) get to know both the school's standards and the students individually. Over the years, during every visit, I have always seen many admissions and scholarship offers made on the spot!

  o In the case of college fairs and college recruiters coming to the school, the CCC should have gone over the rubrics of professional interviewing with the students; don't assume they know what to say and what not say. The college recruiter is working, so it is their job to recruit. Don't waste their time! Don't make their job difficult or uncomfortable; extend every possible courtesy and support. Make sure the college recruiter visit is well-publicized throughout the school prior to their visit. Further, I have not had one college recruiter who visited one of my schools who did not remark about the respectful, polite, and smart manner in which my students carried themselves. I know for a fact that the knowledge of these types of "impressions" are spread throughout the school recruitment/admissions offices community, thus further helping our students in the present and future by building a positive school college-going profile.

  o Our college advisor is able to make a personal connection with

161

the recruiter. This is important when we need to advocate for a borderline student or when scholarship funds become available outside of the normal school admissions timeline. Finally, this contact can lead to some productive and excellent college tours where the colleges have picked up the cost of lunch for the students and staff chaperons.

o   With the individual college recruiter as well as the college recruiters attending the college school-based college fair, you should provide the college recruiters with a nice lunch, a thank you package of school designated items: cups, hats, shirts, pens, journals, etc., along with school publicity materials. Also present them with a framed certificate of appreciation (they really are not obligated to visit your school!).

o   Make sure students who are interested in the particular college and who may have connected well with a particular recruiter send a follow-up thank you note to the recruiter. Help the students with the style and format of the note.

- The school should set up a prominent (front lobby) College Acceptance/Scholarships Awarded Honor Bulletin Board. Post colorful copies of the various acceptance letters. A display next to this board should feature a theme of Dollar Amount of Scholarships earned by Senior Class of X. At Phelps ACE, our art club created the picture of a colorful giant thermostat so that the new total could be added each week. Have students compete (friendly) with last year's class in college acceptances and scholarships earned.

- Have a schoolwide awards assembly recognizing those students who applied and were accepted to city, state, and other in- and out-of-state private colleges. Recognize the top ten scholarship earners of the senior class and all those who have attained full-ride status.

- Encourage and put into place a no-cost standard operational procedure to have all students apply to a city (local) and state colleges. You will get some student and parent pushback on this. Principal, don't get discouraged by the pushback; push forward anyway. I have known many instances in which students' family situations, due to an unforeseen emergency, changed dramatically such that they could no longer go away to that out-of-state college for which they were accepted. But having a local or state college acceptance letter in the bank allowed these students to pursue their college aspirations anyway. (And like a lot of good outcomes of unpopular decisions made by the principal, don't bother to thank me, just have a good life!)

The CCC's strategic approach for obtaining college scholarships for students

There is a terrible disconnect in our society, in which too many working class, working poor, and middle-class families are struggling to pay for college while more affluent families are fully aware of the techniques to lower or eliminate the cost of college. I can't remember the number of times that I have stood before a body of parents and/or students and said, "Going into financial debt over college costs, in almost every case, is a parent-student choice!" Every year, we have that well-publicized article or TV news story about some urban or rural poor student (whose grades are good but not necessarily extraordinary) who amasses millions of dollars in scholarship money, so much that they can't ever hope to utilize it all! And, yet, parents and students continue year after year to willingly climb aboard the college debt train. One of the problems is that professionally we educators have failed to present this parent-school collaboration as one of the real acts of parent engagement. The school must in every sense "tag-team" with parents and guardians in order to convince students to do the college scholarship leg (computer keyboard) work. Perhaps, because the reality of college debt (including graduate and professional school) is too far away and abstract for high school students to grasp or the fact that they are playing the game with somebody else's (their parents) money that allows too many students the luxury of not taking this serious task to heart. But for whatever reason, it is my experience that a large number of high school graduates who go to college, go leaving some money on the table!

I once announced to a group of SSCHS students that there were scholarships for left-handed college students. They naturally looked at me like I was crazy and they probably would have kept that perception if we had not gone on a field trip to the Foundation Center (FC) in Manhattan. (Having membership access to FC data is very expensive, and another reason to create powerful partnerships and a school foundation!) And, of course, being teenagers (meaning their mission was to prove me wrong on the left-hand scholarship assertion), they quickly learned through the FC's data bank that indeed there were foundations, individuals, benefactors, societies, and organizations that provided scholarships for left-handed high school student graduates! They were collectively stunned. But they were even more shocked and excited to find the extensive and often obscure opportunities for acquiring college scholarships. Many years later, several Phelps ACE parents also came to me shocked when they confirmed that just as I had informed them at a senior college meeting, the companies/corporations they worked for offer college grants and scholarships to the children of employees. The same result occurred when I advised them to search out scholarships in national organizations to which they belonged as well as the faith-based institutions of which they were members.

The big three components of the College Scholarship Search Process (CSSP): Knowledge, Information, and Effort

Since we are talking about high school, and thus teenagers, it should be said that the success or failure of the CSSP really does rely on student interests and initiatives. Which is why as a principal I always framed the CSSP as a competitive game with immediate rewards and recognition. In many ways we could substitute the word scholarship for college admissions as many of their required elements are overlapping (and often the same) processes, so:

- There must be a four-year (year-round) CSSP plan as part of the GCPC. Students should stop looking at school hours/days and school-related work as the only efforts that are important for their career objectives. Building a strong senior (profile) portfolio requires the proper and thoughtful management of both in- and out-of-school activities. The summer/weekends/holiday breaks are the times when a student should be building their portfolio/resume by collecting valuable work-learning experiences. Building a well-rounded and balanced personal image, identifying possible sources for contacts and letters of recommendations, expanding general knowledge competency through informal educational institutional visiting experiences and reading, studying (expanding vocabulary and math skills) for the SAT/ACT exams, practicing for AP exams, and, finally, the opportunity to build a bank of scholarship opportunities by starting the search early in high school.

- It would also be a good part of the ninth-grade financial literacy workshop to encourage students and parents to start their own college savings account. There will always be some item, activity, event, or situation that will not be covered by even the most comprehensive and best college scholarship search (e.g., the cost of pledging for a fraternity or sorority).

- Students should check to see if their faith-based institution as well as the larger denomination to which that institution belongs—clubs, fraternity or sorority organizations their parents are members of—provide special government and/or private scholarship monies targeting their school, community, city, region, or state.

Additionally, at the center of that college search is the student's GPA. A primary role of the "forward looking" CSSP and GCPC process is to encourage and inspire students in all grades to take school seriously and pass all of their classes with the highest grades possible. You are starting from a place of disadvantage if your college admissions or scholarship application/essay is explaining failing, low grades or a GPA that was damaged in the early high school grades. The exception would be those scholarships designed to support comeback storylines. But any and every scholarship granted is in some way an investment in the student recipient; the case must be made for the trust in the wisdom of that investment and to also make an argument for why the committee should deny another student of that same scholarship you are receiving. There is a general overuse of a common narrative, "I fell down in the ninth and tenth grades, but I got up!" A good CCC can do his or her best to actually spin that story to a student's advantage. However, a much better scholarships and college admissions-friendly narrative is, "I am a serious mature student, I started strong in the ninth grade, I continued strong throughout my high school career, and finished strong in the twelfth grade!" More on this topic in the chapter on: Practices of a Successful High School Student. But for now, let us look at how another department performs effectively in our "good school"!

Chapter 8:
The Elements of an Effective Visual, Creative, and Performing Arts Department

A school's art programs represent the creative soul of the school. A truly effective school will have the capacity to both bake foundational "academic bread" and at the same time cultivate aesthetic "creativity roses." Our objective as professional educators is to bring the balance of head and heart into the learning experience of the students. And, so, the first priority for the principal and his/her SBL team is to build a culture of importance and essentiality for the visual, creative, and performing arts departments. The principal's words, body language, budgetary priorities, and quality-level of instructional leadership attention go a long way in establishing that the arts are a major component of the school's overarching mission. Again, this is why I am going to return to the need for the development of a school 501c3 foundation and a fundraising supplementary plan/program through partnerships, grants, and gifts to supplement your chronically annual inadequate budget allocation. You will never have enough money to establish and maintain a comprehensive high school arts program from a standard school budget allocation. And even those schools that are designated as specialized arts high schools must often struggle with district and elected policymakers in helping them to understand the true cost of creative space architecture/construction, additional programmatic costs, the need for outside staffing flexibility, equipment/materials/supplies, maintenance of the equipment, and district regulations relief that these specialized arts schools need to operate correctly, effectively, and to fulfill their educational missions.

Funding an effective arts program or any school program/ project/activity not fully covered by a school's budget allocation

I am starting with fundraising for the arts because as a superintendent whenever I spoke to principals about the lack of quality or insufficiency in their creative and performing arts programs, invariably the first words out of their mouths were "budget" or "money," and "time" (away from standardized test-prep). I am starting here also because one of the most common questions from my principal colleagues was, how did you get enough money to fund your extensive arts programs?

I will focus first on the entrepreneurial skills needed to build an effective schoolwide arts program. As a building school leader, you should build three types of arts fundraising pathway procedures: (1) Through the school's 501c3 foundation, hire an experienced professional fundraising/grant/proposal writer who is a full-time budgeted staff person who has been built into the school's standard school budget. Or, find a corporate partner who will pay in part or whole for that position. Obviously, the designated employee must be able to at least raise his or her salary, plus acquire a great deal of additional funding for the school, including raising funds for programs beyond the arts. (2) Seek the commitment of a dedicated volunteer (e.g., retiree, former grants officer, a parent, or an alum with experience in professional grant writing). (3) Contract a professional grant writer who will not charge the school anything, but rather find a way to fundraise an agreed amount (percentage) of money raised to pay for the person's services. Again, this is another reason to form a school 501c3 foundation, since in most cases schools are not allowed to independently enter into contracts with consultants. This approach also points out the importance of having a prominent law firm functioning as one of the school's corporate partners. This firm can manage the negotiations and contract development between the school's foundation and the consultant fundraiser. (4) A grant proposal writer who can have his or her services paid for through a corporate or nonprofit organization partnership as a tax write-off. These grant proposal writing professionals can in partnership with departmental instructional teams translate their needs and professional knowledge into a workable and viable "boilerplate" (general) proposal, or in response to a specific Request for Proposal (RFP) issued from a governmental or private grant entity. They can also properly package your arts department's needs in order to solicit financial donations from private patrons and promoters of the arts; these generous individuals are present in just about every town, community, city, and state in the nation. The principal must professionally develop the staff to effectively cooperate and collaborate with the professional fundraiser. It is difficult but importantly honest to state here that the culture of public education is often out of step with the speed, demands, and standards of private, public, and corporate entities who want to support public schools. You must make the school:

168

proposal-preparing, gift-giving, and grant-receiving friendly!

The key factor here is that a supplemental fundraising plan must be put in place if the school truly desires to have a serious and effective arts program. Looking back at my two schools' arts programs, there was just no way that I could have pulled off establishing an effective program with just a standard high school budget allocation. The principal must be the #1 patron and promoter of the arts in schools. And this is especially important in a Title I high school, where the arts could be viewed by both society and professional educators as inconsequential and superfluous. Leadership style and substance matters a great deal if a school is to have a dynamic creative and performing arts culture, consisting of elective and advanced classes, dramatic plays and performances, film festivals, musical programs, art exhibits, trips to art museums and professional performances, master artist presentations, etc.

Although both of my high schools had a strong STEM focus, I always tried to make sure that students were fully immersed and intellectually enriched with art programs. Upholding this type of educational approach will force the principal to reflect on his or her own philosophy of education, for you either believe that the arts are an essential component in the development of an educated person or you don't. Many principals I have met over the years, who had weak art programs, were not necessarily haters of the arts; they were simply choosing to surrender to the dictates of a chronically unimaginative professional education community. The challenge for every principal is how to respond to the multiple external stakeholders who often verbally champion the arts then routinely underfund them. They also discourage art programs by making it clear to the principal that you will be held solely responsible for only the students' testing performance on "non-arts" academic content areas (e.g., ELA, math, science, history, and foreign language). It is then only the brave, entrepreneurial, and pedagogically wise principal who will fight to establish an effective arts program in his or her school. Wise because he or she knows that the arts actually enhances and supports better performance in all of the other academic areas, including student performance on standardized exams.

Fighting for the instructional integrity of arts courses

One sure way of helping the image, perception, and real immersion of a serious schoolwide arts program in your school is how you view and treat those courses in relationship to the school's instructional and student behavioral standards. First, the principal must insist on the same high curriculum standards (with accompanying rubrics) and the same rigorous performance standards for arts classes as would be found in any academic department in the school. The principal must also insist on the same schoolwide behavioral standards for a quality classroom environment for both art students and teachers. In matters of formal and informal observations of classes, I always gave the arts classes the same amount of attention that I gave all other academic classes. I also made sure that the arts departments received the same amount of meeting sessions with me as all other departments [Full disclosure and a warning to principals: I did not share that information with my superintendent, in part because I did not know how it would be received!]. Here, you need a cooperative art teaching staff who is willing to meet outside of the regular school hours (which I was always fortunate to have). And, of course, you need to triage your school leadership time, though it would be a mistake to not invest a qualitative amount of your intellectual and leadership capital into areas of the school that are not externally assessed, by way of standardized exams. But the reality is that allowing mediocrity in any academic area of the school creates the possibility of that mediocrity infecting other academic areas of the school. Further, there is every indication that the arts will not only enhance and strengthen the school's academic profile but also enable and enrich its students' intellectual capabilities. Academically struggling schools undermine their own academic efforts by traditionally and habitually cutting back and/or eliminating the arts programs in exchange for mostly unproductive test-prep programs and activities Or, because of high student course failure rates, they are "budgetarily" boxed in because money that could be allocated for art electives is needed for credit recovery classes. We can best grow intellectual capability, academic achievement, and, ironically, higher standardized test scores by providing a child's (right and left) learning brain the opportunity to expand through their experience with the creative and performing arts. We want to stimulate and grow the imaginative, analytical, inquisitive, creative, and speculative parts of that child's brain. We also offer the opportunity for more children in the school to display and improve their individual gifts and talents; this helps with self-esteem and gives students another reason to come to school every day. A really good school (and school leader) will work to encourage high learning standards in every subject area, which will raise the academic standards in all academic departments. This means as with every content area the principal is supervising, there is a need to become literate and familiar with the main/trending pedagogical and instructional concepts of the individual content areas. Thus, to be an effective principal, you must be a well-informed academic generalist, and that includes the arts. You don't need to be an expert, but you must have an appreciation and strong enough knowledge base to be able to engage in a meaningful discussion with any subject area teacher or department in the school, and at least be able to grasp the main instructional ideas being expressed by the teachers in those departments. Art is no exception, and the first step in winning over your art faculty is to display knowledge and sincere interest in their work. This, I also believe, is the first step in inspiring your staff to go above and beyond their normal work hours and responsibilities; they will definitely follow your arts passion lead. And, frankly, if they don't choose to go above and beyond their contract and collective barging labor agreement, then there is probably no hope that you will have a dynamic and effective schoolwide arts program anyway! The real amount of work and hours that is required to develop an art exhibit/competition, AP art/music class, art club, performing orchestra, chorus, dance company, or school dramatic play can't "budgetarily" be reasonably completely administered by way of overtime pay and contractual rules. Not going to state here for obvious reasons, but as a principal, you can surely come up with some creative ways to reward those art staff members who go above and beyond their printed duty to make an art activity and/or event work for students!

The principal should also be able to make the pedagogical rationale or case for the importance of the arts programs in the school. Making connections with all academic departments as well as crafting opportunities for integration and collaborative projects go a long way in making art a core rather than an "extracurricular" (a pedagogically incorrect word that I will use for purposes of communicating with educational "laypersons") place of study. This is made so much easier if the school's instructional culture is heavily committed to projects and performance-based practices in all academic departments (e.g., a schoolwide content fair for every academic department). The school must also make sure that the arts programs adhere to the most rigorous core standards for public presentations. If the school puts on a play, dance program, art exhibit, or concert, it should set the highest performance standards that actually reflect the standards set by the artists/professionals in that field. Therefore, by extension, students should be encouraged to engage in the full spectrum of careers in the arts world like writing, choreography, production, management, directing, staging, lighting, stage craft, costumes, curating, marketing/advertising, and finance. This process opens up the real art world career landscape to the students. Too often, particularly for students who are underexposed to careers in the arts, they are only familiar with the performing or exhibiting artists' side of the comprehensive and rich world of art-related careers. These students could also not be familiar with the essential careers that undergird the actual exhibit or performance, and also those careers that merge art and other fields of study such as art restoration science, ethnomusicology (music and anthropology), set design and construction, costume design and development, art-music history, composing, stage craft building and technology, editing, screen writing, production, directing, lighting and sound engineering. By supporting vigorous art productions, programs, and projects in a school, the school, in cooperation with the college/career advisor, is also expanding the future career options for those students whose interests and talents exist outside of being a performing and exhibiting artist.

The presence of a rich offering of art electives is one of those Tonal factors that speak volumes about a school

The establishment of art electives will serve to encourage students to dig deeper into art-related subjects. These electives will also raise the intellectual and creative capacity ("smartness capital") of the students. STEM students will be able to make a connection between the inventive and technical, the imaginative and product. Art electives also raise the academic profile of the school by offering interesting non-required courses, enriching individual student's transcripts. An exciting and rich survey of elective art course offerings also suggests to prospective parents and students, funders, colleges/universities, and external stakeholders that the school is producing a healthy number of students who are passing the required courses; therefore, the school can offer a rich survey of art electives. A sure indication of a good and effective school is its elective course offerings, and art electives suggest that the school has given some thought to the role that art plays in producing an authentic, full academic program and a fully educated human being. Some examples of the art electives I have worked with as a principal are:

Computer Art & Design

Film and Literature

Piano

Creative Writing

Chinese Literature (fiction & poetry)

Chinese Art, Music and Culture

Jazz Band-History of Jazz

African-Modern Dance

Painting

Sculpture

CAD/CAM

Photography

Gospel Chorus-History of African-American Music

AP Studio Art

African-American Literature

A seminar class on Ralph Ellison's: Invisible Man

Spanish Literature (novels, short stories and poetry)

Music History

The schoolwide arts program can also be strengthened by the establishment of clubs relating and connected to the arts activities mentioned above. These out-of-classroom activities place students under the watchful eyes of faculty members who share their artistic interests and also allow students with similar interests and talents to socially support and encourage each other.

The AP art programs (studio art and music) allow students to put their particular talents on display, something a school should encourage at every opportunity. These classes also go a long way in helping the students to build a strong career/college-going transcript and academic profile, including the senior portfolios of students who are interested in pursuing non-art majored STEM-CTE programs. Engaging in serious art programs separates these students from those STEM-CTE students whose transcripts don't demonstrate their ability to develop themselves outside of their "major STEM-CTE-related" courses.

A rich and full liberal arts education has fallen into hard times lately; this attitude is doing a great harm to our students and the nation. I can even say as a committed STEM educator, that we have placed too much emphasis on courses that are solely and directly too focused on current societal employment "need". But as professional educators, we should not give into the unprofessional understanding of the reasons for schooling. But rather we should have an expanded understanding of not only the role art plays in helping students to be both employment ready and employment successful but also having the richness that the arts bring to the professional and private lives of all people, regardless of career choice!

Chapter 9:
The Elements of an Efficient English Language Arts (ELA) Program/ Department

The English Language Arts (ELA) Department influences, interacts, supports, and closely collaborates with a large number of the school's efforts. The ELA department, like the human heart, metaphorically pumps its standards and rubrics throughout every aspect of the school's operational anatomy. By this I mean that a school is only as good as the ability of *all* of its academic departments, not just ELA, to successfully incorporate reading, speaking, and writing skills into its departmental objectives. I also understand and appreciate that every academic department sees itself as the heart of the organization, and in many ways, that positive departmental perception and healthy competition between academic departments can actually be a good thing for the school. But the reality is that the skills and competencies reflected in the ELA curriculum/standards are absolutely reflected in almost everything that takes place in a high school. Students will struggle with mathematical problems, science concepts (including labs), or document-based history studies, or they will be fundamentally challenged because they are unable to fully utilize their subject area textbooks and any other written study materials used in a course. A high school student who is a poor reader will find it extremely difficult to succeed in high school. Further, poor high school readers are aware and sensitive about their inadequacies. This knowledge of not being able to read can create a powerfully negative sense of sadness and despair on the part of the student, and is a great contributor to the high school dropout rate. These students may not be able to express these feelings of inadequacy and will in many situations find extremely creative ways of avoiding having to read out loud in class, including getting themselves into disciplinary problems. Also, students who are unable to transfer knowledge and information from their brains onto paper (or keyboard) or who lack the verbal communication skills to express that same knowledge and information are probably going to struggle in every academic course in high school. Students will surely be hard-pressed to pass any of their courses and will generally academically underperform if they are struggling with ELA competencies and skills. Testing, standardized and the in-school format, will severely challenge students with ELA deficiencies. This problem will fortunately be better revealed in those schools that utilize the same vocabulary-phraseology standards that are found on standardized exams on all classroom exams. Further, the majority of requests and responses received from various external critical decision-makers (e.g., essays for: internships, college admission, scholarships) who will directly affect the lives of high school students will be requested in written form. Standardized exams and the responses to job/internship application questions, resumes, etc., will also need to be in written form. In most cases, that modality will be the students' first, and perhaps, only opportunity to present themselves to these decision-makers. And, so, every teacher and counselor in the school *is* in many ways an ELA teacher. And every ELA teacher is in essence a teacher of every content area and student-related activity in the school. So, let us explore this department that, in a good and necessary way, imposes itself upon every aspect of the school's life.

A departmental strategic plan—no high school academic department should operate without one!

Let's start with two important questions:

"At the end of four years, what conceptual (what they will know and understand) and behavioral (what they are able to do or exhibit) ELA objectives do we want to see represented in the students who have graduated from our ELA program?"

And,

"What ELA skills and competencies will be needed by our graduates to be successful in college, in matters of commerce, in performing on standardized exams (e.g., SAT, ACT, MCATs, PRAXIS LSAT, GRE), in inter-human communication, in future career-employment, as consumers of information-books, as public or private intellectuals, as parents, as informed citizens of their nation and the world, and how will our ELA program help them in being good, thoughtful, and reflective human beings?"

Now that these two foundational questions have been established, the next task of the ELA department is to deconstruct that "model" competent and skilled ELA high school graduate, starting with the end of the twelfth grade and then working backwards through the eleventh, tenth, and ninth grades, taking careful note of the prerequisite skills required at each grade level that would allow students to master the learning objectives of the next grade level. A good and effective ELA department will create a four-year, syllabus pacing calendar consistent with the standard (State) ELA learning objectives that will help students to master the conceptual behavioral objectives of being able to effectively read, speak, and write. Now, inside of these three major categories are a great number of skills and competencies that students will need to master before exiting high school. This means that the department must also carefully deconstruct the ELA curriculum and come up with a common core of standards that must be applied in every ELA classroom and on every grade level. Failing to engage in this necessary deconstruction process will mean that a school can produce graduates but not necessarily ones who are prepared to successfully integrate themselves into the ELA standards as they are applied in the world after high school. And further, a school that depends on employers or college professors to teach their graduates the ELA skills they failed to receive in high school are setting their students up for failure in the post-high school world. This is why the good and effective ELA department must first take a stand for standards!

ELA standards must stand for something!

The ELA department, along with the other academic departments of the school, must reject the current misguided political pushback against curriculum learning standards. As I stated in the chapter on ethics, professional educators are bound by a set of principles that should prevent us from inflicting educational harm on students. Not helping students to master the skills that would allow them to effectively compete in the standards-based world they will enter after graduation places them at a serious disadvantage. And for those students who are not part of the entitled class, that disadvantage can be extremely devastating and dangerous to their life chances. Not improving students' reading comprehension; not teaching cultural-context linguistic "code-switching;" allowing students to write poorly crafted letters and other documents for employment, college, and scholarship applications; not providing students with a rich vocabulary and literature bank of knowledge, thus under-preparing them for the ELA requirements of college and future employment, constitutes educational malpractice. The ELA communication standards of reading, speaking, and vocabulary mastery as well as critical-analytical listening and writing represent an important part of any future job description and surely a component of your job success or failure.

The ninth-grade ELA program should establish some core departmental objectives and principles:

- Having determined no later than the first week of school during the Summer Bridge Program, or by way of an ELA diagnostic exam, those students who are struggling readers. And while keeping those students in their regular ninth-grade English class, they should also be scheduled for an additional reading improvement class.

- All ninth-graders should be assigned a daily independent (out-of-class) fiction reading schedule.

- Assign in- and out-of-class independent nonfiction guidance readings that will assist students in successfully transitioning into high school life.

- All ninth-graders should engage in daily journal writing.

- Establish a fiction classroom library in every ELA classroom. Ninth-grade ELA teachers (and all ELA grade-level teachers) should have their own dedicated classrooms and, thus, able to have classroom libraries. These libraries should contain reference/study books as well as fictional works that students can borrow and take home to support a Readers to Leaders[3] independent reading program. This idea of classroom libraries in every grade-level ELA class is understandably one of my most controversial projects, which will become clearer when I discuss my take on the effective high school library. The moving of literary works of fiction, poetry, and plays out of the school library will be both a financial and organizational challenge. Public schools are perhaps the worst examples of the bureaucratic practice, "This is the way we have done it for X years, and that reason alone is why we should continue to do it that way." But I believe that by placing books near students, along with the driving power of the "Readers to Leaders" project, we will invite students to embark on a reading-for-enjoyment path, which I believe is a core attribute of a "learned" person. Yes, I know that this designation of ELA teachers as deputy librarians who must now keep track of books lent on index cards is extra work, but my experience is that the rewards are so great, and this initiative is a vast contributor to creating an intellectually safe and rich school culture, that it is well worth it. Maybe as a principal, I have just been lucky, but outside of one or two not-so-happy librarians, all of my ELA teachers have been extremely supportive of this project.

- Specific empowering and values-building fictional and nonfictional texts should be assigned.

- The student's fictional and nonfictional readings should complement and reinforce their science and history curriculum pacing calendars.

- Current trends excluded, students will be required to read complete fictional novels, not excerpts.

- Teach the students how to take classroom notes and how to utilize those notes when studying after class. Helpful in all classes! (HIAC)

- Help students to organize for long-term (yearlong) projects and presentations. (HIAC)

- Train students to master PowerPoint and other electronic/computer presentation aids. (HIAC)

- Teach Latin and Greek roots, prefixes, and suffixes, particularly those words that will show up in their ninth-grade science/biology class. (HIAC)

- Go over how to use a dictionary, thesaurus, *The Elements of Style*, and other reading and writing reference sources. (HIAC)

- Provide students with the standards and rubrics for effective oral presentations. (HIAC)

- Teach students how to properly and effectively utilize their high school textbooks. (HIAC)

- Students will master the standards and rubrics of writing an essay. (HIAC)

- Students will learn the standards and rubrics for writing a term paper. (HIAC)

- Students will understand the concept of plagiarism. (HIAC)

- Students will read current and topical editorials; this will greatly complement the history department's learning objective of deconstructing a newspaper.

- A yearlong objective/project is that all ninth-graders will master the vocabulary words of the standardized exams they will be required to take and, in particular, the "turnkey" words and phrases found in standardized exam questions such as "less than," "most likely," "best describes," "represents," etc. (HIAC)

- Students will be exposed to the many career options that are directly connected to ELA such as book writing, editing, screenwriting, K-12 and college instruction, technical writing, journalism, linguistics.

- That wonderful mixture of serious and clear high academic behavioral standards, accompanied with high expectations while being balanced with a spirit of nurturing, concern, and compassion; that is the best profile and professional practice rubric of the most effective ninth-grade teachers I have been fortunate to work with.

Reading competency and confidence as one of the core missions of the ELA department

A prime focus and directive of the ELA department is to proclaim and promote the beauty and power of reading. As I stated earlier, there is no other skill that influences the achievement levels of all content areas. The ELA department must also be cognizant of the political implications of a student not just being able to "read" phonetically but also to be able to read critically and analytically. There was no accident that in our own U.S. slavery history, a great number of prohibitions and restrictions were put in place to prevent kidnapped-enslaved Africans from learning to read or acquire any type of reading material. We know enough through the study of history and current events that authoritarian regimes spend a great deal of time and energy in restricting reading and writers, and destroying certain books. Clearly, there is some connection between reading and an individual thinking about ideas and concepts that would cause them to question that which they see in the present world. But most importantly, reading causes an individual to think about the meaning, purpose, and humanity of their own lives and what those qualities suggest about the quality of life they are living. The ELA departmental staff must see themselves as the "reading activists" of the school, charged with empowering students with the skills to decipher the written and spoken word. We spoke earlier of reading capability serving either as a ladder or obstacle to a successful high school and post-high school education as well as future employment. We should also add that the ability to read is closely associated with good citizenship and good parenting. We outlined earlier the important role that the ninth-grade ELA teacher plays in establishing the theme and culture of the department. Let us now look at the other ways in which the entire ELA department, in cooperation with other academic departments, expands the student's reading capacity:

- Early detection and strategic intervention for students who are struggling readers is critical. ELA teachers (as well as other faculty members) should be on the lookout for students who may have some type of vision or physiological (medical) problem that is interfering with their ability to read.

- Inter-Departmental Collaborations by organizing titles, genres, and authors to match the grade-level parallel courses in history, science, CTE, mathematics, etc., provide students with double academic support. For example, this can help students studying a particular historical era and/or region of the world with the fiction and nonfiction documents and writings from that time period. For the Civil War section of the American history syllabus, the ELA teachers could introduce poetry, speeches, newspaper articles, political documents, and personal letters that would enrich and expand the study in class. On the other hand, with the history class providing much geographical, cultural, political, and historical information about the era, it can only enhance the reading experiences of ELA class students.

- All ELA teachers should have their own (unshared) rooms, with a classroom lending library consisting of works of fiction, poetry, plays, and biographies. The selection should be diverse and student-centered, focused on themes and topics such as sports, teen challenges and social issues, popular events, music, entertainment, and fun. The classroom library should also contain some interesting and traditional fictional works; however, the books students select to read independently should be their own choice.

181

- "Readers to Leaders" program: The key here is to encourage and inspire students to see reading outside of the context of school-assigned activities. The ELA department must lead the fight to establish a school culture in which independent reading for fun, intellectual interests, and curiosity is a normal and acceptable standard of behavior. Each ELA grade-level teacher should post a book-completion achievement chart, complete with stars indicating when students complete an independent reading assignment. Even I was shocked at how serious high school students can get about this stars accumulation. And, of course, you, the principal, will help with creating this spirited and competitive atmosphere by providing gifts and rewards such as gift cards to popular teenage sneaker/clothing stores, online music gift cards, tickets to professional sports events, and discount coupons to fast-food restaurants. It is also important to give a nice awards ceremony where you will invite parents to see their children receive standard certificates, medals, and trophies. Thus, another reason for having corporate/business partnerships and a 501c3 school foundation.

- The students should be knowledgeable and conversant in the different types and sections of newspapers, magazines, journals, and online news and information sources.

- The ELA department should teach students the importance of watching films, television, dramatic plays, dance performances, speeches, and debates as if (and they are) these activities were literary events.

- The school must create and support reading opportunities in every subject area beyond standard textbooks. This could take the form of historical documents in social studies classes, science magazines, and/or science articles in general newspapers and magazines, a local newspaper's "weekly science section," and special films and television broadcasts of science themes and topics.

- The entire student body should be public library cardholders; give students bonus points or extra credit in their ninth-grade ELA class for signing up for public library cards. I have also been fortunate to work with very supportive and accommodating public libraries that were kind enough to actually send library staff to my school where, in the cafeteria and lobby, they were able to sign up and provide students with library cards on site!

Note: School principals should not assume that because of the overwhelming amount of negative publicity given to public education that external institutions, both public and private, are not willing to support your students. In fact, I have found the opposite to be true; there are many people in our society who wish to see public schools be successful!

- An important aspect of the ELA department's drive to enrich and expand the reading capacity of students is the SAT/ACT/AP vocabulary mastery project. In every ELA grade-level course, students will be invited to study and master all of the commonly occurring words and phrases on the beforementioned standardized exams. The ELA teachers should set the following mastery of words and phrases, in and out of a testing context, as a departmental goal:

- "show all work"
- "most likely"
- "least likely"
- "probably"
- "most effective method"
- "does not"
- "represents"
- "prove"
- "best represents"
- "which one does not"
- "best defines"

- "compare"
- "contrast"
- "least reflective of"
- "provide an example"
- "give examples"
- "explain"
- "best"
- "write"
- "demonstrate"
- "given"
- "refer to"

- "describe"
- "best describes"
- "choose the one best"
- "infer"
- "in most cases"
- "theory"
- "hypothesis"
- "evaluate"
- "consider"
- "establish"
- "explains"

In the ninth grade, this project is initiated through the use of flashcards[4], with the word on one side of the card and the definition and the word used in a sentence on the other side of the card. Each student should, in consultation with his or her teacher, establish his or her own realistic individual pace (X words per day) for mastering the words. The teachers should also from time to time set up a fun activity/game when students can test their mastery of the vocabulary in pairs or teams. These cards and the plastic index card holder box should be part of the required materials and supplies list sent along with the reading assignment the students receive upon entering ninth grade, again providing an opportunity for students to earn an encouraging positive grade in their first semester of high school. However, in case a parent is unable for whatever reason to provide these and other supplies, the school should step up and supply these items. (There's that need for external partnerships and a school foundation again!)

- The ELA teachers should, over a four-year period, help students to understand the rubrics of reading comprehension. Being able to properly read and interpret any standardized test question is a critical and core ELA competency that you want every student to master. A deficiency in effectively reading the question can and will negatively offset whatever content knowledge the student may possess. (Poor writing response skills will create the same result, but I touch on that later.)

- The ELA teachers should be given other subject areas' standardized exams vocabulary, word problems and extended/essay questions format so that they can assist students with the reading skills that are needed to decipher and successfully respond to these various prompts. We will return again and again to that critical test-taking mastery question that requires the ELA department's help: "What am I being asked to do?" The effective ELA test-taking skills that students need to employ when they take science and mathematics exams are the same test-taking skills they will need to be successful when facing ELA school-based and/or externally based standardized exams!

The ELA Department's process for effectively teaching the writing process!

As I stated earlier, the ELA department is a rubric-rich environment. One of the best examples of the critical importance of standards and rubrics can be found in the writing process. Standing very close to reading skills in the category of attributive skills for establishing academic success is the competency level of a high school student's writing skills. This important fact is the reason one of my schools adopted a "Nail the essay by ninth grade" campaign. Our careful analysis of student performance on standardized STEM, history, foreign language essay/extended questions sections of exams revealed that students were losing points because they were not successfully transferring the content knowledge in their heads to the answer sheet sections of the exam.

Part of the rubric-rich environment in which the ELA department does its work is the laborious, but extremely important areas of:

- Grammar

- Punctuation

- Spelling

- Style (e.g., expository, persuasive, descriptive, and narrative)

- Sentence, paragraph, essay, research paper standard structures

- Citation, attribution, footnotes, and biographies

- What plagiarism is and is not

The ELA writing program should also help students to master the standards, processes, and techniques of multiple writing projects they will be required to utilize in high school and beyond:

- Letters (of introduction, providing information, thank you, etc.)

- A resume (GCPC)

- Speech writing

- Biographical essay (GCPC)

185

- Science-Technical writing

- Math journals

- Personal journals

- The benefits and dangers of social media writing

- Short story writing

- Playwriting

- Effective note-taking (HIAC)

- Journalistic writing

- Editing (self-editing)

- Poetry (different national and cultural styles)

The ELA department must empower students with confidence, competent awareness, and the technical skills to be able to write clearly, effectively, and appropriately for any type of situation in which writing is necessary (required). If the instructional program is good, students will be able to place writing in its proper position of an important tool in the communication arts toolbox. But they will also be able to combine their strong reading skills and passion with the knowledge to understand and analyze the complex and creative methodology employed by professional writers of any genre and professional field.

Oral communication skills

As professional students of pedagogy, school-based leaders should be familiar with psychologist Lev S. Vygotsky and his important work *Thought and Language*. Our language ability (vocabulary, grammar, and the strategic organization and translation of ideas into words) is inextricably connected to the knowledge and ideas in our brains. In the other direction, the mastery level of our construction and usage of language is a type of exercise machine for brains. These two qualities of speaking and thinking strengthen and enhance each other. This fundamental quality is different from simple oratory skills, which I believe can, to some degree, be improved in everyone through learned techniques. On another level, I think there is some aspect of natural ability that allows some individuals like great writers, sculptors, and musicians to be "naturally" gifted orators. The good school will identify these "orally gifted" students and then provide them with a platform and vehicle (clubs, teams, programs, events, etc.) to practice and perfect those talents. In public education, we need to strengthen the oral communication skills of all students and further provide students with the techniques to fully realize their naturally gifted and talented best oratorical/communication skills.

Oratorical code-switching skills

As a matter of professional ethics, we cannot shy away from a topic because it makes us or others uncomfortable. We must always as professional educators tell students and parents the truth about the world outside of schools. It is understandable that some of these discussions will create some controversy and even pushback. But educators can't run from challenging situations. We must insist that our students be made aware of the standards, rubrics, and expectations of life outside of, and after, school; they are then free to choose their own course of action, but that choice should never be based on a shortage of information. As educators and adults, we are fully aware of the weight that is assigned to the verbal parts of any type of interview, whether it is the gifted and talented elementary screening process or the interviews associated with acquiring a teacher or school administration position. Let us not pretend that oral communication skills are not critical decision-forming factors. For the other side of this concept, the listener's thinking is greatly influenced by the language and speaking mastery of the speaker. If we are to be honest, in everyday communication experiences, we all make assessments (fair or unfair) of individuals based on the quality of their oral communicative skills; and in professional/employment settings, often these initial assessments can be perceptually fatal. Not arming students with the capability to effectively navigate linguistically in different types of settings and environments, places those students at an educational and professional disadvantage. The relationship between speaking/speech and thinking/analyzing must be a critical concern to all professional educators who work in settings where their students' out-of-school experiences don't allow them enough exposure to a wide, diverse, rich vocabulary and language acquisition environment that enables them to effectively communicate outside their social and family circles. This is an honest assessment of the need for many of the students, and their teachers and school administrators, to have the capacity to engage in an effective bilingualism (and I'm speaking of native-born English-speaking students here) in the school setting and to also understand the role of cultural linguistics and code-switching outside of the educational/professional/employment environment. I will further explore these three themes of bilingualism, bi-cultural linguistics, and code-switching later in this chapter, but for now, I want to focus on the ELA department's role in developing the oral communication competency of students. One of the first actions is to disconnect the rubrics of appropriate and context-based affective speaking from a particular group or race. When Black students innocently proclaim that another Black person sounds or is "speaking white," we should analyze that perception in relationship to Vygotsky's theorem that the statement is revealing a great deal about the thinking of the individual hearing that language style and usage. But we should also ask the question, where did that line of thinking come from? This question and its answer must be critical drivers of the teaching philosophy and learning objectives of a high school's ELA department. The ELA teachers should teach students effective oral communication skills while at the same time recognizing the role and validity of colloquial language. No particular race or culture can claim ownership of proper English, particularly since English is spoken properly in different ways, in different parts of the world. And, so, the ELA department should help students to understand the validity of dialect that is utilized in literary works by authors living in different parts of the English-speaking world (e.g., Dennis Walcott and Dylan Thomas). Students should also understand that spoken language is an evolutionary and dynamic activity. It is a constant state of many old words disappearing and new words emerging every year. One of the critical "soft skills" that students must master is the ability to conversationally code-switch, which is to understand the form of language that is appropriate for a particular setting. All educators or professionals in any field should be honest about the different speaking styles one employs on the job and the language utilized at home with family and friends. Therefore, this code-switching activity can't be limited to people of color and for ELA teachers and students of color. I know it is often done, but I think it is a terrible mistake to teach the concept of code-switching as a learning objective that is only connected to Black, Latino, and poor working-class students of any race rather than present this idea as a standard learning objective for all students, for "code switching" is a universal practice.

The good thing about any academic department in a good and effective school is that there is a learning interconnectedness of many different conceptual and performance skills. The vocabulary exposure and expansion project taught as part of reading arts and skills also helps to strengthen oral communication. The standards of self-editing are definitely aligned with helping students to say the same thing in different, or more effective, ways. And just as the goal is to eventually have students self-edit naturally, particularly when they are responding to an exam prompt, we also want students to be able to appropriately adjust their speech when engaging in different types/settings of verbal communication experiences.

Language beyond thought and into behavior

The ELA teaching staff can improve the students' oral communication skills by establishing and teaching the standards/rubrics of good listening. Learning to effectively listen to artists, public speakers, instructors, presenters, and their fellow students are skills that must be taught. Students must also be taught to listen to themselves. I call this the verbal expression of metacognition (thinking about our own thinking); how many times, as a principal, have I asked a student sent to my office, "Are you listening to yourself?" It is not uncommon for teenagers to display a disconnect between what they are saying and what they truly know makes sense. Asking them to "listen to themselves" can often bring them to a place of corrective self-enlightenment. Teaching students to listen to themselves is also a way of making them better communication partners in a classroom, social or non-social dialogue, in meetings and making class oral presentations. In public schools, we often mistakenly place students into paired or group work-study situations but fail to teach them the communication standards and techniques that help to make sure that the work of the pair or group is effective and successful. These communication skills don't emerge naturally; students have to be taught the techniques and skills of things like brainstorming, critical and noncritical listening, speaking in turn, leading a discussion, dissent, consensus, etc.

The ELA department should encourage, as part of their schoolwide departmental fair, for students to think about submitting oral history projects. These projects/presentations would allow students to record and write commentary on interviews of senior citizens, elders in their neighborhood, family members, older members in their faith-based community, etc. Oral history projects, in

my experience, can help to bridge the understanding and appreciation gap between generations of family members. As a college student, I engaged in such
a project and it absolutely enlightened and expanded my appreciation for the
bravery and convictions of my own 1940s-50s Caribbean immigrant family.
This is particularly an excellent project when it helps students to connect their
studies in World History and American History courses with real people who
personally experienced a historical event. For those students who are interested in a career in journalism, fiction or nonfictional writing, this exercise
also provides an opportunity to learn and practice interviewing and editing
techniques. Further, it can be helpful for students to learn and appreciate the
historical struggles that many people faced in the past and that their perseverance and commitment to survival created a foundation upon which the student
presently stands.

   The entire ELA department should promote a curriculum concept of approaching public speeches as literature. Not only should students read (both
silently and aloud) great historical speeches, such as Lincoln's Gettysburg
Address, Frederick Douglass' "The Hypocrisy of American Slavery," Barbara
Jordan's speech on Richard Nixon's Impeachment, Mario Cuomo's Keynote
Speech to the Democratic National Convention (*A Tale of Two Cities*); the
students should also watch, listen, and learn what defines these speeches as
historically great. Which leads me to the next important educational objective
of the ELA department—providing students with the standards and rubrics of
good public speaking skills. This would include teaching students about developing a theme, using rhetorical techniques, the architecture of a speech, writing of a speech; managing the tone, pace and cadence of the speech; methods
of relating and connecting to the audience with physical gestures utilized by
great public speakers. Public speaking studies could also be an excellent con-
nector that would allow ELA teachers to introduce the concept of language and
speaking in the context of body language. Although this linguistic expression
of body language is not usually associated with ELA learning objectives—in
the case of public speaking/presentations, group conversations/meetings, personal and professional two-person dialogues, interviews, and sales pitches—
the connection between one's verbal and physical language is often a critical
factor of success or failure in the particular communication experience. The
ELA department, like any responsible high school academic department, must
always be aware and willing to share with students those soft skills for which
they may not have access to adults who can teach them. This would also include teaching students how to develop and deliver a "thirty-second elevator

speech." Over the years, I have connected many students with powerful and influential people, sometimes on the spot; students then should be able to respond quickly and effectively, meaning clearly and concisely, who they are, what they plan to do (career/study-wise) and what types of resources, experiences, and connections they need to achieve their objectives.

This oratorical exercise can be practiced and perfected in the classroom. And when developed early in the high school experience, it offers students the opportunity to prioritize and focus on their life, education, and career plan. Besides, as many of my former students have learned, you never know when you could meet that resourced individual who will ask you a simple question, "What do you want to do with your life, and how can I help you?" The ELA department should make sure that every student answers those questions in "elevator speech style!"

Note to the entrepreneurial principal: As the Chief Resource Acquisition Officer in the school, you may want to design, practice, and perfect your own version of the thirty-second elevator speech. On many occasions, I often found myself in conversations with the POTUS, cabinet and department heads, U.S. senators, congress persons, governors, mayors, state secretaries of education, state and locally elected officials, chamber of commerce presidents, CEOs of Fortune 500 corporations, and philanthropists, etc. Whether you are meeting these individuals by schedule, or by accident, you should be able to quickly, and in a clear and precise manner, make your case for (your) the school's mission, vision, and the support you need to realize that mission and vision, in thirty seconds!

A major component of the ELA department's communication arts program should also include teaching students how to employ logic, reference information, persuasive techniques, metaphors, allegory, storytelling, psychological techniques, the organization of ideas and objectives when engaged in debates, formal and (positive) informal arguments. In cooperation with the guidance department, students should be taught how to best explain themselves, defend a position or action, and/or the ability to make their case. Finally, the ELA department should collaborate with the guidance department to set up, particularly for juniors and seniors, mock interview sessions. These interviews should be structured and evaluated based on a standards/rubrics system. If a school is in partnership with a corporation or large business, the human resources staff person could be of tremendous assistance in helping students to understand and learn the best practices for the interview process.

The ELA department should develop course electives that are aligned and supportive of the department and school's mission. Electives should add knowledge of ELA topics of study including advance courses (like AP English). These electives should also provide students with the opportunity to fully explore ELA topics that incorporate subjects, content, and topics of other academic departments. Historians, artist, mathematicians and of course scientists must be able to effectively employ ELA skills. But scientists also have their own "language," standards, and practices; and so let us look at the high school department that is responsible for teaching science methodology and thinking.

Chapter 10:
The Operational Structure, Function, and Philosophy of an Effective Science Department

If you are a science educator, you should've picked up on the pattern that every academic department is essential and important. Full disclosure: Science education is my first and lifelong pedagogical passion; and both of my high schools contained a strong science foundation and structure. Beyond my own personal positive experience with science as a K-12 student, I was always interested in the way that the mastery of scientific thinking and methodology produced a confidence and organized thinking process on the part of the students. And, sadly, how discrimination and low expectations was systematically used as a means to keep specific populations in our society out of the science career pipeline. The ability to learn, engage, and practice science is, in many ways, a great dividing line in our nation, and those who were not scientifically literate suffered not only educationally but also in terms of things like health, environmental issues, entrepreneurship and lost employment opportunities. There is also the larger question that all science educators and every science department must ask: Science for what purpose and to what end? Of course, science mastery can be an important catalyst to raise students' self-esteem. And, yes, it can also prepare high school students to fully participate in a very science-dependent society. There is no aspect of life that is untouched and disconnected from some expressions and application of science. This would include the arts, humanities, and social sciences. One of the most important tasks of both the science and guidance departments in a high school is to make students aware of all of the science-related careers that are attached to many of the human activities that emerge from American life and culture. Schools must share the knowledge of these exciting and rewarding science careers. For example, many people enjoy the outstanding sports, music, and performance-related productions while not being fully cognizant of the huge number of science-related jobs that make those productions happen. But there are additional important roles that science plays in the well-being of our nation. There is the science of construction, innovation, and invention that covers every moment of our sleeping and waking existence. Crime and forensic sciences keeps us safe from our fellow humans who may want to do us harm. Science is involved in the safety of our food, water, workplaces and play-places; the word "health" science is connected to all of us prior to, at the moment of our birth, and throughout our lives until death. Medical science, exercise science, pharmaceutical science, biomedical science, and research science plays a major role in helping us to have a healthy, long, and productive life. Although we want to prepare our students for an economically viable post-high school life, we also want them to participate in our civic society as scientifically literate adults; we want our students to pursue and utilize science as a way to serve, heal, improve, and enrich the human experience and for our students to serve as knowledgeable and informed caretakers of our collective home Earth! An effective science curriculum and approach would involve the teaching and learning of scientific principles and methodologies that included good values and scientific knowledge, along with sound scientific techniques. Despite the presently floating, and in many places, popular political (not scientific) trend, an effective high school's science program must resist the teaching of "junk science." The science department must be clear: science is not, and never will be, in competition with religion. Science is science, and religion is religion. School administrators, teachers, students, and parents are free to hold onto any spiritual or religious belief they choose to follow. But in all science classrooms, what must be taught is science concepts and scientific methods for arriving to conclusions. Science is not, nor because of its ever-evolving and dynamic nature, able to explain all of the questions of life. All science can do is give us the value of previously acquired knowledge, combined with a methodology that can help us to inquire and discover new avenues and bodies of knowledge. Science departments also must take care to not degrade, dismiss, or disrespect the religious beliefs of students.

The effective science department must also take a stand in demystifying science and promote the necessity of every citizen being science literate. That old phrase I once heard as a child, "What you don't know won't hurt you," is a lie. Not being able to interpret the hazards and dangers in your immediate environment at home, in your neighborhood, or larger community and not understanding the most basic medical knowledge concerning one's own body can lead to serious illness, injury, and death. Science literacy is not a neutral state of being; real people are hurt, harmed, and die because of incomplete, insufficient, and in some cases flat out wrong ideas that are unscientific. This is why my science education position has always been that all high school students should take at least four years of a lab science with three of those sciences being earth/environmental science, biology, and chemistry; my fourth choice would be one of two physics classes based on the student's level of math proficiency. My ideal sequence would be to offer ninth-grade biology in the same semester as a required health education class. I believe that presenting these two classes at the same time can help students in avoiding many of the pitfalls and tragic dangers of teenage life. These two classes taught in tandem can address alcohol and substance abuse, drunk driving, preconception health, nutrition, good health practices, and illness preventative measures, fitness, chronic and deadly diseases and disorders with high incidence rates in particular populations with hypertension, diabetes, asthma, and violence. Good science education and instruction in a school can be an effective way to immediately improve the personal and physical well-being and lives of the individual student. But raising student science literacy is also the type of information that could spill over into improving the lives of the student's family members, neighbors, and friends. Let us now look more closely at how that science department should be best organized to fulfill the above objectives.

Note to principals: Work with the science department in the effort to plant the seeds of the school's science education learning culture early in every ninth grade cohort, just as in other content areas (e.g., ELA and mathematics). A good place to start is with the curriculum and science instructional practices and objectives for the school's Summer Bridge Academy (SBA). The science classes in this program should employ hands-on experiential science lessons that teach the scientific method by way of simple and fun experiments and projects in life science/biology, environmental/earth science, chemistry, robotics, physics and culminating with each student selecting and developing a presentation on a scientific topic. The SBA can also serve as the first exposure that allows students to learn the school's standards for STEM safety rules, the use of tools and scientific instruments/machines, lab procedures, paired and teamwork in a lab on a project, and the rubrics for writing a lab report. Finally, the hiring of the school's top junior and senior STEM students to work as Summer Youth Employment counselors for the SBA establishes a positive role-modeling opportunity for the incoming freshmen students as well as offering teaching and learning experience to the students who serve as counselors/ assistant SBA teachers.

How students understand the role science plays in their school, as well as the role and responsibility they as students are being asked to play, will lead to a more successful student science achievement outcome at the end of their high school experience. This is extremely important for several reasons and for several different types of schools. For the school that is requiring, at minimum, a four-year science (with accompanying lab) sequence[5], a great deal of problems emerge when students fail classes and fall out of grade level sequence. A required science course failure could mess up their opportunity to take science and other academic department electives. In the case of schools that offer science majors, which might include a certifying exam, science course requirements, and/or a certification of completion for graduation, this means that students will need to successfully pass courses to maintain a course sequence pace but, also, so as not to get knocked out of the opportunity to take science electives and engage in internships. Finally, if the school is in partnership with a college or university, and/or offers AP courses, an early and strong science foundation allows both students and teachers to make the best use of actual college courses as well as college level AP courses. Districts/schools should not just throw dramatically unprepared students into AP courses to simply show good diversity data as well as fool parents and other external stakeholders. I am absolutely in favor of expanding AP course opportunities beyond its present demographic limitations; however, we must sincerely invest the strategic programmatic time in the ninth grade and the financial resources if we truly want to expand the pool of students who are properly prepared to take AP science courses.

Building a powerful and Effective Science Department's (ESD) philosophical and operational mission

The process and frame through which the ESD should establish its departmental mission is to first ground that mission in the fundamental objectives of the school's larger mission. Then the ESD must define what a scientifically literate student graduating from the school will look like.   A primary operational objective connected to that profile says that the ESD's vision of science literacy can best be developed when students take four years of a *lab* science. The next step is to define how the school can effectively prepare students who wish to pursue a science-related post-high school college study path and career. With these objectives in mind, the ESD will need to "plan backwards" to identify programs, courses, course sequences, science electives, advanced and AP courses; develop a science research and competition program; identify how all students will participate in the schoolwide science fair; as well as promote participation in the science curriculum of the Summer Bridge Academy (SBA), science-related internships for tenth- through twelfth-graders, science teams, science clubs and other out-of-classroom science activities, and outside-of-the-school science-related partnerships. If the ESD and school commit to a four-year lab science program, our entrepreneurial principal is again going to need to get to work! Trips for environmental science classes, seminars, lectures, museum visits as well as the purchasing of models, charts, and displays for all courses. Science equipment (e.g., microscopes) will need to be purchased (in the case of microscopes, a class set) and will also require a funding source for repair and replacement. There is also the cost of replenishing the large amount of one time-use supplies. And, of course, the large amounts of lab glass/metal/plasticware that is required for labs and teacher demonstrations. A great deal of instructional approaches and laboratory exercises are now being done with the use of teacher smartboards and students' desktop computers, which means that science classrooms and labs have also become computer labs.

The language of science

We definitely want to start (in the ninth grade) with an ESD commitment to help all students to utilize the generally accepted and shared understandings of the language and vocabulary of science. Such words as:

Inquiry	Micro/Macro	Factor
Investigation	Evidence	Pattern
Influence	Transformation	Experiment-Test
"Outliner"	Cycle	Hypothesis
Speculation	Organization	Theory
Projection	Sample-Example	Proof
Model/Modeling	Classification	Correlation-Causation
Determining	Reaction	Cause and Effect
"Wrong Answer"	Product	Evolution
Innovation	Observation	General & Specific
Change	Trial and Error	Variable (Independent
Assimilation	Objectivity	& Dependent)

It is important that the ESD works to move students out of, and away from, the common non-scientific uses of these words and phrases and transform students into the mindset and language utilized by scientists. Returning to our language and thought continuum hypothesis, the ESD can add another objective to its list of students' learning outcomes it wishes to see: that students are able to think and practice like professional scientists. The mastering of science vocabulary will also help students to understand that a core attribute and quality of any profession is the presence and utilization of a particular language or that profession's ability to redefine words and phrases that commonly exist in the culture. One of the important benefits of utilizing a profession-based vocabulary is that it allows these professionals to be able to communicate with each other as they work in different settings and geographical areas around the world. This capability is critical in the fields of scientific research, as a great deal of the progress (innovation and invention) that is made by all practicing research scientists is made due to their ability to study the work of other scientists. Thus, this peer-acceptable language and vocabulary is essential to the success of science no matter where it is being practiced in the world.

The ESD starts this part of its mission by exposing students to the vocabulary and language of science. But the language and science inquiry skills are not simply limited to the pursuit of scientific content; rather, these skills can be employed in the other content areas such as the different aspects of the human experience: business, the arts, parenting, leadership, and good citizenship. Most people see the term "science skills" and think it to mean a list of technical applications utilized to answer a question or solve a problem related only to science. The ESD must extend the students' understanding of this phrase to also incorporate a way of perceiving, thinking, evaluating, problem-solving, and framing the response to many different phenomena that exist in the world. One of the first conceptual objectives of the ESD is to teach the scientific method or approach. An important ninth-grade departmental objective is that students should be able to "nail" the scientific method—not just as a set of words and phrases but as a logical process and procedure that is methodologically structured to get one to an answer or a question! Now, there may be a general misunderstanding on the part of many students concerning the difference between finding an answer(s) and finding the correct answer(s). The ESD would want to dissuade them from that concept early in their high school science career. It is important that the science teachers let students know that mistakes, overstating or understating a variable, proving your hypothesis to be in part or completely wrong, reconsidering and reconstructing an experiment are often critical and essential parts of scientific work and don't necessarily represent a "wrong" answer. In fact, the history of science is rich with examples of scientists looking for one important thing and ending up "by accident" with discovering a completely different important thing! And, so, the ESD will seek to present the scientific method as both procedurally effective as well as a dynamic process that allows for verification, re-evaluation, alternative testing, and honest analysis.

Students may have heard or even used a term like "hypothesis" in an earlier educational setting. The understanding of this word can vary greatly among students who attended different middle schools. The ninth-grade ESD teachers must clean up the ESD's understanding of all of the categories of the scientific method, including the word "hypothesis." This clarification will greatly assist the students into the practice of placing scientific thinking at the center of their own thought process. And, as stated before, this way of thinking will pay dividends across the many content areas as well as get students to think in a certain analytical way in their personal interactions and social actions outside of school. A strong grounding in the scientific method could allow a student to think about the underlying causes and factors (variables) that significantly contribute to daily human events; to be disciplined and organized in planning for the future; to objectively observe oneself and reflect on one's thoughts and actions, including thinking about the reflection process itself; and to read and process information so as to determine the "turnkey" words and phrases in the text as well as understand the author's meaning, intent, and purpose of a particular text. The ESD should want students to see the world in terms of consistencies and inconsistencies, patterns, and a break in a pattern. All of the beforementioned science thinking skills are critical factors in helping high school teenagers accomplish an important learning objective of high school education, and that is to successfully transition into adult life. One of the major challenges to that learning objective is the student's ability to close the distance in information and knowledge between teen-hood and adulthood; and anything that can help young people to appreciate how present actions will play out in future life conditions is absolutely a gift to a school's successful numerical and qualitative successful graduation rate. Science teachers may only see themselves as science concepts skills teachers, but in fact, those same science concepts and skills are the core competencies we will find in the life skills learning objectives. In short, the ESD should be seeking to help students think in an inquisitive, analytical, testing-evaluating and thoughtful way, both inside and outside of the science classroom.

The next leg of the core ESD's foundational learning objectives is for students to transfer their scientific language and thinking into standardized, yet dynamically creative scientific methodological practices. This behavioral objective should take the ESD to a place that proposes a vital and rich laboratory program that would exist as equally important and in parallel with the classroom-based science courses. The four core science courses (and almost every other of the ESD courses) should include a full period separate graded lab experience. These labs should be organized in such a way that students can't just blow them off; the lab grades must be an important part of the overall course grade, even as it is listed on the report card as a separate course. The science department must make it clear, starting with an incoming class, that any disregard for lab classes will adversely affect the student's ability to pass that science class. Here, again, the principal's knowledge, attention, and commitment to establishing a strong department-wide laboratory program is essential. The science department and science teachers must receive the backing of the school's administration if they are going to be able to raise the importance of science labs in the school. The principal is a critical catalyst in the science department's desire to establish a strong and effective laboratory program. First, by affirming and confirming that lab attendance and performance will be subject to the same performance objectives as in any other class in the school, and that includes penalties for the often-abused make-up lab practices that are not the result of a legitimate emergency. If the lab topics are running parallel to the course-pacing calendar, then "off-sequence" make-up labs will diminish the entire learning objective connected to the curriculum topic area.

The principal must also offer material support, without which a first-class schoolwide laboratory program can't exist. Thus, the need for the principal seeking and acquiring strong external partnership connections with science-related corporate partners. If as a principal you are not constantly thinking about acquiring resources and raising funds, then you will find it difficult to maintain a laboratory-rich science program. A first-class and effective science department must have first-class laboratories, supplies, and equipment. The principal and the science department chairperson must commit to, and invest in, the same level of attention to the laboratory experiences of a ninth-grade biology class as they would to an AP biology class, even as the specific lab cost of those two courses are different. There must also be a budgetary commitment to hire a full-time competent Laboratory Technician (LabTech). A first-class LabTech will essentially serve as a team teacher with every science lab class teacher. And, particularly, with AP science classes, a good LabTech is needed simply because of the huge amount of time that is required in ordering, storage, maintenance, repair, replenishment/replacement, organizing and setting up labs, and the breakdown of those labs. The instructional practices of science teachers will improve greatly if they can devote the majority of their time and energy into lesson planning and teaching a quality laboratory experience; that can only happen when they have an effective LabTech partner who can successfully set up classroom demonstration items as well as facilitate good laboratory exercises. In a school that requires all students to participate in a schoolwide science fair, the LabTech can play an important role in helping students from both a safety and theoretical perspective to design their individual science projects. The LabTech will also play a critical role if the school offers a Science Competition Research Class (SCRC). Those ninth- and tenth-grade SCRC students who may not be assigned to a mentoring lab outside of the school will more than likely need assistance from the LabTech with organizing and acquiring materials and the tools to successfully complete their projects.

The benefits of students engaging in first-rate course/ laboratory exercises

The first set of essential principles and skills the students will learn in these laboratory activities is safety. This immediately helps teenagers adjust to the idea that rules for behavior can, and will, vary from place to place and that there are consequences and rewards for ignoring the rules of behavior. The highly transferable skill of following directions is valuable in all areas of the student's life. Students will also learn to realize, especially in chemistry, that not paying attention to the smallest details can cause a project or plan to completely fail. Finally, students will learn that there is a rationale to practicing procedural integrity and that, like many things in life (e.g., baking a cake, fixing a car, or writing a computer game program), sloppiness will inflict a serious penalty on the negligent practitioner. Laboratory experiences allow students to concretely connect science concepts learned in their theory classes, and equally important, the ability to apply these concepts in a real-world hands-on way. The science lab is a wonderful place to help students clearly define and understand the differences between the micro and macro worlds. I have often spoken to physics students who said that it was the physical and visual interaction of the lab experiment that really helped them to fully understand a concept that was being taught in the physics classroom. This is why the parallel pacing of science classes and science labs are so pedagogically important and why making up labs long after the science concept connected to that lab has been taught defeats the very purpose of having science labs. Science lab classes allow students to enter the special world of scientific work and provides students with a possible future career opportunity. It is not uncommon for students who have little exposure outside of school to science museums and science practitioners to limit their career aspirations to the only science practitioners they encounter (e.g. medical doctor or nurse). Science labs can be an inspiring gateway for students to think about the many career opportunities that are available to do some type of scientific research, either related or totally unrelated, to health and medicine. Science labs offer the opportunity to realize the ideal pedagogical practice of teacher as mentor and guide. Good labs are student taught, led, centered, and driven. And along with a self-evaluation component, science labs provide an evaluative process that involves a partnership with the instructor and the student's fellow class/lab mates.

The instructional practice and lesson plan for any science lab must make sure that girls, ESL, students with disabilities, students of color, and quiet and reserved students are fully engaged as equal participating partners in the lab experience. The ESD chairperson should also work with the Special Ed supervisor and the guidance department to determine if any adaptive technology and/or special support is required for students with physical disabilities to fully participate in lab activities.

The lab activities offer the students an opportunity to practice science in partnership while working in groups and learning the value of teamwork. Students should be taught by their science teachers how to break up and divide a problem into focus-work components while at the same time understanding the overall, overarching objective.

Good science labs can increase student confidence, build student science conceptual competencies, and provide the opportunity for those students who may be struggling with a concept in the lecture class to gain a better understanding of the concept by putting it into practice in a laboratory experience. Science labs that are well-planned, well-organized, well-taught and well-resourced send an important message to the entire student body that the school in general and the ESD department in particular are:

- Absolutely linking science theory and practice by way of science labs.

- Hoping that students can intellectually and procedurally experience and model the experiments and procedural methods utilized by scientists in the past and present and, therefore, appreciate the real work that real scientists do.

- Helping students to appreciate that all human activity throughout history—whether they were our hunter-gathering-farming African ancestors or modern-day astrophysicists—were all in their unique way STEM activity specialists. For they all participated in some form of problem-solving scientific experiments. In other words, scientific experimentation is a natural human survival experience that compels our species to understand the world inside of us and around us.

- Seeking to empower students with the knowledge of what science can do as a vehicle of human and environmental transformation. And that to be a safe, healthy, fully informed and participating citizen means that scientific literacy is a requirement not an option. Equipping students with science experimental, research methodology and testing practices knowledge, so that students can, as either scientists or citizens, effectively evaluate government and private sector policies and their impact on the public and their own lives.

- Inviting students to complete the third leg of science learning that includes science: (1) language, vocabulary, terminology, (2) thinking, observing, planning, and (3) practicing, experimenting, testing, and evaluation.

- Teaching students to think and speak like scientists.

- Expecting students to be able to translate and transfer the terminology and procedures of science experimentation on to other areas of intellectual, artistic, and academic subjects and careers "outside" of science.

- Creating a learning environment where safety, following procedures, intentional observation, a non-commitment to pre-conceptions and assumptions, questioning, and then questioning the result, the discovery of new and different questions is standard.

And, finally,

- Helping students to "discover" an unknown STEM interest, talent, and/ or skill for them to think about pursuing at the college level, essentially expanding the students' career options. The self-affirming aspects and products of engaging in science labs can effectively counter the negative cultural beliefs that seek to restrict the learning and practice of science to a limited number of young people in our nation. Good science labs when combined with good science coursework can be a powerful influential factor in helping students to taking ownership of their future in STEM.

Science clubs, programs, activities, electives, and advance courses

Out-of-classroom, after-school, weekend, and summer science programs and activities are important qualitative indicators of the level of commitment the school is making to formal and informal science teaching and learning. And, of course, the presence of a four-year science research competition program speaks to a serious investment on the part of the school to building future science research/career capacity within the student body. A rich, non-required science menu of programs, clubs, and activities also sends a powerful message to the students attending the school as well as to prospective parents and students considering attending the school. These additional science learning opportunities will, and must, cross several academic departmental boundaries. The school should also encourage friendly competitive and non-competitive science activities such as a science bowl in a game show format, STEM-themed college tours, inviting practicing scientists to do demonstrations/lectures at the school as well as science-related trips. For example, a visit to power plants, local utility companies, military facilities, state or national parks as well as a "science behind the scenes" trip to a play, art museum, music performance, or TV show. Science skills are applicable in almost every aspect of human endeavors. The science department must see itself in the context of science career recruiters who are strategically and constantly reaching out to students who may like and be good at science beyond their knowing.

The project research-based schoolwide approach of requiring (by making it part of the course grade) all students in the school to participate in the schoolwide science fair, regardless of the science course the student is taking, allows students to pick a topic from the course syllabus that particularly interests them. But this practice, because it includes all of the curriculum content areas, requires a strong research support system. And that necessary research resource mechanism is based in the school's library. A high school can't effectively pull off a comprehensive project research-based approach to teaching and learning if the school library is not structured to assist students as they do their research and prepare these projects for public presentation and grades. And thus, the tremendous importance of the next area of the school we explore: The School Library/Research Center.

Chapter 11:
Building an Effective High School Library/Research Center Program

Perhaps, one of the most misunderstood, underutilized, and underfunded resources in too many schools in our nation is the school library. It also follows that a school without an effective and well-supported librarian is placing its students at an academic disadvantage. This deprivation is damaging to students at all grade levels, but an unfocused, underutilized, and/or under-resourced school library presents a tremendous specific educational problem for high schools. The high school library should be a core component of the school's academic mission as these schools should have students spending significant time working on research projects and papers. Title I schools are often being asked to play a dangerous game of "academic achievement Russian roulette" when they want to raise student achievement while at the same time these schools cut the very staffing and programs (e.g., art and libraries) that will help to raise said achievement! Too often school libraries face two fatal assaults on their ability to be effective on behalf of students: (1) School libraries (like the arts) will more than likely bear the brunt of any school budget cutting or tightening measures. (2) School libraries will not rate high on the attention and interest list of ineffective principals. Ironically, those schools having large numbers of students without an adequate home library, good Internet computer and service access, and a quiet place to study and do research are often the schools that house unsupported and underappreciated (by school administrators) libraries. An effective and dynamic school library program can serve as a powerful partner and enhancer for all of the school's academic departments. A further irony, librarians and the library itself can provide students with the resources and technology they need to perform better on standardized exams.

My slightly different approach to building an effective high school library program

I have chosen to take an unconventional, and some would say controversial, approach to the structure and role of the high school library. Now, I understand that this approach may not work for every high school, but I have found that it meets the needs of my former STEM-CTE—Research Project-Based schools. For as previously stated, these two schools also held annual academic curriculum/content/departmental student research project presentation fairs. These academic departmental fairs required that students engage in a great deal of in-depth research on a curriculum topics lifted from the course sylla-bus they were taking. Further, my thinking on libraries also matched my ELA department's initiative of having every grade-level English subject classroom taking on the role of a "decentralized" fiction books lending library. If you visit the average high school library, you'll see that they essentially all look the same. It is not uncommon for principals to not have a vision or strategy as to how the library fits the overall school academic mission and philosophy. And, so, it follows that these principals may go through an entire school year without having regularly scheduled strategic meetings with the library staff or include the library in larger schoolwide academic initiatives. Principals should not underestimate the challenge and work required to radically change the way high school libraries operate and are structured. The reward for that hard work is having a core department in the school seriously empowering and facilitat-ing the achievement of the school's academic mission.

My vision of a high school library is that it should focus on research resourc-es, papers, journals (paper and online), magazine and technology-based resourc-es, and reference books. Essentially, it will be a school library without any fiction books, as the only fiction-related material in the library should be anthologies, biographical works, commentary, and criticism about fiction authors—thus, shifting all fictional works to ELA classrooms. For specialized, themed high schools, there should be a strong concentration and heavy emphasis on reference books that focus on that school's major theme(s) (e.g., the arts, culinary science, STEM, history, law); the first major challenge for the principal is how to sell this idea to librarians. The ELA teachers will probably be much more open to the idea, in part because the classroom libraries will lead to an increased interest in fictional reading on the part of students; also this approach allows these class-room libraries to support the ELA's departmental Readers to Leaders initiative/ competition. The establishment of ELA classroom libraries (and the fact that these works of fiction were literally in arm's length of students) has served as major influencers, we found, of an increased fictional books reading interest on the part of students.

Initially, the librarians were not happy with (and doubted) my hypothesis that this approach would actually increase student engagement with fictional works as opposed to the traditional school library methods. I clearly understood that on the surface my proposal seemed to be counterintuitive because it was based on removing certain fictional content out of the library and into ELA classrooms. How could that possibly increase student interest in reading works of fiction? The justifiably skeptical librarians were basing their disbelief on the fact that it is the traditional role of the school librarian to singularly and/or primarily promote and push the appreciation and love of fictional reading. My thought is that other departments, particularly ELA, should be equal partners in that effort. And while I still believe that the traditional school library structure to be the correct practice in the K-8 world, high school libraries should take on a more specialized and research support and facilitation role. To be honest, no prospective librarians I pitched this idea to initially responded favorably. Those who were kind saw me as well-meaning but clearly wrong on school libraries. Just about all saw the idea of having a high school library without works of fiction as the library science equivalent of a religious abomination! My interpretation is that they saw the high school library as just being an older version of the K-8 school library model. I was finally able to convince two librarians (Lena Barker-Phelps and Emily Francis-SSCHS) to give this experimental approach a chance. But if the principal chooses this specialized and focused route, you should harbor no illusions that you are not only challenging the general public education aversion to radical change but also the strongly held professional/historical beliefs of the school librarian community.

Thus, in the initial planning stages of the school's library program, we set forth a series of assertions, questions, concerns, and objectives that we hoped our library program would achieve. The first assertion is the belief that our school library, like any other academic and/or non-academic department and activity in the school, must make its own unique contribution to the realization of the school's overarching academic mission—and equally important, the degree of attention and support that is required from the school's principal. For there is another historical cultural practice found in every public education system, and that is the staff will gauge the level of leadership interests in a particular work effort by the level of strategic-planning and principal leadership energy that is invested in that particular schoolwork effort. By simply having a strategic planning meeting about your school's library program, you send an important message to the entire staff as to the importance of the school library that the principal attaches to the overarching school mission. Here are several ideas that can emerge from these strategic sessions concerning the purpose and structure of the school's library program:

- At the end of four years, what learning objectives do we want students to acquire from their experience and interaction with our school library? Learning research methodology skills, specifically how to search, find, and utilize information, are some core competencies we want for every student graduate.

- What type of library program can best support our school's academic program? Should not our library program place a heavy operational focus on responding to the school's heavy emphasis on students producing end-of-course research papers, term papers, and all students required to participate in departmental-course curriculum fairs and presentation projects?

- Do we want to duplicate or complement the public library services?

- How can we take advantage of our corporate and university partnerships to enrich and expand our access to online library services?

- How do we begin to build and catalog an informative, useful, and productive bank of Internet-based research sites?

- How can the library support our college/career guidance programs and objectives?

- What would it mean for us to envision the school library as a type of classroom? And, actually develop library course electives?

- What type of organizational institutional support, materials, and resources will be needed with the shifting of works of fiction from the library to the grade-level ELA classrooms?

- What would be the political (school district's) response to our unique school library program?

- Where will we find the funding to support a technology-rich school library?

- How should we respond (as a Title I school) to the research, study, projects, and written paper resource needs of the less-affluent members of the student body?

- Where will we find the external funding to pay for the very expensive cost of a library primarily stocked with expensive journals (paper and online), biographies, textbooks, reference books? A large number (class set) of computers and multimedia equipment.

- What type of professional development, reorientation information sessions, and communication work will be required to get members of an entire school family to rethink how they believe a school library should function?

- Following the scientific concept for the relationship of function and form, if our library is to act different, then in what ways should it look different? And what does that "different" look like?

- What does it mean to truly see a librarian as a member of the instructional team?

- How can the library support school activities, clubs, teams, and programs outside of the regular classrooms? What about support for The Science Fair Competition Program, Law and Debate team, Robotics, CTE senior projects, et cetera?

- How could both individual students and whole classes (from different academic departments) effectively utilize the library?

- Does (should) the school library have a role in after-school programs?

- What type of student out-of-classroom (lunch time, after school) independent learning activity access do we envision for the school library?

- How can the classroom teachers and a librarian collaborate in organizing a team-teaching activity around a particular topic allowing students to engage in individual and group research projects?

- What kind of technical support and capacity will a school library need that is technology-rich and heavily dependent on online resources?

- If our library will rely heavily on technology and the Internet, what does that mean for the library staff's skills capability, staff recruitment, and professional development?

- Because we require research projects in so many classes in our school, how can the school technology support and library aides best organize its staff to support this schoolwide effort?

- Will the library play a role in staff professional development?

- Are there library models in other places—both in and outside of public school system—that could offer us insight on how to build and organize our unique school library?

- In what way could our library program support the Summer Bridge Academy and Saturday tutorials, AP/ACT/SAT prep, etc.?

- With a library so heavily dependent on computer-Internet resources, what hardware, operational, and maintenance costs will such a system generate? (And how will we meet these costs?)

- How will we technically manage the possible safety and off-task negative behaviors that students might engage in when having access to a computer system that provides a great deal of Internet search freedom?

- One of our objectives for the library program was to create a librarian-designed and taught elective curriculum/course in research methodology. This class would not only help students with their ongoing required class projects but also provide students with an opportunity to study and explore the deeper methodologies and techniques utilized by researchers. The course should cover various writing approaches to research as well as the latest and best practices in audio, visual, and technology-assisted presentations.

- Use Student Technical and Resource Organization Library Aides (STROLA). Can we design a student services/learning program that would allow students to provide organizational and technical support for the library program as well as expand the student's technical and research methodology knowledge? Can we utilize this service project to interest students into thinking about pursuing library science/research/research center work as a career? Engaging students in STROLA accomplishes several objectives: (1) It forms another protective and supportive organization of students who have similar interests. (2) Since both of my schools were extremely computer hardware-rich, there was a need on the part of the technology coordinator to get some assistance with the tremendous workload! The expanded and expansive use of library services by so many students and classes meant that the library staff could definitely use some help! (3) Students can earn service credit and enhance their career-college portfolios and resumes. (4) The best defense against student vandalism, material and equipment loss, online off-task behavior, and hardware/software safety is to allow students to be part of the security, development, and maintenance of whatever it is that the school wishes to protect! Besides, you don't want your top "student techies" freelancing; you want them under expert adult supervision.

After addressing all of the above questions and concerns, we went forward to create our vision of a high school library focused on study and research support. This library would strongly depend on the utilization of computer technology/Internet reference resources, nonfiction reference books, biographies, how-to study resource books and textbooks, and standardized exam review and study books. The library would also contain materials to support our schoolwide initiative of content-departmental research project fairs. The library would also include audio/visual sources for learning, a career-college section including virtual and hardcover directories for college admissions and scholarships. This section also compiled useful information on city, state, and federal civil service jobs, and civil service test information. Reference books that covered a wide spectrum of information, including books on geography, arts, STEM, CTE, research methodology, anthologies, research writing, how-to study guides, SAT-ACT preparation manuals, presentation-project development, personal development, career development, historical documents, and maps. Also, there are samples of textbooks from every class taught in the school as well as stocked different textbooks (from other publishers) covering the major courses being taught in the school. By providing access to textbooks covering the same subject but from different publishers, that was our way of formalizing a little-known study technique utilized by high-performing students—and that is to read a concept or topic in multiple textbooks as a way of gaining an understanding or greater insight into that concept or topic. Sometimes the light bulb of understanding will ignite simply by a student hearing a concept or topic in a different textbook author's voice. Finally, we acquired a large number of computer stations. And, as previously mentioned, we moved the works of fiction into the grade level required English classrooms where those teachers set up a basic index card, sign-out book loan system.

The librarian was naturally a central part of all of the various academic departments in the school. It was therefore necessary for all of those departments to continually communicate with the librarian so that he or she could help to facilitate and support student access to information concerning academic activities, fairs, research papers, class projects, etc. The librarian also, over time, compiled a bank/catalog of useful research Internet sites for students' use.

A teacher instructional resource reference section was set up in the library that could also double as a career information section for students.

And, of course, the question of how we finance and support such an ambitious library program came to mind as there is just no way around this. A library program of the type I am suggesting absolutely costs more money. There were the easy-to-solve problems like acquiring book cases/shelves for the ELA classes, which was solved by way of a supportive district storage facility director and staff. But then there were the expenses that had to be covered by sources outside of the school system. Obviously, the first thing we realized was that nonfiction/reference books were extremely expensive. In addition, the result of diversifying and distributing the fiction collection throughout the school would mean that we would need to acquire multiple copies of single works of fiction. It became clear very early that in building such a school library program, we were absolutely going to blow through our paltry district library book allocation quickly and annually. Our response was to turn this problem into an opportunity. Many members of the public, civic/ religious, community organizations, the business community, universities, and foundations all appreciate the importance of libraries and reading as a path to a more-informed, educated, and decent human being. Most people, in general, and especially those in positions of authority and leadership, place a high value on reading and books. There is a wealth of resources to be had by public schools; all that is needed is a school having a sense of entrepreneurial clarity of purpose. Every successful partnership I have ever experienced as a principal all enjoyed working with our school because we had a well-organized purpose and plan of action.

If as a principal you want to be a successful fundraiser, you must develop a successful business- fundraising plan, which means thinking like the people from which you are soliciting support; your plan should be focused, measurable, goal-orientated, and not overly bureaucratic. The first thing we did was to use this specialized library idea as a marketing fundraising tool. We organized a book acquisition campaign drive through Amazon. Our supporters were provided with an easily accessible online site to pay for the requested books we listed. We used this method to acquire reference books; maps; journal and magazine subscriptions; films (e.g., *Stand and Deliver*); and educational DVDs and software for the library itself as well as works of fiction for the ELA classroom libraries. With just a few clicks, donors could easily purchase a book(s), and that book(s) would be automatically shipped to the school. Our school 501c3 foundation allowed those donors to designate (for tax purposes) these purchases as a nonprofit educational institution donation. We acquired textbooks by writing to textbook publishing company's sales divisions and asking for textbook samples (both student and teacher editions). We also took advantage of the book sales of public libraries where book prices were dramatically reduced. We received donations from professional organizations, corporate libraries, universities as well as from estate sales of personal libraries and individuals who had extensive home libraries.

The point I am trying to make here is that no matter the type of library in the school, it will require additional funding to start and maintain it. It is of little value to students if the library resource materials are outdated, badly maintained, and/or missing completely. The principal must also show an interest in the school's library program. And by "showing an interest," I mean in things like working with the librarian in the annual strategic resource acquisition planning of said library as well as providing a serious standards-based, year-end evaluation and assessment. The principal must also encourage and facilitate communication between the librarian and other departmental leaders and teachers in the school. The principal's presence is critical; visiting the library at various times of the school week sends an important message to everyone: that what is going on in the school library is important!

Finally, as principal you should know that the "focus of your attention and time" is being closely monitored by the school family. Does the principal's "rhetoric" match up, and is followed up, with a certain level of involvement and engagement? You, in a real and symbolic way can set the positive *Tone*, guide by example the perception (*Climate*), and ultimately help to encourage and establish a school *Culture* of seeing the school library beyond the mere traditional-statutorily mandated space in the building, and instead see it as a core partner in the school's mission march toward high student academic achievement. Yes, you are always being watch by the members of the school family so that they can gain clues about what you have determined is important and of value in the school. And so it would not be unusual for these "observations" to also cover the treatment and attention given to different cohorts and categories of students in the school.

As a superintendent visiting schools, I always wanted to walk around unescorted by the principal. This, I suspect from observing the body-language response on the part of most principals made them uncomfortable. They all eventually got accustomed to it (or maybe they didn't), but in any event I did not need a "tour guide" for I always knew where I wanted to go in the building. And in every school visit, at the top of my "must see" list was the school's library; also near the top of my "must see" list was the school's approach to Special Education. And just like the curious members of the school family, I wanted to see how the principal addressed (not just talked about) these "special" members of the school family. So in the next section, let's look at how I think a positive and productive Special Education program should operate.

Chapter 12:
A Productive Special Education Program/Department

If you want to get a good and quick *Tone* assessment of a school, then observe how that school treats its Special Needs/Special Education (SNSPED) students. In most cases, the level of attention shown to these students is a good indication of the concern shown to the entire student body. Schools are in many ways like all human societies; they can easily be revealed (or exposed) as to their commitment to compassion based on how they treat their most vulnerable populations. If the school does not sincerely and strategically support SNSPED students by way of an individual student and schoolwide plan/culture of Pro-action that will help them to achieve academically, then that will tell you a great deal about the school's approach to supporting non-SNSPED, academically struggling students. The first job of the principal and his or her SBL team is to initiate some meaningful professional development (PD) for the entire school teaching staff. You would think given its primary role and place in our professional mission (teaching and learning) that we would be more effective in designing professional development activities, but that does not always happen. In fact, more often than not, we don't do a good job of PD in public education. The first step is to fully immerse and commit both the SNSPED department and the non-SNSPED academic departments into the overarching academic mission of the school. Not only are their departmental objectives not in conflict, they are mutually codependent on each other for individual departmental and schoolwide success. The SNSPED department must fully appreciate the need for collaboration with all of the academic departments in the school, and that part of their evaluation will be based on their ability to effectively work in productive partnership with those departments. The ultimate act of advocacy is to put SNSPED students in a position to succeed academically, successfully graduate, and then move on to the next arena of a productive life. There is no such thing as the special education department (SPED) losing and the school winning. Therefore, it also follows for the majority of academic departments, that not supporting the SPED department and SNSPED students does not translate into a victory for one or more content area

217

departments in the school. In fact, there is a good political military concept for this type of thinking when two nations have the nuclear capability to destroy each other along with the entire planet that is accurately called Mutually Assured Destruction (MAD). Since special education students will also be taking departmental courses and standardized exams, their performance in these two areas will serve as the evaluative measures of the department's leadership and the level of departmental instructional quality by the principal. The general education teaching staff must be made aware of what SNSPED students need to be successful in their classrooms. And in both a slightly practical, but largely theoretical sense, all teachers in the school, regardless of their subject area, must function as deputized Special Education teachers. For the high school principal, this is a particular challenge, for as I stated earlier, high school teachers tend to be focused on content, as opposed to the singular needs of individual students; this is not a professional defect, rather it is a rational response to the difference between having twenty-five students for an entire year, and having 150 students for half, or an entire year. We are further challenged by the fact that even if a teacher arrived to your school having experienced a traditional college teacher education program (which unfortunately is not always true), the average content specialist General Education (GENED) high school teacher will need, through PD to have their SNSPED undergraduate course based instructional-information and knowledge recalled and upgraded. Professional development activities led by the SNSPED staff, or special invited cognitive specialists, could engage GENED teachers in an exercise that will allow them to see the world from the sensory perspective of a Special Ed student. I have found that it is often a lack of awareness, not callous disregard, that prevents GENED teachers from being able to objectively see how particular instructional methods are harmful and nonproductive for Special Ed students, and as I will explain a little later how this harm is visited on those students without IEPs, who are struggling with undiagnosed, unaddressed, or mild (almost undetectable) forms of learning disabilities. The first "sale" the principal must nail is to convince the GENED teachers that being aware of teaching methodologies that are successful with Special Ed students will increase their course pass rate, because those adaptive methods will also help academically students who are not designated Special Ed to perform better in the class.

I don't want to replay the historical conflicts that can often arise in a school where the SNSPED folks will see themselves as the sole protectors and defenders of SNSPED students, thus removing those students from the supportive umbrella of the entire GENED teaching staff; while at the same time, I have spent a great deal of time explaining to sometimes annoyed GENED teachers the reasons for some modifications or accommodations that a student may need and is entitled to based on the student's documented IEP. As a principal, I understood and appreciated both sides; like the GENED teachers often felt that both the academic behavioral standards for SNSPED students was in many cases too low. But I also understand how these students could be facing serious learning challenges and, therefore, needed a creative methodological approach as well as committed advocates in the school if they are to achieve academically.

The problem is further complicated by the large numbers of teachers who are entering teaching without having taken any SNSPED courses or any education courses at all. This means that the principal must empower the SNSPED supervisor in the school along with the SNSPED teaching staff to become SNSPED trainers, educators, and staff developers for the entire teaching staff. You, the principal, might even have them educate yourself if SNSPED is not your area of expertise. The principal, and other members of the SBL team, should establish their own group and individual study program to make themselves better acquainted with SNSPED pedagogy, laws, and regulations. Every superintendent (including me) has had their time and resources wasted by that principal who failed to properly read, understand, and follow a simple IEP mandate or who purposely or through ignorance did not properly follow the SNSPED regulations concerning student discipline procedures. Trust me, this is not the best way to endear yourself to your superintendent or district SPED director. My advice, if you want to send SNSPED students, advocates, attorneys, or parents a message is to write a book after you retire, but don't do it by ignoring SNSPED IEP's, laws, regulations, and mandates; judges are often not amused, and they may even choose to send the school district their own punitive and costly message.

Part of the schoolwide SNSPED education programs should include eliminating myths like the majority of students misbehaving in your school are SNSPED students or that learning and testing accommodations are some kind of unfair advantage given to SNSPED students.

Now, it is true, that I have received too many incoming ninth-graders who bring silly and non-productive IEPs. For example, the obvious re-copying of the same goals year after year or having goals that don't truly challenge the child. In most cases, these bad IEPs were crafted by lazy, ill-informed, or visionless middle school leadership teams. This is, unfortunately, a part of our world that is in desperate need of fixing, especially in high schools. The principal should seek some balance here. We should be honest about what parts of our profession are not always where they should be while at the same time focusing on what support mechanisms we need to put in place to correct those profession deficiencies. Further, the principal should be careful about what he or she says about the SNSPED world, either in jest or frustration. Your comments about SNSPED students can greatly influence the SBL team as well as the GENED teaching staff's level of commitment in supporting these students. Your philosophical/ethical approach to serving SNSPED students will frame and drive the entire school's approach to how these students are treated. If your SNSPED staff feels that they must assume an aggressive defensive posture on behalf of SNSPED students, then the entire schoolwide academic mission is in serious trouble. The support and success of the school's SNSPED student population must be seen by both SPED and GENED teachers as a primary component of the school's pedagogical vision and mission.

Along with helping the GENED staff by way of PD, to understand the full spectrum of personalities and learning challenges that exist in the SNSPED student world, we should also make sure that they are prepared to handle students with various (sometimes undiagnosed) disabilities, physiological health, and academic deficiency challenges. As principal, you want to encourage the development of a schoolwide *Cultural* approach that seeks to meet individual students at the point of their educational need. Again, a doable but not easy task to accomplish in the complex world of high schools. Creating accommodations and interventions that allow different cohorts of students to succeed academically should be the entire school's mission, not just the SNSPED folks!

Our most important operational response to supporting SENSPED students was our Team-Teaching Inclusion Model (TTIM). The first major challenge for the principal is to change the *Climatic* perception (reflective of a systemic *Culture*) held by teachers, students, and parents that the second SNSPED co-teacher in the room was indeed a teacher and not a teacher's aide. But the primary work of this *Cultural* change must be done first with both GENED and SPED teachers themselves. As always, high schools present their own unique challenges. In the early developmental stages of instituting a TTIM, it is imperative that the principal must first convince the two classroom teachers that the initiative leads with the word "Team" for good, practical, and operational reasons; they are in every way working as a team! This would suggest that the principal may want to pick a confident and cooperative GENED teacher for a "pilot" class. It won't hurt if you provide this and all future TTIM classes with a dedicated classroom and some material and equipment resources, for you are really asking a high school GENED teacher to go counter to the prevailing culture! It is not uncommon for high school teachers to share a room; it is, however, a unique challenge to convince two teachers to share a room during the same class period. In a high school, the staff organizational structure itself is a major contributor to the challenges of creating an effective co-teaching inclusion model. For example, the SNSPED co-teacher in a biology, chemistry, or geometry class may not necessarily have the sufficient content knowledge or certification to actually get up in front of the entire class and teach a lesson. But I have found that when the TTIM model is really working, and the two teachers are truly a team, they seem to be able to organize a significant number of class activities that provide the SNSPED teacher with the opportunity to lead the lesson. In most cases, this lesson was a paired or group activity project. These activities not only allowed the students to see the SNSPED teacher perform as a traditional classroom teacher; these jointly planned lessons also allowed the GENED teacher to walk around the classroom and see students from a different perspective. Instructional models that utilize the TTIM classroom approach can, as I witnessed, improve learning capacity for all of the students in the classroom, not just the SNSPED students. Clearly, there is a need for a strong sense of staff camaraderie, mutual respect, and appreciation to create a successful TTIM classroom. As the principal, you must encourage, strengthen, recognize, and reward these positive working partnerships by materially (classroom technology, additional funds for projects, extra teaching supplies and materials, etc.) and professionally by way of favorable letters in the teachers' files, pedagogical books, magazines, and special professional development activities (e.g., conferences). It is also essential that you provided these teachers with the same prep and lunch periods. The first for the practical reasons of joint lesson planning; the second because for a different practical reason these two teachers must actually develop a professional respect, appreciation, and liking for each other.

As every high school principal knows, any type of co-teaching SPED-GENED inclusion model creates a scheduling nightmare for several reasons. First, creating a schedule of TTIM classes that can match SNSPED student schedules and the availability of a limited number of SNSPED teachers and paraprofessionals was described by one of my APs as the scheduling puzzle challenge of her life! Further, high schools exist in a subject-dominated environment. Students move from one classroom (and teacher) to the next. Thus, a challenge arose because a certified SNSPED teacher may not necessarily be a content specialist in that subject area for which they were available. The entire affair can and will turn into a principal triage problem since you don't have the true number of special education teachers that you truly need, so the question becomes, what courses do you concentrate these teachers in? Finally, this TTIM must allow time in the school day for the students to have exclusive learning sessions with certified SNSPED teachers or they will get lost in the fog of the high school environment. This creates a scheduling challenge since pulling students out of their high school courses causes them to miss important instructional time. This, unfortunately, will only complicate whatever academic challenges they already face. Listed below is the TTIM development plan we provided SNSPED students, which allowed them the best opportunity at academic achievement we thought possible:

- Given budgetary limits, we selected the courses we wanted to invest the greatest TTIM resources in. Then, we began with ninth-grade SNSPED students who were at the greatest risk of failing a course. This is important because a student failing a class will present an additional scheduling challenge when organizing TTIM classes. The scheduler will need to cluster SNSPED students in classes with an assigned special education teacher, and/or paraprofessional; a few students falling out of course sequence could mean they would also not be able to take advantage of a TTIM scheduled course. Ninth-grade TTIM priority scheduling increases the odds for successful graduation and building student confidence and self-esteem in SNSPED students, which is critical in the first year. And, like all pedagogical budgetary decisions in public education, there are always institutional consequences. In this case, it meant a concentration of TTIM classes in ninth grade, a smaller number in tenth grade, and a few almost exclusively Education Paraprofessionals (EDPARAS) in TTIM classes for the eleventh and twelfth grades. There was also thought given to the subject areas that would receive TTIM classes. In order of priority, the TTIM classes were concentrated in math, ELA, science, and history. It was our experience that it was these classes that SNSPED students found the most challenging and were in the most danger of getting lost in and failing. Therefore, specifically in the cases of mathematics and ELA, an additional review/tutorial/instructional course was added to those ninth-grade students' schedules who entered high school with severe mathematics and/or reading skills deficiencies. The additional mathematics and/or ELA SNSPED support class at the end of the day obviously works best in those settings where the students are able to travel independently (e.g., urban settings). But even in more rural and suburban districts, schools find ways of accommodating the transportation needs created by students attending many different types of after-school activities, so why not academic support? Students can be assigned either a daily mathematics course or a daily reading skills course, or a combination of the two. It has been my experience that when trying to provide support for the academically weakest students in a given ninth-grade cohort, in most cases, the deficiencies will exist in both math and ELA. One of the benefits of these additional courses, particularly when they are combined with something like a one-and-a-half-year or two-year algebra course, is that they slow down the learning pace of the high school experience. It is very easy for any ninth-grader, with or without an IEP, to become confused, overwhelmed, and disorganized in the face of all that they are responsible for from different classes. The additional math and ELA classes should include some elements of the college recitation class style with a high school tutorial approach; this allows student groups to work on a focused content area/skill for an entire period.

- Recruit SNSPED teachers who are double-certified in Special Education and a subject area. Where that optimal situation is not possible, recruit and assign the SNSPED teachers to a TTIM team based on transcript/content/course strength in a particular subject area; and, of course, investigate teacher interest in particular content areas as well. When recruiting GENED teachers generally, not just for membership on a TTIM team, you'll want to probe for number of Special Education courses taken, knowledge and awareness of special education pedagogy, and a professional interest in helping students who are struggling to succeed. (Their knowledge of and ability to practice efficacy.)

- In those classes where we could not schedule a SNSPED teacher, we placed a paraprofessional (educational aide) who could take notes (or collect class notes summaries provided by the teachers), help students to get and stay organized, and keep track of students' SNSPED short- and long-term assignments. Giving the SNSPED students (and other students who are struggling academically) a summary of the class notes allows them to give their focused attention on the lesson. Also the GENED-SPED teachers, and/or the EDPARA can teach a simplified system of note-taking while encouraging students to pay attention to the lesson, demonstration, or classroom activity. Or, incorporate adaptive technology into the class notes-taking process. The educators in the classroom could also supply the entire class with bulleted formatted notes of the important takeaways from the lesson. Class note-taking skills, as with other effective study habits, must be taught. The important point here, particularly with SNSPED and all academically struggling students, is that our goal is not for them to write beautiful notes and then completely miss the learning objectives of the lesson.

- *(Don't want to go into this too deeply here, but I am wondering if ninth-graders in general, who we ask to take class notes, where we have not taught them how to efficiently and effectively take class notes, are in actuality doing more harm than good to their ability to absorb the objectives of the lesson being taught.)*

- When organizing the TTIM classes, the principal should hold separate meetings with the prospective parents of the regular education students and SNSPED students. This should only be done separately in the planning stages of the program and at the beginning of the school year. In this way, their concerns can be addressed openly and honestly. The different parent concerns can be summarized as the following:

  - Regular education parents:

    - Will the class be (academically) slowed down?

    - Will class standards (level of rigor) be lowered?

    - Will there be a high level of distractive behavior in the class?

  - For the SNSPED parent:

    - Will my child receive the academic support and services they need in this full inclusion (TTIM) class?

- o Will the other students make fun of my child? (Or, will my child be identified as the "SPED kid in the class?")

- o Will the accommodations (including those relating to testing) listed in my child's IEP be provided?

- o How can a (regular education) teacher effectively teach my child?

All of these questions must be heard and effectively answered. Don't take the concerns of each parent group personally; it is not a referendum on your leadership but rather their lived experience with a system that does not always get the entire Special Education effort quite right. The key is to demonstrate the benefits of the TTIM program to both groups of parents and how their child will greatly benefit from being in a TTIM class. A major part of marketing the TTIM class to GENED parents is to show how the program's teacher planning and training, additional academic support, materials, equipment and activities, and, finally, the principal's personal investment in wanting to see the program succeed will benefit students at all academic levels in the class. For our SNSPED parents, the TTIM classes seeks to be true and consistent with the principles of providing SNSPED students with the Least Restrictive Learning Environment (LRE). More importantly, not just to follow the LRE "letter of the law" but to work in such a committed way that every effort is being made to help these SNSPED students to succeed academically.

Parents and staff will always have concerns about something new, but like anything different and challenging in education. If the proposal is discussed thoroughly and honestly (including the possible difficulties) at the very beginning, it will help address any potential misunderstandings that may emerge later. It is particularly important to have these extended conversations in a smaller, more productive environment where all questions and concerns can be addressed. In high schools, team teaching of any type can present its own unique challenges; therefore, the emotional investment and attention provided by the principal is critical to the success of a TTIM classroom. A team-teaching model, like most initiatives, can only work if it is "sold," not mandated, by the principal.

Final words on building an effective Special Education program/department

The critical factor for the establishment of any school initiative is the level of commitment in its success that is displayed by the principal. The entire staff is going to assess your true views on any topic based on your budget priorities, time-interest allocation, formal and informal observations, body and verbal language, recognition, and reward. We wrongly think the staff is not watching, but they are always watching, waiting to take their cues (pro or con) based on their observations of you. I must admit, many years into my tenure as a principal, I wrongly maintained a visible oppositional attitude with many of the Special Education rules and regulations, particularly those related to discipline. I believe that my attitude had a profound effect on the members of my staff, some of whom were looking to me to model their own future careers in school administration and supervision. The truth is, Special Education, like so many bureaucratic products of public education will, depending on the situation, display both good and bad attributes. A great deal of what is not working in Special Education has been influenced by bad actions (poor treatment of SNSPED students) in the past. Many of these "past bad acts" by schools and school districts have led to some regulatory and statutory mandates that could—if taken out of their proper context and purpose—indeed academically hurt SNSPED students. Like most things in life, there is a need for balance. But the principal must rise above and go beyond the often wrongly formatted, Special Education/Regular Education debates, creating instead an integration of a purposeful strategy that would include SNSPED-GENED teachers when discussing academic achievement, student scheduling, credit-earning initiatives, professional development, a ninth grade success plan, tutorials and after-school programs, and finally, the budget. At the end the school year, during your self-reflective review and evaluation of the school, the topic of how you and the school performed with SNSPED students is a necessary part of that assessment. To put it in a practical job and non-professional ethical context, the high school principal who ignores *any* standardized testing or graduation statistical rate cohort of students does so at his or her own professional peril. Your good works may or may not be known, but your school performance statistics will be well known annually because they will be published widely!

The progress and ultimate success of SNSPED students must be an essential part of the evaluation of the principal, the school's SBL team, and all academic departments. I know the "how well did you do with your SNSPED students" was, for me, a critical school leadership effectiveness rubric when I was a superintendent evaluating and rating principals.

Chapter 13:
The Effective Health and Physical Education Department

The school's standards are the standards for every academic department in the school.

If we begin with the above affirmation as an evaluative tool for establishing the foundational operating principles of all academic departments in the school, we will be led to the best approach in developing and supervising these departments. It is important that the principal establish a high academic standards Health and Physical Education department (HPED). This department should be held to the same instructional standards as any other academic department in the school. Unfortunately, you may be forced to convince some members of the HPED that you are serious about holding them to the school's standard academic expectations. An important schoolwide message can be sent here by defining the HPED as a full-fledged academic department, along with all of the responsibilities that follow that designation. This principle pedagogical and uncompromising position will spread throughout the school: If PE teachers are expected to follow a curriculum, teach to the standards, and have a formal lesson plan crafted in the same standard school lesson plan format, then the conversation about instructional standards in other academic departments will quickly and qualitatively shift upward. The key factor in establishing such a *Culture* of excellence in any school is that students encounter rigorous standards no matter the classroom they enter. I have no problem in proclaiming that there should be no "free classes" (absent standards and rigor) in a school. And the amazing thing about young people is that they easily adjust to whatever level of academic rigor exists in a school. Unfortunately, that level of academic rigor could be low or high, but regardless of its descriptive and operational quality, the students will adjust to it. School *Culture* is powerful like that! This practice of taking the HPED seriously can also help to eliminate that guidance nightmare of students arriving to their senior year missing required graduation HPED credit because they did not take the class

229

seriously. I love teenagers, and I have chosen to spend large segments of my professional life working to make them successful, but they can sometimes exhibit a nonsensical, self-destructive approach to important matters. I have seen smart students fail gym for something like too many "unprepared" days. The failing of any required (for graduation) courses, as I stated earlier, is not a penalty-free act in a high school. Students who have failed an HPED course and are now juniors and seniors must be given scheduling priority to make up that required HPED course; this clogs up the system by them unnecessarily occupying a costly seat in the class or, in the case of the gym, a space. These students would have been better served by passing their required HPED courses on schedule and freeing themselves up to take electives. The making up of failed HPED classes can also make scheduling classes difficult for the rising classmates behind those students, and all of the above problems will cost the school unnecessary money. By setting the standard that the "gym is the largest classroom in the school," students will get the message that just like any other classroom, there are standards and expectations to be met in HPED classes. The principal should personally set the *Tone* here. Each semester I would ask for the list of students who were in danger of failing an HPED course; in health class, this usually meant a missing assignment or failing class exams; for PE, this often showed up as students who were one or two "unprepareds" away from failing the class. To establish a *Culture* of excellence, starting in the first marking period, the principal must empower the HPED faculty to actually fail students who choose to not perform and produce at a passing grade standard. It was also common for me to go into the gym and challenge individual students who were sitting in the bleachers for unexcused reasons. I eventually evolved in this process; I dealt with the "bleacher sitters" by mandating that any student who was unprepared for a PE class and who did not have an official excuse would be referred to the ARC (attitude readjustment center, or as it is sometimes defined, ISS), where the rule was that every student assigned had to engage in a full class period of academic work; thus, the ARC could never serve as some kind of illusionary break from class work. Going to the ARC meant moving to another hard-working classroom, albeit missing the normal classroom niceties. This action seemed to dramatically help students in making better choices when it came to being prepared for PE class! In a Title I school, you could also encounter more than a few students who just don't care about their grades or failing classes. If you have a school where there are a lot of students who for many different political, historical, and socio-economic reasons don't feel the need to seek and maintain a high GPA, you as the principal must force and manufacture that need with the hope that the instinct to survive and thrive will kick in. Of course, the sooner it kicks in, the better—which is why the principal must push early and hard for a schoolwide adherence to high academic and performance standards. The HPED must not be exempt from that principal principle-pushing effort.

Further, serious standards must be established for the required Health Education course. This class is really important because it offers important hygiene and life-saving information for students, which is why I always thought that pairing this course with biology was a great way of teaching students the psychological and physiological facts of life. A great deal of what students think they know and/or actually know about human anatomy and physiology can vary greatly in any grade-level cohort. The spectrum can range from absolute facts to absolute fiction. And, so, the Health Education class in cooperation with biology class is an excellent place to clarify and correct any misconceptions students have about the human body as well as the health dangers, safety risks, and challenging issues (e.g., maturing, sex, drugs and alcohol, diet, violence) relating to those bodies. A third collaborator with the required health education class should be the guidance counseling department. It is not uncommon for questions, or written responses to prompts, reveal to the health education teacher a health issue/crisis a particular student may be facing. These revelations provide the opportunity for a guidance counseling intervention, which is often a much better option than peer advice or incorrect adult/parent advice. It is also true that these health education classes can serve as tripwires to get students the health or psychological support they need through outside referrals from the guidance department. This is particularly true in those situations in which the communication channel between parent and child is either weak or nonexistent. All of this to say that the principal, SBL team, and HPED chairperson must see the required health education course as an opportunity to save students. Now, this is true for all teenage students regardless of their social and economic status, but it takes on a greater sense of urgency in those communities where there is a shortage and lack of access to healthcare and health education and information. Finally, this class can also establish a schoolwide *Culture* where equivalent value is given to both physical and mental health. Every year, we are forced to read about the terrible tragedies that occur in high schools. The health education course could help to remove the stigma and negative perceptions concerning counseling and psychotherapy and place good mental health as a core curriculum objective. That translates into making the conversation concerning mental health, a positive and judgment-free process throughout the school. It also means getting students the support and help they need when they feel emotionally overwhelmed or challenged; the health education discussions, questions, and written responses on mental health topics can serve as a safe conduit of support for the student and as collaboration with the health education teacher and guidance counseling department.

The health education class is also suited for a guest speakers' program. First, because very often students will feel more comfortable asking a difficult question of a visiting professional as opposed to the regularly assigned teacher. Second, a guest speaker's presentation adds excitement and interest to the class; teenagers find it interesting to receive information from an experienced firsthand source. Finally, an invited expert allows for out-of-school resource information to be provided to students. I have also found that health education CBOs, hospitals, dental clinics health departments, etc. have been more than supportive in their willingness to send speakers. And be sure to brief the speaker on the regulations that govern the school in regards to the dissemination of information to students; don't assume they know! In some cases, you may need to offer a parental "opt out" or "opt in" procedure (check with the district's legal department). Some possible presentation topics that could even be offered to students generally outside of the health education class format are:

- "A Beautiful Smile" (Dental care information)

- "Seeing is Achieving" (Why being able to properly see in school is important)

- "Marijuana High and Driving" (Students are very confused about impairment here)

- "The Science of STDs"

- "What's happening to my body?" (Physiological-Psychological maturity)

- "I don't like the way I…" (Look, feel, am being treated, etc.)

- "What should I do when my best friend says_____" (Or, what secrets should I keep?)

- "When helping you is hurting me!" (How not to be taken advantage of)

- "The effects of drinking alcohol short/long term"

- "Addictive/Hallucinatory Drug Dangers"

- "Mental Stimulants and Muscle-Building Stimulants Dangers"

- "How much sleep do I need? What foods empower us?" (Rest and nutrition)

- "Depression and Sadness"

- "Psychological bullying: The dangerous effects"

- "That dangerous medicine cabinet at home"

- "Suicide"

- "Neighborhood/community violence as a health crisis"

These, and other topical areas, help to frame the meaning and purpose of the required health education course, but they also signal the importance the principal and his/her SBL team must attach to the organization and actual daily instructional practices in this course. The scope is wide and extensive, yet extremely important. Supervisory support and professional development will be required to make this project work. Health education teachers are in fact teachers, so we must constantly remind them of that fact as we help them to improve the instructional quality of their practice. One option is to apply the team-teaching format, utilizing a guidance counselor and physical education teacher. In any event, the principal and SBL team must not see this health education course as just another check-off point on the list of required classes for graduation. With students facing daily mental and physical health challenges and decisions, the school must use every resource available to maximize the potential for a healthy student graduation outcome.

A pre-semester, pre-observation discussion with the PE teachers and having the PE curriculum and standards as the reference points for the conversation is a good place for the principal to establish clear expectations for PE instructional practices. There were always some important fundamental learning and behavioral objectives that I felt should emerge from any semester-long PE course:

- To enhance student health and fitness.

- To be modeled (following the curriculum) on the survey exposure model such that teachers are able to spend a meaningful amount of time covering multiple sporting and competitive events.

- To teach students the fundamental techniques, rules, and strategies that govern particular competitive sports activities.

- To translate the positive competitive sports/athletic values of sportsmanship, hard work, practice, teamwork, friendly competition, pursuing a personal best, and goal formation.

- To expand student awareness and knowledge concerning the vast spectrum of sports from around the world and the historical/cultural explanations for the evolution of these unique sporting activities.

- To expose and invite students to engage in sports activities outside of the limited stereotypical sports activities they may have been exposed to prior to the class.

- To make students aware of the many career opportunities in the "allied sports" fields, including the fact that for every job as a player in a professional sporting event, multiple well-paying jobs in support of that player and the sport is created.

- HPED electives should provide the opportunity for students to be able to dig deeper into the operational techniques and practices of a particular sports activity (e.g., tennis, gulf, weightlifting, volleyball). This course should expose students to the complexity of the different player positions, the practice and preparation for competition, the "subtle" and creative techniques utilized by the best practitioners of a sporting event, and finally, the successful competition strategies that are employed by players and coaches.

It is critically important to include the PE classes in the principal/SBL team's rigorous formal and informal observations schedule. Several veteran PE teachers have told me over the years that they have never had so many principal visits and in some cases no formal observation by a principal in their entire career. The principal should make sure that PE classes are following the standard work product driven by high expectations that is required for all other academic courses in the school. That means a standards-based syllabus, a pacing calendar, a lesson plan, and planned assessments in addition to providing feedback to the students on those assessments, participation and behavioral standards, midterm and final exams, a curriculum fair, projects, and research term papers. Even if the state and/or district policy is that the class be structured as "Pass or Fail," the students should not be under the illusion that passing means just showing up for class. Every class in the HPED department, including the electives, must be driven by both the school instructional practice standards as well as the district's content standards. In the PE survey classes, students should cover a diverse menu of sporting activities, paying particular attention to the non-stereotypical sports often not offered to Title 1 children. Students should leave these classes with an understanding of the names, vocabulary, national origins, equipment required, techniques, rules, scoring system, and how the particular sport fits into the worldwide system of international competition. The students should leave the PE program with the knowledge of sports such as tennis, soccer, all parts of track and field, golf, bowling, table tennis, cricket, rugby, Olympic events, etc. Even in those situations that the school does not have access to either equipment or a venue to teach a particular sport or competition, the students should still be made aware of those activities. Students should have knowledge of the major sporting events/competitions that occur in, and outside of, the United States (e.g., the World Cup of Soccer).

When the Winter and Summer Olympics come around, students should, through a graded research paper, make themselves aware of the diverse categories of sports competition connected to these two important events. The opportunity provided (every four years) by an Olympic research project allows students to learn a great deal about history and geography by way of studying the evolution of these various competitive events.

It is always nice to have professional and college athletes visit schools, particularly when they place a great deal of emphasis on academics and scholar athleticism. But the HPED can expand this career week activity by inviting to the school sports journalists, sports statisticians, orthopedic medical professionals connected to professional and college teams, sports nutritionists, sporting equipment engineers and manufactures, athletic shoe company executives, creative designers and marketers, sports agents and attorneys, and local sports television technical staff persons.

PE electives should focus on sports that are not as traditionally popular as others in school, such as Tai Chi, Yoga, tennis, fencing, gymnastics, archery, golf, the decathlon, etc.

There should be an overall departmental goal for personal fitness standards, good nutritional habits, weight reduction, toning, physical stamina, and strengthening. As opposed to focusing on a few students who will benefit from the varsity teams model, the HPED department should give equal organizational attention to developing a schoolwide team-based intramurals program for sports like volleyball, basketball, flag football, softball, bowling soccer, etc. The purpose here is to get large numbers of students who are not on a varsity team to get involved in improving their fitness, building camaraderie among the student body through fun, friendly sports competitions. Intramurals can provide students recognition and reward, who may not have received that recognition in any other part of the school's activities. Intramurals can also be another tool to dismantle any artificial wall between Special Education and General Education students. This schoolwide intramural activity can serve to build a spirit of cooperation and connectedness, particularly with those students who sometimes get lost in the "bigness" of the high school environment. One of the great dangers of high school, both from a group safety and individual psychological health perspective, is the ever-present challenge of trying to keep students from being isolated even in crowded places where the crowd itself can dangerously hide that isolated loneliness. A schoolwide intramural program, if done well, will cost some money. So, perhaps, it is best to start with two sports that can fully engage both girls and boys. Some of the cost of the program can be raised by the teams and their parents—for example, allowing individual teams to have a fundraising day in places like the cafeteria in order to raise money for competition T-shirts. But other costs generated by the schoolwide intramural program for things like equipment/materials, referees, custodial building opening, teacher coaching overtime, and awards (medals, certificates, and trophies) must all be identified and raised by that entrepreneurial principal.

Finally, it is important to establish the school's academic mission beachhead in the HPED department because this effort will set the *Tone* for the important establishment of a varsity scholar-athletic sports program. Winning that victory is critical, particularly in a majority-minority Title I school where the male students may see their only path to economic success in America is through the "terrible odds" professional sports route. As this department takes the lead in saying that we are always students and scholars first and athletes second as well as promoting the thinking and intellectual skills associated with sports, this will affirm and empower the school's mission of placing one's life options primarily in the basket of education and academic achievement. If the departmental objectives are the balance of the physical, mental, and spiritual, then the varsity sports program will follow that philosophy because more than likely the coaches will emerge from the HPED faculty. They should promote a set of principles such that even if the Division 1 college sports route is the objective for a student, they want these athletes to be thinkers, both inside and outside of the playing fields; be responsible to themselves and their community; be entrepreneurially wise in their dealings with colleges and professional sports organizations; be disciplined and principled in all of their interactions; be of high moral character and able to conduct themselves with dignity and respect at all times; and to serve as positive role models for the young people following in their footsteps, for it also connects to the school's mission of pursing excellence in every endeavor of one's (and the school's) life.

Chapter 14:
Building an Effective Foreign Language/Cultural Studies Department

We must create a school learning community of world-learning leaders. In order to do that, we must invite students to explore the rich diversity of knowledge that is actualized and best expressed through the study of the history, culture, and languages of our planetary neighbors. As educators, we should be ethically inclined toward seeing the diverse rainbow of the human experience as a positive strength, not a negative weakness. I have this nagging belief that the best way to quickly learn about a nation other than your own is through food or language; since I've never been principal of a culinary school, I will focus here on the language acquisition part. A nation's language carries with it all of its history, joys, rituals, disappointments, heroic deeds, fears/hopes, collective sacred sayings, geography, art as well as that nation's past pains and inspiring aspirations. This is why our nation's public education approach to foreign language fluency is sadly a model of underachievement. In part, it is out of an ignorant arrogance that wrongly pushes us to believe that learning about our world community neighbors is beneath us. While we ignore learning the language, and therefore the history and culture of other people, they are definitely strategically and advantageously (for reasons of commerce) learning our language and, therefore, better understanding our history and culture.

As I traveled around the world over the last forty years, one thing has become consistently clear, and that is how ordinary people in many parts of the world are extremely fluent and knowledgeable of languages and cultures beyond their own, and many particularly have a good working knowledge of English. Unfortunately, for the majority of American students, what passes for linguistic and cultural literacy is really only being able to speak (badly) a few words and phrases of another nation's language along with the few historical/cultural concepts they can pick up in passing from their K-8 geography, social studies and high school history classes. The task then of an effective Foreign Language Department (FLD) is to challenge and raise those poor learning standards. All of the academic departments have unique yet connecting mission statements; all of the academic departments in a school serve as members

239

of a larger orchestra of a larger programmatic purpose. As a core mission, the FLD must reflect and project the school's larger academic mission, creating a "well-educated graduate," translated through its own departmental message. To realize its operational objectives, the following questions must be asked and answered by the school's FLD team and the other academic departments:

- What does a foreign language studies graduate of our school look like? To push or not to push for a schoolwide graduation standard of a four-year foreign language study program? How do we define foreign language fluency in our school? How does our school, in co-operation with the FLD, define what it means to know and speak a foreign language? How does the FLD philosophy and approach to real language learning align with the school's mission of graduating the best exemplars of U.S. and world citizenry? What are the budgetary, staffing, and academic implications of a four-year foreign language study program?

- What is our responsibility as American educators to the well-being of the nation? This is an important school culture question, particularly because most school districts only require two to three years of foreign language study as a graduation requirement for the majority of their high school students, a terrible mistake in my view. In most U.S. high school cases, if one compares the quality and quantity of actual functional and useful foreign language acquisition on the part of students, with the budgetary expenditures, it is in essence a waste of money. Too many of our high school graduates simply can't read, write, and surely not speak a foreign language competently. An additional problem is that we are not producing an adequate number of fluent foreign language graduates that is needed for the U.S.: foreign, military, diplomatic, intelligence, and foreign assistance/aid services.

- Private sector-business community linguistic competency needs: How do we prepare students to be effective communicators of world languages; to be fluent and confident when conversing in meetings where the language spoken is not English? How do we expand and strengthen the resumes of our students for the business and employment opportunities of the present and future? Can we empower them with knowledge and skills to be adaptable global citizens who can effectively function in an increasingly integrated global economic community?

- Cultural literacy and good national/global citizenship: In what ways can we best expand and enhance the student's level of cultural appreciation, knowledge, and information about other nations and other members of the world community living in those nations, with the understanding that this knowledge will make a graduate of our school a more informed voting U.S. citizen?

- Language and thinking: How do we design an unbreakable learning link between the study of a nation's: history, current events, geography, literature, art, music, political system, favorite sports, dance, food, rituals and belief systems, to the study of that nation's language?

- Schoolwide Readers to Leaders initiative: What effective methods can we utilize to give students the ability to read non-English authors and foreign language works of poetry, journalism, fiction and non-fictional works.

- Connecting foreign language study to future college/career study/career objectives: How do we convince students that foreign language/cultural studies are a critical component for strengthening an internship and scholarship/college/job application?

- The FLD's approach to selecting foreign language study offerings: Can the FLD be bold and strategically thoughtful in its selection of what foreign languages the school can and should offer (e.g., Chinese, Korean, Russian, Arabic, and Yoruba)? Can the FLD effectively respond to the dynamically changing future needs of the student, city/state, nation, U.S., and world economy?

- Interdisciplinary study opportunities: How can the FLD complement, cooperate, enhance, and expand on the work being done by the other academic departments (e.g., history, ELA)?

- Support for out-of-classroom activities, clubs, and programs: How can the FLD support informal/formal school activities such as a travel club, a non-U.S. menu restaurant and dining club, community service projects (e.g., serving as translators for senior citizens), world literature club, etc.?

- Fighting against summer foreign language loss: Can the FLD design a program utilizing summer foreign language immersion projects, periodic summer foreign language institutional get-togethers (e.g., colleges and foreign language institutes), foreign language practice at home DVDs and software as well as online foreign language teaching and learning sites to maintain the high level of foreign language acquisition when school is closed and classes are out of session?

- Celebrating diversity and nations study: How can the FLD support an annual FLD curriculum fair as well as a school Family International Food Celebration Day?

- A foreign language and cultural studies institute: Can we set up a system of FLD electives? What approaches, methods, and courses should be established that would prepare our students for internships, summer employment, study abroad programs, and future international college courses?

- The four-year requirement for foreign language study future benefits: Enhancing the student's college scholarship profile for future employment in situations such as the Peace Corps, governmental and private international aid and development agencies, the U.S. military intelligence services, international government agencies (e.g., NATO, the UN), the U.S. foreign service, foreign companies investing in the U.S. and/or U.S. companies operating outside of the U.S., health and literacy NGOs, etc. How does foreign language mastery enhance the student's personal/professional senior portfolio? But how do we "sell" the need for a four-year foreign language study sequence to students, parents, and in many cases the district?

- Identifying foreign language acquisition gifted and talented skills: Do we have a departmental strategy or plan to identify those students who are particularly good, gifted, and talented in foreign language and cultural studies? And, what do we do (programmatically) with those students once we identify them?

- Can the FLD offer advanced level foreign language classes and AP courses? Is there a standards-driven methodological instructional process by which we can effectively prepare students to take and pass advanced local, state, and national foreign language exams?

- How can a "study abroad" school semester break and/or summer program be part of the operational (credit earning) mission and purpose (knowledge and skills development) of the FLD?

The start of wisdom in public education is to be able to ask the right questions. So much of what does not work in our profession is due to the fact that we are either not asking the right questions or providing answers to good questions that are counterproductive and meaningless. A school's response to the above questions will serve as the blueprint for the philosophical and operational structure of its FLD. As with all academic departments in the school, it is critical to join the school's mission to the FLD's departmental mission, for that work will ultimately determine the success or failure of the school's foreign language program. And, so, the next step is the implementation of the responses to the critical FLD pedagogical questions.

Let's begin with the principal's leadership role! As mentioned previously, the principal sets the *Tone* for the level of serious attention that is paid to any effort, activity, or department in the school, based on the attention they give to that entity. In the case of high schools, there is an important organizational problem of understanding the difference between taking classes to simply fulfill a graduation requirement (important as that objective is) and taking classes to actually learn and hopefully master the content standards being taught. This is part of the reason why high school students can take three years of Spanish and then, at the end of those years, barely be able to even pretend to speak convincingly or read a nonfiction/fictional text written in Spanish! Holding the FLD to the same teaching, learning, and behavioral standards as other academic departments means the FLD must follow a curriculum pacing calendar, standards-based lesson plans, and engage in weekly rigorous written, reading, and verbal weekly assessments.

It is important to again note here, principals who consciously or unconsciously communicate through words and/or deeds that only those departments, classes, and content areas connected to an externally generated standardized (school performance assessment) exam are important, then the opportunity to create a *Culture* of academic excellence in departments like the FLD will be lost, which translates into an intellectual growing and cultural/linguistic loss for the students.

Okay, so let's go!

- Starting in the ninth grade, students must be welcomed into the world of serious Foreign Language Studies (FLS) as it is defined in your school. Perhaps, they experienced a less than (or even no) rigorous middle school FLS program of instruction. An aura and environment of high standards and expectations must be established early and often, as this department may not feel the pressure of having to face a graduation required standardized exam. The principal and the FLD team must create that academic pressure 'artificially' if you want students, parents, and some staff members to take these classes seriously. As is the theme throughout this book, the words, body language, and attention shown by the principal is a critical determining factor. If the principal sends the message that these classes are not important, then the entire school family will follow the principal's lead.

- Talking/Listening/Talking to Learn: Learning a language should be an active dynamically communicative experience. In every FLD class, including the ninth grade, the FLD teacher must appropriately utilize the foreign language immersion techniques of providing only the necessary minimum amount of English words during classroom instruction; and the FLD should have an organizational objective of maximizing the words and idioms of the foreign language being learned and minimizing the use of English as students progress upward in courses and grades. It has been my experience that this approach can be successful through the assistance of visual aids, teacher body language, helpful English (scaffolding) words that gives students hints and clues as to the meaning of the foreign word or phrase being used or studied. The FLD should have a well-thought-out strategic plan to ween students off of English in FLD classes over the course of four years. The underlying theory here is that humans don't attend a school to learn their native speaking language; language learning is a natural cultural experience that is best learned by way of the action-orientated verbal communication-community shared exercise.

- Principal and SBL team sets the *Tone* for student FLS seriousness in the general start of the school year orientation, Summer Bridge Program, and throughout the school year. Staff should stress the importance of the pursuit of a GPA, which can be strongly reinforced by establishing a school-based honor society (even as the school participates in the National Honor Society.) And starting in the ninth grade, the school must hold public academic award ceremonies, which have a broad spectrum of award categories, including recognizing students who have made meaningful progress to those who are top academic performers. As principal, you want to establish and maintain a culture of rigorous teaching and learning in every department and in every course in the school. The idea is to get all students into the habit of attempting to pass all of their classes with the highest grade possible. This is in furtherance of a school mission for each individual student, and that is to pursue personal excellence in every worthwhile and positive activity and effort!

- The principal should spend as much informal visitation time in as many FLD classes as any other academic class in the school building. As a principal, I made it a habit to personally perform informal and formal observations in classes that in no way were connected to any school evaluation-related standardized exam (e.g., Spanish 1, Chinese 2 as well as an elective offered by the FLD). This made both teachers and students in these classes aware that I was taking their teaching and learning seriously. And one of the best-kept secrets of successfully leading a school is to push for high academic rigor and expectations in those classes in which teachers and students might feel it is not necessary to put forth their best efforts. In an interesting way, the high stakes testing-related classes will generate their own organic sense of academic rigor intensity; but if you can build high academic standards "energy" in all classes, including electives, the level of rigor expectations will be distributed across all departments and school activities. Because a great deal of our instructional practices were linked to a project-based learning approach, this allowed me to observe (often at the request of students) many classroom student(s) project presentations. This action always provided a double reward: (1) My presence says that what the FLD is doing is important. (2) Despite what they say about "old folks," teenagers like to be recognized for their efforts. Over the years, so many students have tracked me down in the hall to say something like, "Mr. Johnson, please come to my fourth-period Spanish class to see my presentation on the agricultural economics of Peru." (They won't invite me unless they know that their presentation will be "slamming"!) How could I say no?

- As principal, I took the time (over several evenings and weekends) after every marking period to review the print-out of post-report card grades of all students. My practice was to have discussions with students about slipping and failing grades. To inspire this culture of schoolwide high academic achievement, it was important that I also discuss poor or failing FLD grades with the student earners of those grades. By not making a distinction between an unacceptable mathematics, science, PE, or foreign language grade, the message is sent and received; every department, content area, and class in this school is important!

- In staff meetings, the agenda and discussion should send the clear message that the FLD, what they do, and their contribution to the school's mission is vital. You must invest in professional development and long-term strategic plans with the leadership of that department. As a principled-principal habit, I rotated myself from time to time in order to attend different academic departmental meetings. Not only does this practice allow teachers in that department to have your undivided attention concerning their particular departmental concerns and needs, it also allows you as a leader to gain critical and important insight as to the unique challenges that each academic department faces as they all try to achieve the larger mission. And, as in any relationship, principal, you can't just say how much you love the FLD, you must show it, and that is primarily demonstrated by your presence from time to time in their departmental meetings!

- The principal must invest time, money, equipment, and material resources for in-class, out-of-class, and outside programs and activities for the FLD. A computer-based teaching/study foreign language learning lab is one of the ways that students can begin to think about perfecting their foreign language arts skills and to also think about the type of future career activities that will be available to those who are fluent in more than their native language.

- All students must be presented with a general FLD brochure (as with all departments), presenting the grading policies, departmental goals, objectives, expectations, electives, and advanced courses, academic competitions, classroom clubs, activities and programs sponsored in whole, or in part, by the FLD. All of these potential and real areas of interest should be reiterated in the orientation speech for each class. A syllabus is distributed for each course at the beginning of each semester and should include class objectives, expectations, grade-scoring rubrics for every aspect of the class, grading policies, study guides, due dates of papers, projects and presentations.

- The effective FLD must create a body of electives that could also strengthen the academic studies in other departments, as these courses provide the talented and interested FLD students with an opportunity to enjoy an advanced course of study related to their talents and interests in foreign language acquisition. For example, elective classes in Chinese Literature, Chinese History, or reading the works of Cervantes and Lorca. By offering these electives, the FLD is also making a statement about the serious work involved in learning and studying the language of another nation and its people.

- The FLD's program of foreign language study cannot be separated and, in fact, is fully immersed in cultural studies. The primary focus of the annual FLD curriculum/content fair is the exploration of not just a nation's language but also that nation's history, food/agriculture, music, dance, art, mythological, religious, moral, ethical belief systems, geological, anthropological, and archaeological distinct profiles of the nation. In other words, to fully appreciate and understand the language of the people, students must understand all of those cultural expressions that are created by, from, for, and explained by that nation's people.

- The FLD should be instrumental in setting up "Sister School" relationships, utilizing video conferencing technology. Not only will students be able to practice the language skills with high school students their own ages, they will also be able to engage in vigorous discussion as they compare and contrast teenage life in their distinctive countries. An added value for this program is for students to see how their counterparts in other countries take learning English (and schooling in general) so seriously, particularly when the Sister School partnerships are made with schools in countries that don't have the level of financial and material resources available to American students. These school partnerships/exchange programs will probably shock and slightly embarrass your students when they realize the amount of systemic, instructional, and learning investment made by the staff and students of other countries in their pursuit of mastering the English language!

- The FLD would be an excellent incubator and collaborator for school clubs and activities like International Electronic Pen Pals; A Travel

247

Club; an International Food Celebration; International Art, Dance, and Music Fair; United Nations Day Celebration; or an International Cuisine Club.

- The FLD should make sure they are part of the Career Day and College Week planning activities team to ensure that representatives connected to a foreign language study career (we invited members of the U.S. State Department) are present to make students aware of the many career options available for second-language learners. These include, translators, foreign language teachers, U.S. military services, journalism and broadcasting, domestic and international intelligence services, international corporate business persons, scientists, engineers, the Peace Corps, and U.S. citizen entrepreneurs who work in other countries.

- The FLD in cooperation with the History and English departments should lead the push to expand language/cultural studies through in-school and distance learning special seminars and presentations for nations that will play a critical future role in American foreign policy/economic relationships like Iran, Korea, Germany, Russia, China, Israel and other nations in the middle east, France, Japan, Canada, Brazil, Mexico, Caribbean nations, India, Pakistan, South and Central American nations, Nigeria, Egypt, South Africa, Ghana and other nations on the African continent.

- The FLD must establish important external partnerships as every department should have its own list of collaborative partnerships. These partnerships can provide multiple levels of financial, information, programmatic, and foreign country connections. Every foreign language being taught in our schools is also represented in multiple places in the U.S. by a friendship organization or society. One of the missions of these fraternal-friendship-societal organizations is to expand the learning of that nation's language and culture in the U.S.; they have a great deal of connections and could help with fundraising and proposal writing. There are also groups that encourage and support the expansion of global literacy on the part of American students like D.C.'s Center for Global Education and Leadership (CGEL). This is an excellent organization that is dedicated to improving international cultural literacy among U.S. citizens in general, and U.S. students in particular. There are many foundations that fund foreign language study fellowships, study abroad language and cultural studies, school-based and summer foreign language study programs, college scholarships, and the full funding of foreign language teachers and cultural studies. And, finally, there is the U.S. Department of State that funds and encourages through programs, the expansion of foreign language acquisition among American students.

Note to principals: There are many organizations, individuals, government and private agencies, and foundations that are extremely anxious about the terrible learning deficiency gap when it comes to American students and foreign language speaking and literacy. A great deal of this support and funding often goes unnoticed in many of our Title I school districts. One of the best and most productive tasks on the part of the entrepreneurial principal is to find a partner who will purchase, on behalf of the school, an online membership account to the Foundation Center (http://foundationcenter.org/). This resource will provide you with a large survey of foundational grant sources of support for all of the great in-school and outside FLD programs.

- Finally, the FLD must be a central player in the building of the school's mission of promoting the student personality profile that fully represents the school's definition of a truly educated human being. And being "truly educated" means being well versed in the language and culture of those who are outside of your circle of family, friends, community, state, and nation. The world is rapidly shrinking due to the expansion of technological communication innovation. Various places and fields are in desperate need of foreign language knowledge-competency practitioners. A high school that prepares its graduates to only be able to communicate with other English-language speakers and with little to no awareness of how people outside of the U.S. borders live their lives is underpreparing them no matter what domestic or foreign-based career they pursue. How often have we seen the job requirements change from the time a student enters in the ninth grade and then walks across the stage at graduation four years later; or the new fields and careers that emerge in one, five, or ten years! The effective school (and effective FLD) prepares students to succeed in the present as well as the future. The future suggests that linguistic and cultural literacy and proficiency will be a prized skillset (for workers

249

and managers). We also want our students to graduate with a sense of belonging to a worldwide community. No longer can nations through real or imaginary walls separate themselves from events occurring in other parts of the globe. The more our students are able to understand their planetary neighbors, the better the chances for mutually beneficial outcomes, as these different people encounter each other in moments of peace, war, natural disasters, health crises, economic, educational, sports and scientific research exchange. A cross-borders cultural-linguistic literacy effort is one of the best opportunities for promoting peace and prosperity between different nations. I have always believed that education is the fundamental key to a better world, and that better world begins with students who have a grasp of another nation's language and culture. The FLD is a critical department whose work is to make that part of the school's mission; the creation of competent and skilled cultural-linguists who can enhance communication and understanding across national borders promotes international peace, reduces world poverty and suffering, increases our national security as well as our capacity to work with other nations, while at the same time providing these linguists with opportunities to nurture and practice their own individual careers and personal aspirations. That is what we call a "win" in public education!

Chapter 15:
The Importance of the
History Department (HD)

"History is a clock that people use to tell their political and cultural time of day. It is a compass they use to find themselves on the map of human geography. It tells them where they are but, more importantly, what they must be."
— *John Henrik Clarke*

"We must go beyond textbooks, go out into the bypaths and untrodden depths of the wilderness and travel and explore and tell the world the glories of our journey." — *John Hope Franklin*

One of the joys of the principalship is that you get the chance to continuously fall in love with the many content/subject departments in your school. In fact, I believe the key to being an effective school-based leader is to feel a strong sense of appreciation and affection, especially for those departments outside of your specific content specialty area. As I stated earlier, the principal sets the tone with both the staff and students as to the level of importance of any school activity. Oftentimes, the importance of past events, people, and places is missed by high school students as they don't understand the relevance of something that has already happened. (But also because history education is too often presented so boringly poor in the K-12 educational world.) This means that every high school history department must be able to effectively respond to that possible "lack of interest" on the part of students, in a meaningful, powerfully dynamic and purposeful way. When developing or refocusing a history department, some of the questions the faculty must pose and answer are:

- Why are we requiring students to study past topics in the world, America, state, local, and civics-economics studies? Why is geography and cultural literacy important? Is this just about studying: "Dead people, dead places, and dead times?" Or, is there a larger and more important purpose at work here?

- What are the conceptual standards that would define the level of historical literacy required for a graduate of our school? What are the major (defining) historical movements, places, events, and people that we believe they should be familiar?

- How will the history department weave the study of anthropology, geology, political science, economics, social psychology, and social movements/ideas into the course of study?

- Very important, what is the history department's approach to current events, an important study that I believe has become a lost instructional art. Also can the history department link current events to past events and further to their possible influence on future events.

- How will the department pedagogically, and in a safe and productive way, address the difficult past and current conversations around topics of race, economics, ethnicity, LGBTQ, gender studies, immigration, religion, and power?

- If the high school has a theme (e.g., STEM-CTE, performing arts, fashion, and culinary arts), how can the history department reflect, reinforce, and enhance the school's thematic mission?

- In a Title I school, or a school with large numbers of students of color, or in racially, culturally, and economically diverse schools, what role (if any) should the history department play in empowering students for whom the larger society (as well as public education systems) has systematically and historically denied access to the full fruits of the American Dream? And how do we address these issues while fulfilling our ethical requirements of making the school a safe and comfortable space for White students and staff persons?

- How will the history department address the issues of the curriculum cultural deficiencies, inaccuracies, falsehoods, and in some cases, demeaning historical portrayals and treatment of certain people; regions and nations of the world; Central and South America; and the many regions of our own nation?

- What role will external resources and informal education institutions (e.g., museums, theatrical plays, and libraries) play in the realization and enhancement of the history department's academic mission?

- In what way will the history department courses, activities, and programs prepare students to become well-informed local, state, national, and world citizens?

- Can the history department establish and promote a curriculum and instructional approach that would create the opportunity for students to become well-informed voters, leaders, and politically conscious U.S. citizens in the democratic electoral process? Very important: How do we make sure that that every student graduates with a standard and/or working knowledge and understanding of the U.S. Constitution? The knowledge of the operational structure and organization of our national, state, and local government? An understanding of how the judicial, legislative, and executive branches of our government operate and interact?

- Can we provide them with a core political scientific literacy that would allow them to be knowledgeable of and be able to compare and contrast various systems of government in the past and present world?

- How can the history department collaborate with other academic departments? And how will this collaboration play out in a specialized and theme-focused (STEM-CTE, business-economics, art, drama, dance and music, ELA, culinary, etc.) high school?

- In what way can every history class in the school be an operational model of the techniques and methodologies that represent standards of the science of historiography (the study of history)? In other words, how do we get students to methodologically, analytically, and critically think and work like professional historians? In a school that is heavily driven by projects and research, how will that be demonstrated in our history classes?

- As in every department, we always want to make future career awareness a core learning objective. What career information can we make available to students in the specific (historian) or related (law, political science, etc.) areas of historiography, and how do we strategically plan to make students aware of those career opportunities? Further, also those careers that link historical studies with other careers interests (e.g., art historian, historical fiction and nonfiction writer, sociologist, or anthropologist)?

- What learning and behavioral objectives do we hope every student will master by the end of their high school experience? What are the standards and rubrics that define their level of historical literacy? How will we measure our success with the students beyond standardized exams?

The answers to these basic questions become the foundational and organizational principles and practices of the school's history department. They frame the department's identity, purpose, and mission. They should also be aligned with the school's overall mission.

The History Department's mission will drive its form and function

As is always the case, the *Cultural* establishment of an academic department's belief system begins in the ninth grade. That theoretical beachhead is established by making the case in the departmental brochure, course syllabus, and at the beginning of each class in the fall semester the important link between current, future, and historical events. This is an important starting place for the department and individual class teachers because it confronts the primary question of the students as to why they're there. "Because it's on your schedule" or "it's required" is not a sufficient response. The opportunity for a more effective learning environment occurs when the learner is personally invested, not just in the process, but in the acquisition of the learning objectives, concepts, and skills. There is evidence that a great deal of student enthusiasm for learning is based on the question of practical relevancy. Further, the lack of enthusiasm and the inability to make a personal connection to the subject matter will often fuel classroom discipline problems. Now, is every student in every class going to immediately become personally and passionately engaged with every academic topic? Perhaps not, for one of the purposes of education is to confront students with ideas, information, and knowledge they may feel (now) is irrelevant. Yes, it is their job as the emerging next generation to ask, "Why am I studying this?" And it is our job to answer that question in the best way possible. A *Cultural* characteristic of a highly effective history department is its ability to make the case to students as to why the study and analysis of "old places," past events, and "dead people" is critical to understanding our present state of affairs as well as greatly influencing our future and that the past itself is one big important learning lesson for so many spheres of life and human activities. We need, for example, to help students to understand how past wars have shaped the present geo-political-economic state of the world. That all of the laws, regulations and statues the students are subject to as young persons and as citizens are connected to acts (good and bad), events (some happy, some sad), and people (famous and infamous) from the past. The "why are we here" question must be answered before the students ask it (because they are thinking it even if they don't ask), on the first day of class, in every history class in the school, from ninth grade world history/civilizations courses to AP U.S. history! And one of the unifying answers delivered in all subject/content areas is that a thoughtful and working knowledge of (in this case) history is an attribute of what this school defines as an "educated human being."

Now that the department's teachers have established the rationale for the history course, the question now is, "What, and how, should they teach that history?"

The study of history (historiography) must be an honest effort, in both truth telling and truth revealing. Studying history should reveal the full and wonderful arc of human progress and development. However, it should also honestly confront when human behavior in the past displayed a deficiency of character, kindness, and compassion. We cannot design a pedagogy of history teaching that assumes that the students' intellects are too incapable or fragile to deal with the highs and lows of humanity's behavior throughout history. What we don't want to see is an American version of the kind of K-12 history syllabus that you see in places like North Korea. We can't avoid topics like the Armenian genocide, U.S. slavery, the past and continuing to present-day devastating effects of European colonialism, the terrible "ethnic cleansing" campaigns in many parts of the world, the treatment of Native Americans, or the unjust internment of WWII Japanese Americans. An important learning objective for all history classes is to expose students to those moments in history when we humans failed to display our bravest, compassionate, and best selves as well as those wonderful heroic moments when individuals and groups of people put forth great efforts to uphold and/or correct an injustice. Both those moments when we built "walls" of indifference and hatred as well

255

as those moments when we built bridges of love and concern.

I know that there is a current debate about how to best present American history. It should be said that historiography is not the same as cheerleading. We can teach students to celebrate America while at the same time applying the techniques of historical critical analysis in order to make the U.S. a better nation. We should resist any curriculum standards or textbooks that don't tell the truth about history. Any history curriculum that seeks to overstate the greatness and goodness of one group of people while diminishing and demonizing others is political propaganda and not good history pedagogy. A nation's history is essentially a story about that nation's human beings; and just like humans are not perfect, human history is not always a perfect story. But I think we make students better world and national citizens if we present U.S. or any nation's history in all of its full complexity, contradictions, strengths, and weaknesses. In this way, we can help students as they transition into adulthood to select what is true and good in their time period of history-making. We should also take care to correct any attempt to exclude the suffering, contributions, and triumphs of particular groups of Americans.

The Effective History Department (EHD) must also link its historiography to other content areas. A school should have as part of the EHD's syllabus a main theme/approach to the study of history, both required and elective courses that include important elements of the history of (in my case) science, technology, biographies of STEM practitioners, invention, and innovation. Any theme-based school can utilize that school's theme as a driver and focus of any history course's curriculum topics without abandoning the generally acceptable topic standards for the course. The great thing about historiography is that it is also a study of the culture of a continent, region, nation, and people. It is the study of creative and performing arts, agriculture, politics, sports, customs, language, commerce-economics, and its secular and non-secular belief systems. And so any specialized theme school can find topics in all history course curriculum for which the school can place a special emphasis. In the examples of my former schools, any historical study could be easily linked to understanding STEM as a critical variable and driver of historical events.

The study of history is not an abstract exercise that is value-free. The "whose history is it" question must be addressed in EHD classes. There must be an ethical conversation that runs throughout all classes; a reminder of how we should treat each other as fellow world citizens; a sense of the need for economic and social justice; and always important, the telling of necessary and sometimes inconvenient truths. For the authentic teaching of history, the "his" and "story" must be separated and deconstructed. In the telling of His-story, a discussion of who the *His* is, is (including asking why the "His" is even a His!) essential to the understanding of the purpose and meaning of the *story*. Equally important are those people who were/are unable to tell their (side of) the story.

The EHD curriculum must also seek to explain the present economic and geopolitical structures in which we presently live. For example, we had one Germany and Viet Nam and then two, and now one again. The EHD should reveal the social, political, cultural, religious, etc., evolutionary principles that created our present city, state, and world. And in what way will our present history (current events) determine our future, which will continue to affect the students, in many different and significant ways, long after they have left our school.

The effective EHD must be able to link, in a thoughtful and analytical way, the major current events and their historical "ancestors." It is impossible to understand and interact with nations like Nigeria, Russia, China, Japan, Germany, or our next-door neighbors Canada and Mexico without first understanding the historical process that led up to the present state of their relationship with the United States and other nations in the world. The EHD should employ a core teaching strategy that calls for a research methodology and analysis approach to the study of history. Always demonstrating that current events and conditions don't ever emerge without prior particular events and conditions.

The EHD must expose students to the instruments used to gather information on historical and current historical events. Students should be able to effectively read past and current newspaper articles and editorial content and know the difference! This exposure should also include other paper and online sources including magazines, journals, political commentary-essays, political cartoons, and photojournalism. Students should also be aware of the various multimedia sources of news and topical information such as National Public Radio/TV, film documentaries, cable news stations, CSPAN, and the History and National Geographic channels. Here two collaborations are important: (1) The need for the EHD to work in partnership with the school library/research center. (2) If the district does not provide it, the school should identify funding through a grant or partnerships to install teleconferencing/distant video learning centers along with the school having access to cable TV.

Important principal: The cable technology must be properly/restrictively man-

aged and monitored, just as you would student Internet use, or you might find yourself in the uncomfortable position of having to answer a reporter's (and your superintendent's) questions about why your students were watching an "unsuitable for children under 17" program in a school. Remember, it is not a contradiction to love them and at the same time not ever forget that they are teenagers!

The EHD can help with one of the biggest challenges high school educators face, and that is by utilizing an instructional approach to teaching history that helps students to clearly understand that past acts and decisions have profound and serious effects on future acts and decisions, particularly as it pertains to fully understanding one's available options. And just like we want the graduates of our science department to be able to think like a scientist, we want our EHD graduates to be able to think like historians. This is why the standard instructional approach to the EHD in all classes must be dynamic, document-rich, multisensory, and technology Internet-based. An EHD class should be able to transition between past and current events, compare and contrast past events in different eras and geographies. Making the same case that the science department's biology/environmental studies are making that ultimately there are no truly isolated events in the world. European ship building and navigational science and technology is absolutely linked to colonialism and the African slave trade. The history department of any high school runs a risk of producing "boredom studies" if it is promoting the teaching of history as old and insignificant news.

Professional historian skills should be central to the mission of the EHD's work, which means the bulk of the work done in EHD classes must be individual/group research project-driven. And as previously stated, the EHD must teach students to approach the study of history in the same way that they approach a STEM class. That means employing similar problem-posing-solving skills and methodology. We want students to gather information from a variety of sources; be open to counter narratives; form and test hypotheticals to go where the data, facts, and research leads them and to essentially model the work of a research historian. We start with global history because it is the best primer for American history, for you can't truly understand American history without understanding the influences of world historical events in the making of America. Global history also links the students to a strong cultural literacy foundation. And as a nation of immigrants, in every true sense of the words, world history is inseparable from American history!

The EHD must also provide students with a launching pad for civic involvement. There are ideas (and specifically American history and civics courses) that should encourage students to know and understand their local, state, and federal system of government. How is power exercised, expressed, manipulated, and utilized in these various governmental branches? We want students to emerge from EHD classes with a clear answer to the questions: what is executive, legislative, and judicial power, and how is it practiced and exercised? How, when, and why must these three centers of government interact with each other. Students should understand that even those who are not of voting age, or those who are, but choose not to vote, are not exempt from the decisions made by those citizens who do vote, as well as actions, policies, and laws enacted by our three branches of government. They should understand that these governmental decisions, in one way or another, will in a profound and personal way, dramatically affect every individual student in the class.

In summary: What operational practices should be put in place by the EHD team?

- Go beyond the textbook! Make sure the class is largely problem-solving, research/project-based, utilizing multisensory instructional methodology as well as multiple source materials and documents required as part of every course syllabus.

- Teach the students how to analytically consume and deconstruct the various sources of news. How to separate news reporting from editorial commentary and opinion. How to identify "fake" or incomplete news information. And in cooperation with the mathematics and science departments, how to properly read polling data, graphs, charts, research studies, and statistical information.

- The history classes in cooperation with the school library should rely heavily on research/project-based (both group and individual) activities in which students can actually engage in the work practiced by professional historians. After receiving the proper background information as well as being well-grounded in standardized research methodology techniques, students should be presented with challenging historical questions based on the course learning objectives. Rather than memorizing dates, places, and people, students should be asked to go deeper into analyzing the causes and drivers of historical eras; the role of geography in the shaping of human history and how human political economic history helped to shape geography; what people, organizations, secular and non-secular movements, political science theories, and philosophies helped to create historical events while at the same time shaping and influencing current and future events.

- The EHD (like all academic departments) should host a schoolwide history fair at which every student taking a history class must produce a research project/paper related to a major theme in that course. The entire history department should utilize a standard format (with the accompanying rubrics) for both the board and research paper presentations. Don't have students floundering around trying to individually "invent" the best practices for research paper presentations. The history class teachers should give them the standards for research paper presentations as well as the accompanying rubrics so that they can independently measure their own work product before it is presented publicly.

- The EHD should teach students how to conduct an oral history research/ interview project as an elective, or one of the required assignments in American history. This activity is also a wonderful intergenerational project when done in collaboration with a senior citizen center. It could help both teens and elders see each other in a more positive light.

- During the school day as well as a part of a spring/winter out-of-school assignment, each EHD class should assign a project on some aspect of local neighborhood history, historical architecture, and the changing community environment. All communities, whether urban or rural, are living historical, geographical, environmental, genealogical, and architectural historical lessons. And in almost every city and town in the U.S., there are always formal or informal local historians and historical societies; these individuals and organizations are more than happy to share their information with students. I've also found that local schools of architecture will have faculty and graduate students who can assist as teaching tour guides on a class historical architecture study trip. It is also an excellent opportunity for students to study the science of map making and using. (Many public libraries will have maps and archival photographs of neighborhoods and buildings very often including archival pictures of the school the students presently attend!)

- During the career day/college week, the EHD must take the lead in recruiting presenters and designing activities that inform students of the career opportunities that exist for history majors. Don't forget public school history teaching! Students should be exposed to history-related careers such as law, political science, economics sociology, social psychology, fiction/nonfiction writing, library science, natural historical museums, and historical (graduate school) research.

- The EHD should create partnerships with natural and specialized history museums, libraries, local landmark commissions, and the librarians/archivists that maintain the archives of local newspapers. These partnerships can include inviting guest lecturers/presenters to speak to classes, class trips, or acquiring assistance for students with their class and EHD curriculum fair research projects.

- Through the use of Internet teleconferencing, the EHD should form partnerships with a local college history department for topical presentations in history. (This is an excellent resource for advanced, elective, and AP history classes.) In NYC, we formed a teleconferencing partnership with the Columbia University (CU) History Project, which gave our students access to CU faculty members who possessed a deep understanding and knowledge of a particular historical event or person. The good news is that these professors could make their presentations directly from their office, and the students felt like they were sitting in a college class—and they were!

Note to principals: One important thing you must do with all of your AP classes is to actually make them feel and act like a college class. I always met with my AP teachers at the beginning of the school year to see how we could get the classes to really "feel" and perform like a college course. This was also part of the AP course student orientation where they were informed that this class was going to be very different from all the other classes they had been taking in high school. That means more independence, more student responsibility, and a rigorous testing and evaluation system that is based on the standards and expectations of the AP exam. I know it is popular in some districts to just dump students of color (no matter how unprepared) into AP classes so as to make the access equality numbers look good. But these (costly) classes should be approached in a serious manner with the thought of having all of the students in the class pass the course and the AP exam with a valid transferable score. Even if the college they plan to attend does not accept AP credit, having AP course credit on their transcript is a big plus. Also, the AP course should position the student to perform at a high level when taking that course again in college. If the AP credit is accepted and used for a college transcript, students can use this AP course credit to their advantage. By having one less class on their schedule they could devote more time to their other college classes and thus drive up their GPA. And AP course credit is also a way for students to reduce their college cost and debt after they graduate.

- The EHD should be the organizers of a "Time Capsule" project club for students. This club, in cooperation with civil engineers from the military or construction companies, can organize a schoolwide project that every department can participate in preparing digital documents, music, pictures, and videos placed in a specially designed metal container with instructions to open by a team of archaeologists, anthropologists, and historians in some designated future date. Not only will students gain a familiarity with the beforementioned career opportunities, they will also gain a greater understanding and appreciation for the historical artifacts they explore during the course of their history classes. This project in one of my schools also generated many interesting class discussions around a conceptual understanding of "the future," artifacts, and archeology. "But we won't be around to see when they dig it up!" One practically minded teenager mentioned to me one day in the hall; "But you will be there," I responded, "just maybe not in person!" With this club/project forcing the students themselves to become subjects and creators of history, both the present and future value of historical activities becomes something real and personal.

- The EHD should offer in cooperation with other department elective courses The History of Science, Technology and Innovation, African-American History, a women's history/studies course, Labor history, Chinese history, The History of Architecture, and Military History.

- There is a great possibility that the EHD and that entrepreneurial principal can recruit a presently working or retired expert in one of these specialized areas to teach a volunteer single elective course (for the cost of lunch).

Note to principal: The SBL team should develop a school volunteer plan/orientation. Providing a volunteer package including a brochure and a quick answers guide (who to reach out to, what to do, what not to do, what to do when or if...). A comprehensive school volunteer plan must be designed and completed before you recruit volunteers. Many talented, knowledgeable, and skilled Americans are presently retiring in great physical condition. They may have spent a lifetime in a rewarding private-public sector, college teaching, the military, or some professional career, and now they are in a place to donate their services and wisdom in a positive and productive setting. Recruiting one or two of these individuals to teach a single class is no small matter, as it amounts to saving the school one class percentage of a full-time teacher's salary. You'll need to provide a separate orientation for them and the students, because you don't want the students to provide their version of the rules, procedures, policies, and regulations to the volunteer instructor. You will also need to follow the standard school district fingerprinting/background screening procedure (check your school district, local and state regulations and procedures, as they pertain to volunteers working and/or teaching classes in a public school). In their orientation students should be made to understand that admission to this elective class being taught by a visiting scholar is a privilege, and there will be no tolerance for that privilege being abused—that is, put the fear of the principal in them! Some professionals who I have been able to recruit to volunteer in one of my schools told me that the reason they stopped volunteering at a previous school was due to student disciplinary behavior issues. People who are retired from a stressful and strenuous career don't want to volunteer in a place of turmoil, confusion, and disorder. You will need a coordinator or assistant principal to closely monitor the class for the first few weeks. And, finally, you should put a tough school aide or para in the room to manage the logistics and paperwork of the class but also to keep the students in check! This volunteer teaching project can become a critical part of the school's instructional program and mission. At Phelps ACE, we actually had a ninth grade-required CTE majors survey class that was taught completely by volunteers from places like Diversified Educational Systems, Inc. (DES), Clark and Turner construction companies, the office of the Architect of The Capitol, The American Institute of Architects, Construction Trade Unions, etc. That wonderful volunteering activity represented a free full teacher position (a "unit" in principal budget speak)!

Chapter 16:
Creating an Effective Career Technical Education (CTE) Program

The "shop" classes at my 1960s Brooklyn's Simon F. Rothschild Junior High School taught me an early lesson about public education's approach to "physical" and "mental" work. For the gifted and talented students, it was an opportunity for us to connect our academic and creative educational experiences into some practical application. But for some classes (and students) in the school, the shop class experience was seen as an entry portal into some kind of vocational field that was characterized by physical, not mental, skills. That experience reflected the terrible and destructive divide that existed, and to a lesser damaging extent, still exist in public education. This is the false divide between the works a person does with their hands, as opposed to the work that is done with their brains. This artificial division has severely limited the emergence and development of a promising effort in the educational field that recognizes that "hands" and "minds" can't be disconnected, and that idea is one of the core assertions of a really good Career Technical Education (CTE) program.

I realized painfully in one school district how hard it is to move the public's (and professional educators') misunderstanding and collective belief system away from the traditional "vocational educational" model into the modern ideas of Career Technical Education. At this very moment, professional "experienced educators," working and retired, all over this nation are saying, with good intentions, that for students who are struggling academically, poor readers, unable to pass standardized exams, etc., that we need a program that will allow these students to "work with their hands!" This is essentially, the modern version of the approach of my 1960s vocational education thinking era.

The overwhelming majority of us working in the education profession are more than likely the products of a liberal arts education with a strong emphasis on the humanities. Now, I actually believe that an educational program rich in arts and humanities is essential for the education of all students. But often wrongly and quietly embedded in this approach is a pronounced bias that favors mental labor over physical labor. In public education, our primary currency is books and reading, theoretical math algorithms over functional applications—the college track has always been the major leagues of public high school learning, despite our pronouncements to the contrary. And we professional educators are probably the products of a private or public school system that promoted the idea that smart kids focus on academic classes (working with their brains) and "slower kids" need to focus on shop/vocational classes (working with their hands). Of course, since race and class are always in play in America, the kids who were more likely to be better at working with their hands than their brains, and therefore assigned to vocational programs, would be students who were poor Whites, Black, and Latino. But ironically, we now find ourselves in a position of asking an authentic CTE approach to rescue our nation from a deeply applied technical skills readiness hole in which our public and professional misconceptions of how academic knowledge is expressed has placed us. We have lost all sense as to the many ways in which art, science, and mathematics are utilized in solving real-world day-to-day problems. As a teacher taking students on a 1980s college tour, I was able to fully appreciate the tremendous applied STEM work of those 1890s Tuskegee University students in designing and building the still-standing structures on that campus. But my experience of seriously learning about the unbreakable link between theoretical and practical work would emerge when I became principal of a STEM-CTE high school, for there is no better classroom for an educator to fully understand and appreciate the level of complexity found in many educational initiatives than when you are responsible for a young person's future success or failure. It is at that moment when I came into a full understanding of the pedagogical mess we professional educators made of vocational education. These mixed and wrong messages are deeply embedded in our pedagogical language; a common phrase voiced by educators, "All students (re: the "dumb and dumber") need not or should not go to college!" This statement is dangerous only because the concept is really motivated by the belief that the primary reason for not being "college worthy" is due to a "natural lack of academic capability." And then what is also often connected to that assertion is a second well-meaning, but poorly thought out, embedded belief. "We need to have eighth- through twelfth-grade programs that would allow the chronically truant SPED, ADHD, and the persistent and incurably misbehaving students to have a pathway to graduation and a useful life after high school." Two immediate problems emerge from these two bad assertions, the second being fatal to the image of vocational education: (1) The fact is that pursuing a professional career in any applied technology-construction skills field does in fact

266

require a high school-level mathematics and reading literacy skills, the ability to apply (even if it is not named) the scientific method, discipline, creativity, and thoughtful problem-solving skills. And with computer-related technology entering every aspect of the construction trades, there is a requirement that skills trades' persons also grow their technical skills, as the role of technology grows in their profession. (2) With such negative recruitment criteria (the "academically slow" and/or the behaviorally and disciplined challenged) for admission to a vocational education middle or high school program, it would not be strange that a large segment of parents and/or students would not find these programs attractive. The hope and promise of CTE is that we can revisit, restart, and revolutionize our entire thinking and approach to vocational education. And based on my previous experience with this effort, no CTE program can be truly successful in a school district unless that district engages in a system-wide and community-wide explanation as to what CTE is and what it is not.

Clarifying the differences between vocational and career/ technical education

One of the great challenges we face (and too often fail at) in public education is the organization of our pedagogical practices and curriculum theory in such a way that it matches up with the world and society the student will be facing in the near and far future after they graduate from our school system. It is extremely difficult to identify new careers that will be added, or in many cases, modified and/or eliminated in the next five years; so, projecting twenty or thirty years into the future is really difficult. Which is why an effective school's academic program will seek to equip students with a bank of skills and competencies that are flexible enough to transfer over time to many possible career opportunities. Further, for many of us school-based leaders who happen to be baby boomers (and even those "baby boomer lite" folks who were born five to ten years after us), we must fully appreciate the amazing seismic shift that has occurred in the world of careers and work. My professional work life story of entering a specific career early in life, and then sticking with that same career until retirement, may in fact become a societal behavioral artifact; indeed, most of the young people in the 2019 high school graduating class will probably face a future where employment is translated to mean being seriously engaged in multiple different assignments on a single job and/or multiple jobs as well as careers over the course of a work-lifespan. Being able to transfer and translate a "survey" of applicable skills in multiple employment settings could be seen as a positive employable attribute. There could be a declining interest on the part of employers as to the specific undergraduate and graduate/professional school degree that is earned. Specialized training (e.g., nursing, computer coding, forest ranger, environmental biologist, anthropology, or civil engineering) will still exist, but individuals may decide to take advantage of longer and healthier life spans by spending a third of their employment life in a field like the above professions, a third in law, teaching, or some combined extension of their career choice with another professional career. It is also clear that technology will continue to assert its ever-growing presence in the world of manufacturing. Increasingly, many corporations and the stockholders and investors they serve will find it simply irresistible to not build manufacturing production centers that, in part or whole, employ shift robots to maximize profits and minimize human issues. The great danger we face in public education is not just the unprepared students that we send into the present job market, but it is also not graduating students equipped with a set of skills and competencies that will make these students employment relevant and competent for future job markets. In the construction trade industry, science, technology, and mathematics continue to influence and drive the speed, efficiency, and effectiveness in many of the traditional construction trades like carpentry, plumbing, welding, HVAC/R, electricity and masonry. Not only are STEM principles and practices gaining a greater theoretical foothold into the operational practices of these career fields, the skills trades are also finding that there is an ever-expanding connection to different areas of academic study: health, safety, and environmental concerns; invention and innovative ideas for tools and equipment; the use of laser technology and robots; sophisticated technical probes and measuring instruments; and the almost universal expansion of computers in construction equipment; computer usage by way of desktop, laptop, and handheld machines. Further, students who want to translate their skills trades knowledge into an opportunity to serve in a supervisory and/or an entrepreneurial role will need an academic foundation that will give them the capacity to expand their non-skills trades competencies (e.g., business management; human relations-psychology; customer service; job proposal writing; the ability to read, interpret, and respond to codified labor agreements as well as governmental laws and regulations; mastering the rubrics of budgeting; time management; and cost analysis). It is also probably true that the best creative, dynamic managers and entrepreneurs are those individuals who have been exposed to the arts, literature, philosophy, psychology, history, and ideas, people, and cultures other than their own. As greater communication and human interaction increases, success in the world of business for both employees and employers will favor those with the largest cultural-linguistic literacy capacity. Finally, there is without a doubt a growing societal and economic need for the development of a cohort in our labor force whose knowledge and skills capabilities consist of a high school education CTE education and a two-year technical/community college skills professional certification program. In STEM careers there is a tremendous need for non-engineering applied technology manufacturing positions that cover everything from biomedical engineering, computer-aided manufacturing, automated farming and food production, computer-based products, software/programming skills, building automated machines that build other machines, Cisco networking, robotics development, maintenance and repair. Needless to say, all of these high-demand employment opportunities require students to have more than the basic hands-on skills.

This is also true of four-year and post-graduate professional education programs. In medicine, our rapidly expanding (and longer-living) senior population could mean that we may want to expand the numbers of nurse practitioner and physician assistants to meet this growing medical need. The positive growth of complex technology-based solutions to everyday human needs will also require a greater level of problem-solving skills on the part of the technical support and maintenance practitioners. As society creates an environment where more and more citizens find themselves in an expanded integrated relationship with technology, outsourcing to foreign nations will neither be viable, customer-friendly, desirable, or even safe for national security. The U.S. will absolutely need to step up its STEM game to stop the denigration of applied STEM employment.

I learned an important lesson as a principal in partnership with skills trades unions. And that is the awareness that even the traditional trades' skills apprenticeship programs require a strong foundation in good reading and reasoning ability, problem posing-solving skills, and mathematics applications knowledge and skills. One needs only to take a moment to review the standard construction trades apprenticeship program syllabus and take a second visual walk through the different construction trade apprenticeship program textbooks. Once in frustration as a principal of a CTE school, I was trying to convince a group of middle school educators that pursuing a high school CTE program was difficult and challenging. They were confused about the difference between vocational education and career/technical education. Since everything you need to know in life you learn as a teacher, I thought this was a great time in this lesson for visual aids. I pulled from the bookshelf in my office the various CTE majors' textbooks our students would be utilizing during their four years at Phelps ACE high school. I also shared with them a few of the textbooks that are utilized in the trade union apprenticeship programs. Because they were professional educators, there was an immediate awareness (and surprise) at the required reading level of the books, the extent of required safety information, the huge amount of technical knowledge required of a welder, carpenter, electrician or plumber, and further, the amount of general science and mathematics knowledge that was required of the students. I spent that day, and many of my days, in Washington, D.C., explaining to people that preparing young people for admission to a trade skill apprenticeship program was a serious and challenging task as students had to master both theoretical and practical (application) objectives. Students who chronically failed classes had poor attendance and punctuality, exhibited a lack of discipline, and engaged in habitual behavioral problems were not the standards for a model high school CTE candidate. In fact, an individual student with severe control and behavioral problems constituted a greater danger to themselves and other students if they pursued a CTE program. I finally went on to explain that the way standardized assessments work in the CTE world is that they are equally divided between written Q&A and extended answers exams, and individual demonstrated proficiency of skills and procedures; the CTE students are required to pass all of these different and challenging assessment tools.

Unfortunately, liberal political progressive good intentions have often been the greatest contributors, particularly in the case of poor students and students of color, of a great source of student academic failure and underachievement. Career Technical Education is the true educationally progressive alternative to this line of thinking. In part, because CTE does not begin in a place of "fixing student brokenness." CTE seeks to match talent and skills with a strong balance of theory and practice. CTE also affirms what many of us professional educators always believed, that the definitions of learning, "intelligence," talents, and gifts were too narrowly defined. And, further, many of us suspect that these definitions have their origins in gender, race, and class discriminatory theories. Finally, the greatest gift of CTE to students is that unlike the old vocational education that existed on the outskirts (exile) of the public education mission, Career Technical Education, if done properly, forces itself to be placed in the center of the school's academic work and mission. Students who are enrolled in CTE courses and programs, more likely than not have a strong sense of what they want to do after high school graduation. Linking high school work to a career in the world after high school is that critical connection every effective high school educator is passionately working hard to establish. And having a CTE major family of teachers and fellow students gives the CTE student a sense of camaraderie, shared purpose, and mutual support on the high school path to graduation. The special presentations and lectures, internships, industry-related summer jobs, and CTE-focused field trips, along with the continual exposure and interaction with powerful and influential industry leaders and skilled professional practitioners, provide students with a daily reminder of that goal they are pursuing. In fact, I would take a chance and go even further here and say those students I observed who were serious and fully engaged in a CTE program were the most focused, goal-orientated, and "end objective" minded students in my high school! The structure of the CTE program positively affected their punctuality, attendance, and behavior during the course of a year. The CTE program was also a great incentive for the enrolled students to successfully pass all of their academic subjects since the CTE classes are rigidly sequentially structured for each of the four grade levels; failing a class and then being forced to take that class the next semester when a CTE-required course could be scheduled at the same time could cause havoc on a student's schedule and even create a danger of not being able to acquire the CTE certification by the twelfth grade. I have employed a lot of techniques over my eleven years as a principal to get students to pass classes, but one of the most powerful influencers and enforcers were when the students exhibited a self-directed and self-managed response to the high school experience. And no one was better at this than that CTE student who feared falling out of CTE program completion sequence by failing some non-CTE course. Failing any class on their schedule placed a CTE student in danger of not receiving a CTE diploma, not being able to take a certification exam, thus weakening their chances of gaining admission to the competitive post-high school trade skills apprenticeship programs.

Baking bread and growing roses: Why a joint study program of CTE courses and the school's other academic offerings are a good and necessary fit!

My school CTE program students face three important challenges on their path to high school graduation. The first is that they must satisfy the district admission graduation requirements. The second is the successful completion of their CTE major requirements (certification exams, departmental course of study, and/or project development). And the third is that all graduates must be "college ready" and eligible to attend a two- or four-year college, even if they choose to not do so. It is important that the school establish these graduation requirements if they expect to truly operate and function, in deeds not just words, as an authentic and highly successful CTE school. This academic profile automatically demands that a CTE school not be bound by the standard staffing, labor, and work schedule agreements and restrictions. The most obvious reason is that CTE students can't possibly complete all three graduation requirements in a normal school day. The second requirement of such a school is that they must have the flexibility to employ CTE departmental teachers with specialized skills who may or may not fit the "standard" academic profile of a public school licensed teacher. Optimally, a CTE program with these type of teachers should have a director or AP with a certified teacher background and, depending on the size of the department, a dedicated instructional coach. The third challenge for a CTE school is that by definition they cost more to operate; there is just no way around this reality. These schools have unique but necessary architectural (specially designed learning spaces) requirements. CTE schools require specialized equipment, furniture, and often unique electrical wiring. There are machine and equipment servicing contracts as well as the replenishment supply costs. The building operational and maintenance costs for the schools are also higher. The district must make a long-term budgetary commitment to the success of the school, if it is to work. Additionally, any district hoping to create or redesign a CTE school must include for both academic and financial reasons a strong industry partnership program, access to a full-time grant writer who could also coordinate an alumni organization, multiple fundraising campaigns, a resource and materials acquisition rolodex of supporters, and a "connections-rich" financial fundraising nonprofit foundation that is separate and independent from the school district's fundraising efforts. The funds raised by the school's various CTE programs and activities should not substitute for the district's long-term additional funding for the school; funds raised by the school should supplement and not replace the district's special allocation. It is critically important that a board of education (local school district), district leadership officials, teacher unions, elected officials, parents, and the community at large understand how CTE schools/programs are different and what that difference means for prospective students, admission requirements, graduation requirements, summer and weekend programs, organization and scheduling, school building leadership, budget, scheduling, labor-contract agreements, instructional and non-instructional staffing.

Managing and leading a CTE high school staff

One of the key components of a CTE high school leadership team is the expanded commitment that must be made to instructional coaching. In almost every situation, a CTE school will need to employ a considerable number of non-traditional teachers. These teachers may have spent a previous professional life in a particular industry or have been engaged in a specific skill or craft area other than professional education. The school must craft a comprehensive pre-assignment and ongoing professional development plan for these teachers. I understand that there is this popular notion held by those outside of professional education that anybody can teach. For sure, the myth that anybody can teach (or be a principal) has done great harm to the profession, and even greater harm to children. Teaching is a difficult and complex craft, even for those who have graduated from a conventional undergraduate teacher education program. Obviously, the long-term and sensible plan for the development of CTE teachers is to provide ongoing professional development; another possibility is to provide in-school, after-school and weekend course offerings found in traditional teacher education programs. Ideally, these "uncertified" CTE teachers can earn official teacher certification if the project is done in partnership with a local college that offers a teacher education program. Perhaps the agreement with the district could be something like: For every year the CTE teacher spends in the teacher education program, he or she must in turn commit to work in the district/school for a year or repay the tuition. And "super-ideally" would be for the colleges to set up a teacher education program specifically focused on producing CTE teachers!

But in the present and immediate future, CTE schools more than likely will need to recruit CTE teachers who have no prior training in pedagogy. And, so, the school must set up an "in-house" concentrated professional develop-

273

ment "mini-course" if these teachers are to be successful. This course should start over the summer prior to the fall semester of their teaching assignments (more, but necessary cost) I would in some cases even say that these pre-teaching classes would be equally beneficial to first-year teachers emerging from a traditional teacher training program. Further, placing these two groups of teachers together can be mutually helpful, particularly with the inclusion of a rigorous and robust standard teacher routines, a crash course in adolescent stages psychology and a "What to do when and if" component. Below are the key topic areas that should be covered in these pre-teaching classes:

- There should be a new teacher "this is how we do it" handbook that covers everything from attendance taking/recording procedures to bulletin board standards.

- What is the school's mission, and how is that mission actualized and duplicated in every classroom?

- An overview of the key developmental psychology issues that particularly pertain to teenagers.

- The legal and ethical responsibilities of a mandated reporter.

- "Who is who" in the school, and what is their role and function? Who is the principal, assistant principal, departmental chairperson, program coordinators, guidance counselors, Special ED supervisors and teachers, school nurse, Dean-ISS coordinator, school safety officers, custodians, payroll officer, et cetera?

- What is curriculum? What are standards? What are rubrics? What is a pacing calendar? Why is a pacing calendar important?

- Special Education.

- School lesson plan standards: sections of the lesson plan, how to write a lesson plan, and how to deliver a lesson plan.

- How we approach exams and student assessments in this school.

- Overview of our student population.

- Legal issues: the do's and don'ts of being a teacher. The written and "unwritten" rules concerning teacher-student relationships (even new teachers who graduate from formal teacher education programs are sometimes sketchy on this topic). Those subtle and not-so-subtle, seemingly helpful, and sometimes well-meaning things that get teachers into trouble! The guidelines for appropriate and inappropriate teacher-student interactions.

- Working effectively with your department chair and departmental colleagues.

- What is effectiveness, efficiency, and efficacy?

- Professional dress attire, language, and behavior.

- Effective partnership strategies for working with the school-based instructional coach.

- What are formal and informal observations?

- How to make the most out of an assigned teacher/mentor experience? In some districts, mentors are assigned by the central office or college program. I didn't get in the way of that process even though I didn't particularly like it. However, I always, in addition to the district assigned mentor, assigned my own teacher-mentor to first-year teachers because this particular teacher would understand and be able to convey our school's mission and culture to that new teacher.

- Classroom safety and behavioral standards. School discipline expectations, codes, and procedures.

- Why our academic rigor and high expectations philosophy is to "Teach them hard and make them like it!"

- Security and safety procedures (e.g., fire drills, intruder alerts and procedures, student illness or injury).

- Classroom management.

- Effective parent communication/dialogue.

- "Open School" day or night, parent conferences, practices and procedures.

- "What to do when _____" (e.g., you get sick at the start or in the middle of class, you call a student's house and a parent curses you out, a student cheats on an exam or commits plagiary on a research paper, a student asks for a loan, etc.).

- Q&A session: the only bad questions are the ones you should have asked (but didn't) before you started teaching your class!

The initial sessions can serve as the general overview of the most critical areas of interest and concern for the new teacher. But these topics should continue to be covered in greater depth by way of weekly professional development sessions for CTE and first-year teachers. These sessions should be a joint effort of the principal and rotating teams of departmental chairpersons and the school-based instructional coach. The principal, APs, departmental chairpersons, and the instructional coach should also offer a daily (voluntary for the teachers) debriefing and Q&A session for CTE and first-year teachers. This after-school support meeting should be made available for the CTE/first-year teachers' entire first year of service. At the beginning of the school year, differentiate most of the professional development sessions. Placing veteran teachers in the same professional development settings as CTE or first-year teachers wastes the veteran teachers' time and stifles the asking of critical and necessary "rookie" questions by new teachers. If possible, the school should also create a dedicated Teacher Professional Development Center (TPDC), which can serve as the working and resource hub of the school-based instructional coach; the principal will need to invest in equipment and materials for the instructional coaches' workshops and for teacher acquisition of classroom/lesson plan/lesson presentation resources. For CTE teachers in particular, the TPDC can be an extremely vital resource, as they attempt to quickly learn pedagogy as well as school practices and procedures. It is also important that as the principal and the SBL team sets up the formal and informal classroom visitation schedule for the year, the CTE teachers, particularly those who are teaching for the first time, will receive the bulk of formal and informal observation, time, and feedback. The CTE departmental chair, the principal, and AP or instructional coach should literally collaborate with the CTE teachers (and first-year teachers to the extent that they need that level of support) in the development and writing of their first two to three months of lesson plans. The objective here is to be proactive in the professional development effort. You absolutely don't want CTE/new teachers to "drift," get frustrated, and struggle unnecessarily; and we don't want teachers to fail because that means students fail!

Note to principals: If you and your SBL team don't have a prudent system of triaging your informal and formal observations/classroom visits for the first half of the school year, then you are, as they say, "cruising for a bruising!" You can always modify the plan in the first or second half of the school year—that is, push a veteran teacher up in the schedule who is showing some signs of instructional practice/classroom management "fatigue" and/or weakness. Or, pull back slightly, but not completely in intensity, for that first- to third-year teacher who is performing like an instructional all-star. But in every case, and for every year, you will surely need to get into the classes of CTE teachers and first-year (as well as second- to third-year) teachers early and often. I would also add to that list veteran teachers who transfer into your school. Bad pedagogical thinking can be (fatal to the school's Culture) "contagious," the breeding medium often being the teacher cafeteria/lounge. Also get in quickly because poor instructional practices can quickly and easily become bad work habits; those bad instructional habits are much easier to detect and eliminate when they occur early in a teacher's career. Conversely, they are harder to eliminate once they become a comfortable and reliable part of a teacher's standard teaching repertoire.

The profile of a CTE high school student and graduate

As with any effective high school academic department, the place to begin its overarching philosophical, structural, and operational strategy is to ask the important question, "What are the characteristics that describe and define a graduate of our CTE department?" For that student who successfully completes a four-year CTE major program, the following expectations should be realized:

- All CTE students must take and pass a first (ninth grade) full year CTE survey class. The rationale and purposes of this class are:

  - Allow students to learn a particular CTE area of study once they are exposed to that CTE topic. Students are surprised during the CTE survey class experience that they not only discover an unknown passion for a CTE topic, they often also discover a dormant talent during the course. The CTE survey class offers students a "time-safe" second chance to re-select their area of CTE concentration.

  - The CTE survey class offers students the chance to see the interaction and inter-relatedness of seemingly different careers; it also gives students the opportunity to think about combining two presently existing career objectives or creating a completely new job description.

o   A ninth grade, one-year CTE survey class will allow students to rotate and take an introductory class in each of the content areas of the CTE program. Based on this one-year experience, students will be asked to select a CTE path of study. This class can take place in a normal forty- to forty-five-minute class period, and the credit earned in this class will go toward satisfying the CTE graduation requirements. This will add an additional class to every ninth-grader's schedule. The only exception would be the engineering CTE sequence; this should start in the ninth grade, preferably with students who have taken algebra 1 in the eighth grade or algebra in the high school's Summer Bridge Program. The reason is that students seeking to be admitted to a college engineering program should have taken calculus no later than the twelfth grade. The CTE survey class rotation can last anywhere from three days to three weeks based on the information and skills requirements for the topic and should include a wide spectrum of presenters from specialty areas within that job description. For example, carpenters who make furniture and those who work in building construction. Or, masons who work on housing-related structures like walls and paved walkways, and those who do historical building restoration. In this way, the students can be exposed to the full diversity of job categories in the field. In the ninth-grade engineering program, the students should be exposed to the many categories of engineering (civil, electrical, chemical, transportation, industrial, etc.) All of these ninth-grade introductory classes can be co-taught utilizing a skilled practitioner in the particular CTE category along with a traditionally licensed teacher in the CTE department. All visiting instructors should receive a brief orientation to familiarize them with the school's practices/procedures, rules, and regulations that govern public school education. The success of this survey class also depends on the school/CTE department building strong collaborative partnerships. Although these visiting professional experts are volunteering their time, the school community should appreciate the tremendous donated sacrifice and cost these companies and government agencies are making by providing their paid employees time off to teach at a public school. Although it is not a qualifying criterion for the success of the CTE survey course, if at all possible, the school and CTE department should hint carefully that a diversity of professionals (presenters of color, women, and those with disabilities) would be greatly appreciated.

- o Finally, in the construction trades sections of the CTE survey class, girls are forced to discover how talented and gifted they are in areas often identified as male careers. I have seen girls excel in areas like the welding and plumbing sections of the yearlong CTE survey class, and then those same girls go on to be top welders and plumbers as they make a full commitment to a CTE certification program.

- If a district is building a brand-new CTE high school or refurbishing an existing school building, the investment must be made to make the architecture and construction of the building itself a major part of the CTE teaching curriculum, and that would include putting the school in position to seek and achieve LEED (Leadership in Energy and Environmental Design) platinum status.

- There is a dual-certification graduation requirement for CTE students. This means that the students have met the college-going requirements for admission to either a two-year or four-year college as well as meeting the specific credit CTE graduation requirements.

- The school's Construction Trades CTE course of study follows, in a prerequisite format, for the course of study found in the post-high school skills trades' apprenticeship school curriculum—except in certification programs such as Cisco and Microsoft, where students can actually be fully certified to work by the time they graduate from high school.

- Students should be exposed to many different aspects, skill levels, supervisory and job categories, descriptions in a given industry or trade (e.g., underwater welding, historical maintenance and restoration in masonry and carpentry).

- The CTE program must utilize to the greatest extent possible, the actual tools and equipment that are used by professionals working in the field and where that is a challenge (e.g., heavy construction vehicles and equipment), field trips and simulation technology should be employed.

- A senior project should be completed when it is required, for example, a performance, culinary presentation, original fashion design, architectural "green building" design or engineering innovation service project. Or, the students can do a group senior project across many different CTE major areas of concentration, like designing and building a school campus green house.

- Students should successfully pass the CTE major certification exams, end-of-course assessments, written and practicum admission-qualifying exams for admission to a CTE post-high school training program, and/or a specific construction trades apprenticeship school.

- Optimally, a CTE student will be able to spend at least one semester or enroll during the summer in a mentorship program, internship, work study experience that is connected to that student's CTE area of concentration.

- The CTE program's instructional model challenges and ultimately empowers students to be equally proficient in theoretical and project/performance-based learning and assessment. There is no learning they engage in that is not connected to practice and no practice that is disconnected from the theoretical learning. The CTE department is essentially the praxis heart of the school.

- All CTE students should complete some community/school service project before graduation, for example serving as an assistant coach for a middle school robotics team; membership on the school's LEED team; beautifying, upgrading, renovating, and restoring parts of the school building and the school building grounds; performing (under teacher supervision), house repairs for senior citizens, etc.

- All CTE students should build their senior portfolios by to the degree possible participating in some non-CTE school activities, programs, or teams.

- The model CTE student will be fully grounded in non-STEM-CTE subject areas such as fictional literature, poetry, plays and essays, creative-design and performance arts.

- All CTE students will complete a GCPC, a professional senior portfolio as well as a resume. Principals must make sure that the school's guidance counselors, and more importantly the CCC is thoroughly familiar with the unique four-year and post-high school needs of the CTE students. This will require that you facilitate some joint (CTE-Guidance) departmental meetings.

- Over the course of four years, the school's CTE graduates would have participated in many individually assigned or school-sponsored and organized CTE careers-related trips.

- CTE graduates will be well informed and well rehearsed in resume writing/job interview standards and techniques. The CTE department will also familiarize students with the professional work environment soft skills that would allow them to be successful in any internship or employment setting. The departmental objective is to have the student "job ready" by graduation.

The CTE Departmental-Operational Philosophy

The power and effectiveness of CTE is that it radically redefines and transforms the old concept of vocational education. It's because CTE seeks to remove that false divide between the analytical and the practical: the creative genius of the brain and the applications genius of applied operational techniques. CTE reunites and reaffirms the need for whole body intelligence and learning. CTE presents the idea that we are multisensory and creative beings; we are metaphysical thinkers who must create and act in a physical world. We bring our complete (mind and body) selves when we seek to transform and better our day-to-day living reality. Music and art are great revealers of this joint effort of imagination and technical skill. But so is carpentry, plumbing, electricity, and masonry. CTE destroys the false educational concept of mindless bodies and prepares students for a world that has become increasingly reliant on applied technical knowledge. I can remember two cars ago when I brought my car to the mechanic for routine maintenance work. The mechanic proceeded to get under the hood and chassis to do the evaluation. These days, the mechanic connects my current car to a diagnostic computer that is able to analyze places and parts that were previously inaccessible to human eyes. If anyone wanted convincing that CTE is the evolutionary expression of vocational education, they only needed to be in my basement as the plumber gave me a lesson on the physical and chemical properties of PEX versus copper. My car and house insurance company constantly remind me that I am in "good hands," but in the modern world of skilled craftsmanship, more and more of the work product will require the application of both good hands and good brains.

We have a very bad habit in public education, we too often hold on to old "ideas" and "beliefs" long after their original intent and/or practical value have disappeared. While at the same time, we resist new ideas even as the conditions call for their adoption. When my eighth grade JHS 294 classmate informed me that the eighth grade would be his last year in school, and that he would be joining a family member to take a job in their construction company, I tried to talk him out of it. Despite all of my arguments of the great possibilities (both academic and social) that awaited us in high school, I was not successful and my friend dropped out to go into construction work. But that was 1960s Brooklyn and many people were able to get good-paying, "labor-intensive" jobs with or without a high school diploma. That was an age when manual labor dominated, but that era and its job requirements have evolved. To not be replaced by a machine, a worker with a "strong back" will need that back to be connected to a strong brain that is able to negotiate applied STEM technical skills and analytical knowledge. That connection between STEM and the skills trades would grow over time, and it is my belief that the STEM connections to CTE will only increase as we move into the future, particularly a future when robotics and computerized tools and machinery will be major players in the workforce. The key then is for educators to approach the vocations curriculum with the concept that students must be able to understand the theory behind and the technical applications for production, manufacturing, construction, maintenance, and be capable when necessary to easily and confidently upgrade their personal skills and knowledge portfolios.

Career Technical Education is a transformative experience for a school

The introduction of a high school CTE program or the building of a CTE school could immediately transform the graduation and life success options for the students involved. CTE pulls together and engages the multiple skills and talents of students while greatly improving punctuality, attendance, and the GPA of students as they are under self-directed pressure to pass all of their classes. A CTE experience offers its graduates the power of having managed a complex and rigorous academic schedule; and more than any of their high school peers, they have a better sense of the standards and expectations of the adult/professional "real" world of work. For those students who complete a Cisco computer networking certification or who will transition into a construction trades apprenticeship program, there is a combination of pride, sense of accomplishment, and comfort about the future as they walk across the graduation stage to receive their dual-graduation recognition. The students are confident because having the evidence from two accreditation agencies not only speaks to their strength and discipline as students, but also gives them the confidence of knowing they have multiple life-career options after graduation. Leaving high school with a quantifiable practiced job readiness skill, along with a college readiness diploma, means that the two accomplishments will presently, and into the future, empower and enrich each other. It will also send a clear message to the world that this young person is serious and prepared for success!

It has been the struggle of all educators for so many generations to make those important motivational links between school life, work life, and adult life. It goes without saying that for underprivileged students, a CTE program can literally serve as a life trajectory game changer—providing the student with the opportunity to break the cycles of unemployment, low-wage employment, and the absence of "marketable" skills and qualifications. These students can see themselves in a positive, rewarding, and productive future. Those wonderful outcomes are some of the great overarching and most sought-after learning objectives of our profession.

Chapter 17:
The Effective High School Mathematics Department

An effective high school mathematics department is the combination of good principal leadership, thoughtful and committed departmental chairpersonship, a sound and strategic departmental plan, and a cohort of methodologically effective mathematics teachers. And working with students who may have spent their entire pre-high school lives being convinced that mathematics, and more importantly success at mathematics is not part of their "culture," you will absolutely need a strong, skilled, and committed team of instructors since these teachers must not only teach well but also inspire mathematical confidence and courage in their students.

Mathematics is the great post-high school professional STEM recruitment or rejection center. As a principal, you want every academic department to feel that what they do in their classrooms is the most important area of study in education (while at the same time not putting down other content areas). This high level of pride and confidence in their chosen field of study and teaching is wonderfully passed on in every class that the department sponsors. Students wanting to learn begins when they perceive the fiery glow of passion that starts somewhere inside their teacher's heart and then is powerful enough to make its way to the surface through teaching methodology; these are the teachers who literally take student failure personally.

The most effective high schools appear to practice high standards and high expectations in every subject area classroom. One of the important objectives of the Title I school Effective Mathematics Department (EMD) is to flip that narrative concerning students of color and the study of mathematics. If mathematics proficiency in general, and algebra in particular, is the great gatekeeper on the path to pursuing careers in STEM, accounting, economics, medicine, etc., then the teaching of mathematics is going to require a sense of urgency in that school. Math confidence and competency-building activities represent a form of academic advocacy whose aim is a more empowered mathematics-learning student. Providing students of color (particularly, males of color) with a safe space to embrace and take ownership of mathematics study and success will have a positive effect in other subject areas and will also help to establish and strengthen the school's culture of high academic achievement.

The principal must join and support this effort by turning the "math is not us" myth upside down. The passion that is needed for any affirmative academic movement must start at the top then flow down to the departmental leadership, teachers, and then students who will embrace that passion from their teachers.

The place to start this ownership of mathematics effort is to first establish a four-year rigorous mathematics program of courses, regardless of the student's future post-graduation plans. This process is greatly helped by the EMD that offers a rich survey of academically challenging, interesting, and diverse list of mathematics core and elective classes. The next EMD objective is to get every student to first "nail" algebra, as early as possible in their high school tenure, regardless of their career aspirations.

The academic, political, and school cultural significance of a strong and dynamic schoolwide mathematics program

Mathematics education is important in every school, but it represents a particular importance for STEM departments in all schools and especially in those high schools that have a STEM/CTE-themed focus, for these are the departments and institutions where mathematical calculations applications are the daily currency of so many classes. Further, for those non-STEM/CTE students, mathematics mastery adds critical attributes to the students' intellectual and transcript repertoire. First, mathematics applications require that one think analytically, systematically, orderly, and logically; it also forces students to make sure to use the proper application of an algorithmic process, formula, law, and principle to solve a particular problem. At the same time, the individual engaged in these mathematical problem-solving processes is called upon to be imaginative, speculative, and in some cases, creatively artful in one's thinking. Doing things like visualizing and contemplating the relationships between triangles inside of circles and polygons; understanding the meaning and role of negative numbers, symmetry, real numbers, rational numbers, etc. It is in the mindset and formulated practices that the study of mathematics allows us to transfer those skills to other areas of research and study, like economics, political science, art, music, dance, history, linguistics, anthropology, sociology, philosophy, and medicine. Further, I have found that students having the ability to master mathematics had a confidence about them that led them to believe that they could pass all of their classes and conquer many different challenges, including those students who were English-language learners. These students utilized the universality of the mathematics curriculum language to give them confidence and solace as they did well in math classes, which then motivated them to work harder to master the English language. It has been my experience over decades that many students of color actually enjoy the study of science. But many of these students could not fully embrace that love of science because they struggled with the mathematical principles applied by, and attached to, those scientific topics. High school students who loved microscopy studies (utilizing the microscope) and chemistry activities struggled with understanding microscopic measurements, reactions not visible to the naked eye, and analyzing organisms that existed and lived in a single drop of water. These were often the students who never mastered measurement, multiplication and division, the metric system, percentages, fractions, place value, or decimals. Getting eliminated in large numbers from the public school STEM pipeline are those students who love biology, earth science, and chemistry but get tripped up on algebra! The Effective Mathematics Department (EMD) must understand both the determining power and the associated political power of mathematics in those STEM fields that require the application of mathematical principles as well as math applications required in many other fields (e.g., statistics, actuary science, accounting, market research, or political science polling).

In the high school world, the school and the EMD can essentially predict the advantages and disadvantages a student will encounter in pursuing a successful future STEM college/major/career based on the student's relationship to the following pre-high school mathematics-related factors:

- The student who enters the ninth grade having successfully taken a middle school (high school content and topics, not an algebra-like (lite) course) algebra 1 class in the eighth grade. This student may have an additional advantage of having parents who engage them in informal educational experiences (e.g., science and natural history museums) where math-strengthening skills can be absorbed by the child, the access to a computer and math-related games, educational toys and games that teach and reinforce math concepts.

- The student who enters the ninth grade having successfully taken a yearlong algebra 1 course in middle school and who passed the high school standardized algebra 1 exam. (Students in groups one and two may also be fortunate to have been enrolled in an out-of-school STEM or mathematics after-school, weekend, or summer program such as math summer camp.)

- The student who enters the ninth grade who is prepared to take algebra in the ninth grade, having fully mastered the pre-algebra (arithmetic) skills of elementary and middle school.

- The student who enters the ninth grade who is really unprepared to take algebra in the ninth grade (having completely missed some or a lot of critical K-8 arithmetic concepts).

- Those students who can mechanically stumble through to solving a simple and basic arithmetic problem but struggle if the problem is worded in a slightly less straightforward and more complex format. This usually shows up in word problems in which, in many cases, reading skills may be the actual culprit. The student knows the applicable algorithm and could solve the problem, if only he or she could adequately translate the question and correctly understand what is being asked.

- Students who were exposed and can name mathematical concepts but lack the adequate deep and thoughtful understanding of concepts like addition, subtraction, division, and multiplication; negative-positive numbers, equal, less than, more than, the number line and an equation. Whatever the level of poor quality teaching of reading skills in elementary school, the teaching of mathematics skills will probably be much worse. No malicious intent on the part of teachers here, for as a superintendent who has reviewed many prospective elementary teachers' transcripts, the vast majority of them revealed either a transcript deficiency in college math courses (including math education for elementary teachers), or they took the minimum mathematics courses required for graduation. Even with general education elementary teachers, the curriculum and pedagogy are weighed heavily toward ELA and/or reading skills.

- The students who may have been exposed to a "disrupted" and disorganized middle school experience, classes in which there is a great deal of student distractive behavior, long periods in a school without the same teacher, the teacher is hired a month into the year, or students spending one or three years (sixth through eighth grades) with a mathematics teacher who is not fully certified and/or with inadequate teaching experience. Unfortunately, this factor can render even the most mathematically capable student unprepared to fully engage high school algebra 1, even if the student is able to pass the eighth-grade standardized exam.

The EMD must first come up with a strategy to fix the many mathematics deficiencies students can bring with them to high school. And that would include addressing an insufficient/incomplete algebra class the students may have taken in middle school or the "less rigorous" algebra 1 course taken from a high school they transferred from. A weak algebra 1 foundation may hide itself temporarily in geometry during the tenth grade, but left uncorrected it will only show up to hurt the students in the upper-level mathematics courses, including, and especially, algebra 2, pre-calculus, and calculus. It's the professional ethical responsibility of the EMD to understand that a student's mathematics preparedness is in most cases not a reflection of the student's innate capabilities but may have more to do with having access to an early and consistently strong mathematics educational experience from pre-K to eighth grade. Perhaps these "algebra ready" students were simply fortunate to be living in a strong mathematics school zone, possibly including elementary and middle school gifted and talented programs. For the less fortunate, a math-phobia mindset can both consciously and unconsciously be transferred to young people by adults. I can't remember when, as a former principal, the number of parents (who clearly skipped their high school biology class when genetics was covered) who voiced that the problem their child was having in algebra was caused by the "bad math genes" the parents passed on to them! The EMD must understand that this pre-high school exposure to a quality mathematics instructional program and access to informal STEM-related activities and resources are the driving forces that determine the quality of the student's algebra 1 preparedness. But the lack of access to this entitlement, enrichment, and standards-based instructional learning opportunities does not necessarily speak to a child's undiscovered mathematics capabilities.

The EMD working in a Title I school must be prepared to address the large number of entering students who may disproportionally fall into any of these categories of unpreparedness to do high school-level mathematics; some institutional (school) and organizational (district) changes are needed:

- The school does not have a teacher qualified to teach eighth-grade algebra, even if students are willing and able to take the course. These middle schools can't offer algebra, or in some cases even a strong pre-algebra course. The school has a cohort of students entering the middle school who could take algebra, but the school does not have a plan for these students beyond passing the eighth-grade standardized exam; thus, the students may be exposed to a great deal of mindless, monotonous, and unproductive test-prep instruction and very little mathematics (pre-algebra) enrichment work.

- The middle school has an algebra class, but large numbers of students who are capable are negatively tracked out of the course (perhaps there is an inadequate number of teachers). A larger number of students in many of these Title I middle schools could in fact take a robust eighth-grade pre-algebra/algebra course with the proper instructor, an additional class period, and/or after-school Saturday programming. Ironically, this approach would be both financially and educationally sound versus the time and resources spent on senseless test-taking prep exercises. These rigorous pre-algebra/algebra classes would not conflict with the school's desire to have students pass the eighth-grade standardized exam, since all of the topics they will cover are lifted directly from the eighth-grade math curriculum. It also provides the opportunity for students to receive some real qualitative and test-taking skills that are well thought out.

- The middle school needs an instructional, focused approach to mathematics concepts. For example, instead of having students do twenty problems for which they don't fully understand the algorithm required to arrive at a solution, students can do two or three problems in a teacher-directed group activity in which they can both dissect and deconstruct every part of the problem being posed, and fully analyze and understand the process by which the answer is discovered.

- An enriched middle school mathematics program has both strong pre-algebra classes as well as rigorous high school-level algebra classes.

- For those middle schools that do not have an eighth-grade algebra program, there must be a strategic school leadership plan to identify those students who are below, proficient, or above grade-level standards, and then adequately prepare them for a high school algebra 1 course. This means, when required, placing them in some type of extended-time or tutorial-support classes.

Note to principals: There is a legitimate pedagogical debate concerning the taking of algebra in the eighth grade. My position is based on two factors: (1) College admissions offices exercise a great deal of control over the general STEM and engineering admissions game; in order for students to get to calculus or AP calculus by their senior year of high school, they must have algebra in the bank by the ninth grade or do some kind of math course taking adjustments such as taking an advanced math course in the summer, after school, or weekends. Those high school students wishing to pursue a STEM college major and scholarships are at an advantage if they enter the ninth grade having already successfully taken algebra 1. (2) It is also helpful for students to take algebra 1 in a known and comfortable environment like their middle school, without having the strain of adjusting to being in a new high school building setting and taking four to six other rigorous high school courses.

The EMD must come up with a strategic plan to address the mathematics success and future college and career needs of all these different cohorts of students. Schools or EMDs that are stuck on the conversation, "They ain't sending them prepared to do high school math work," doom themselves and the students; some positive and proactive steps the EMD must take are the following:

- Review incoming students' elementary and middle school math performance records (give standardized exam scores more weight than report card grades, and know the quality of math instruction from your various feeder middle schools); as soon as possible get the elementary and middle school (eighth grade) standardized exam scores. For those students who received the lowest (or barely met the standards) scores on these standardized exams, which can translate to mean that their math education did not reach the eighth-grade pre-algebra standards, the Summer Bridge Program must be used. These students would then transition into a double-period algebra 1 course for the school year.

- Set up an all ninth-graders' elementary pre-algebra diagnostic exam to see what mathematics learning objectives, skills, and concepts the students are missing. Start with easy questions somewhere around the third-grade math standards and continue with questions from the fourth-, fifth-, sixth-, and seventh-grade math standards, and then end the exam with a section on the eighth-grade math standards. The key here is to see where the student drops off the mathematics conceptual and achievement wagon. This diagnostic exam will also let the EMD staff know which specific topic areas of the elementary/middle school math curriculum the student is missing and therefore set up *at the be-ginning of the school year* a proactive tutorial program. The results of this diagnostic exam could also guide the EMD's decision on which students will receive a priority seat in a double or extended (over three terms) algebra 1 course. The first class must be a crash course in pre-algebra skills acquisition on the part of the student. This process is not as difficult as it might sound; after all, it is not like these students have never heard of a decimal point or negative-positive numbers. It may be that they did not completely learn these concepts, or they are a little confused about what they mean.

- For those students who took an algebra course in middle school but did not take the high school standardized algebra exam, give them that exam and see how they perform. If necessary, a tutorial program (start-ing with the first semester) should also be set up for these students. If a student does not do well on the algebra diagnostic exam, there are two options. If a student scores very low on the exam, you must im-mediately bring in the parent(s) for a conference. Have a mathematics teacher sit down with the student, go over the exam verbally to ascer-tain the student's grasp of algebra 1 concepts. After that verbal diag-nostic discussion, and it is determined that the student has not really learned the algebra curriculum concepts, you must again immediately bring in the parent(s) for a conference. This can often be a difficult dis-cussion, since you must keep it professional and not bad-mouth your middle school colleagues by informing the parent that what their child took was an algebra-like (lite) course but not a real high school-stan-dards algebra course. Say it carefully and gently as it has also been my unfortunate experience that the parent(s) will see (in their eyes) the recommendation for the retaking of algebra in your school as an academic setback for the child. But letting the student go forward with major algebra deficiencies is the cruelest act of all. It would help if the EMD had a plan and program to get these students back on their eighth-grade algebra track by way of after-school, weekend, or summer courses. This meeting will go easier if your school is in a district that requires a centralized standardized high school end-of-course algebra 1 exam for middle school algebra students in order for them to earn high school algebra Carnegie unit credit. In any event, some type of algebra 1 after-school tutorial-enrichment program must be set up to clear any algebra 1 conceptual deficiencies that will come back to hurt the student when he or she enrolls in higher-level mathematics.

• Review the mathematics performance levels of incoming students as early as possible, as it is critical. Part of the Summer Bridge Program for incoming ninth-graders can in actuality be the first semester of a "tri-semester algebra course." This course will help those students (based on the diagnostic exam) who display some deficiencies in pre-algebra concept areas and, therefore, would benefit from a one-year algebra course spread over three continuous semesters. For those students who successfully passed a high school algebra course and standardized exam in middle school, attending the Summer Bridge Program meant putting those math skills to work on STEM research and projects as well as engaging in a hands-on introduction to applying the principles and concepts of geometry.

Based on how students perform on the post-Summer Bridge Program mathematics diagnostic exam given at the end of the program, the school should assign students to one of the following classes in the fall:

• Level 1: Small classes of no more than fifteen students. These students will have one year of double-period algebra, along with an additional math tutorial course at the end of the day; yes, they will scream, but meet with parents to explain your reasons. You need a really strong and effective teacher for this class, especially in a high school that is introducing students to challenging academic standards. That teacher should be specially selected and professionally developed (and like working with) former middle schoolers and now ninth-graders. These teachers must have the combined gifts of middle school nurturing and high school tough love. Since we have found that very often many students who are the lowest K-8 math performers are also struggling in reading, I would keep that fifteen-student cohort together for their ninth-grade ELA classes.

- Level 2: A math team (certified math teacher and a Special Ed teacher) algebra course. With the same double-period and mandatory last period of the day math tutorial class.

- Level 3: The beforementioned group of students who will be scheduled to take a one-year algebra course over three semesters. The first semester (summer) of the course should be dedicated to building the student's pre-algebra competency. They should also be enrolled in a math support class, which means placing a math tutorial course as the last (after-school) class period on their schedule.

- Level 4: Start any and all math tutorial classes at the beginning of the first semester of the school year, just as any other class. Now, I know this will sound strange to both professional educators and civilian stakeholders, but waiting until students fail the first or second marking period is playing academic achievement catch-up. Proactive tutorials can help pre-algebra skills-deficient students to maintain the syllabus pace with the class. Further, so much of math learning is based on mastering a prerequisite skill or concept; students who get lost early in the semester tend to stay lost as they try to comprehend and master topics that rely on the knowledge and skills of previous topics.

In all of these ninth-grade classes as well as the extended "last period" tutorial classes, there must be a serious investment made by the school for purchasing math learning manipulatives, computers, and software. If the funds could be raised, the school should set up a student Mathematics Study Center (MSC). The tutorials could be held there, where the space is large enough for computers (with headphones), worktables, and well-organized labeled shelves of manipulatives in baskets, tutorial software, class notes, and summaries of topics (students who have excellent class notes could earn service credits by providing their notes for other students to review), text and workbooks, and written source material for all of the mathematics courses taught in the school. The center should be open and available to students an hour before the start of school and three hours after the end of the school day. Student peer tutors should not be assigned based solely on grades and test scores; just like adults, good grades and test scores don't automatically mean that they will be good tutors! Tutoring, like teaching, is a skill that requires technique and a set of standards. In fact, I have found over the years that many of the high-performance students actually lack the patience and personality to tutor their peers. All peer tutors should be interviewed and selected by the staff of the EMD and then professionally developed through workshops to serve as teaching assistants to teachers, volunteers, or paraprofessionals assigned to the MSC. The service credit and the resume-building part of tutoring is excellent for those students who serve as tutors, but organizing these activities in a professional way—including supervision, evaluative feedback, and letters of recommendation—will also help these students to be better prepared for the world after high school. Peer tutoring also helps with the school's academic mission because student tutors develop a deeper understanding of their own math knowledge by having to explain concepts in a fundamental and developmental way. The students being tutored benefit by having fellow student tutors who, unlike their teachers, are closer (having recently learned the material themselves) to the topics being reviewed.

Remember, when it comes to school culture, words and labels matter. I would officially refer to and label the MSC as a study, not tutorial center, even if tutoring is the main activity that takes place in the center. First, the MSC should be available to all students not just those who are struggling. Besides, the word "struggling" could simply mean that a student was taking a difficult mathematics course while taking several other difficult and challenging academic courses; getting a little professional help with a particularly difficult topic or concept as well as having a space where a study group can be formed to do their study work is the most productive use of the MSC.

Further, the word "study" changes everything for teenagers who might be more encouraged to visit the MSC if the stigma of "this is where failing students go" is removed. This concept must also be reflected in the language of the EMD staff. For example, no EMD teacher should reprimand a student privately or in class and suggest that he or she needs to go to the MSC as a form of punishment! The MSC should not be seen as the place a student runs to at the end of a semester for not working hard in class, not doing homework or projects, and not studying. At the core of the MSC's philosophy is the student taking personal responsibility for doing his or her best to raise the level of his or her own academic achievement. The MSC can then do its best work by providing the student with a place of support to make that high academic achievement a reality. As I explained in the section on school *Culture*, words, labels, titles, and designations greatly influence the thinking of the internal school family as well as the external stakeholders. Great attention must be paid to the implications of the political, cultural, and linguistics aspects of the school's *Culture*. The MSC, like the school's Teacher Resource Center, should be seen as a place where a "learner-practitioner" at any level can go early and often to receive support in realizing and achieving his or her personal best.

The EMD use of additional teaching and learning time

An unfortunate habit in public education is the terrible myth that additional money and time (without a strategic vision) will lead to greater student and/ or school academic outcomes. And, so, also related, a common mistake practiced in many supplemental, double classes, and tutorial classes is that the extra or additional class time utilizes the same style, structure, and format as the student's regular class where the student is struggling. Not only is this a waste of money, it wastes teacher time and is not academically helpful to students. If a student is struggling to comprehend a concept in his regular class, then an additional class time utilizing the same teaching methodology will be of little or no help. When you combine this wrong approach with the beforementioned absence of a strategic plan to close learning gaps quickly, the "wasting" part becomes clear.

The key factors when setting up any type of mathematics academic intervention program are the following:

- It must look, act, and be different from the classroom experience that created the need for the student to seek, or be referred for, academic intervention services in the first place.

- An effective academic intervention program (before school, during school, after school, weekends, summer, etc.) must be linked to the school's effective theory and approach to helping students be successful on both internal and external standardized exams. It must build skills and conceptual knowledge as well as incorporate effective test-taking skills.

- The academic intervention or tutoring program must be based on concepts and skills diagnostic prescriptive model. In other words, specifically identify and target the student's conceptual and skills deficiencies. And this includes identifying if the "blockage" is due to missing math knowledge from the student's K-8 learning experience.

- The school should seek to set up an MSC that can provide services and support for students, regardless of where they fall on the academic performance hierarchy as well as support for students in any level of math courses. One of the objectives of the MSC is to particularly teach potential STEM students (as well as those in other graduate and professional programs) in the art and science of forming effective study groups.

- There must be a strategic approach, curriculum, operational and teaching standard for a school's academic intervention program. Tutoring should be framed by a set of conceptual behavioral standards, recognized and evaluated by a series of rubrics. Peer tutoring should not be based simply on assigning students with high grades; in fact, the peer tutoring program should be thought out well, and the tutors interviewed and screened. Peer tutors should also receive some kind of professional development. One of the few public education advantages a poor school has is Title I academic intervention funding; but as a superintendent, I have witnessed a wide spectrum of approaches for the qualitative use of these funds. Any aspect of a school's operational or academic culture that is not strategically well planned will naturally incline toward ineffectiveness, mediocrity, and failure. Understand, principals, that investing time and money alone will not automatically produce positive academic intervention outcomes.

The EMD must take on the primary task of making the school's mathematics program both accessible and challenging.

The reason for mandating a four-year high school mathematics program as stated in the previous section is to expand students' college and career options after graduation, including giving them the option to make a college major or career shift in the future. High school students are also always in the process of strengthening and enhancing their transcripts, so we want students to take the highest mathematics course that matches their personal best ability. There is very often a terrible instinct in the high school world of seeking to get through, as opposed to gaining a great deal of knowledge, information, and skills. Therefore, at times, the local/state-mandated minimum credits required become the overwhelming objective. I am fully sensitive to the challenges high school educators face when trying to graduate students who may often arrive to high school totally unprepared to engage in legitimate high school mathematics work. Schools ultimately are not buildings, programs, initiatives, slogans, and activities. In the final analysis, schools are really about students and, to be more precise, each individual student in the school. Our primary, professional, ethical responsibility is to get students to the point where they can walk across that stage and receive a graduation diploma. But "primary" does not mean only; an additional objective is to graduate students in such a way that they are empowered to access the most and best post-graduation life and career options. In short, do what you have to do, principals, but push for all of your students to take four years of serious and challenging math courses.

The EMD must also promote and build two types of excellence of practice: instructional excellence and learning excellence. The first is based on efficacy, content knowledge, and sound teaching methodology. The second is based on self-appreciation, attitude, and attention to classwork, along with a serious approach to study and achieving the highest score possible. In some schools, we find ourselves up against some ugly and debilitating social/cultural narratives such as "mathematics is not a Black thing." We often use the phrase "best practices" in education, but to create a school of mathematical excellence, school administrators, teachers, students, and parents must reach a collective understanding and determination to all practice their best efforts to dismantle all mathematical gates and roadblocks that stand in the way of students realizing their full intellectual and gifted personalities.

The EMD's weekly use of standardized assessment formatted questions to inform and guide teaching and study

- I believe all high school's academic departments should have a strategic schoolwide designated day each week for testing and assessment. I will explain the pedagogical rationale for how less turns into more by having four days of instruction instead of five and how this approach can actually lead to more instruction and learning time; just work with me until you get to that chapter! But the reason these exams take a complete class period (day) is because they are linguistically (question formatted), in wording, phrasing, terms, and rigor as would be found on the end of year: school, local district, city, state, and national (AP/SAT/ACT) final standardized exams. Essentially, every week the students are taking the curriculum pacing calendar section of where they are in the section of the course culminating exam. These are subject-weekly exams (we organized our weekly testing schedule for mathematics exams to occur on Friday); in actuality, this approach helped us to have a really great Monday-Friday student attendance record-statistics.

Also:

- In the above approach, teacher-designed exams are basically eliminated, and different classes of the same subject are all offered the same rigorous learning standards and instructional practices. And this is accomplished by way of instituting departmentally designed curriculum pacing classroom exams. The principal should expect some "pushback" on this. But you must hold the line here, as it is the only way that you can ensure that every student in the school who is taking the same math course, but in different classes, is receiving the same standards-based curriculum.

- Grades are important, but the diagnostic value (to inform instructional practices and tutorial support needs) of these exams are what was most important to us.

- These weekly exams energized group and individual study habits, since every week was a "high stakes" testing experience.

The EMD must expand and enrich the school's mathematical experience for all students.

The act of establishing and solidifying a school culture in which mathematics education can flourish, not just for STEM-CTE aspiring students but also for all students in the school, requires the development of in-class and out-of-class programs, clubs, and activities:

- In a Title I school, an important ninth-grade classroom, library, home work, in-school or break project could be to allow students to research the "odds" of successfully becoming a professional athlete in the NFL, NBA, or MLB.

- The EMD should, like all academic departments, create and maintain its own departmental website. This would include career information, math articles, special math-related events, math study and tutorial resources for students and other family members.

- A rich offering of rigorous mathematics electives should include courses that are not specifically limited to those interested in pursuing a STEM-focused career: for example, Statistics and Probability, Logic, The History of Mathematics, The Mathematics of Chess, and An Advance Geometry Art course, etc.

- Like all departments in the school, the EMD should sponsor a school-wide content area fair. This fair would not only stretch the mathematics knowledge of the fair participants but would also present interesting topics and concepts to schoolmates in other classes. These academic fairs also allow the EMD and school family to bring in distinguished judges in the mathematics field who can inspire students who are interested in pursuing a professional career in mathematics research. This EMD curriculum fair should be connected to a school-wide multifaceted celebration of "Math Week!"

- The EMD should sponsor an annual award-granting game show-style mathematics competition in the auditorium where students and parents could be invited.

- On career day, the EMD must work with the college/career advisor to make sure that mathematics career-related professionals are invited to participate.

- The EMD should offer advice and suggestions to the librarian for setting up the mathematics reference section and website resources in the library.

- The EMD should cooperate and coordinate with the school Science, Technology and Mathematics Fair Research Program (STMFRP) in helping to define and refine topics; finding university or private industry mentors and overall support; and scheduling the students for in- and after-school classes that support student participation in the STMFRP.

- The EMD staff should serve as faculty advisors for the Math Team as well as A Future Mathematicians Club.

- The principal should fund and support all of these great and wonderful programs through their entrepreneurial efforts-based school 501c3 foundation, for they represent the attributes of a great mathematics school! Much of this funding would go toward the acquisition of mathematics learning technology hardware and software. And so for the EMD and all other academic departments in the school, a technology-rich high school is essential. And this is why our next chapter defines what "technology rich" looks like in a high-performing school!

Chapter 18:
Schoolwide Technology Program and Department

A school's technology program should enrich and enhance all teaching and learning experiences in the building.

All high schools, STEM-CTE theme-focused or not, must have a comprehensive, well-designed and well-distributed (throughout academic departments) technology program. It does not matter what career objective the student plans to pursue, for their career options are enhanced with a strong conceptual and applications knowledge of technology. I have noticed recently how even my standard doctor's office checkups include an expansive use of technology by the nursing and medical support staff. I am not sure that anyone could work in a doctor's office these days without some minimum standard of technical computer application skills! Technology in schools can no longer be thought of as extracurricular or elective study. Technology is an essential component, collaborating with all content/subject areas in the school. Adaptive and supportive technology is also an indispensable tool in the area of Special Disability Needs-Special Education. And we are also learning that many of these learning-enhancing tech tools can help students who do not have a formal IEP, like teacher voice-recognition translating/writing programs that can produce "written class notes," which eliminates the problem faced by students who are unable to write or find it difficult to follow a lesson and take notes at the same time. Technology can also extend the school instructional period beyond the classroom and school day/week; a student having access to a lesson-tutorial online allows them to stop, slow down, replay, and even ask questions at key points in the lesson. It provides students with the power to take ownership and manage their own learning in the safe, uncritical comfort of home, a computer room in the school, or on their laptop or phone sitting in the park. Technology can open up some wonderful avenues for communication between teachers, administrators, and parents. An annual common complaint of high school parents—who may interact infrequently with school staff for many logistical and practical reasons—is not knowing the present academic status of their child before they receive the information by way of a failing grade on the report card or a not-so-good result on a major exam. High schools are extremely vulnerable to this parent-information deficit because of the psychological development of teenagers who are unconsciously trying to construct an independent personality from adults, which often results in them not wanting to be fully and honestly communitive with their parents about their true academic performance status. Technology can be helpful in closing the teacher-parent communication divide via a class website, text messaging, and e-mail. On the website, there can be a section where parents and their children both have independent password-protected access to student academic-performance data. Parents and students can also access the course syllabus, homework/projects assignments, grades earned, a copy of the latest transcript, the student's Graduation Critical Path Chart, test scores, school break and summer assignments, and parent meeting information. Many parents are legitimately very busy, and so even mobile phone technology can empower these parents to know "what is going on" with their child's education, but the school must be willing and able to raise its technology capability to meet that parent need!

Note to parents: What parents don't know can hurt their child's education. A very common conversation in the principal's office after a student has "forgotten" to share an important out-of-school assignment information with their parent: "Mr. Johnson, I had no idea my child had a (weekend, winter-spring break, summer) project to complete before returning to school; he/she sat around the house all day, talked with friends on the phone, watched TV, etc. I would have been more than happy (and very happy) to give my child the public transportation money to go to the museum and complete that assignment!" And music to my ears: "Guess what Mr. Johnson, my child will be going to the museum this weekend to complete that assignment, that was hidden from me, and yes miss the roller-skating with friends event planned for Saturday afternoon, that I have been passionately informed and reminded about, over and over for weeks!" Principal (forgive me Lord) inward smile moment! Cue principal in serious voice: "You are so fortunate to have a good and wonderful parent who cares so much about your education!" Parent smiles outwardly.

Through electronic attendance taking, the school's attendance teacher should have the technical ability to inform a parent in real time (same day) of their child being late to, or absent from, school or a class. This could be done via text messaging and e-mail.

I have found as a principal of a Title I school that both (rapidly disap-

304

pearing) landline home phones as well as constantly changing cellular phone numbers can create a notification-communication gap with large numbers of the parent body. For purposes of emergency and school/academic information, the school should design a parent phone number updating plan/system. Include incentives if you must! I would then add the management of that updating plan/system to the job description of the school's attendance teacher. I know that boards of education, like most government/civil service bureaucracies, can often offer "anemic" and/or inadequate job descriptions. These bare-minimum duty requirements often seek to maintain the bureaucracy, or to justify the existence of a job title, rather than really servicing the customer. In fact, there are many public education employees who are better at telling you what they are not required to do than what they are actually required to do based on their official job description, or what they should be doing to really make themselves indispensable and effective. As a principal, you know that if you truly followed the "letter of the law" of your own labor contract, the school would fail and children would be lost. As a school building leader, you must seek to creatively interpret a labor contract by expanding job descriptions to make the school work for children, not the adults in the system. This must be done in a strategic and thoughtful way and without malicious and mean-spirited intent. If there is any hope of your leading a high-achieving school, especially one that is burdened with large numbers of poor children, then you will absolutely need all members of the staff to go beyond their official limited job descriptions.

Students can also greatly benefit from having technology avenues of communication with their teachers[6] because a high school student will often rather leave the class not understanding something than asking an embarrassing question in front of the class (often a question that one-third of the class also wanted to ask)! Something like a class website can also facilitate online student study groups[7], best practice postings, a way for a student who is forced to be absent to stay current with the class, a summer or school break resource for study and review, and a way to build a community of student learners who can support each with tough course topics.

As a STEM-CTE person, I believe that every academic department should fully integrate technology into their daily instructional practices. And just as I believe that technology should be an integral "member" of every academic department, in a school rich with technology assets, it should also function as an independent department (with a full-time, non-teaching coordinator). The higher the number of machines, the diversity and complexity of technology us-age, the greater the need for a knowledgeable, skilled, resourceful and creative Technology Coordinator (TC). The principal should be aware of the possible gap between the district's HR official job description for technology coordina-tor and the real job requirements needed by an advanced and technology-rich school. The job of a good high school TC is to manage the school-based server, the school's and course websites as well as classroom and library technolo-gy, the installation of hardware and software, maintenance, upgrading, and the protection and security of all technology equipment and Internet-based resources. Both of my high schools featured an enormous amount and usage of technological resources, including teachers having classroom laptops and smartboards, state-of-the-art applied technology robotics lab, multiple com-puter labs, and a distance learning teleconferencing center. As computer tech-nology becomes more and more complex, school districts need to adjust by upgrading their TC job descriptions as well as distinguishing the difference between a school TC and a technology teacher; the hiring of the TC should not be restricted to the teacher hiring seniority pay contract format. Without those changes (and some principals have figured out how to circumvent the present systems restrictions), public schools won't be able to recruit the kind of indi-viduals who are needed to be an effective TC.

The profile and attributes of an effective high school TC

- The job of a STEM-CTE high school or a technology-enriched regular school TC should be a full-time, non-classroom teaching position. If any school is both administratively and educationally fully immersed with some aspect of technology use, then there is a need for a dedicat-ed point person who can manage this technology-diverse institution. The greater the engagement with technology, the greater the need for a TC with a rich portfolio of technical expertise.

- You may need to do an outside-of-the-box recruitment and hiring pro-cess. First of all, in most school districts, there is a tremendous un-derestimation and lack of understanding of the technical knowledge and skills required to manage an effective high school technology pro-gram. A part of this misunderstanding is on purpose as public school systems try to fit a specialized and complicated job requirement into a regular teacher's position. Districts don't want to pay the true salary cost for the level of technology expertise the school really requires. Thus, across a school district, you will find a wide spectrum of knowledge, expertise, and skill levels among TCs in the schools. For a quick confirmation review of this reality, just look at the quality of each school's website, or the absence of same! I have also sadly seen situations in some schools where a (usually new) teacher in a non-technology academic department will have the same, or greater, level of computer-tech knowledge and skills as the school's TC. The administration and staff could then overburden that new teacher with a lot of technology tasks that should fall under the TC's job duties. If as a principal you envision a dynamic schoolwide technology program, then you may need to look outside of the traditional college technology education programs; or if you are fortunate, you will find a graduate of one of these programs who also has advanced (private industry-level) applied technology skills. In any event, you will more than likely need to substantially upgrade the district TC's job description in terms of tech knowledge and skills, duties, and responsibilities. Make it more of a job analysis of the type of tech support you need in the present as well as what you need for the technological evolution of your school.

Note to principals: (That "entrepreneurial principal" thing again!) You are going to need to find supplementary funds to be able to pay a good TC at least 75% of what they can make in the private sector (and hope he or she is responding to a compassionate calling); this can best be done through some type of per-session, overtime, or after-school pay, since there is no way he or she can do all that is required in the course of a regular school day.

- Smart person with a strong academic background. I was fortunate at SSCHS to have a person who was extremely knowledgeable in advanced technology theory and practices as well as being a chemistry major. The double-education/technology major TC candidate is obviously the ideal. But an important find is the degree of richness and well-roundedness in the candidate's undergraduate and graduate transcript. The TC will need to interact with the full academic spectrum of the school; and you need to know if the candidate can at least appreciate the work of the ELA, art, music, etc., departments in the school. In so many ways, an effective TC will need to possess a few of the attributes and skills of the principalship. For example, the TC is working in a school building full of people utilizing technology, who see their individual technology-Internet crisis as the school's #1 technology problem at that moment. Properly (politely as possible) managing the school family members' expectations while strategically "triaging" and working through each school technology problem is an important and necessary skill for the TC to have.

- The TC should be tech savvy, meaning being conversant in multiple areas of technology (e.g., Internet, safety and security, hardware and software) as well as abreast of the latest trends and where technology is going in the future. The TC should also be familiar with wide usage (sites and techniques), tech language, and methods that young people are currently using, which may be totally unknown to most adults, in or out of education. The TC should have the ability to match wits and monitor those students who possess advanced computer knowledge and skills that under certain conditions can be problematic. At both of my high schools, I had to unfortunately (and for different reasons) suspend a few students with temporary or permanent bans from the use of any of the school's computers because of some technical infractions discovered by the TC. One way the TC can neutralize bad temptations and keep an eye on tech-savvy kids is to fully engage their knowledge and skills in a positive and productive way (e.g., Robotics team, computer club, school or course website development and management, Cisco or Microsoft certification courses, online college computer science classes, schoolwide technical assistance [AV] team, cyber-forensics team).

- The TC must see the total school technology picture, which means seeing how technology is integrated into every operational and academic effort of the school. In short, the TC should be able to comprehend and execute the school's mission as it is expressed through applied technology.

- Most principals will need a capable TC who can effectively negotiate with the many hardware, software, and Internet-related technology vendors. For even the most successful models of entrepreneurial principalship, there is still an ongoing search for significant savings, the overflow which can be applied to a larger array of programs. A really knowledgeable TC who is also a good negotiator can go toe to toe with a vendor, getting the best "bang for the buck" for the school.

- The list of stakeholders and partners, particularly, in a STEM-CTE school, can be long and complex (diverse). A good TC will be able to effectively "code-switch" and serve as a communication bridge between the language of the non-public school actors and the internal professional school community. Corporate partners in particular will show very little patience with the bureaucratic obstructionist structure that is often negatively associated with public education. The TC should be able to speak their language as well as work at their level of expected efficiency, professionalism, and excellence.

  Note to principals: I have been able to snatch corporate partners from other schools because of one overall simple complaint the company would voice to me: Communication problems. Schools could not successfully articulate their needs or challenges to the corporate partners. In some cases, their former school partners weren't getting back to them or getting them the information they requested in a timely manner. Schools also engaged the corporate partners unproductively in our labyrinth of bureaucratic rules and regulations.

- Again, specifically in a STEM-CTE school, a great deal of the fundraising efforts are directed toward the acquisition of STEM-CTE equipment and supportive Internet software resources. It is critical that the TC serves as a major, important, permanent member of the school's proposal/grant writing team. And even in non-STEM-CTE schools, those academic departments who wish to make technology a part of their instructional program will need the TC to help translate their academic objectives into technology hardware and software language by way of equipment and products. When seeking a gift or grant or responding to a private sector or governmental technology proposal (RFP), your TC is critical in helping the school-based educators to refine and focus the budget and projected outcomes of your proposal narrative.

- The TC must play an important role in assisting teachers with the training and professional development (PD) required for the successful integration of technology into their instructional content area. As part of the school's technology plan, the TC should strive to grow the staff's technology competency and capabilities to reduce the need for the TC to assist with minor technology issues that individual staff members could easily fix themselves. This will allow the TC to devote more time to upgrade, prevent, and maintain the school's technology, thus preventing an influx of minor technology problems. No names, but in one school, a teacher called the TC because a classroom's wireless printer was out; the TC arrived to only discover that the printer's AC plug had been accidently pulled out of the wall socket!

- I will talk about the important schoolwide technology plan in the next section. For now, it is enough to say that the TC is the key custodian of that plan. The TC must have an ongoing strategic systems review process, such that he or she can make changes to the technology resources and programs, with minimal interruptions and negative effects on the school's daily operational and educational programs.

- The TC must be familiar with the multilayered and sometimes conflicting (school, district, local, state, and federal) laws and regulations that apply to Internet use for and by students and adult staff. As principal, you may want to either share your copy or give the TC his or her own copy of the monthly Education Law Review Journal, so that he or she can be familiar with any possible changes in the law. Another option is for the principal to ask the district's central legal department to update you on any major changes in laws relating to Internet usage in schools. Wearing my superintendent's hat, this is something the legal department may want to do on its own by sending an "Internet usage" information update memo to all schools when there is a significant change in the law based on a recent higher court ruling.

- The TC must be personable, service-orientated, patient, and have a rich reservoir of people skills. A huge amount of the TC's day is spent problem-solving. When a staff person calls the technology department, it is usually because something has gone wrong. Or they need assistance in getting some uncooperative computer, piece of technology, or software to cooperate. The upside is that everybody in the building loves the tech person who solves their problems, but to get to that praiseful state of collective appreciation, the TC must first get through the many daily anxious calls they receive. Sometimes these callers fail to understand that their call is not the only call, nor may it be the most urgent at that moment. But the TC, like the principal, must be in the moment with each person's concerns and not take their frustration personally.

- The TC should be able to serve as teacher/mentor for those students who wish to pursue a computer science-related career. The TC is needed as an essential primary or assistant coach for multiple technology-related activities and teams such as robotics, cyber forensics, STEM competition program, etc.

- (If the school has one) the TC, in cooperation with a school administrator and business manager, supervises the Computer (student and teacher) Laptop Lending Program.

- The TC must have the technical knowledge and skill to effectively manage the school's dedicated Internet server.

- The TC should be available to provide a series of generally announced, hardware and software orientation workshops, technology safety and security sessions, and professional development classes for all members of the school family (including parents), and categories of staff (including school administrators)!

- The TC, in cooperation with the SBL team and the college career counselor, should lead the effort in organizing a schoolwide technology fair. This fair is a little different from the standard departmental fairs in that the focus will be on careers in technology. This fair can be one of the activities of Career Week. Recruit professionals from many different areas who also utilize various types of technology as well as companies that either manufacture or that are major users of technology (medical, transportation, government, communication, sports and entertainment, manufacturing, construction, security, military, etc.).

- The TC is the primary person to manage all of the school's websites and Internet use, and should be given powerful authority and access over both staff and student school computer and Internet usage. Everyone in the school family should be made aware of the TC's access and oversight; this will serve as a disincentive for doing the "wrong thing."

- In every case of a school employing a really great and first-rate TC, it often boils down to either the luck and/or skill of the principal; yet a position that is so important in our modern era should not be reduced to such a random process.

Summing up the TC recruitment/hiring process, the person must understand and embrace the school's technology vision. The integrational power of a school's technology program means that it is the essential connective life force of the modern high school. If any school invests in the total integration of technology into every academic and administrative operational department of the school, then as stated earlier, the school will need a highly skilled, full-time person who can facilitate, expand, monitor, and maintain those various technology computer-based systems. To get the type of person you need, you may need to look hard and deep inside, or outside, of the school system. As a superintendent, I have read many ambitious, wonderful, dare I even say, poetic schoolwide technology plans submitted by principals. The fail, however, is that the school did not have the appropriate TC person who could effectively and efficaciously put that plan into action. The effective school will wisely approach technology as one of many important tools in the school's (principal's) strategic building management and academic achievement tool kit. Any good (or bad) pedagogical practice must be firmly rooted in a sound theoretical and philosophical foundation. The difference between good or bad school practices is that a bad practice will emerge in a school with little to no thoughtful planning while a good practice will only emerge through a process of thoughtful planning and a clear understanding of what constitutes the "good." A school's theory and philosophy of technology use must be expressed through a written plan of action that places the school on a path where the technology program and the school's overarching operational and academic mission can meet and join forces at a workable praxis intersection. And, so, let us explore the elements of a Schoolwide Technology Plan.

When Building an Effective School Technology Program (ESTP), start with a well-conceived and well-designed Schoolwide Technology **PLAN**:

Purpose and rationale for technology in our school!

Long-term objectives for building technology literacy for staff, students, and parents!

Applications on a practical daily basis in, and outside of, the classroom and school building.

Nexus to the overarching schoolwide academic mission and meaning.

312

A school's technology plan and program must be dynamic, comprehensive, present, and forward-looking, and should prepare students for the next technological career frontier. We must always return to the central questions for any school initiative—how does this technology effort support or detract from the school's larger primary academic objectives of:

- Creating the optimum conditions and school environment where effective teaching and learning can go forward.

- Raising academic achievement, which implies reducing the possibilities and conditions for underachievement.

- Assisting students in successfully passing classes, performing well on internal and external standardized assessments, successfully completing academic projects and assignments.

- Moving and annually increasing the number of students toward, and into, graduation.

- Asking, how does this action empower and enhance the quality of our students' post-high school college and career options?

The school's TC, SBL team, clerical/administrative and security teams, the members of the Technology department staff as well as faculty representatives from every academic department must start the process of Technology Plan Building by addressing several important questions.

When we envision a senior graduate of our school, what level of technological knowledge and skills will they have mastered by graduation date?

What does "technology literacy competency" mean in this school? With high schools, the "end" is actually the beginning. For once we have discovered the attributes and qualities that would empower that young person walking across the stage to receive his or her diploma, we must then go back to the beginning of that student's journey in order to construct the path by which that student can reach that positive graduation profile. But how do we accomplish this? One way is to institute a written graduation requirement that all students must meet. That stated requirement will always lead to some task, product development, a series of work projects/activities, a senior production and/or project assignment, or a list of required courses or exams that must be taken and passed. Highly effective schools already engage in the practice of enriching and expanding the already standard local and state requirements for graduation (e.g., requiring students to take four years of a rigorous math course, four years of a laboratory science course, a pre-law/medical program, IB programs, credit/degree earning college or high school partnerships), and in the case of a STEM–CTE school, students may already have additional certifications and qualifications (e.g., EMT certification, construction trades pre-apprenticeship qualification, IBM, Cisco or Microsoft certification programs). These students, in most cases, will be required to meet one of the beforementioned graduation obligations, along with earning a college admissions-ready diploma. Adding an additional technology literacy course as a graduation requirement, as opposed to an elective, could present certain time, credit earning, and schedule space challenges for the students in these schools. One piece of good modern generational news, when it comes to technology education, is that even though some students may not have performed at their full academic potential prior to reaching high school, they may still possess a high level of tech savviness and feel comfortable engaging with technology. If a school designs the right plan of action, a list of technology courses required for graduation may not be necessary. Some of these steps are as follows:

- The school immerses itself and its instructional programs around the use of technology in the areas of teaching and learning. In such a school, "technology literacy" would not be an elective option, rather it would be a standard requirement for the student to be able to function as a member of that school community. The school's mission, philosophy, theme, and instructional and learning methodology is heavily inclined toward the active use of technology.

- In both of the schools where I served as principal, we were able to introduce in every academic department a serious research projects-based learning format; thus, students were essentially "forced" to actively engage with computers and Internet-based resources.

- To accommodate students in a rich, research-project development environment, the school library must be focused on serving as technology-based informational resource and research centers.

- All teachers and educational paraprofessionals were issued a laptop computer. This allows the teaching staff to standardize and coordinate a great deal of administrative and instructional tasks, such as atten-

314

dance taking, managing electronic grade books/report cards, collecting and translation testing data, and accessing smartboards and other school-based equipment and technology. The standardized electronic administrative equipment and procedures are extremely helpful in departmental meetings, pre- and post-formal classroom observation meetings, parent meetings, open school day/night meetings, Special Education pre-referral meetings as well as IEP meetings, or when a student is challenging a final grade. These laptops (as strongly emphasized in the required orientation taught by the TC) are to be used for school-related business only. The principal may need to raise funds beyond the allocated district budget to make this teacher laptop lending program work.

Note to principals: Make sure that the "limited usage" clause is part of the acceptance of responsibility agreement that the teacher must sign before taking possession of the laptop. Your school district's legal officer should have a standard equipment loan form on file as well as the district's policy on staff usage of the Internet. Both the equipment release form and an orientation covering the district use of equipment policy should be part of the required pre-release of equipment orientation, and a dated orientation attendance sheet should also be signed. This will eliminate most of the misunderstandings that can emerge from a staff laptop lending project.

- In a STEM-CTE program or themed school, the role of technology is inseparable from the programmatic learning objectives and outcomes being sought. Technology is not an add-on or an academic enhancement to the instructional program and mission; technology is an instructional program and mission! The required themed programs, the courses that are associated with these programs, and/or student majors alone ensure that students are intensely utilizing technology for the major part of the school day.

- Elective courses are an additional option by which students can grow their technology intelligence. And these technology-related courses can be offered across academic department boundaries, for example, the Computer-Internet Research (Library), the role of technology in the history of human events (History department), computer art (Art department), the technology of set design, sound and lighting systems (Drama department), and the technology of producing music (Music department).

- If there is an expectation (even in a non-STEM-CTE school) that students will, in every class, be required in some way to engage with computers and the Internet, then the school should make sure that students are not disadvantaged based on parent resources and/or the quality of technology education in their K-8 experience. The school must make sure (starting in the Summer Bridge Program) that all students receive the requisite instructional information on how to effectively engage the equipment and online resources. Please don't assume that a recent arrival from a middle school will automatically know how to use computers and the Internet properly (or safely!) and more importantly how to use them to do proper research. In public education, equity is often confused with equality, to the detriment of those students who live on the "less than" end of the wealth-entitlement equation. If a school commits to the development of the effective technology school model, then it must also commit to closing the access to technology divide that exists in our nation. And that might happen programmatically by way of an extended after-school program in which students can have access to Internet-linked computers, or weekend access to computers and the Internet, or a laptop lending program. If a school chooses only to create a rich and dynamic school day technology program and ignore the built-in societal technology inequalities, then that school is an active participant in building and reinforcing the national economic entitlement technology divide.

As a specialized STEM, CTE, or a STEM-CTE school, technology and its applications go to the very core of the meaning and purpose for the school; how is this centrality of technology in the schoolwide curriculum theme reflected in our schoolwide technology plan?

The answer to this question must be in the form of standards, along with their descriptive, measurable, and explanatory rubrics. As with any set of adoptive school standards, when thinking about technology competency, the school's instructional-administrative community should not feel shy about going, when appropriate, beyond the district, state, and national standards; or to match those technology standards with the specific mission and theme of the school. For example, at a STEM-CTE school like Phelps ACE, it was impossible for a student to go through a school day without the hands-on engagement of some type of technology-based equipment, machine, or tool. That means that the school could ill afford too much maintenance downtime, because that could translate into instructional lost time. Part of the TC's operational part of the technology plan must address the need to keep the school's technology program moving forward with as little disruption as possible. There is a natural wear and tear problem with all machinery and equipment, and when you have a school full of these items that are being used approximately six or more hours a day for an entire school year, replacement and maintenance issues will emerge. To accomplish this, there must be an extensive "spare parts" storage-inventory system that may not make sense to the district's budget department. Also complicated, for large equipment and machinery items, the TC is going to need to maintain and manage multiple service and maintenance contracts by outside vendors.

The expanded graduation expectations and requirements in a STEM, CTE, and STEM-CTE school will define the school's expectations as to the depth and width of the amount of technical knowledge that is needed to successfully study at the school as well as what is expected by the time a student graduates from the school. There are some general skills that cut across all majors (e.g., pre-engineering, aeronautics, electricity and welding) like keyboarding and having the knowledge to do Internet research. And then there is the specific technical knowledge that is required in a specific area of concentration. These types of schools will need an ambitious and ongoing skills upgrading: program/professional development/classes/workshops/training budget.

Every school must create its own definition of technical literacy based on the school's theme, focus, human, equipment, financial resources, and overall mission. Technology literacy in a STEM-CTE program or school will (and should) look different from a general/comprehensive (or performance, creative arts-themed) high school's definition of technical literacy. *How much technology is enough?* This question alone will make the case for the need to have a full-time, tech savvy, fully trained TC. And definitely why the TC position must have a high degree of technical expertise. For beyond the daily tech-troubleshooting, the TC must also serve as the chief technology educator/trainer in the building. There may also be a need, depending on the size of the school, for additional members of a technical team. Also, since these tech-themed programs/schools are heavily dependent on a large amount of working equipment, part of the school's technology plan is the: what for, how much, by when and how of raising external (to the school's budget) the funds needed to acquire, continually upgrade, support, and maintain such an ambitious technology program!

Putting the school's technology plan into practice

Putting parts (segments incrementally over time), or the whole technology plan into action, should be strategically organized over a long, step-by-step process. At the same time, the evolutionary nature of technological innovation and tech-related careers suggests that the plan should also be flexible, adaptive, and dynamic. Four years is a lifetime in the world of technological invention and innovation. Schools must make sure that students are not being prepared only for the present economic-industrial period; the technology plan must always have its eyes on new and future technologic trends. The library must make sure to keep a current technology innovation, information magazine section in the library, for example *Popular Science, Science, MIT Technology Review, Wired, Computer World*, etc.

Strategic steps in operationalizing the schoolwide technology plan in a non-specialized or STEM, CTE themed school

The first objective is to start the process of the integration of technology into every academic department in the school, such that the lessons, learning, the in- and out-of-classroom experiences should involve the students and staff in some aspect of technology. Along with smartboards, there will be the need to invest in the hiring and professional development of tech-smart teachers and administrators.

Establish of an Applied Technology Learning Lab that incorporates the following and/or similar technology content work areas/stations:

- Biomedical/health and physical fitness science.

- Robotics.

- Biotechnology-micro video systems.

- Gaming creation technology.

- Forensic science: cyber and bio-chem lab applications.

- Rocketry-space technology.

- Aerodynamics-flight simulation.

- Communication technology: video, photography, recording-broadcasting, online/off-line publishing, etc.

- Elements of electrical, mechanical, computer, industrial and civil engineering.

- Automated manufacturing technology—CAD, CNC and CIM.

Satellite/National Oceanic and Atmospheric Administration (http://www.noaa.gov/)/ national weather service (http://www.weather.gov/) linked weather station.

A National Oceanic and Atmospheric Administration (NOAA: http://www.education.noaa.gov/noaa_educ.html#nesdis) satellite linked school weather station.

The school may also want to include other dedicated technology-based learning labs/classrooms:

- A dedicated (with recessed computers stations at each desk) or mobile Distance Learning-Teleconferencing system.

- A digital photography, video, sound, lighting production center. This program can support many activities in the school as well as generate funding by producing items like a digital senior yearbook.

Designing dedicated computer labs to support the various school's academic programs as a place to teach computer concepts and skills provide student self-directed and directed academic tutorials; and to support, (along with the library) computer-based research, writing, and editing. This option presents another opportunity for grant seeking with both software and system licenses in research-based informational systems, such as ERIC as well as the numerous free and open access sites (such as Library of Congress https://www.loc.gov/maps/collections/).

In the Art department, a tech component or lab specializing in:

- School art magazine production.

- Computer-generated Art and Imagery.

- Graphics and Animation.

- Cartoon and comic book production.

- Virtual tours of art museums and works of art.

- Computer-generated architectural and landscaping design.

Even as all high schools strengthened their engagement, education, strategic application, and operational commitment to the use of technology and technology education, let us not jump on the ever-arriving and ever-changing (and often wrong) societal hot careers' bandwagons. Each child is individually gifted, individually talented, and individually interested in pursuing a particular life path. We should not be party to an effort for having all students follow economic employment projections data rather than their own mind and heart. We can balance counseling them to pursue their dreams with the financial reality and odds of entering a particular career path. Which is why it is important for the school to have a philosophy of technology education that teaches the use of technology in multiple career avenues, rather than just limiting students to a singular focus on a specific STEM vocation. One of the jobs of the school in general, and the College/Career Guidance Counseling program, is to help students fully understand how technology, going forward, will dramatically impact whatever career they choose to pursue and that their adaptive technology knowledge and skills will greatly determine how successful they are in that given and ever-changing career option. As ethical educational professionals, we want to be responsible and help students to fulfill their dreams in whatever career they select to pursue. And part of that responsibility is to teach students the many technology links in every future career option they may choose. We also want them to be able to take advantage of any technological innovation that enters their career. I say this as an educator whose major professional interests, love, and primary focus is STEM education, schools cannot allow themselves to be turned into technology jobs factories. Our primary task is to fully prepare students to be technology-competent citizens in all aspects of their lives, including wherever they choose to present their personal career interests, gifts, and talents to the world.

Financing a schoolwide technology department plan and program

Resources are always critical in any educational initiative. And, so, how a principal organizes financial, equipment/materials, human, internal (district) and external organizational/institutional support is necessary for a successful and effective schoolwide technology program. A first-class, effective high school technology program cannot exist without the appropriate financial support. Which means that the best visionary and thoughtful technology plan must include an acquisition plan that would allow the school to gain access to the necessary resources, so that the school can move the vision from potentiality on paper, to the productive reality of actual programs that serve students, staff, and parents. No high school's effective technology program was built in a day, so the technology plan must be co-partnered with a fundraising capacity plan that will pay for the necessary resource requirements of the technology plan even as this resource acquisition plan seeks to maintain an ongoing high standard of operational technology excellence. In other words, the schoolwide technology program cannot lose ground as it seeks to gain ground. It is important for the principal, the SBL team, and the TC to understand that a huge percentage of the resources generated by this technology fundraising plan will not necessarily be expressed as cash. Indeed, a great deal of the elements of a school's technology fundraising plan will be received by way of STEM professionals volunteering their time (e.g., setting up and networking a computer lab); university students volunteering and doing internships (e.g., National Association of Black engineers—http://www.nsbe.org); corporate STEM employees volunteering as mentors and coaches for robotics and cyber forensics teams; free online technology-related courses such as Cisco, Microsoft, and Columbia University History Project; corporate equipment donations; and in one situation at Phelps ACE, a corporation allowing (donating) one of its STEM-CTE employees to spend a year teaching full-time at the high school without any cost to the school or district. The principal must also organize a "Power Rangers Rolodex." These are the resource-rich contacts you have cultivated and nurtured over the years. They are the individuals who passionately believe in the mission and promise of your school. The rule is that you don't call them for something you can get done with your regular budget, and you don't call them on any matter of personal gain. There is a large and rich reservoir of skilled, talented, and connected people who actually want to see our public schools succeed and specifically succeed for those young people who were born on the downside of the disenfranchised track. The list covers many different job descriptions, professional fields, and socio-political endeavors. Its list is diverse from Fortune 500 executives, local, state, and nationally appointed officials, the military branches of the U.S. government, retired educators, skilled construction trades people, university administrators and faculty, informal educational institutions and CBO directors and employees, entertainers and professional athletes. What all of these individuals have in common is that they want a good reason to help a public school, which means they want to see a vision, a plan, and an operational organizational structure that could make that vision work. Here, the school's grant writer is essential for the creation of a boilerplate technology proposal that covers all of the school's technology needs. The strength of this document is that in the hands of a good grant writer this document can be retrofitted and modified quickly to address any and all types of gift or grant offers, or any governmental, foundation, or private sector RFP.

With a solid foundation of technology funding sources and connected-people resources secured, the next step is to review and make the necessary adjustments, particularly in the area of long-term objectives for the technology plan. Also, think about how the plan will succeed without (beyond) you. To be honest, many corporate and government partnerships are made and sealed based on personal relationships—the vision and entrepreneurial energy invested and expressed by the principal. An important question you want to ask yourself is, what happens to this fund-resource raising program if I retire or accept a promotion? This is probably the title of a separate book or seminar, but you need to think about how you can document and pass on the productive aspects of your principal's entrepreneurial practices that are utilized to support a dynamic technology program to the staff or your successor.

Chapter 19:
The Importance of Building Maintenance and the Custodial Services Department

The first, and most important, principle that must be established with the building maintenance and custodial services team is that they are a key part of the pedagogical staff and academic achievement effort—that, in fact, the physical condition of the school will work for or against the realization of the school's mission. This is the point that must be firmly planted and continually pressed by the SBL team. I understand that the custodial staff may not have a background of formal pedagogical training, so it is left to the principal to make the case, as it must be made with all non-classroom instructional staff that the tasks they perform are directly connected to raising academic achievement in the school. The school's physical condition and appearance is a *Tonal, Climatic,* and *Culturally* accurate and revelatory comment on what that school truly holds dear. Further, how the school looks is a visible commentary on how that school feels about, and honors, the people who work, teach, and learn inside of its walls. It is a definitive proclamation to those who visit the school, "This is what we think of ourselves, and this is what we want you to leave thinking about us!" As with any educational initiative or goal, there must be clear standards, rubrics, and an evaluative process in place to define what is a clean and well-maintained building that is supportive and conducive to good working and living conditions as well as an effective teaching and learning environment. The principal should have no illusions about how hard it is to successfully accomplish this goal. Like most departments, operational areas, and job categories in public education, there are cultural beliefs that fuel and drive work habits, practices, and procedures. Many of these operational work habits are outdated and/or ineffective, and they could be protected by contractual, state, city, district rules and regulations, or labor organizational (union) agreements. Public education can also exhibit all of the worst traits of a bad, entrenched, and entranced bureaucracy where employees do things "a certain way," not because it makes sense or is productive but because it's the way it has always been done! Such is the case in how school building cleaning and maintenance is too often approached and practiced. The principal must first establish the fundamental standards by which the custodial leader and his or her staff will be evaluated. Unless you are extremely lucky, you will surely hit an oppositional wall. Even in a place like NYC (and from my experience, a place with one of the best approaches to school building maintenance in the nation) that prides itself on the wonderful maintenance of some very old school buildings, I drew complaints from the custodial staff when I initially proposed my different philosophical approach and definition of a clean school. Fortunately, in both NYC and Washington, D.C., I had district directors of school facilities who backed me up. Having a school district facility director who shares your cleaning and maintenance standards can make a critically important difference in this clean and well-maintained school effort! Start with discussing the most problematic fundamental assumptions, those bad, habitual and wrong practices about how a school should be cleaned and maintained by the custodial staff. For example:

- Start with asking them what major concerns they have and the challenges they face as a custodial team. You will immediately begin to hear their understanding and definition of what constitutes a clean and well-maintained school building. The principal acquiring this data is critical in designing a building culture where good maintenance is the standard. Another piece of important information you can gather from this phase is the identification of those principal, staff, and student decisions and behaviors that prevent them from performing and producing at their best. (Or maybe they think they are already the best.) This information can help you to formulate the strategies needed to integrate the custodial staff and the rest of the school family into a single mission, a clean and well-maintained school that supports academic achievement.

- Have the serious talk about why and how the role of the custodial department is making the school mission successful. This conversation must be had in an extended meeting with the custodial staff. Promote the idea in this meeting of having an Effective Building Maintenance and Custodial Services Department (EBMCSD). You must have this conversation, even if you face a sea of misbelieving and confused faces. Be patient, and remember they may have never heard of their work being defined in such a way or had a similar meeting with a former principal. Turn the idea of making sure the school is well-maintained into a schoolwide learning objective and mission. This is important in that the custodial staff will take the lead in this mission, though it is the responsibility of the entire school family to serve as members of the school beatification clean team! It is at this part of the conversation where you usually get the full attention of the custodial staff. For it is at this point you outline your short and long-term school building cleaning and maintenance plan. And most importantly, the distribution of responsibility assignments and expectations for you, the SBL team, instructional and non-classroom administrative/support staff, and students. The radical idea of engaging an entire school family into taking collective responsibility for the physical condition of a school helps to break the custodial staff away from the old "them versus us" historical approach to school cleaning and maintenance. This philosophy also pulls the custodial staff into the family of institutional departments who may have their own individual operational objectives, and yet they are all equally committed to helping the school realize its overarching academic achievement mission. Without diving deep into pedagogical terms like "standards," "rubrics," and "assessments," it must be made clear to the custodial staff that their department, like any other department, must achieve, and will be evaluated based on a set of clear, mutually understood standards and high expectations. And, further, make it clear in this session by stating that for you, school and learning isn't just what happens inside a classroom. Schooling and learning is also the physical state of classrooms, halls, bathrooms, floors, ceilings, walls, and the absence of a broken look permeating the building. As with its scholastic (academic study and learning) ability, a school is defined by its cleanliness, level of comfort, beauty, and the amount of maintenance care that is invested in its upkeep. How a school looks and is maintained speaks to the pride, appreciation, and sense of ownership that the school family holds for the institution. Finally, you should make a partnership agreement with them that just as you are asking them to step up as clean, school mission achievement team leaders, you will also present concrete plans, policies, and procedures that will encourage and inspire staff and students to become active partners and advocates of a clean and well-maintained school.

- Have an honest conversation that clearly defines your standards for preventative maintenance, the rubrics or the descriptive conditions (evidence) for determining when something is considered cleaned, fixed (quality and effective completion time), or well-maintained. (This is one of the good reasons to have a woman as part of the custodial staff; my experience is that they almost always have higher standards for what is considered clean. Sorry, guys…), and most importantly, it is those standards that will be used for purposes of departmental and individual professional evaluations and ratings. These standards will (if they are good) no doubt go beyond the district's regulatory standards or the acceptable practices of the custodial community. Like all work efforts that operate in a school, each principal must make a personal decision about choosing the level of ineffectiveness and incompetence they are willing to tolerate for the sake of a false sense of peace.

- Turn the meeting into a walk-and-talk session (preferably at the end of the school day). When a superintendent or principal walks around a school, there are important places to look when determining the custodial staff's understanding and commitment to being an EBMCSD. The students' bathrooms are a clear indication of the quality of cleaning and maintenance. A smelly bathroom environment, dirty floors and walls, broken and/or not properly functioning fixtures, toilets and urinals that don't flush properly, missing or broken toilet stall doors, graffiti, missing or malfunctioning apparatuses for washing and drying hands, no soap and soap dispensers, or toilet paper in toilet paper dispensers are big problems. A clean and functional bathroom system must be an organizational priority for the principal and SBL team. The other areas of a school building that reveal poor cleaning and maintenance practices are dust-covered areas, dirty glass areas, small or large elements of graffiti, small broken or missing fixtures, particularly easily fixable items like door knobs, missing ceiling tiles, light bulb replacement, the presence of old, long-term dirt, floor tiles/carpet damage, broken/damaged furniture, holes in walls, areas in need of painting, the (floor) waxing over of dirt practice. One of the problems in many school systems is the improper and ill-advised contractual agreements that limit what custodians can do, along with the non-productive bureaucratic repair structure that severely hurts and prevents good school maintenance. It is understandable that for particularly complicated jobs, bringing in a district licensed plumber or painter may be necessary; but for the majority of things that are in need of fixing, repairing/replacing, painting, and correcting in a school, most of it should be able to be done by a member of the custodial staff. Waiting for a centralized district painting, locksmith, etc., repair and replace team to get to a school can often be challenging, as these teams are more likely triaged to address emergency safety items. But that can leave a school in the long-term state of living daily with an unsightly, inaccessible, malfunctioning, demoralizing, deteriorating building. The custodial staff's job description and requirements include the addition of a "repair and replace" person(s) who is skilled to perform many of the minor repairs that occur daily in the school. Many school custodial staff already engage in this practice, as I was fortunate to have such skilled and talented individuals in my schools. But this good custodial practice should not be arbitrary or based on principal's luck; rather, it should be a standard operating procedure in every school. But until that happens, the principal should do an informal (verbal) skills survey of your present custodial staff, and then figure out how to "win them over" and reward them for taking on minor repairs and maintenance work outside of their contracted job description.

- We need to challenge the idea of how the custodial staff utilizes its time. The standard practice is for the custodial staff to clean up the building at the end of the day; meanwhile, sit somewhere on accident duty and wait to be called to clean a "spilled" something up. That approach poses particular problems for high schools since the end of the day is oftentimes stretched into the evening. So, if dirt is left to accumulate over the course of an entire day, by the end of the day, large numbers of students in after-school activities will be swimming in dirt!

- Like all public education employees, the custodial staff should be expected to work (minus their lunch and statutory breaks) the entire workday. The custodial supervisor should create a priority list of "fixing" and ongoing building maintenance items as well as a daily cleaning and replenishment in the building schedule.

- Discuss preventative maintenance and repair time. Also in need of a challenge is the idea of waiting for things to happen and then take a long time to repair the situation. My thinking is that fixing, repairing, and replacing as quickly as possible during the course of the day will not only make the school more aesthetically pleasing and comfortable but would also create a collective psychology (particularly with the student body) that we should all care and take responsibility for the physical well-being of the school building.

- Share the good news, which they won't believe at first hearing! By following your lead in making the school a model of a clean and well-maintained school, the staff and students will join in and also work hard to keep the school clean and well-maintained, thus ultimately making their work easier!

- The meeting(s) must not end until everyone (principal and custodial staff) is clear about the definitional standards of what is meant by preventative maintenance, proactive cleaning, well-maintained, in a timely manner, ready, finished, and complete.

Once these cleaning and maintenance standards and expectations are thoroughly discussed with the custodial staff, the next step is to propose schoolwide positive solutions.

Present the custodial team to the school (at the opening assembly of the year and at subsequent rewards ceremonies) as part of the educational team. Publicly announce that the condition of the school building is a lesson in what and how the school family members feel about the work that is done there— and even more importantly, how they feel about themselves. That this is the team who will lead those lessons and efforts in making the physical school reflect our internal striving for academic excellence.

The custodial staff are also the clean building leaders, but they don't work alone. Every member of the school family from administrators, teachers, and security personnel, administrative staff, parents and students will be held responsible for the cleanliness and beautification of the building. For most hours of the day, this is everyone's home, and it is in everyone's power to live in a clean and inspiring home.

The principal must observe and evaluate the work of the custodial supervisor as well as the entire custodial staff. This is made easy if floors and/or designated sections of the interior and exterior of the building are assigned to specific custodial staff members. Importantly, the principal must give equal attention to the cleanliness and upkeep of both the exterior and interior parts of the building.

Getting the custodial staff to buy into the proactive clean and well-maintained school philosophy is critical and difficult. But here again is the *carrot*. I offered to both my school's custodial staffs the following promise: If they follow my plan of action, along with my commitment to convince the students to be good caretaking partners of the school building, then their work would by the end of the year be easier, less stressful, and more rewarding. Essentially, I proposed that if they worked harder and more focused upfront (early in the school year), this would make keeping the building clean and well-maintained much easier later in the school year. Further, I asserted that going forward, the school would become much cleaner and better maintained, not because of the actions of the custodial staff alone, but due to the change in the attitude and behavior of the staff and student body. The truth is that the first time I proposed this approach to a custodial staff, it was an untested hypothesis. I really had no way of knowing if it would actually work. And it was in many ways similar to convincing my teachers to go to a "four days of instruction and one day of assessment" instructional model. Historically, public education systems have engaged in the bad institutional habit of investing in high energy, low results activities and programs. I knew (based on the looks on the faces of the custodial staff members) that what I was suggesting sounded contradictory and counterintuitive (like less instructional time turning into more instructional time). Very often, a principal who truly hopes to help young people must go beyond the standard acceptance of how a task or job title in the school is defined. And when working with at-risk students (Black, Brown, and Latino, recent emigrants, the poor of any color, the financially "unentitled" and disenfranchised), employing the standard operating procedures and practices will not work. The use of the public school operational norm or "business as usual" approach means that these at-risk students will succeed only by accident. But understandably, the looks I received from the custodial staff was a response to my idea that we do something completely different from how it was traditionally done. And, so, I proposed:

- That we continually clean the school, making cleanliness the standard in the minds of the entire school family. That meant sweeping the halls between each passing of classes as well as engaging in minor repairs and building maintenance throughout the day. It could be anything from a missing doorknob, broken window shade, a loosely hanging exit sign, or a missing ceiling tile. Over time, I insisted that clean would become the comfortable norm and everybody in the building would work to maintain that norm. Humans (consciously or not) follow the rules of biological, historical, social customs, and habits. They will adjust and adapt (in both a positive and negative way) to the reality of the psychological, social, cultural norms in which they are immersed every day and then become (again for good or bad) both passive and active contributors to a long-term condition that they have come to accept as normal. Being forced to live in an environment with large amounts of trash and debris encourages additional contributions of trash and debris. A major component of a schoolwide clean school effort is to raise the collective self-esteem and pride level of the entire school family. In essence, we are all saying that we are worthy and deserve a school that is well-maintained and clean.

- Make small things big things—no job or "minor repair" is too small to clean and fix. Bathrooms were to be cleaned and checked for soap and toilet paper throughout the day; continuing through to the last class of the day. Students who study or attend after-school programs and activities, and the staff members who work with them should not be subjected to a filthy building; places like the faculty and student bathrooms should be clean and well stocked the first period of the school day until the last student and staff person leaves the building's after-school programs. All graffiti (no matter how small) was to be removed (after taking a photo for disciplinary reasons) immediately, even if it meant painting it over during the school day; depriving the graffiti perpetrator what they seek the most, recognition and attention. Not waiting for the end of the day (to push large amounts of dirt and debris), or week (except in special circumstances) to fix, repair, clean, or replace something should end as a practice. The idea here is to shift cleaning and maintenance from reactive to proactive activity. The team should engage in actual intense cleaning often, not wait for the major school breaks to launch a massive cleaning initiative. By then, the dirt has literally "dug in!"

- We need a strategic plan with a triage component for making larger repairs in the building. I was fortunate at both of my high schools that the staff stepped up, particularly in the area of repairs, where they could have easily submitted a "request for repair" form to the central maintenance administration, then wait for months (if it is not determined to be an emergency) for them to show up. With the custodial staff taking on a lot of small to medium repairs, the perception that items in need of repair lingered as eyesores and inconveniences for months, stopped. Two important custodian qualities are necessary for this to work, and those same two important attributes should help guide the SBL team in the hiring of custodial staff: (1) the willingness to go above or beyond the job description and contract, and (2) having a basic working knowledge and skill of a particular trade (carpentry, plumbing, painting, locksmith, etc.).

- My long-term view is that the custodial position must be totally redefined, such that each person who is hired comes in with an established level of competency in a particular skill trade area, thus, allowing them to be able to do more repair work in the school; this, of course, will mean more staff positions, but the long-term savings for this approach would easily pay for that extra position. If a school offers a large survey of after-school, school breaks, and weekend activities, then there is absolutely a need for an evening (night) cleaning shift.

What happened when we undertook this clean and well-maintained school building initiative?

- The students responded to the clean environment by taking ownership of their own disposing of trash. Placing trash collectors conspicuously throughout the building helped!

- The teachers had each student pick up any paper near their desks at the end of each class period.

- Students were encouraged to thoroughly clean off their tables during the lunch periods.

- Having art, including the work of students, displayed on the school walls creates an atmosphere that says, this school is a special place. (It also offers a creative and positive outlet for the graffiti folks!)

- Just about everyone, including the principal, engaged in the practice of picking up any paper or trash from the floor, no matter how small. The extra garbage cans throughout the building incentivized the school family to see that paper ended up in trash cans and not on the floor.

- No designs or markings on lockers were allowed.

331

- Because of the rigorous academic program, very few students actually went to the bathroom during class time, which meant less bathroom cleaning.

- Increasingly, over time (and faster than my projected schedule), the building was much easier for the custodians to clean at the end of the day/week/holiday/summer breaks.

- The custodial staff shifted out of reactive mode and were able to effectively address the normal wear and tear and repair issues of the building. Yes, milk or juice still from time to time spilled in the cafeteria. But because the building was always in a relatively clean state, these occasional custodial emergencies did not have the effect of causing a deterioration in the schoolwide cleaning and maintained plan.

Note to principals: Effectively manage the "knowable problem stuff" and you will be better prepared to meet and conquer the "unknowable problem stuff" that always seems to emerge at the most inopportune times. Effective school building maintenance is a lot like the principal and SBL's approach to effective school operational management. Unplanned emergencies are destined to show up daily (students or staff members get sick in the middle of the school day; a parent/child conflict spills over into the school, etc.), and so the key is to be proactive about the issues you know are coming your way. By doing so, you will have ample time and the psychological capacity to deal with any unforeseen emergency that inconveniently shows up in a school on a regular basis. Underperforming and ineffective schools are characterized by a Culture that is constantly in emergency-reactive mode. They can't invest in serious planning and building for a positive future because they are constantly battling for survival in the immediate now; these schools expend all of their emotional and physical energy only to live and get through that present school day.

Every plan/strategy (classroom lesson or building management/operations) requires: Standards and a set of rubrics by which the "action taken" can be measured and evaluative. And, so, I informed the custodial foreman separately that at least once a week, the two of us would do a before or after-school evaluation of every part of the school building. Any corrections, improvements, or upgrades would first be handled by the foreman; if that failed to produce the desired results, I would communicate (in writing) with the individual custodial staff person as well as the foreman. This is the opportunity for you to coach the coach; however, you should inform the custodial foreperson and every person in a supervisory role in your building that if you, the principal, must take on the job of directly supervising staff members assigned to their supervision, then it raises a question about what their role is at the institution. As the principal, you are (always) ultimately responsible for the physical state and condition of the building. But that does not mean that you don't hold those who have a maintenance supervisory role fully responsible for the work product quality of the people they supervise.

Cleanliness is a habit, which has the power to reinforce itself until it becomes a part of the unconscious acts of institutional Culture

Humans are habit-forming creatures. Like all things in public education (and life), the standards and definition of "accustomed to" is a matter of the collective will and the collective sense of self-worth. When a school lives and practices a *Culture* where "broken, disrepair, cleaning neglect, and in need of replacement" is the standard expectation, they will then see dirty and broken things as a "normal" way of living. They will also see the custodial staff as charged with cleaning up after them, as opposed to a clean and well-maintained building being a collective school family effort. The opposite is also true; when a school *Culture* enforces the importance of maintaining a clean, emotionally healthy atmosphere, then those staff members will naturally reinforce that *Culture* through their individual practices and habits. A school building must "say" in its presentation that it honors the people who work and learn there! Utilizing the principles of Proactive Cleaning and Maintenance is the complimentary factor to a peaceful, respectful, and productive learning environment. One cannot exist without the other since they emerge from the same core central school *Culture* of effectiveness in the pursuit of excellence. A clean and well-maintained school building is the companion and champion of the school's high academic achievement mission. A principal should also know that morale matters and nothing undermines morale more than going to work and learning every day in a building that does not honor your presence. The principal should have no illusions, workplace habits, and cultural traditions are extremely hard to break; but you will find this is true of every department and job category in public education, even when something is not working and is clearly no longer productive, people will still stubbornly engage in that behavior and/or practice. This can produce a culture of low expectations and complacency. You must take the lead because everyone will follow your lead, even if you unfortunately lead in the wrong direction. By asking that every department in the school redefine and reinvent themselves out of the public education standard practice of verbal and symbolic gestures into doing real and meaningful work for children, transitional pains will emerge. But we must lead by encouraging professional courage and discouraging the love and worship of old procedures and practices, many of which were put in place not only before the students were born, but before the current crop of custodians were born!

My hypothesis proved right (at both schools!): Aggressive, proactive cleaning and school building maintenance does eventually make the custodial work easier and dramatically reduces the need for major building repairs. Also, making students partners, as opposed to building care adversaries, connects the larger mission of raising their self-esteem and sense of self-worth among the school family members. Any people who love themselves feel that their living, learning, and working environment should love them back. They truly believe that they are worthy and deserve nice things, and a clean, inspiring, and uplifting school building environment is just that. Students destroy, injure, dirty, and break a school when they feel that the school and the adults working there are their enemy; and what better place to take out their anger and resentment than on the inanimate building itself. After all, the school is not welcoming; it is not honoring and loving them. The principal's job is to encourage and help all of the members of the school family to see the mastery, pride of work, and accomplishment inside of themselves, even when they themselves are unable to see those attributes of excellence. That they are deserving of everything a clean and aesthetically pleasing space can offer in the way of inspiration. I am not going to pretend that this task is easy, but it must be undertaken. Self-loving and empowered people care for and maintain their environment; they feel they deserve cleanliness. Fully actualized humans also protect themselves and the environment for which they feel is an important contributor to their actualization; and so in the next chapter we'll look at what good schools do to protect their mission, along with the school family members who live out that mission.

Chapter 20:
High School Safety and Security Services Department

The principal's fundamental approach to leading the security team is to define and establish, as a core departmental cultural value, what it means to *Serve* and *Protect* the school community! Not necessarily an easy task since many school safety and police officers bring a conscious or unconscious "lock 'em up" mentality into the school in which they are assigned. The principal must fully destroy (yes, I said destroy) that ideology if there is any hope of your students being treated like full human beings. The security *Serving* and *Protecting* profile for schools will vary greatly; disenfranchised and disentitled school security presenting as pre-prison while enfranchised and entitled school security reflecting a pre-college approach. The principal of even the poorest, most populated with students of color high school in the nation must resist the former pre-prison security approach and uphold the later pre-college approach school atmosphere! This is of critical importance in schools that educate large numbers of students who, because of many historical-political reasons, are seen by too many in law enforcement agencies and official public policy positions as citizens in need of containment and punishment rather than service and protection. The principal of a Title I (poor) school must promote and uphold the U.S. legal ideal of a person not being guilty or a criminal simply based on the individual's race, religion, nationality, ethnicity, economic status, and/or zip code in which they reside even when these "truths" are not self-evident and held sacred by the government that oversees the district where the school is located. A school must protect itself and the members of the school family from any harm, hurt, loss, and any danger or threat to that school's ability to engage in teaching and learning in the most peaceful and productive way. However, the school must display (and the principal must model) the best attributes of justice, fairness, compassion, and equality under the laws that govern behaviors of staff and students. Finally, it is our ethical and philosophical duty to fully educate, serve, and protect all students in our care, regardless of their (or their parents') U.S. citizenship-residency status. The doors of the school are open, let all children who want to be educated come and be safe.

The art and heart of serving and protecting

Serving: In the eyes of many in this nation, the mere existence and presence of some children in our society defines and designates them as criminal (or at the very least, criminally prone) simply based on their social, ethnicity, racial, or economic status. The problem can emerge from them observing normal teenage behaviors like the inability to moderate the volume of their voices during a group discussion, the sometimes culturally based use of animated body or hand gestures while talking, the inability on the part of observing adults to understand slang, horseplay, the assumed dressing in a "hoodlum" fashion, appearing like they are looking for trouble when in fact their grouping, bold gestures, and loud words could actually be defensive and protectionary actions in response to other violent and predatory teenagers. The bottom line is that Black and Brown teenagers are often not allowed to be teenagers. Sometimes, it is just about the adult observers forgetting when they were once teenagers and how their public behaviors may have caused adults to shake their heads in worry and despair about the present and future state of our nation and world! To get to *Service* as an operational approach, the principal must openly and honestly discuss with the security team this complicated perception problem that exists in our nation. First, as in any society, the problem of adults not understanding the innate developmental behaviors and complex emotional stages of being teenagers, the perception problem is exacerbated by those same adults suffering from a form of collective social amnesia (or fictional remembrance) about their own teenaged lives. Teenage behaviors can often be annoying for us adults, and perhaps even uncomfortable; but they don't necessarily rise to the level of danger or criminality.

The second part of opening the *Service* conversation is the frank and honest discussion about how race, class, "body type," culture, gender, religion, zip code, style, and dressing preferences play out and into the perceptions and responses of law enforcement personnel and agencies. And, principal, please don't make the tragic mistake of thinking that a security officer (or teacher, AP, school aide, etc.) of color is going to automatically agree with, or even accept, that your "Students of Color Matter!" philosophy of school security. For I have found over the years that even officers of color must be assisted in shifting out of a military policing style response-thinking mode whenever a problem or conflict emerges in the school. *Serving* then is defined as the response to any security threat between students, always starting and inclines toward de-escalation as opposed to confrontation and escalation. *Serving* the student body actually gives power and meaning to the phrase "Peace Officers." *Serving* suggests that the security staff sees the students as worthy inheritors of the human and planetary progress experience and, therefore, worth saving. *Serving* behaviors on the part of security officers affirms full human and citizen rights upon the students. Our most professional and effective *Service* to the public (in this case students) is the highest and best good practice and expression of all of us (including police and security officers) who are public civil *servants*!

Effective Service in school security is consistent with the school's academic mission!

The school's mission and culture should push every department, including school security, toward a practice and belief system that says we must honor and value our students and staff, as we also honor their humanity and the rights and privileges associated with that humanity. Part of those rights and privileges includes guaranteeing that the teaching and learning environment can be safe and protected. It has been my experience that unpredictable, unsafe, chaotic, flying from one crisis response to another schools are always associated with chronic and pervasive academic underachievement. Serving the humanity of all students while protecting the human right of the entire student body to acquire a useful and rigorous education is not easy. It is a challenging balance but it must be achieved, which is why the screening and selection process for school safety officers is so critical. The *Service* as security philosophy also means that schools actually need less muscle enforcement as an approach and more strategically thoughtful counseling personality types as security personnel. In any school, the students will always have an overwhelming "military" advantage based on the sheer numbers ratio of students to adults in the building. The best school safety plan and team will come up with a strategy to enroll the student body in taking ownership of their own safety and security. The principal only needs to be clear, convincing, and consistent. You really want to open the door to the student body making a collective commitment to a safe and secure school. This is a critical security department objective that must be sought and won, and it absolutely can't be won if the security team sees and treats all students like potential perpetrators or criminals. The school safety officers will need to treat the students as partners in the plan for effective schoolwide security. This can be accomplished because, as I have always said, even in the most safety challenged and academically underperforming schools, the vast majority of students just want to attend a safe and protective school every day, and they want to learn in a peaceful and productive classroom.

Protecting: The next step in the establishment of an Effective High School Safety and Security Services Department (EHSSS) is to define as one of their primary objectives to physically protect the school family members and to secure the school from damage and theft. *Service* and *Protection* are inextricably linked. Because *Service* frames and defines the thinking and actions of the security teams approach to *Protection.* If the operating philosophy is that staff and students deserve to be safe and secure and further that they have a right to experience the full benefits of the school's material resources, then the "protection from" what and whom clarifies the problem. The problem or threat to the security of people and things in the school is anyone who disturbs the peace and learning productive environment of the school. That concept places *Protection* within the context of the school's overarching academic mission. If students are intimidated from "acting smart"; if (verbal, social media, or physical) bullies keep students from attending school in peace (or in some cases even showing up to school); students who are reluctant for safety reasons to utilize the bathrooms, locker room, hallways, and cafeteria; those students who can't focus in class because a potential fight is waiting for them after dismissal; if teachers and students are unable to enjoy a full period of instruction and learning; if students and staff are restricted or removed from being able to take advantage of the school's material resources because they have been stolen or vandalized; it should be said that although all of these acts may fall under the umbrella of school security, they are in actual fact also issues that fall under the purview of the school meeting its academic achievement objectives. *Protection* then, is the school security team protecting the school's ability and right to be primarily a safe, secure, and effectual teaching and learning institution. I am not really sure what protection could mean outside of that fundamentally critical primary mission!

Protection extends to proactive and prevent actions that secure people, places, and things in the building.

The EHSSS team, along with the teachers, can serve as the first line of recognition concerning the financial, social, emotional, health, and psychological challenges children may bring to a school. They could be the first to notice that child entering the school who is not properly attired for the season. Or that student who looks afraid, troubled, and/or agitated when arriving to school in the morning. In that sense, they must have an effective line of communication between themselves and the guidance counseling office. It is critical for principals to extend the reach of the school's guidance counseling services and designate all staff members, including school safety officers, as observers and reporters of students who may exhibit the stress and strain of some internal or external challenge. You want the EHSSS team to identify that student who may have an alcohol or drug problem (and this is a challenge for all high schools regardless of the wealth and/or entitlement of their student body), not so much to make a substance abuse bust, but to serve the purpose of getting that student to the counseling department for therapeutic resources. This is especially serious in high schools, where many of the students could be automobile drivers, thus placing themselves, other teenagers, and members of the public in danger. Very often, school staff members, like security officers, can have a unique relationship with students simply because they don't give students grades; these individuals can form critical supportive connections to students who can then treat the EHSSS team as guardians as opposed to arresting officers. You want the EHSSS team to develop positive and trusting relationships with students. For that to happen, they must be professional and polite and interact with students as a thoughtful force for peace, not people who just guard things! It is also true that principals should not, under any condition, allow members of the EHSSS team to be disrespected. Just as you insist that the EHSSS team give respect, you must also insist that they receive respect from every member of the school family, which is why I prefer the title of School Safety Officer, not "guard." The EHSSS should be friendly, but not friends, with students. They must also be fair and impartial and balance justice with mercy. Whether or not the school has metal detectors is not important. The key to creating a safe and secure building is the quality of people-to-people relationships between the members of that school family society. I know of no better force danger detector or preventer of safety issues than students alerting an adult in the building to a potential problem (preferably in its early stages). The EHSSS team must form positive and productive informational (intelligence gathering) bonds with students and staff, and that can only happen via mutual respect and collective self-protection. How many acts of violence in, or outside, of a high school were known beforehand by someone other than the participating individual? Answer: the majority of them! To keep a school and its family truly safe and secure, the EHSSS team must act with, and have access to, intelligence. I can't remember the number of times over my eleven-year period as a principal that I have walked with security officers to have a student open their locker, open their bags, or empty their pockets only to find some "offending/violation" item. And how many times have I heard the guilty student ask, "But how did you find out that?" And we respond, "Never mind how we found out, just open your locker!" Access to intelligence means acquiring important "pre-incident" information. The process could include "informers" who are not themselves always angelic, but they can provide information in exchange for "punishment consideration" for some small school infraction they have committed. For every school infraction, the principal is provided with a discretionary range of punishments. But gathering useful intelligence also speaks to strategic school security planning; students can be extremely smart in detecting and deciphering the security team's patrol patterns or those areas in the school where there is the least number of adult eyes or security cameras. It is therefore necessary to continually change and alter the security team's surveillance program. From time to time, over the course of a school year, completely change the patrol pattern of the security team and slightly move camera angles on a regular basis. The custodial staff's cleaning, repairing, and performance of building maintenance tasks around the building also provides the school with an additional set of adult eyes and ears throughout the day. One of the purposes of a weekly principal's SBL cabinet meeting is that you have the custodial foreperson and the school safety officers' supervisor in the same room where critical and important information can be exchanged that greatly enhances the quality of work produced by these two departments. These cabinet meetings make the important point to the SBL team that departmental success is linked to schoolwide success, and that schoolwide success is impossible without the awareness of the interconnectedness and dependence that all departments have for each other.

As principal, you and other members of the SBL team should often change your building walk procedures and times daily. For example, some days I started my walks on the fourth floor south, the next day second floor east, third day locker room gym area, etc. To serve in your important role as the chief security officer of the school, and to really see what's going on in the building, the principal must come up with multiple clever strategies to escape from the comfortable clutches of your (and the main) office. In matters of school safety and security, the predictability of the official response, punishments, and consequences for rule-breaking must be known by everyone. On the other hand, many of the SBL and EHSSS teams' strategy for keeping the school safe and secure must be totally unpredictable and known only to them or to any other adult staff member who is a partner to the particular process.

Establishing official school-safety standards

A primary task of the EHSSS team is to master and practice school-safety standards and the rubrics that define those standards. As with any academic department or job classification in the school, these standards must be guided and expressed through a series of clear conceptual and behavioral objectives. It is in many ways professionally unethical for a principal to lead and evaluate an employee if there are no mutually understood standards, even if these standards are not mutually agreed upon. And, so, what are the school's School-Safety Standards:

- The operational functions, practices, and goals of the security and safety plan as well as the work of the school safety team must be consistent with the school's overarching operational and educational missions of the school.

- Those standards should define, affirm, explain, and ensure the concretization of a core value of the school—that adults have a right to work and teach without negative behavioral interference, and students have the right to learn and attend school in peace and security. Establish, effectively enforce, and maintain an emotionally healthy, positive, and productive learning environment in every part of the interior and exterior of the school building.

- Safety and security must enhance the academic achievement goals and support the realization of a successful graduation for every student. The school building, furniture, equipment, and supplies are essential components of the educational program. The protection of these resources from theft or damage is of critical importance in the realization of the school's high achievement academic goals.

- The standards must speak specifically to the detecting, stopping, and elimination of any real or proposed verbal and/or physical threat of emotional or physical violence, fear, intimidation, or bullying in any form. Further, these standards must address a serious problem that may exist in many high schools, and that is the ridiculing and intimidation of students who are and/or seek to be smart. Those students seeking to perform at a high academic achievement level should feel free to do so without the fear of intimidation. There should be a "non-publicized" safe haven protective plan for those students of color who do not fit the stereotypical profile; these students should feel free to pursue a wide category of interests without facing ridicule. Students who choose to get involved with academic-related clubs and activities (e.g., robotics team, law and debate team, Shakespeare scholars, newspaper); the students who come to school every day just wanting to learn, and have simply decided to follow the school's rules and regulations, should be protected.

- The effective, efficient, and professional screening of all visitors to the school. Be sure to provide a series of clear rubrics that can explain the EHSSS member's role as the first face of the school. Also, the prevention of external threats to the school and its family posed by any unauthorized persons gaining access to the school.

- Special school activities and events can present unique security challenges for a school. Some of these events—which may include athletic/academic competitions, fundraising events/concerts, dance/orchestra performances—will more than likely involve admitting large numbers of non-school family members into the building. Further, in the case of both of my high schools, institutional uniqueness and high academic achievement generated a vibrant and recurrent school visitation schedule during the school day. My security team had to deal with a huge number of international, U.S., state, and city government officials; educators from all over the U.S. and world; members of the print and electronic news media as well as corporate and non-profit sector executives. In these situations, the (professionally developed and well-briefed) school safety security team had to balance the role of school family protectors and ambassadors. The standards should inform and guide a strategic plan that provides for flexible responses that allows adjustment for different school events and activities (including those events "outside of the norm"). These standards will also ensure maximum safety and security for all after-school/weekend/evening events and activities, and make sure that they can exist in a safe and protected environment.

- The standards should provide guidelines to the security team as to how to best investigate, de-escalate, contain, minimize, and stop any potential threat to a peaceful school environment. The school (guided by the standards) should provide professional development opportunities for the EHSSS team as to how to de-escalate any situation by way of words and actions. Physical force for reasons of protection and restraint should be the last and least desirable of actions. The EHSSS team must also be conversant of the rules and regulations that protect the rights of students. Any real or alleged rule-breakers has the right to a fair, transparent (to student and parent), just, and respectful disciplinary process. The student's right to confidentiality (including official records of the disciplinary process and outcome), must be respected and adhered to.

- The standards should outline the coordination plan with the dean and the Attitude Readjustment Center (ARC) aka ISS room. The dean should be part of the security team's departmental meetings, and it is essential that they communicate on a regular basis. The EHSSS team should have a daily updated list of those students who are assigned to the ARC, or those students who have been suspended from school or from specific places, equipment, trips, activities, or programs.

- The standards should clearly outline the expectations and evaluation process of the EHSSS department: The team leader, security team officers, as a group and individually, will be subject to a standards-based (demonstrated/performance) evaluation system. In some school systems, security officers are not part of the school employees that a principal can evaluate. Ignore that. You can, and should, essentially evaluate and supervise anyone working in your building, even if it only means a letter of praise and commendation to their supervisor or a letter of concern to that same supervisor.

- The security standards should clearly define "Good Customer Service" as a theory, practice, and an essential EHSS departmental objective. Good customer service must be a core standard and an essential expectation of every security officer's job description and evaluation. Once, on a trip to Barbados, it was interesting to observe how the Barbadian Police went about their work. It was clear as I watched them that they were well-trained to know that an important part of their duties involved assisting tourists, not just catching bad guys and preventing crime. And because of the special place that schools represent in our society, the EHSSS team must also see themselves in the dual role of serving as well as protecting the student family and visitors. Particularly, those officers assigned to front entrance security duties. These welcoming and greeting entrance door officers have the unique power to frame the first impression attitudes and expectations of all those who come to visit. School security can either negatively stir up a parent who has been called for a conference to the principal or dean's office or help to bring them down a notch by way of their professional attitude. At that front entrance, several important statements must be made regarding the safety and security standards of the school:

o   This is a welcoming place. As professionals, we are here to protect everyone, including you. Our procedures are designed not to harass, but to accomplish that stated goal of safety and security for everyone.

o   (To parents) Based on our professionalism and performance, you have good reason to believe that your child is safe here.

o   The security area is neat and clean. The officers don't present a sloppy or slovenly-attired appearance. The language (body and verbal) is professional. The safety security officer is helpful. They have a good working knowledge of the school's structure, organization, procedures and protocols. The front entrance officers are problem solvers, so you should have a discussion and PD session on "what to do if or when" a particular situation arises. Examples include: an upset parent, a parent who is not fluent in English, a parent who does not understand how schools/school districts are organized and operational structures, etc. The officer must be a guide to those who are seeking assistance and a barrier to any who come to the school to cause harm. The model front entrance officer is a positive representation, in voice and action, of the School Security Safety Standards!

Note to principals: establish subdivisions of excellence in every part of the school's operational, academic, and administrative spaces. Set a high standard of performance for the appearance and/or behavior at the front entrance, main office, and lobby area, etc. No aspect of a school's life is too small for you to pay attention to how well it is operating, performing, and looking; how that segment of school operations is meeting its singular objectives is helping to support the school's overall academic achievement mission. Subdivisions of excellence translates into framing an entire school's vision of excellence!

Police officers stationed in public schools: A word of caution and advice...

A thought on Municipal Police Officers/Sherriff's Deputies assigned to serve in a public school. First, the law enforcement agency must do some upfront critical work of screening these officers. Select these officers in the same way you would select personnel for specialized units (e.g., undercover work, hostage negotiators, community affairs) This assignment should carry with it prestige and be on the promotional path to a higher rank and similar assignments. There are also a few major processes and procedures for police departments to seriously think about when assigning law enforcement officers to schools: (1) The Screening and Selection Process, (2) Training and Education, (3) Supervision and Evaluation.

Screen out those officers who carry a personal philosophy/psychology, which says particular racial/ethnic groups, neighborhoods, and communities are by nature criminal, or at the very least, inclined toward criminality. Further, screen out those officers who believe that every rule broken in a school requires a military punitive response and solution. That schools (unlike the streets) are primarily in the teaching and character development business. Don't select officers who lack multicultural-linguistic competency skills.

And most importantly, we in education are seeking (at least we should be) to divert students away from, rather than direct them, into the criminal justice system.

Offer selection-hiring "Preference Points," (not absolute disqualifiers):

- A college education; an officer who reads books and who is intellectually curious.

- Officers who live in the same, or similar neighborhoods, as the students.

- Some type of community service history, such as coaching, volunteering, Girl or Boy Scout leaders, served in the community affairs division of the force, etc.

- (And oddly enough) Those officers who had a "troubled or challenging" teenage life, but something or someone mentored and/or helped them to turn their lives around. Retired NYC police commander, Corey Pegues, author of *Once a Cop*, offers such a life story.

Training and education in the areas of:

- Clarifying the phrase: "Serve and Protect" (all citizens!)

- Fundamentals of "Education Law" and how it differs from regular (street) law.

- Understanding the present state of police student community relations.

- Major themes and outline of Adolescent/Teen psychology.

- Why Black Lives Matter, anti-brutality, and other social justice movements are not anti-police.

- Crisis de-escalation skills.

- Conflict resolution skills.

- Mediation/Negotiation skills.

Supervision and Evaluation:

First, some important factors that can greatly influence and enhance the Principal-Police Department relationship (and you will need a good and respectful relationship), is for the principal: (1) To have a sound philosophy and theory as to school building, staff, and student safety and security. (2) To translate those ideas into a thoughtful and strategic schoolwide operational plan for safety and security. (3) The plan is fairly and consistently applied. (4) The plan clearly outlines the desired optimal role, relationship, and responsibilities of the police officer assigned to the school. (5) That the plan is actually (demonstrably) effective as a working philosophy, which means it is working in its daily application.

The principal should schedule regular short check-in meetings with the police officer's supervisor (sergeant or lieutenant); get to know the precinct commander. These meetings can help to make sure that the police department and the school are on the same page. They can also serve as a setting to revisit the expectations and standards for police/school relationships that you have outlined in the school's safety and security plan (e.g., an intruder alert, a "lockdown," or an evacuation). It is the principal's hope that the assigned officer will be evaluated, recognized, and rewarded for their faithfulness to the plan. In other words, school-based officers should be evaluated differently from public law officers, which means they should not be judged on the number of arrests they make, but, rather, on things like the number of incidents they are able to successfully prevent or de-escalate, their ability to successfully mentor those students who are confused and struggling with social interactions, following school rules and regulations. Finally, the principal, the EHSSS, and the public law enforcement officer assigned to the school, must all work together to make sure that their collective goal of a safe and peaceful school, and the development of good and productive citizens, represents the best safety and security outcome in the present and for the future. This means we are all on the same team, and therefore all responsible for *Serving* and *Protecting* each other's professional goals and objectives!

Chapter 21:
The Effective High School Health Center/Nursing Office

A comprehensive high school health education program

Any principal leading a high school must understand the connection between general health education and care (medical, dental, reproductive education, substance abuse, etc.) and the goal of achieving academic success for all students. It is also critical to understand how the health and medical issues that affect the parents and siblings of your students can seriously impact your students' ability to concentrate on their academic achievement potential. For example, during my tenure as a principal, I always had a significant number of grandparents, aunts, and uncles who were doing their second tour of childrearing duty. Many of these guardians had reached senior-hood and were facing their own serious medical challenges. I came to realize that they also needed counseling support to help them to cope with raising a teenager, who in many ways, was more confusing to them than the children (the child's parents) that the grandparents had previously raised. Physical and psychological healthcare are inseparable from academic performance—a point that is lost on all of those governors and states who claim they want to create a more knowledgeable and skilled citizenry/workforce, and then undermine that effort by failing to expand Medicaid healthcare services to families by way of the Affordable Care Act (Obamacare). The public schools face the reality of serving large numbers of students and families who are the working poor, the underemployed and unemployed, who suffer from having sketchy, incomplete, or inadequate access to healthcare services, especially services linked to counseling or psychological health services. Those schools, for both humanitarian and pedagogical reasons, can't just take the role of interested observers; strategic action must be taken! For some poor families, the cost of a simple health insurance provider deductible is a financial struggle; and the additional cost of a medical specialist could further drain a family's meager financial resources. Further, the school could be serving students who, due to their family's undocumented residency status, may face serious challenges in gaining access to government public healthcare services. Our students don't exist in isolation, they are a part of a family; so when parents, live-in family members, or siblings have serious, and perhaps, chronic health challenges, this can place a tremendous burden on the family's financial, including healthcare budget. This can sometimes force families to make tough decisions just to keep the most vulnerable family members alive (an older high school child may be asked to "hang in there" health wise because a younger sibling is severely suffering from asthma, diabetes, or sickle cell disease). We should know that students living below, in, or just above poverty, are not mere numerical statistics. Poverty is not an abstraction, it adversely affects real people and real students, with real and terrible human and academic outcomes. Poverty carries some severe, painful, and deadly negative associations that students can bring with them to school. Students facing health challenges that are either caused by, or made worse by, poverty will sometimes struggle daily just to learn their school lessons, or they will miss significant days due to health issues. There is even the reality of a health service inadequacy-insufficiency that significantly contribute to the academic learning achievement gap among students. One way in which it is expressed is how students whose families have access to private healthcare insurance can schedule healthcare and dental appointments on weekends or after school, thus not missing critical instructional class time. It also helps when a family can afford to obtain prescription medication quickly and not wait for the next payroll check. Many poor families find themselves utilizing the hospital emergency room as their primary healthcare provider. And then there is the severely unaddressed problem/crisis afflicting affluent, middle class and poor children, the failure to seek and/or receive vital and necessary mental health services. This is a national crisis in schools that goes beyond access to financial resources. But, of course, like most bad things, it hits the poor the hardest. A lot of schools in America suffer from a chronic inattention to counseling and mental health services. And we are paying a heavy student self-inflicted and group projected acts of violence price for this abdication of our responsibility to young people. Every school district and school maintains a clear, organized, step-by-step process in response to a student who accidentally fractures a wrist or ankle in the gymnasium. However, for those students in a school who may be suffering from some type of emotional "brokenness," historical or present abuse, depression, and/or emotional suffering, there is no consistent systematic and operational response to the mental and emotional injuries that afflict so many of our young people. And this is after so many years of students cutting themselves, purposely engaging in destructive, dangerous, or risky lifestyle behaviors, running away from home, becoming dropouts, illegal self-medication with alcohol and drugs, threating or actually committing suicide, substance-related car accidents and fatalities, school violence, and mass school shootings. Meanwhile, we are also suspending a lot of (particularly poor, male children of color) students on a daily basis because they are just not receiving even the most basic mental healthcare intervention services. We are further challenged in high schools by the susceptibility on the part of many of our teenage students to make bad, uninformed/misinformed health and life choices. A critical component of the school's health education program is pre-conception health and sex education. This initiative must be presented in a scientifically serious, honest, and relevant way, less the school's underground and unofficial sex education curriculum serve as the primary source of information for students; the results are almost always tragic, painful, and a future career expectations distraction and derailment.

High school students can be forced to go untreated for serious health problems because of poverty. Or, unfortunately, in some cases they can opt to undermine their own good health possibilities. They will go for long periods of time without proper vision care (glasses), hearing, dental, and general health services. Very often the symptoms of poor health situations will show up as misbehavior, and ultimately academic failure. It was common in my high schools to discover a child who had a health challenge that adversely affected their learning (perhaps for many of their K-8 years), and went undetected, students with hearing problems, students who were in need of glasses, who were either unable to acquire glasses, or refused to wear the glasses provided because the public health service did not give them stylish eyewear. And what can one say here, except that this is teenage psychology, and for them peer acceptance is real, even if it is self-defeating!

Poor diet and the lack of exercise are also a major reality for many high school students. I observed and remarked early in my 1990s' principalship that although the price of athletic footwear was skyrocketing, the amount of meaningful physical exercise students engaged in while wearing these expensive sneakers was dramatically dropping, in some cases to "0" outside of their PE classes. Long gone was the practice of my 1950-60s childhood, when sneakers served a practical, not just stylistic, purpose. Back then, we engaged in physical activity year-round and played multiple sports in season, some adult-supervised (Sandlot Baseball, Pop Warner Football, Basketball leagues, middle school/high school Track), others (handball, stickball, touch and tackle football, softball, box ball and playground basketball), we organized ourselves. The dangerous mixture of a lack of exercise, in some cases obesity, combined with poor dietary habits, exacerbates existing health problems and creates an opportunistic opening for both intermittent and long-term chronic diseases. None of the beforementioned statuses of a student's health is a friend to quality learning and academic achievement. A sizeable number of students on any school day will be struggling to learn while in some state of illness-poor health conditions; or will completely miss critical days of learning. All high school subject curricula should be based on a paced teaching calendar, which can prove difficult when students are trying to learn while sick or in pain, or lose class time altogether due to absences.

Diet issues bring their own unique challenges to learning. We are perhaps servicing countless children who are suffering from food allergies of some kind and we only address this problem in the most extreme cases (peanut allergies or lactose intolerance). This can prove dangerous if food item selections during the lunch period were chosen with a lack of knowledge as to an individual student's allergenic profile.

Dr. Gerald Deas on the faculty of Downstate Medical Center, Brooklyn has been desperately trying for years to make educators aware of the link between diet and a student's ability to academically perform and behave well in school. Dr. Deas has used the work of The Feingold Association (www.feingold.org) to help prove his theory about this important connection. Either independently or with the cooperation of their parents, young people are ingesting huge amounts of sugar, sodium, chemically-based artificial colorings, and taste enhancers in large quantities. In high schools, it is worse because of the greater degree of freedom of movement and the independent decision-making power on the part of teenagers. We have also seen the sunset of the family sit-down-to-dinner era. And, so, high school students in too many cases have the time and ability to frame their own diets. Understandably, there is a lot of bad choosing that occurs as they pursue high sodium and high sugar selections and avoid nutritious options. Ill-health and illness factors will ultimately adversely affect their capacity to learn. How many times have we seen students falling into negative disciplinary cycles in our public school systems that unfortunately leads to suspensions, which leads to not learning, which leads to further suspensions: I am inclined to propose a full health screening procedure as part of the academically struggling, or behaviorally challenged, students as the first step in the academic support needs assessment intervention plan (Pre-IEP development stage). For are we mistakenly misaddressing diet and healthcare issues through the disciplinary codes? And are we always sure that a "learning issue" is not somehow connected to diet, allergies or an undiagnosed physical and mental health ailment?

Good health and hygiene information is critical.

There is also the issue of having good knowledge and the correct information concerning matters of hygiene, health, and sex. Again, it was shocking for me to encounter students in high school who were lacking the fundamental information concerning hygiene. And further frightening, were the number of students who either had incomplete or completely wrong information concerning the human sexual and/or reproductive systems.

Daily poverty, or living on the margins of the poverty line, can have a deleterious effect on the capacity to live and learn normally. This poverty, even when it is survived, does not leave families without depositing some deep and painful scars. When everything relating to existence is a struggle, when every moment of playing, talking, sharing a laugh walking down the street, going to visit friends, sitting in front of the house or on a park bench presents the possibility for violent victimhood exposure—including those acts perpetrated by law enforcement—a school (particularly a Title I school), must effectively respond to those potential and actual negative effects. We must fully explore the exposure results of constantly being bombarded by verbal, mental, and physical neighborhood violence. The stressful, deleterious psychological and physical effects on the young people who are exposed over long periods of time to these conditions, and especially important, how this health crisis hinders and damages academic achievement potential.

All of the various health issues must be part of the conversation by the SBL team as to how the school's Effective High School Health/Nursing Office (EHSNO) should be constructed, and also how the EHSNO should go about its work. As with all departments, all initiatives, all projects and decisions, the purpose of the EHSNO must be seen and assessed through the singular uncompromising lens of the school's primary mission: how does the EHSNO enhance and build, or delay and detract, from the work of realizing academic achievement, and increase the potential for a student to successfully graduate?

Now, the model EHSNO and ideal healthy school solution is one I fleshed out in great detail in a section of an earlier paper titled "School as Community, Community as School." I asserted in the paper that every Title I school should have a school-based clinic (SBC) attached to it. And that this clinic should not only serve the students in the school, but also their families, because the lack of access and options to good health providers are ultimately shared as a family unit. I think this can be done without extra cost by shifting primary care

353

service from the public health centers to a school-based clinic. Not only would this greatly improve the health and well-being of students and their families, it would also reduce the loss of learning time as well as loss of wages and work-time for parents. Further, these SBCs could target and treat those students suffering from asthma in schools with high concentrations of students suffering from this ailment. Imagine how productive, stress-reducing, and timesaving that would be! We could dramatically reduce the loss of class and school time for these students! And because of the geographical convenience and access to patients' factors, I believe that a SBC would actually save the local, state, and federal government money because we would then be able to screen and detect many chronic illnesses in their earlier, easier (and cheaper) treatment medical stages. We could also redirect these families from utilizing the very costly hospital emergency rooms for general healthcare needs. Finally, SBCs could serve as health education hubs of the community in the challenging pursuit of good health and wellness and in the battle against misinformation. At the same time, good and timely health information is the best path to a winning wellness outcome. Effectively educating students, their parents, and the community could transform entire communities for the better and make a way for the children to realize better learning opportunities!

Back to the (un)real world

But until that practical, sensible (and money-saving) plan of having a SBC in every Title I school can excite, or even interest the minds of our elected leadership class, school leaders must do their best with what they have. Most high schools, if they are lucky, will be forced to make do with a full or part-time nurse (and nurse's office). And, so, what is a principal to do with that important, but limited reality, especially in the face of the long list of student health challenges I have previously outlined?

The first step is to make your nurse's office focused, effective, and efficient as it can be. Invite and include your nurse into the conversation as to how the school can make health and wellness a central component of the school's academic mission. There should be a conversation as to why and how the nurse's office should function as a health and wellness center, a treatment and prevention center, and also as a center of health education and information. This fits the standard school affirmative mission principles that every functional space in the school is both a classroom, and more importantly, a contributor to the collective achievement of the school's academic graduation objectives! This, therefore, suggests that with all aspects of schooling, measurable standards are the guiding tools of practice, performance, and evaluation. The nurse's office area (bulletin boards, waiting area walls, and tables) should be rich with information that can encourage students to ask the nurse critical questions or find resources to help with any type of health issue. The school must also invest in brochure and magazine racks for the waiting area; there are a huge number of free health education informational magazines printed by professional health organizations, the city, state, and federal government health agencies, advocacy groups (e.g., Mothers Against Drunk Driving [MADD]), that must all be fully screened. The waiting area should also have a VCR/Screen that can play looped health, nutrition, and wellness information videos. The walls outside of the nurse's office should also have bulletin boards. The information posted should have the purpose of reaching the casual passerby students and the reluctant or shy students with important health questions. This bulletin board should also have Hotline Help numbers, a "Did you know" health and nutrition advisory posting, and also how the guidance and nursing offices can provide you with confidential[8] advice, services, and outside referrals.

The nurse's reception area and office should not only be a center of health education, but a center of health resources. Depending on the local and school district rules and regulations, the nurse's office should be a place where students have access to condoms without having to go through a formal request process. An easy way to do this is putting them in a large, easily-accessible bowl. Or, allow students to meet with the nurse in their office where they could be given condoms privately and confidentially. The nurse and librarian should collaborate on developing a Health Information Reference Section in the School Library. This section should be a free and open-access shelves unit that does not require the students to identify themselves or publicly request a particular book. It also represents a safe space where young people can pursue and read books on romantic relationships, health, preconception and/or sexual reproductive education questions or concerns in private. The resources in this section of the library will include well-screened fiction and nonfiction books and pamphlets on topics that emerge as critical concerns during the teenage years, such as:

- Depression
- Peer pressure
- Physical/emotional attractiveness
- Sexually-transmitted diseases (STDs)
- Anger
- Hygiene
- Sexual abuse
- Suicide
- Grooming
- Same-sex attraction/relationships
- Verbal/Physical abusive relationships
- Alcohol abuse/addiction
- Drug abuse/addiction
- Pregnancy prevention myths and facts
- Loneliness and isolation
- Nutrition and exercise for teenagers

An important task the school nurse should organize is the visual and hearing testing for all students in the school, starting with the incoming ninth graders and transfer students during their PE class period. Vision and hearing testing should also be part of the initial stages of a student referral for academic intervention services (Pre-IEP development stage). The nurse could also help the school leadership and instructional team to identify those students who: (a) Need an ophthalmologist-optometry referral/appointment. (b) Have a prescription for glasses, but for one or more reasons, the prescription does not turn into actual glasses. (c) Have glasses but refuse to wear them.

This expansive screening initiative will require the establishment of external health and medical institutions partnerships; one nurse alone cannot accomplish this in a reasonable and realistic timeframe. These partnerships (along with others) could also be expanded beyond screening and into the area of actual service/product providing. To be totally effective, the school that is serving financially struggling working-class and unemployed families, should think about this process in a full-service comprehensive way. In other words, there may be a need to have a program that takes some students from nurse vision screening to: an optometrist referral, the optometric doctor's visit, a prescription, and then actually finding the resources for purchasing the glasses (a similar procedure could be organized for something like dental care). As you can see, we are constantly returning to the concept of the indispensable: Entrepreneurial Resource Gathering Principal! Some students will suffer, physically or emotionally quietly, even as they are forced to endure a solvable health issue. And predictably their academic capabilities will be diminished without the internal support of the school, along with the acquisition of external funding and resources to augment, compliment, and in some cases, totally pay for health-related services a student may need.

In order to build a culture of excellence when it comes to health and wellness in the school, a principal must ensure that all staff members are working as a collective unit for students' best interests. Without this, the students cannot succeed. The nurse must share in, and be part of, that understanding.

Note to Principal: Teachers are very often the first line of discovery of a health and/or wellness deficiency a student might be facing; good schools will make this "look-for" approach a part of the school's Culture. But that can only happen if the school's administrative leadership team has a health-medical problem-solving plan in place; and then the staff must see the SBL team effectively and consistently act (follow-up) on that plan.

In cooperation with the guidance counseling department, there should be an organized system of collaboration between the school and the local public health services organization, health-related CBO's, clinics, and the local hospitals. The nurse and guidance department should invite district-certified (and sanctioned) health officials, presenters, and educators to make presentations to students during the school day in PE or HE classes. Special "lunch-time talks" and after-school presentations can be made by inviting outside health speakers. The nurse in cooperation with the guidance department should also set up a "no judgement-no disciplinary action" system, where students who are suffering from any form of alcohol or drug abuse, can refer themselves to the nurse or a guidance counselor for outside follow-up treatment and therapy resources (Don't take it personal principal, but for a lot of reasons, including the fear of disappointment, these students may not want to come to you or a teacher). Health information tables can be set up at back-to-school night, parent-teacher conference days and evenings, PA/PTA monthly meetings, daytime or evening workshops. The nurse should be part of the team that organizes an annual schoolwide Saturday Health Fair that would provide information and special free health screenings and referrals for the entire family. One way of helping to draw a large crowd to this event is to first provide food (breakfast and lunch); but also offer door prizes consisting of free giveaways from local merchants and school partners, a non-stop raffle of "health aids" (e.g., family box of dental floss, health screening gift cards). Students working at the event can earn "credit" toward reducing the cost of their senior dues. Also invite speakers who might excite the students like a local professional athlete. This event could also feature award and credit-earning projects and presentation boards by students taking HE classes. Make sure that mental health awareness/information tables are a prominent part of the event.

With the help of an academic AP or teacher, a series of demonstrations and lessons can be developed by the nurse. From time to time, opportunities will arise where a nurse is able to make a presentation to a class (HE or PE class). If the nurse does not feel comfortable making these presentations, an informational video followed by a Q&A session will suffice. One of the critical objectives here is to make the nurse (in classes and in her office) a member of the instructional team—with good health education being her learning objectives. It is amazing how good health information can be transferred from students experiencing the presentation firsthand to other students in the school. It's important for students to see the nurse and the nurse's office, not just as a place to go when one is sick or injured, but as a place where a student can receive a wide spectrum of health education, including preventative-proactive health information.

As part of the school's commitment to parent/community education and empowerment, health and nutrition could be one of the featured topics for the monthly parent meetings. The nurse, along with other health professionals, could be invited to make (fifteen minutes max) presentations concerning critical health issues. Information tables could be set up at all school events involving parents such as orientations, open houses, parent-teacher conferences, competitions, exhibitions and performances. (no condom giveaways at these multi-age public invited events.)

Another important health objective is the nurse using his/her presentations and individual/group sessions to demystify counseling support and mental healthcare, removing the untrue stigmas that make many young people feel that they are alone and helpless in the face of any emotional pain or discomfort. This negative thinking can hinder both parents and students from realizing their highest productive potential, and achieving a fulfilling state of mental wellness.

The principal must (particularly in a Title I school) make physical, mental health and nutrition a core component of the strategy to raise and sustain the academic achievement level of the students. The nurse, and if you're fortunate, the school-based health clinic staff are critical actors in the linkage of health-nutrition to academic achievement. You must also think of health and wellness, in both a proactive and promotional way. Good health, fitness, and nutrition must be grounded in initiatives or campaigns that would make its objectives foundational elements of the school's working (operational) *Culture*. This means that every staff person in the building is in some way engaged with, and connected to, the schoolwide good health initiative mission. Physical and mental health, nutrition and fitness questions should be part of all discussions concerning student academic success in school. One example is including health-nutrition assessment procedures in any discussion of academic underperformance by a student. Is the student overly tired, listless, and suffering from a prolonged state of sadness? Is the student easily distracted or struggling to study and focus in class? We must understand that some students deal with mental health issues, which can often be a contributing, or a primary, underlying cause for negative behaviors such as making bad and self-defeating, destructive decisions during their high school years. We should ask the question, are lunch periods and what is being served during those periods adversely affecting the post-lunch classroom learning environment in the school? What about the growing negative impact of high school students engaging in alcohol consumption and illegal drug usage, and their access to the legally prescribed medications of others? Or our plan for those students who live in high poverty areas where there is also a high level of random mental, verbal, and physical violence, and perhaps despair and hopelessness due to prolong periods of under and/or no employment. Students (teenagers), in general, face a large number of mental stressors. We should stop saying that young people don't have real problems because these emotional challenges are real to them, as is the pain that is often associated with these problems. When you combine the external societal pressures with the internal struggles of transitioning from one stage of human evolution (childhood), to the next (adulthood), it can be easy to see life as overwhelming and unmanageable. And for reasons of humanitarian concern as well as for the purposes of raising and maintaining academic performance, we should ask the same question that we ask of our other operational and academic departments: What is the mental, physical, health, nutrition awareness, fitness, health-wellness literacy profile we hope to see in students while they attend our school and after they graduate from our school? And, equally, important, what is the quality level of their mental and emotional state as we send them out into the world to become managers, politicians, nurses, supervisors, coworkers, police officers, teachers, engineers, neighbors, citizens, and parents?

A broken arm can heal, but that which is emotionally broken and untreated in a child, can cause for pain and suffering that is self-inflicted and/or projected onto others in society. The physical and mental well-being of our students is consistent with our desire to see them achieve academically. But it is also part of our professional ethical (and humanitarian) responsibility to ensure that they experience healthy and good lives while they are in our care. The Effective High School Health/Nursing Office are the key school departments that are specifically designed to achieve those educational and humanitarian objectives.

Chapter 22:
Building an Efficient
Main Office/Administrative Staff

The principal who aspires to lead a good and effective school, must respect and appreciate the critical work and professional responsibilities of the main office staff. Their level of efficiency will greatly determine to what extent the SBL team can avoid time-wasting activities that remove them from their primary task of serving as teaching and learning leaders; also how effective you are able to be as a principal as you devote your finite time to all of the attention-seeking areas of the school's life. More importantly, it is critical for a principal to understand why a good principal's secretary is worth double their weight in gold!

When I first became a superintendent, one method I utilized to learn about my schools was to observe the main office operations, its "look," architecture, staff practices and procedures right before the start of classes. You can learn so much about a school (*Tone*, *Climate* and with additional information, the school's true operational *Culture*) from those main office operations observations. How students, staff, and parents are treated in the general office, how they are spoken to, responded to, provides an important insight as to the entire school's operational belief system and the leadership capability of the principal. An important tool that is missing from too many of our public schools is this private sector concept of the critical need for good customer service. To be honest (because I want aspiring principals to be fully prepared for what they will face), teaching good customer service skills is not impossible, but it is very difficult to teach public civil servants the meaning of the words "public servant." The fundamental problem in public education is that we simply don't see the public in general, and parents in particular, as customers, who can take their business somewhere else. There is the sense that because of legislative mandates, protections, tenure-seniority rules, unions, labor contracts, etc., and that by law students must attend a school, that the employees (including administrators) need not concern themselves with how the public feels about how they are treated. This has caused many civil service bureaucratic systems to lose their true purpose for the job they are performing. Unfortunately, at times both the "civil" and "servant" has been removed from the process. These civil servants can easily, through practiced bad habits, transfer their interpretation of public service into a self-serving service. They arrive at the place where the position, job, contract agreements, and labor organization, takes on a greater importance and loyalty than the citizens they are paid (by the citizens themselves) to serve. One excellent professional development experience I offered by way of one of the school's corporate partnerships, was to have my front office staff engage in a professional development activity at the company's corporate headquarters. It was important for the staff to see how a front office staff operates when customer satisfaction is an organizational requirement-necessity, mission. It was also important for them to observe how the initial or second contact a person has with an institution can greatly improve (or deteriorate) any situation; and how that initial "bad" impression is very often hard to change. The simple act of directing parents (customers) to the appropriate staff member (not necessarily the principal), who can actually solve their problem, can greatly improve the parent-school communication relationship. Again, wearing my superintendent's hat, it was not uncommon for a parent complaint about how they were treated (badly) at a school, to start in the main office, after which the situation went terribly downhill. Vocabulary and phrasing (what is said, and how it is said) is critical in these situations, which is why as a principal I banned phrases like, "Do you have an appointment?" My directive was that any parent who takes the time to come up to the school, will within a reasonable amount of time, have the ability to meet face-to-face with a school administrator.

I can honestly say that in both of my schools, I was fortunate enough to have an effective front office staff, who could direct parents and visitors to the person best suited to assist them; since I spent most of my day engaged in: school leadership by walking around. These talented staff persons were also skilled in checking in with parents while they waited to be seen, even if those parents came up to the school without giving notice. It is very common in schools that parents and visitors will arrive to the main office asking to speak to the principal. In the overwhelming majority of these situations, the person who could actually address the concern, question, and/or request, is a staff person other than the principal. To the extent that the main office staff can problem-solve and direct the individual to the right staff person, not only helps the parent, but also increases the amount of time that the principal can engage in other leadership activities that require their personal attention. There is also a good customer linguistic skill required to politely explain to the parent that,

"Yes, the principal is in charge of the school, but the best staff person who is able to solve your particular concern or problem is ____; and of course, you can always have a meeting with the principal if you are not satisfied with the results of your meeting." This means that the Effective Main Office Staff (EMOS) must be fully knowledgeable and conversant in all aspects of the school's operations and procedures—understanding who in the building is directly responsible for what program or activity. They should not only know every staff person's job description (title and area of responsibly), but their job analysis; what they actually do that goes beyond their job description. In both of my high schools, I have watched the main office staff solve (both phone and visiting) parent concerns and problems, often without the help of a school administrator. These pro-actions saved the school administrators' hours of important work time. Remember what we said about an attribute of an underperforming school, the school administrators have limited time to serve in the capacity of instructional coaches. The level of main office efficiency translates into a key factor affecting students' academic achievement and keeps you out of your superintendent's "doghouse" when those ill-served angry parents show up or call their office. Know, principal, that the vital organizational-operational information you don't share with the main office staff will ultimately hurt the school and your leadership objectives. The EMOS must also practice an approach that seeks to de-escalate all stressful situations. Again, going back to both of my high schools, I can remember on numerous occasions when a parent came into the main office ready for war. But through the excellent work of the EMOS, their attitudes were completely changed, or at the very least, less hostile and confrontational. Treating parents with the respect, dignity, and professionalism they deserve will usually garner a positive response. As the principal, you must support the EMOS in this effort by also demanding that parents adhere to a clearly established (at the orientation) list of behavioral standards when they visit the school. The flipside of poor customer service, is customer bad behavior. The principal (even with threats by a parent to call the superintendent, a school board member, or politician) must stand their ground on the respectful behavior that is expected of all who visit the school and main office. I have always insisted that cursing, belligerence, threatening or in any way, disrespectful behavior will not be tolerated by parents or staff. Another revealing EMOS behavior is how long does it takes for the main office staff to recognize a visitor. It can be as simple as a greeting or informing the visitor that all staff persons are on the phone, working with another visitor, and that they will be with the visitor in a moment. A parent, student, or visitor should never see the main office staff engaging in social calls or conversations while they are forced to wait. Again, as with the school security team, the main office staff must never bring fire to put out a fire. At the same time that the principal empowers and supports them in not being disrespected, you must establish procedures and practices that can de-escalate a difficult situation without the professionals involved being disrespectful. In my eleven years as principal, I've found that parents are good at figuring out the school's operational culture when it comes to their treatment; in high schools, there may be a period of time for the first-year parents (including transferees) where they learn the behavioral standards-expectations of my schools. Perhaps, in a previous K-8 experience, a parent may have received what they interpreted as results by engaging in loud confrontational behavior and/or intimidating language in the main office, or by threatening to call an elected official, a board member, or superintendent. The staff should, of course, in a professional manner, always provide any parent with the telephone number and address of the person responsible for parent complaints at the district level; and that information should be provided without a tone of sarcasm, anger, or malice. But it is the principal who must establish the *Tone* in the new parent orientation, and every school year's opening parent back-to-school meeting. If the school staff can provide parents with multiple avenues by which their concerns can be heard and acted on, the inspiration to "act out" will disappear. The school can't always give the concerned or complaining parent exactly what they want, but they can sincerely listen, engage in respectful dialogue, give attention to, and to some extent, provide an explanation as to the decision you have taken concerning the matter that disturbs them. I will not make the claim that this approach will always work; the end result that the parent is seeking may be unreasonable, illegal or just flat-out harmful to their child. But it is seriously important, to listen and take their concerns seriously.

The phones are another revelatory example of a school's character. As in the case of physical visits, the rules for respectful engagement still apply. "If you are going to use that language and tone, I will not be able to continue this phone conversation. I would be more than happy to help you when you call back with a different tone and using respectful language." This is how the main office staff should handle abusive calls. This approach could literally mean the difference between solving a problem and frustrating an already upset parent who feels that they must now come up to the school or call someone in authority at the district level. In any event, being forced to have an unnecessary parent conference or taking the time to respond to a complaint, is time the principal or AP could be spending observing classroom instruction, or handling other matters in the school building. The principal, SBL team, and the EMOS must establish the ground rules for parent-school communication behaviors early and then practice them consistently. If the school has a parent coordinator on staff, a major part of that person's job duties should be to serve in an ombudsman capacity and continually work to improve the quality of the school parent communication process. In order for the parent coordinator to properly achieve the beforementioned objective, the principal and school staff can't be more committed to being emotional and "right" as opposed to being committed to creating an effective and positive parent-school partnership. The school administrators and staff will need to show professional and compassionate patience. Knowing how to effectively communicate with your child's school is not a skill that is granted to each parent upon the birth of their child; this can sometimes be a long and extended educational learning process. But helping parents with this skill (as I cover in a later chapter) is not an insurmountable problem. After all, we are professional educators!

Unfortunately, too many school building administrators pay little attention to how the main office operates until something goes dramatically wrong! A principal's disengagement from this critical area could lead to the office staff desperately seeking, and sadly sometime finding their own not so professional-operational standards to guide their practice. In any organizational effort, unclear or the absence of standards will cause those staff members to invent or create their own operational standards; and there is no guarantee that their decision will be the best one for them or the school. A culture of individual personality-driven ineffective, unproductive and random practices, can take root. This will, of course, invite disorder and dysfunction to trickle down and cause the entire school and its mission to suffer, all for the principal's disinterest and non-involvement.

It is critical that the main office staff not just have a staff listing or organization sheet, but know who works in the building, where they work, and the titles they hold. Either the principal or an AP assigned full-time to administrative, operational, and organizational management, should work to develop a more expansive (internal) building organizational directory. Through a series of meetings with the main office staff, they should know exactly who in the building is assigned to handle any given situation. A sure way to make sure that a parent becomes frustrated and angry is to direct them to a person who does not have the responsibility or information to solve their particular concern or problem. These school personnel, job description-analysis meetings with the school administrators and EMOS team will also offer the principal and SBL team the important opportunity to discover any responsibility gaps, unclaimed or mis-assigned task, and any unclear chain of command issues that exists in the school.

A great deal of the communication failures that occur in a school can be avoided by having a thorough and comprehensive parent and student hand-book: every class having a syllabus with academic/behavioral class expecta-tions, a fully explained schoolwide grading policy (to students and parents), and preferably having all of this information in written form (in multiple lan-guages as is needed), and also posted on the school's website. The more clear information provided to parents and students upfront, the less calls and school visits later by confused and upset parents. Further, having a comprehensive parent handbook counteracts the accidental, or on purpose, practice of students providing missing or incomplete information to their parents. While on the topic of phone issues, it is extremely critical that the main office staff under-stands and follows the rules concerning confidentiality. It is not uncommon for one legally-restricted and/or physically abusive parent to use the school to find the location of a victimized partner/spouse and/or child. I always informed my main front office staff to error on the side of caution, and that I would back them up if any issue occurred. You, as principal, are not under any obligation to provide personal information, no matter how "official" the caller sounds or claims to be.

On a more upbeat note, the effective entrepreneurial principal will re-ceive many calls offering funding opportunities, support, and various types of resources. There is already a not-so-good perception in the world outside of public education that bureaucratically we are a mess. Many organizations, non-public and public-private institutions, and members of the business com-munity have told me that their efforts to help public schools began and ended with a single phone call. The main office staff must be fully briefed on all of the school's resource-fundraising activities and partnerships in which the school is engaged. The EMOS must be able to triage all internal and external calls coming into the main office, while at the same time allowing each caller to feel that their call is being responded to professionally. Hopefully, you are a principal who is not mistakenly stuck in your office. This means that that you are going to need a thoughtful and knowledgeable EMOS to effectively problem-solve the many issues that are directed to the main office. The EMOS should share a standard understanding and approach that speaks to a general phone protocol of knowledgeable professionalism. It only takes one office person with the wrong customer service attitude to make it hard for the entire staff, including you, the principal.

It goes without saying that the main office staff must establish a good processes and procedures environment. The main office must be clean, attractive, neat and well-organized. A filing system catalogued so well that any EMOS person can direct the principal over the phone, at any time, to whatever document or piece of information that is needed. The point here is that a well-organized filing system is essential to the effective running of a main office, particularly since the Board of Education uses an abundance of official forms. Knowing where the school's essential operational and administrative documents are located, and making sure forms are always in stock, is critical for the smooth operation of the main office. The counter should always be neat and clean. Bulletin boards should be up to date with useful visitor information as well as the waiting/sitting area being aesthetically attractive and comfortable. People will more likely respond positively to the level of professional organization and structure they encounter. The opposite, unfortunately, also occurs when the response is, "Well, since it is obvious that they don't care how they present themselves, why should I?" The office should have art, comfortable furniture, magazine racks, and leveled book shelves and educational puzzles and games for younger children who are accompanying their parents. We are professional educators, and that includes the younger siblings of our students! Corporate partners can be helpful here as well as federal agencies that have giveaway programs for office supplies and furniture in excellent condition (http://www.gsa.gov/portal/category/21045). You could also make friends with the district warehouse folks for you would be shocked to know what they have in storage! The look, atmosphere, and operational smoothness of the main office not only reflects the school's level of effectiveness and professional excellence, it influences the school itself. For many of the daily visitors, the main office might be their first and only stop. Why not welcome them with a warm atmosphere, plants, magazines and informational brochures, a pleasant greeting and a smile?

The competence of the EMOS may have the ability to fix things before they reach your desk, which will allow you to work more effectively on bigger issues. More importantly, they must accomplish this at the same time that they are trying to complete their own administrative job responsibilities. Understaffing the main office is a recipe for disaster. As the principal, you should be aware of the multiple day-to-day tasks they must perform, even as they are being constantly interrupted. Not only should you not understaff the main office, you should also make sure that they have the equipment, software, and supplies they need to properly perform their assigned tasks. I have seen too many main office staff persons burnt out because the work never stops and they are constantly shifting back and forth between their administrative duties and incoming (telephone and walk-ins) responsibilities. The better the main office is organized, the better they are able to address urgent matters that occur every day in school. Since these EMOS folks rarely get their entitled breaks, it's important that you allow them to have a lunch break away from their desks. Besides, eating at their desk in the main office sends the wrong (terrible) message to visitors.

Another key to creating a proactive and effective main office is leadership. I believe that leadership should come from an office manager and/or the principal's secretary. I have also long argued that in this modern era where the principal must play a public and entrepreneurial role, the principal's secretary position should be raised to the level of Executive Assistant with vastly increased pay and responsibilities based on an enhanced job description. The truth (and if most principals are honest) is that all of my secretaries functioned in that capacity, without the matching commensurate pay, or the job classification of "Executive Assistant." This fact is a disappointing one because there was no way that I could have accomplished all of my daily tasks without the skillful work of two (SSCHS-Phelps ACE) ladies, Ms. Jodi Chandler and Ms. Maria Figueroa. On a daily basis as they were informing me of a serious problem, they were also providing me with several solutions to solve those problems. They saved me from countless wasteful meetings and effectively managed the communication between the school and corporate partners, funders, elected officials, the school's foundation, alumni, parents, the central office, unions and government agencies. Having an excellent rapport with parents, they could often fix potentially negative issues that were caused, accidently or on purpose by any members of the staff. The effective principal's secretary should also have a good relationship with the staff and students, which translates into them serving as a communication bridge between the principal and the school internal and external community. Note, because you, as the principal, are the chief rating officer (and sometimes enforcer of the unpopular) in the building, you will need a good and thoughtful executive secretary who can present you with a perspective you had not considered; or some possible outcomes of your decisions that you may have overlooked.

Principals think long and hard about various staff positions, but you'd better think extra-long and hard about the principal's secretary position, because that person can make or break you. The principal should select a person with high spiritual moral and ethical standards; a person with a commitment to, and compassion for, children, parents, staff, and the school. Someone you can trust to know your weaknesses and deficiencies and someone you trust to have the courage to tell you the truth, even when no one else in the building will. And pray that you have the courage and sense to receive that spoken truth in the positive spirit in which it is given. The principalship is a lonely and, in many ways, isolated position. You will need at least one person in the building who can take you into your office and speak candidly with you about important matters. It is my firm belief that without a great executive secretary, you will be struggling to be effective in your position as principal. Which is why, when you do have a wonderful executive security, you better come up with some "creative" ways to fix public education's secretary staffing-compensation flaw, and appropriately reward her.

Chapter 23:
Cafeteria[9] and Food Services

What's that old military saying, "An army marches on its stomach?" Well, in many ways a school's march toward effectiveness is in part dependent on the quality of the school cafeteria service and food, the lunchroom period as a whole, and the rejuvenating feel of the cafeteria environment itself.

As I stated earlier in the sections on *Tone*, *Climate*, and *Culture*, every space in the school is a teaching and learning environment; and the care, atmosphere, and the behaviors in those spaces support or detract from the school's primary mission. The cafeteria is no different; it is in essence a large classroom. Attention then must first be given to how it looks. Is it a pleasant place to eat? Are the wall exhibits rich in both aesthetic and informational value? Is it safe for students and assigned staff? Creating a safe school, and by extension, safe spaces inside of that school, will never happen by accident. The lunch periods, assemblies, dismissal, or sporting events are moments when the school's respect and discipline values will truly be tested. This is due in part to the sheer number of students gathered in the same place, offering, so they believe, a sense of anonymity for misbehaviors. These are also moments when misleaders will take advantage of the "herd" mentality to misdirect students who, depending on their own initiative, would never break a rule. Providing a quality eating experience is a unique challenge for any public entity that seeks to feed a large number of people in a single, large space.

In the cafeteria multiple objectives are being sought at the same time:

- The lunch period "lesson plan": What habits, values and behaviors do we want students to practice during the lunch periods?

- Health and food safety.

- Providing a "break" for students from the academic tension.

- Responding to school, local, state, and federal guidelines and regulations.

- Planning, purchasing, and storage of food and dining supplies.

- The challenges of cooking (tasty and enjoyable) food, and serving, a large group.

- Healthy food options, particularly in high schools where students have greater personal control over menu decisions.

- In public schools, a dual (and sometimes dueling) line of supervision and rating of the cafeteria staff.

- In public schools, a tremendous "food-wasting" problem.

- Efficiency of the lunch operation. (Less serving line time and more eating and relaxing time). And the serving-eating time constraints. (e.g., 45-min. period)

- Variety in choices to meet the desires of a diverse group of students.

- Safety and security.

- Nutritional objectives.

The high school cafeteria and lunch program offers a unique set of challenges that require a unique set of solutions.

The beginning of establishing a positive and productive cafeteria lunch period culture is to start with transforming the thinking of the people who work there.

It is important to meet with the cafeteria supervisor alone; they should not hear your lunch period philosophy (assuming you have formulated one) for the first time when you speak with the entire cafeteria staff. You should start with asking the supervisor what her vision is for an effective school cafeteria and lunch period. As the school building leader, you may possess some degree of a SuperVision, but don't assume that you are the only person in the building who has one. Many public education employees who work in specialty job classifications very often have excellent ideas on how to improve the qualitative outcomes in their work areas. The problem is that no one may have taken the time to ask them. You should then share your ideas, particularly outlining your school's academic, behavioral, and disciplinary missions and how you both can make sure the cafeteria is a safe, respectful place for staff and students. It is always important in these types of discussions to let staff members know that you respect what they do and that you will remove all possible obstacles to them performing at their best. Additionally, you will insist that this respect is practiced by other members of the school family. It is also critical to make the "cafeteria as classroom" case. The lunch period must be seen as a way of achieving several objectives: (1) Give the students an opportunity to take a breather from the intense and rigorous academic program (again assuming that is the organizational practice of your school). (2) To provide students with a nourishing and enjoyable meal that will rejuvenate them for the rest of the school day. (3) The opportunity to teach students about nutrition and healthy eating habits. (4) To expose students to the soft skills, competencies, and responsibilities that involve social activities like eating in public and sharing an eating space and table. The conversation should also cover and expand on the beforementioned essential objectives of the lunch period:

- Your standards for defining a good lunch period and positive and productive cafeteria. The associated rubrics that will define effective implementation and practice of those standards; and the evaluation process by which those standards are measured.

- The cafeteria environment and food services as expressions and extensions of the school's culture.

- The school's (principal's) ethical position that all children should be allowed to eat without prejudice, ridicule, or punishment.

- A salad and sandwich bar/station.

- The cafeteria supervisor and the staff as part of the school's instructional team.

- Health and food safety education.

- The cafeteria disciplinary action plan and process.

- The operational, academic, social, nutritional, and emotional value and goals of the (before school) breakfast and (after-school evening) supper programs.

- Providing Halal-Kosher and vegan/vegetarian menu options.

- Refreshments for special events such as parent meetings, exhibitions, performances, open school day and evening, visiting guests and dignitaries, etc.

- Creative projects and activities like "Meatless Monday," Italian, Caribbean, Chinese, and Spanish menu days as well as "Guest Chef" days and food-tasting events.

- Emergency procedures/plans (e.g., fire drill, power outage, loss of water)

- The discipline code for a safe, secure, respectful, and inspiring cafeteria environment.

- Planning, purchasing, and storage.

- The ARC (ISS) students' basic menu plan procedures and schedule. (A legally basic nutritional but "unexciting" lunch—those students eat in the ARC room.)

- How to respond to high school students having a greater authority over lunch decisions.

- How to best stop the public school's tremendous "food-wasting" (food into the garbage) problem.

- The plan for running an efficient service operation (less line waiting time to eat).

- Can we make the physical space look more inviting and attractive?

- Food "Tastiness" and "Aesthetics" (Can the food look and taste good!)

- How can we expand the variety of choices to meet the desires of a culturally diverse student group?

- Can we teach healthy eating habits and share nutritional concepts with the students?

- Healthy and natural snacks/juice plan.

- A quality "bag lunch" program, particularly in schools where students take a lot of fieldtrips. Note to principals: Students in my schools went on a lot of trips. The cafeteria staff may not be accustomed to preparing take-out lunches for high schoolers; or they may follow the district's basic (elementary school) bag lunch menu. This is one of the cafeteria bureaucratic norms that you might want to discuss with the cafeteria supervisor, where you both can raise the bag lunch menu standard.

Students who go on trips should not be deprived of a quality lunch.

* The necessary but difficult and controversial discussion about how students in this school will be allowed to take their lunches out of the cafeteria to places like club meeting rooms, the college/career center, to eat while attending lunch time classroom tutorials, or seminars/lectures, and in my case, for even being allowed to eat and meet in the principal's conference room. Students will (as in all high performing academic schools), after eating their lunch in the cafeteria, be allowed to leave and visit the college/career center, attend classroom tutorials, work on projects and papers, meet with their student study group, complete weekly exams, computer rooms, the library, art, music, dance studio areas. Thus, the need for an efficient lunch serving line, and a quick salad or sandwich bar alternative feeding area. Of course, this type of lunch period environment must be strategically designed and implemented by the principal, SBL, and staff. Some students who may have only experienced lunch time in the past as a "lock-down" in the cafeteria period will need help adjusting to this new standard of responsibility; you may in fact find yourself restricting some students to the cafeteria because of their inability to properly utilize this new freedom. You will also need to transition the ninth graders slowly into this system by allowing them to earn these rights based on teacher recommendations (empowers teachers and improves the classroom learning environment), school academic and behavioral performance. If you don't think this a powerful motivator for good behavior and high academic achievement, just wait for those calls from parents whose "hurt feelings" behaviorally challenged children, are forced to prove themselves worthy of the school's lunch period freedom policy. Principal, you should not even attempt this without a powerful, dedicated, and efficacious staff, who respects and expects you to really hold and maintain a strong and consistent discipline line. I got lucky at my two schools for having such a staff!

A follow-up meeting should be organized to bring the custodial foreman, dean, the security team's commanding officer, and the cafeteria supervisor together. There is a great deal of overlap between their cafeteria periods work responsibilities, and it is always easier to start out by having all four leaders on the same page.

The next step is to meet with the entire cafeteria staff, not just the supervisor. As principal, you want to encourage and engage them as an important part of the academic team. You want them to be able to go about their duties in the most positive and rewarding way. If students have a positive lunch experience, that feeling will spill over into their classroom experiences. Further, in Title I schools, the breakfast, lunch, and supper meals programs can often take on a tremendous nutritional and psychological meaning for students. These meals could be the most complete, fulfilling, and peaceful meals of their day. The cafeteria staff must fully come to an understanding that food and eating is of great cultural significance in our society and this school; and it not something that just insignificantly and routinely happens during the school day. The idea is to create a restaurant-like feel in the cafeteria. I always tried to make the point that school cafeterias don't necessarily need to look like prison cafeterias simply because a large number of people are eating at one time. Our goals are bigger and greater than stuffing young people with food, not really caring whether they enjoyed it or not, and then pushing them out the door to their next destination. As principal, you should know that making the cafeteria feel more restaurant-like, will be difficult. Historically in public education there has always been an intentional or unintentional effort to make school lunch periods as miserable and unlikable as possible for students, which often leads (especially in high schools) to large numbers of students not eating at all. This hurts them nutritionally and academically because of the dramatic drop in their blood sugar. Or, the opposite occurs where instead of consuming the "tasteless" lunch, they eat unhealthy foods and sugary drinks and snacks they bring from outside of the school, meaning many of them are "sugar-hyped" and distracted during their post-lunch classrooms. Speaking of real data you can use, principals should compare and contrast your pre- and post-lunch student disciplinary problems. Also, observe the huge amount of food being thrown away. This behavioral practice of students wasting and throwing away a great deal of food is not only nutritionally hurtful, but also undermines a school's efforts to teach empathy and compassion. On the one hand, we speak of the problem of hunger in the U.S. and abroad, yet at the same time teach students to waste large amounts of food each day. The best way to make the cafeteria experience financially, emotionally, nutritionally, and academically more positive and productive is to remove many of the unnecessary cooking and preparation regulations that stand in the way of making the lunch period an appealing and enjoyable experience. Allow professional educators, dieticians, students, and nutritionists to plan menu offerings that would inspire students to not only eat but also to eat healthy. I would also engage culinary schools and master chefs in the certification and ongoing professional development of school cafeteria cooks. In my view, there is no sense in having a culture where food that is costly and healthy goes to waste because it does not taste good. Improve the diversity and taste quality of cafeteria food, and this will help to improve the attitude and behaviors of the students who utilize those school cafeterias.

Teaching students the school's positive cafeteria and lunch period culture

- First, help students to know, follow, and ultimately, self-regulate the health and safety cafeteria rules. This process begins in the new student's orientation (and is repeated to the entire student body at the beginning of every school year), that some of the common shenanigans and misbehaviors that can occur in many school cafeterias will not be tolerated in this school. The penalties and punishments for the violation of these cafeteria rules and regulations should be clearly outlined in your presentations as well as the student/parent handbook; however, more importantly, since the cornerstone of good discipline is consistency, these penalties must be enforced when violations occur. I offer a bit of cautionary advice to new students, pick your friends and cafeteria table mates carefully, for I believe in administering a "group-table" system of justice (I will touch on that a little later). As far as disciplinary codes go, make small things, big things, which will have the effect of making big things that much more out of the norm and unacceptable.

- The annual ninth grade cafeteria disciplinary action volunteer. It is guaranteed that some student(s) will offer you the opportunity to make an example of what not to do in the cafeteria. As principal, you should quickly and effectively seize upon this unfortunate (for the person) and yet fortunate (for the collective good) opportunity as a "Teachable Moment" that no other students observing will ever want to experience.

- If the school is academically rigorous and does not allow for a lot of lesson-distracting "social talk" in classrooms, then the cafeteria

377

(lunch period) will serve as an important and necessary opportunity for student relaxation. Students should be allowed to socialize within sensible audible limits. The school must also support that reality by providing positive games (e.g., chess, checkers, Connect Four, GO, Dominoes, Scrabble). No gambling! It is a Jazz model: Tension (the classrooms) and Release (the cafeteria)!

- Lunch outside of the cafeteria: This is an important discussion you must have with the custodial staff since their work culture is opposed to this. But the school must make spaces available for students who, for personality reasons, do not like the crowdedness of the cafeteria. This approach also assumes that the high school is creating and en-couraging a college atmosphere, where students are held to a higher level of personal responsibility. High-performing schools focus on lunch time student contentment. Low-performing schools focus on lunch time student containment. To rightfully and fairly keep the cus-todians happy, a serious "keep clean and clean-up" campaign/educa-tion program must be in place. Finally, having secondary eating spaces relieved some of the pressure on the cafeteria, thus, the school being able to have a much smaller and more manageable cafeteria environ-ment.

- Not accepting disrespect from, or by, any member of the school fam-ily. Due to some distorted sense of classism, students are sometimes confused (often by the school culture itself) as to whom to respect in a school. This is a principal's red line; cafeteria staff must receive the same level of respect that would be accorded to any other staff person. As the principal, you must quickly, decisively and consistently, uti-lizing the appropriate disciplinary procedures, clear up any confusion that students might have concerning these matters! And prepare your-self for that parental call: "You mean you sent my child to in-school suspension lunch because he disrespected a cafeteria worker?" Yes, I did!

- Students have a right to eat and relax during their lunch period in the cafeteria. Staff monitoring the lunch periods (through profession-al development), must be alerted to any open, subtle, or the smallest forms of "microaggressions," pre-conflict body or verbal language, or bullying actions.

- Having lunch in the cafeteria is a privilege, not a right; therefore, that privilege can be rescinded at any time if a student lacks the discipline and the moral fortitude to carry themselves properly in the company of other students. We will (by law) feed you (in the ARC); it just won't be in the cafeteria, and will more than likely not be the level of menu choice a student might enjoy as a normal lunchroom participant.

- Cleanliness is part of the criteria and qualification for cafeteria usage. Students should enter a clean space to eat and should leave that space as clean as reasonably possible. Eating space cleanliness contributes and encourages an attitude of peaceful environmentalism on the part of those who eat and work in that space.

- The cafeteria functioning as a proactive force, providing a school breakfast and supper program. These meals can go a long way in reducing student stress, provide daily nutritional requirements, and prevent unnecessary disciplinary problems.

- The cafeteria monitoring staff should not assume things like a person knows how to properly eat in the company of others. That they know what a "restaurant voice" is. Set and explain the cafeteria standards and rubrics by which adherence to those standards will be measured; as well as the rewards and penalties for a student's response to those standards.

- Make the cafeteria a more interesting, exciting, and inviting place to eat. Have specialty items and meal days. Let the lunch menu offer surprises. Treat students as if they were customers, like they have options to eat somewhere else. Start by expanding cafeteria/lunchroom options: salad bars, "make your own" sandwich stations, healthy snacks, natural fruit drinks, etc.

- Let the lunch periods be the launching pad for a positive and productive post-lunch period learning school day!

Finally principal, and it is worth repeating, what you don't effectively manage, will become unmanageable, and therefore ultimately undermine your operational and academic objectives. You must lead with a strategically intelligent plan executed without fear, and keep open communication between you and school employees. The cafeteria and lunch periods are a critical part of a school's day; a great deal can go right or terribly wrong; and, principal, it is only your attention and planning that will be the determining factors as to which path this important time and place will take.

Chapter 24:
The Dean's Office,
In-School Suspension (ISS), and
Attitude Readjustment Center (ARC)

An important principle that the school must uphold is that, "We are in the education, not punishment business!" In order to achieve the first part of this objective, the school must provide a safe, protected educational environment where teaching and learning can effectively go forward without hindrance or unnecessary interruptions. That first part of the statement also suggests that an effective school would want students to miss the least amount of instructional time as possible. Thus, finding the delicate balance begins; the need to have a safe and productive learning environment while at the same time holding students accountable who attempt to disrupt that safe and productive learning environment. As with just about everything else that occurs in schools, you must create a standard of behavioral expectations, the rewards for meeting those expectations, and the consequences of not meeting them. If a principal believes that she can talk about school behavioral standards once, or print them in a student handbook (that few students will thoroughly read), then that principal is headed for self-designed disappointment. With behavioral standards, the name of the game is redundancy, consistency, and predictability. You know you are in the right place, principal, when students who have been sent to your office start explaining their "crime and punishment" before you speak. Students should be able to deconstruct their own misbehavior without much prompting. This ability on the student's part is actually a first step on the road to properly aligning themselves with the school's rules and regulations. An effective dean must understand this concept of attitude and behavioral re-alignment with the school for both the community and the student's well-being. Therefore, the dean is in every way a teacher and brain of the school's moral values, not just the muscle. Every encounter with the dean should be a cause for student introspection and the creation of a strategy that will allow the student to not end up in the same place again. Unfortunately, sometimes the nature of the bad act, and the time required to complete an effective introspection process, means that the student will be removed from regular classes for a definite period of time. But before I discuss that suspension experience, let me complete the concepts on the prevention side of the equation. There are several standards that the dean must establish and enforce that will keep students *out* of the dean's office. These standards unfortunately tend to bump into pre-conditioned, family, or external standards that students may bring into the school, often leading to disciplinary problems.

- The school is some kind of a democracy, not a place where adults make the ultimate decisions.

- Students (even before they get to American History or Civics class) feel they understand the concept of "free speech" as meaning saying whatever they want, where, when, and to whom they want.

- Whatever knowledge (or misunderstanding) of the principle of "free speech"; that thought does not carry over to an understanding that their classmates have a right to an education without their interruption or distraction.

- A rule or a decision must always make sense to them; we adults try, but can't always accomplish that goal.

- High school students' thinking, perceptions, motivations, actions, responses to situations, and problem/conflict resolution strategies, can often be driven by peer influential factors. This can lead to the misinformed leading the less-informed, which sometimes results in the less-informed group making some bad decisions.

- A great cause of school disciplinary problems is because of that period of the natural and necessary teenage psychological separation, disengagement, and disagreement from adult oversight. This creates an interesting dynamic when adult rules and ruler-ship is resisted by the emerging adult personality. There is, however, some sense-making for adults to point out the dangers they have encountered on their path to adulthood, thus helping young people avoid unnecessary hardships and setbacks. I have always said to students, "You don't need to experience everything in life (in fact there are definitely some things you don't ever want to experience). You can, however, learn from the negative experiences of others, specifically to not have that experience!"

- The fact is that schooling, high schools in particular, are "rehearsal" sessions for independent professional and family adult life. For example, getting to work on time, positively managing the communication and work relationships with colleagues and supervisors, having your concerns become secondary to the concerns of your children as a parent, mastering the soft-skills of professional life, etc.

- Some students mistakenly arrive to high school with the idea that school should be easy and that the learning and behavioral standards already in place can be altered to meet their personal (or parental) standards.

- We are solidly in the era that wrongly informs young people that their internal reality is the external reality. "Being me" means that I can impose my "me" on others, regardless of the consequences.

- Many students have heard too many times, "It's the teacher, principal, and school's fault!" Sometimes, it is one or all three, but not always, and students, along with some unproductive enabling parents, can't always tell the difference!

- Many believe that they must like the teachers and the teachers are required to like them. There is a wide spectrum of understanding among teenagers (and their parents) as to what "like" is. There is also a common misconception that the student must be in agreement with the teacher's lesson plan, methodology, and approach in the classroom. (Back to that democracy problem!)

- The concept of a student taking responsibility for a bad grade is missing. "He (the teacher) failed me!"

- Students severely lacking in productive and proper protest skills when they feel (sometimes with justification) that they have been wronged.

- Lacking the necessary skills to manage the teacher-student relationship.

- Receiving advice from parents as to how to handle situations in school that are counter to the school's rules, district statues, and regulatory process.

- All decisions and actions have consequences. How many times have we heard adults say, "If only I knew then that it would turn out this way, I would have made another decision!" Teenagers are especially challenged with this natural short-sightedness because they don't have a large experience bank to draw on during the pre-adult decision-making phase of the process. A core learning objective of the dean's office is to help students to see clearly and act thoughtfully at the beginning of the process or proposed action; to think about, where this can go and how their actions might hurt or help them. Finally, we are a social/ communal species, which suggests that as we act, we must take into account the feelings, aspirations, safety, rights, and well-being of our fellow school family members as well as our human family members outside of the school.

"...not in the punishment business!"

I always cringed internally as a principal when a parent, who in reality was more frustrated with their child then with me or the school, would say, "you just like suspending my child!" The cause of the cringing was that somewhere near the bottom of the list of things I liked the least about the principalship was dealing with student disciplinary issues; and that was because disciplinary issues often took me away from things I loved doing like talking and getting to know students, finding internships and college scholarships, and observing classes. But just as we teach students that real life is dealing with the pleasant and unpleasant aspects of life, maturity is not only about doing what you want to do, but what you must do. And, so, one of the ways I changed my thinking and sought to change the thinking of my deans about school discipline is to see these challenges as teachable moments. This means that the school must take *punishment* off the list of objectives. Even if parents and students think that is what we are all about, they may not be aware that the other contributor to my cringe moment was how this present disciplinary situation will affect academic achievement, including the academic progress of the student being disciplined, who by way of a suspension, could even miss one day from their classes.

As we look at some of the above primary communication misunderstandings that could lead to student misbehaviors and ultimately disciplinary sanctions, we cannot as professionals and human beings, approach these problems with anger, malice, or insensitivity. A dean must seek to balance mercy with justice, but also see themselves in the role of educators charged with upholding the moral and ethical standards of the school while ensuring that as much teaching and learning can successfully take place as possible. The In-School Suspension program (ISS) should also reflect those important goals and objectives. If we start with its name "in-school," that should suggest that the school is first pursuing the educational needs of the students. We also know that putting a kid in the street, or having them at home unsupervised for any amount of time, could lead to dangerous and life-threatening situations. Suspension out of school harms the child educationally as well as the school's educational mission. ISS should not serve as an instrument of punishment, for again both the child and the school will be punished academically. Rather, ISS should be a place where the student can reflect on, and rework, their plan for maintaining their role as productive members of the school learning community. One of the evaluations I had of both the dean and ISS, is whether its door was a path to redemption or a revolving door. If too many students assigned to ISS are not redeemed to a serious educational purpose, then that is a demonstration of our collective staff failure; or, as sometimes is the case, the school is the wrong place for the student. This is why the guidance counseling department must work hand-in-hand with the dean and the ISS program. This is also why I prefer the title Attitude Readjustment Center (ARC) for the ISS program. First, because as I stated in the section on *Culture*, what you call a thing in a school is important and speaks to its intent and purpose. So, we start off with the ARC looking and behaving like a classroom (because the ARC team has a lesson plan to redeem and guide misguided students); there are workstations, desks, textbooks and reference books, computers, and a clear understanding that being "assigned" to the ARC is not a vacation from schoolwork. That last assertion alone, along with cafeteria banishment, is a great incentive for a student to not want to return to the ARC! I have also been fortunate to have a teaching staff who did not mind going the extra distance to provide the current class work assignments to students who unfortunately found themselves in the ARC; and that included the teachers who might have been the very staff person who recommended them to the ARC. Some teachers have even visited the ARC during their free periods in order to help a student with a difficult topic or question from the day's lesson. The "stay" in ISS or ARC should be seamless in terms of academic instruction. The academic work produced, collected, graded, and counting toward the report card grade should match the rigor standards of any classroom in the school. And, of course, the guidance counseling team along with the ARC staff should add on the additional instructional objectives designed to help the student discover why they were there and how never to return.

Finally, the principal must take on the never-ending role of bureaucracy buster. As the chief bureaucracy buster, you must do something radically different and important with the dean and ARC staff. You must evaluate them on the goal of less students returning to ISS or the ARC. At the same time, you must assure them that just because there are days where there are few, or no students in ISS or the ARC, they won't lose their jobs. If you don't establish that trustful agreement with them, the entire mission and purpose of an ARC will be lost which means its value to students and the academic mission of the school will be lost. You can confidently assure them that as long as teenagers and adults occupy the same space for many hours of the day, there will probably be a need for a dean!

Chapter 25:
Standardized Testing Preparation and Analysis

Preparing for the rigor and challenges of the external standardized assessments should be reflected in the school's approach to structuring and preparing for the school's internal standardized assessments!

A high-powered, high academically achieving high school will set the standard for the school's approach to standardized testing by designing a plan to help students to do well on external advanced standardized exams, thus sending the message that the expectation is that students and staff will go all out in their attempts to do well on all (external and internal) standardized exams. The mathematics and ELA departments can jointly offer an ACT/SAT preparation elective where the class can rotate or flip between Math and ELA for one week each, or by semester. If the course is offered after school, or weekends it will help those students with already packed schedules. As helpful as this elective course can be, it won't be enough to properly prepare your students. The advance test-prep-tutorial program will require an after-school and weekend program plan. This plan will be costly, so this is where the school's 501c3 foundation can be of great assistance. In order to prepare students to be competitive when taking these exams, the school will need to contract with a reputable professional test preparation company. The school (particularly in Title I schools) will need to pay part or the entire cost depending upon the number of participating students. In addition, test-prep materials, software, and review books can mean additional costs. If the school already has a robust after-school evening educational program, that cost is covered; but the students will need access to the school on Saturdays and/or Sundays to be fully able to take advantage of the intense work hours required by the test-prep company instructors. The school should also provide in-classroom snacks and lunch to create the most productive environment. After these Saturday sessions, I would allow them to play basketball in the gym or have a small study party. And, so, the cost of staff supervision and chaperoning must be added to the budget. As the principal you want to encourage students to attend these voluntary test-prep sessions, so you want to make it as enjoyable as possible (which means giving them the food they want—pizza!) One of the good aspects of the informal student communication system is that the news of the "fun and food" aspects of the sessions, along with a relaxation of the drees code will spread throughout the school; ninth and tenth graders will begin to ask you when they will be able to attend such sessions. My answer, "Well, to get to the SAT/ACT/AP/etc., exams, first you must pass and do well on your present exams!" Make the preparation, taking, and passing of standardized exams a central cultural mission of the school. But to do that you will need to work hard at shutting down a great deal of the "noise" outside of your school!

Principal, be very careful and analytically critical of the advice you receive from folks whose children have options your students don't enjoy.

Be wary of the "entitled parents" and sometimes in cooperation with teacher labor unions-led anti-standardized testing movement. The truly effective school always seeks to define every policy, plan, and initiative that is mandated by external "political forces" (e.g., national, state, and local school district stakeholders) in its own terms. The truly effective school and school leader also seeks to remain true to the authentic and useful purposes of all pedagogical activities. To be honest and fair to the "anti-testers" coalition, the entire standardized testing system has been badly hijacked and harmed by visionless educational veterans and misinformed and cynical so-called "reformers." The true educational worth and practice of standardized testing should never be used to bully, belittle, and mislabel schools as well as the people who work and learn in them. The purpose of standardized testing should also never be used as a single indicator of a school's progress or lack thereof. Teaching and learning is a serious, complex activity as students don't stay with the same teacher from kindergarten to twelfth grade. The evaluation of a teacher's capability can be reflected in part by standardized test results, which is an important factor in the evaluative process, but it is only one factor of many different evaluative tools. The critical point here is that we waste an opportunity to improve instructional practice when we don't utilize standardized testing properly, which means using it to define and refine the quality of instructional practice. And, of course, no professional will get better if they believe that the evaluative process is structured to destroy (fire) them rather than make them better professionals.

388

Worse, we have lost the other important value of standardized testing as a diagnostic tool for identifying student conceptual and behavioral "misunderstandings" and the pace and progress of their learning and mastering the curriculum, course, and/or grade-level standards. This loss of the true meaning and purpose of standardized testing has hurt teaching and learning rather than improved it, and this is also terribly true in how they are applied to schools. The effective principal and school can do very little about the external policies and regulations, even if these policies and regulations are misguided and not well-thought-out. But what we can do is to make every effort to "make lemonade" out of the lame and lemon proposals we have been handed. The effective school is always in the state of redefinition and self-determination; and there is always the challenge of where a school leader would like to put their efforts in relationship to bad policies from above. What we do know is that standardized testing is here until it is not. It is the effective school leader who will always try to keep the school focused on methods that will help students to be academically successful, in the present. Just because some aspect of education is being utilized poorly or improperly does not give us the right to ignore its real implications in the lives of students. Like it or not, we presently live in a standardized testing-results world, and our students will be evaluated by that world. Our students' futures will be determined by their performance on high school and beyond standardized exams such as the ACT, SAT, AP, LSAT, MCAT, GRE, etc. *And, so, until we live in a society where those exams disappear and don't matter, it is our professional ethical responsibility to prepare students to perform well on these exams!* We should appropriately respond to society's incorrect definition of an operational activity in education, even as we reject its underlining bad pedagogy. We know, for example, that comparing the test scores of two different cohorts of students a year apart is not really useful to teachers or schools in the way it is being used. The effective school should set up its own test results analysis that best informs the teachers in that school as to what kind of methodological modifications, pacing, and instructional approach changes they should make when reviewing, reteaching as they move forward in the syllabus. If schools are utilizing local newspapers to evaluate and explain test results, then they are in trouble. The improper response to test results has led us to a bad place in education where some schools engage in never-ending test prep and/or the destruction and dismissal of art, music, dance, library activity, or any other activity that is thought not directly related to preparing for an exam. Ironically, this terrible response has actually led to lower student academic achievement because students are missing an education that provides imaginative, inquisitive, reflective, and creative learning experiences—the very things that actually help to make students smarter! The effective school must be intelligent when it comes to standardized exams; take from them what you need and reject the rest; design your own philosophy of standardized testing. So what kinds of things should the effective school be doing as they place standardized testing under their internal supervision and control?

- They could start by first restoring and returning standardized testing to its true pedagogical purpose. At the same time, the school should not choose to fight the external policies and regulations relating to standardized testing; nothing can prevent them from interpreting and defining the external standardized testing reality in accordance with their internal reality of how they choose to make students successful in their school. The best test prep is to teach students to exceed the standards being tested by the exam, while also teaching them the how to take a test.

- Since standardized testing is a present reality, I say turn it into a school effort relating to the mission. If standardized testing results are going to be used in society as a national measuring tool, then the school can choose not to place their students at an academic disadvantage. Now, over the years I have taken a great deal of heat for that position, but I'm keenly aware that much of that heat comes from people for whom public or private education has been a nurturing friend to their children, and to the children who live like their children. Privilege has its benefits, and one is the choice to ignore, avoid, and/or dismiss standardized testing because the expectations, curriculum, and instructional practices at the school your child attends meets and exceeds the learning standards that are being tested in the standardized exams.

- For external standardized testing, the effective school must deconstruct both the mechanics (test-taking skills) and the content standards involved. Success on these exams requires a combination of strong content knowledge and good test-taking "technology" skills. Both of these requirements can be taught and improved if it is done in a strategic way (which is not the way it is done unfortunately in many of our schools). Smart schools don't play the grueling test-prep approach to performance success on these exams. What these schools do, and what all schools should do, is to integrate the conceptual behavioral standards into the daily instructional program of the school in *all* subject areas. This is a good way of "teaching to the test," because the school is aggressively going after and beyond the curriculum standards by pushing students to go deeper and wider than the test questions. When students are able to face rigorous and challenging instruction on a daily basis, the rigor and challenge that shows up on the standardized exams is much easily addressed by students. The problem with too many schools is that students in underperforming schools encounter rigorous and challenging concepts for the first time when they sit down to take a standardized exam and with the predictable outcome. This also explains why the "test-prep all the time" approach in many schools is such a dismal failure. Piling question after question into a child's head while they have not mastered the underlining concepts does more harm than good. Good and effective schools know that test-prep begins on day one in every classroom in the school, and when students are empowered with a strong conceptual foundation built throughout the school year, the second part of test-prep is easy. That second part consists of teaching students the secret (to some people) mechanics of test-taking. Professional educators have known for years, especially those who have taken a commercial test-prep course (e.g., Princeton Review), that you can raise the achievement level for any student by simply teaching them how to better interpret, translate and properly respond to the test questions. These techniques are actually more effective than just feeding students' endless questions that they may or may not get right, and then giving them the right answers. As a high school principal, you should have a commercial test prep program in your school for the taking of the SAT and ACT. You should also take time to sit and observe these classes, for you will see many important instructional strategies that should be employed in every classroom in the school. Some important learning strategies will emerge as you observe these commercial test-prep classes in action:

o The role of ELA language, vocabulary, etymology, Greek and Latin prefixes and suffixes, reading and writing skills. A critical part of test-taking is being able to properly read and translate the questions; and then being able to effectively convey your ideas in writing.

o The all-important skill of knowing and understanding the: "What am I being asked to do?" And then knowing and faithfully doing it to (the satisfaction of the test grader) its completion!

o The ability, through the use of standards and their defining rubrics, for the students to be able to "grade and evaluate," their own responses to test questions, in their heads, while they are taking an exam. Or, the "good test-takers" internal test taking-talking dialogue.

o Strategies and methods to identify one's strengths and weaknesses, and, therefore, making study time more efficient.

o Mastering the critical turnkey words and phrases, sentence determiners and/or distractors, and the meaning of words to the test-giver and scorer.

o Knowing and understanding the type of exam being given, how it is scored, and whether or not there are penalties for omitting questions.

o The anatomy of a test question. What are the different "working-operational" parts of a question, and how can that information be used to help answer that question, including one in which the student may not be fully aware of the answer? Let us not pretend that the act of "strategic guessing" is not an essential part of successful test-taking. Besides, if a student gets the question correct, the overall test score does not indicate on which questions they employed strategic guessing!

o The "standardized appearance" (format) of questions over many years. Students can be taught how to recognize a question by its format and attributes; the student can then apply the correct algorithm, or strategic approach to answering those sets of questions.

o Test-taking time management and the prioritizing and triaging of answering questions.

o The separation of conceptual knowledge skills and behavioral test-taking skills, and how the student can improve both in class and on their own. The standardized test score raising role of seemingly unrelated activities (e.g., participation in a science, history fair, membership on the cyber forensics or robotics team, independent reading) along with out-of-school informal educational activities (e.g., dance/music/art lessons, museums, hobbies).

○ The test-taking empowerment factor; test confidence, the development of the idea that the test-taker is not a passive player in the process, but can in fact take control of their own testing experience, given the discipline and willingness to put in the proper learning-preparation work. In many schools, there is a great deal of foreboding around test season, which is different from healthy nervousness. The truth is that raising academic achievement scores on standardized exams is much easier than we make it out to be, if we take a strategic approach.

We mentioned earlier the importance of having a consistent and diversified rigorous and challenging classroom culture consistent throughout the school. And "consistent" means in every classroom in the school. Rigorous teaching and learning that is connected to the standards should be the number one test-prep strategy of the school. At the beginning, students may feel uncomfortable and even complain; but, eventually, as it becomes part of the school's *Culture*, students will feel uncomfortable (and complain), if they are not challenged with rigorous class work. Students (and all humans for that matter) are amazingly adaptable. Students who transferred out of one of my schools, have on many occasions, expressed the disappointment they felt when not challenged in their new school. Comparing the same course syllabus in different schools should never be confused with the knowing the level of rigor that takes place in each of those schools. Schools offering the same course is only part of the story; there is also the level of depth, rigor, and the extent to which the entire syllabus is covered and completed, can vary greatly. The transcripts of two students say that they took and passed the same course, but in reality, they took different courses; and one of the places where that "different" reality is exposed is on standardized exams.

Make the course work hard up front!

Parents, and perhaps, students may complain at first, but three things will eventually happen: (1) The students over time will adjust to the quality and quantity of serious academic work. (2) The rigorous academic standards will become a natural attribute of the school, and the normal state of expectations. (3) The students will be better prepared when they face the rigors of standardized exams; and do better in their post-high school, college/career experience.

Teach students how to study!

We should not assume that students know how to study for an exam. This is critically important for those students arriving from a middle school experience where studying (if it existed) may have meant studying the day/evening before an exam. They also may not know how to study (throughout the year) for a standardized exam that they will take at the end of a yearlong course. Or in the case of some high school world history courses, at the end of two years of course work. We should start with teaching students how to take notes and how to properly use the textbook. We should also teach them about the many study guides and support sites that are useful for studying. One of the techniques I advise students to use is reading a similar concept in different textbooks, which is why I always maintain a strong diverse representation of textbooks on the same subject areas and topics in the school library. It is amazing how a concept in math or science can become much clearer when the student reads the explanation in a different textbook, and therefore, in a different author's voice. We must also teach students how to study alone and in groups. Knowing how to study is not a natural experience, it must be taught. The study expectations differ greatly between the K–8 system, where short-term memory can be king, and high schools where it is not as helpful.

The important power of language in test-taking skills mastery

A second good place to start is teaching students to master the vocabulary and linguistic style of exams. There is a certain logic and flow to all exams, and

394

good test-takers are aware, even if it is unconscious, of the feel and direction in which the exam is moving. Good test-takers are able to put themselves in the mind of the test creator and a test grader; while talking (guiding) themselves through each question on the exam, they also have the skill to mentally evaluate and "grade" their answers as they put those answers down. This is why (remember from the ninth grade learning objectives) students must be taught to understand and effectively work with rubrics on their own. Vocabulary also comes into play as a major component of standardized test-taking, regardless of the subject area. A weakness in the ability to read and understand the question will also cause students to perform poorly and far below their conceptual capability on a standardized exam. Further, it is important to be able to write, when it is required, a clear and concise answer. This ELA skill is a critical component of good test-takers. Students should be taught (rubrics again) how to edit their own writing in real test time, essentially as they are writing the answer, knowing what to say, what amount of information to provide, and whether or not they have effectively and sufficiently answered the question. Very often we see poor student performance on standardized exams due to the above ELA factors alone, so the school must take these factors into account as part of test preparation. As I stated in the ELA section, an effective school must have a ninth grade vocabulary project. All of the words, including those critical turnkey words and phrases that are found on the local/state/national standardized exams, the ACT and SAT, must be mastered by the end of the ninth grade English class.

"Teacher-Made Test"

The effective school will also seek to minimize and/or eliminate the use of teacher-created exams. Now, I'm not talking about small quizzes or in-class assessments; and this is in no way a casting of dispersions on those great people who belong to the teaching profession. But it is my experience that in most cases teacher-created exams will often contain many fatal flaws. I say "fatal" because they often create an unconscious bias toward designing instructional confirming questions that help students to pass the exam. These teacher-made exams (not all) can dangerously disconnect from the rigor, complexity, and challenge of a standardized exam that is created by utilizing the curriculum standards. I have always preferred departmental-designed exams for weekly, monthly midterms and term-ending assessments. This approach also ensures that all teachers teaching the same subjects are covering the standards and learning objectives for those subjects, and that they are on the same pacing

calendar. Finally, it allows both teachers and administrators to assess and compare students covering the same subject areas and topics. My exception cases
for teacher-made exams would be the electives, technical, CTE, creative, and
performance arts classes. However, the exams that are given in these classes
should still cover the curriculum standards of those subject areas, meaning
they must pass the "rigor test"!

Giving ELA, Science, Mathematics, History and the Foreign Language departments a full period standardized exam on a designated day every week

Each class exam should contain questions that are worded in the exact or
similar vocabulary, format, and difficulty as the end-of-course standardized
exam. For example, at SSCHS we created a subject-specific Regents Exam
Questions bank, and then organized these questions to align with the curriculum topic-pacing calendar; those questions then become the questions for
the weekly exams. The students should not see the vocabulary, phraseology,
test format, and degree of difficulty of the end-of-course standardized exam
questions for the first time when they sit down to take that exam at the end
of the year. Classroom exams should be designed and organized around the
standards and vocabulary-phraseology of the curriculum, along with exposing
students to the way the questions will be structured-formatted on the end of
the course standardized exam. This is not teachers going over standardized
test-like questions; rather this is forcing the standards into the daily instructional program. The ELA teachers will continue to play an important role here,
from the first ninth grade standardized exam to the last AP exam a twelfth
grader may take before graduation. The ELA team in cooperation with the
other academic departments must make sure that at every grade level where
a standardized exam is administered, there is not one word, term, phrase or
sentence on that exam for which the student can't read and interpret. This strategic process will also include the weekly/monthly public posting of classes
and individual students (without names or any other type of identifier) performance scores on the school's internal standardized exams. This means that
the pacing calendar becomes more than a suggested schedule since all of the
students in every Geometry class will be taking the same exam. For example,
on the week four exam of the first semester, all of the Algebra, Chemistry,
and American History teachers will be testing their students on topics they

have all covered based on the fact that every teacher teaching the same course will be at the same place on the curriculum pacing calendar by the end of week four. Depending on the specific needs of the school, this testing schedule can be modified to cover every other week; however, once you get into the three-to-four-week testing schedule, the school is coming dangerously close to inviting some teachers (particularly first-year and inexperienced teachers) to arrive to the middle (midterms), or end of the course year having not covered major sections of the syllabus. These exams should encompass the entire class period. If the questions mirror, or are lifted from (if the department has legal access to) previous end-of-course standardized exams, then the questions are going to be more difficult, and require more time to answer. This format also means that there are some numerical restrictions on the number of questions that can be asked. However, the class midterms and final exams can be given over two days; or in some subject areas (e.g., ELA or history), midterms and finals can be given in part as a take-home exam. (I have seen students in both of my schools get prematurely happy when they heard that they had a take-home exam option; that happiness did not last long after they got a chance to review that selected take home option!) Another factor is my proposed four days of instruction, is, as I stated earlier in the book, requires that the principal and SBL team performs a Quality of Instruction-Time Audit in all classrooms, at least three times a year—beginning, middle, and when you get toward the end of the school year. The reason for this audit is to find out how much actual quality instructional time students are receiving in your school. This can be easily done during an informal or formal observation visit where you time at what point after the second bell when instruction actually begins. I have visited hundreds of schools and classrooms, even in those schools that had large numbers of teachers really maximizing their allotted classroom time (including my own two high schools), you can walk around the school and see teachers who have different levels of quality instruction time. I am convinced based on my observations that two teachers, students being relatively equally prepared, (teaching the same subject/course), having a class five days a week for forty-three minutes a day, can arrive at the end of the month with one teacher providing additional days of instruction. Now, there are many factors for less quality teaching time, which does not fall fully on the teacher. For example, a veteran teacher may have a classroom routines down and working well. And very important, how effective is the principal and SBL staff in establishing and enforcing quality instructional classroom behavioral standards? There are some areas of the classroom management program for which we need to take ownership in supporting the teacher's right to not be forced to teach in a chaotic and discipline challenged school environment. It is also my hypothesis concerning the amount of teaching time required that: (1) the various curriculum syllabi are constructed to capture the learning abilities of a wide spectrum of students. The underlying design means that some students/classes will finish the syllabus just on time, and others will finish early and perhaps engage in review and/or enrichment during the course year. Therefore, (2) teachers have the capability to adjust, contract, or stretch the syllabus based on the number of teaching days they know they have. (3) I think that it is a human trait to fill (or expand) the time you utilize to complete a given task, based on the time you are given to complete that task.

In summary: The four days of instruction and one day of testing can work to the students' academic achievement benefit, given it is supported by effective lesson planning and teaching delivery, teacher classroom management effectiveness, the school's disciplinary culture is highly responsive and resistant to student "off-task" classroom misbehaviors, really good teacher-student attendance, and students getting to class on time. Once they are there, the learning process quality and quantity (time) is "maxed out," and the school culture utilizes these weekly standardized exams to drive a rigorous and dynamic approach to study.

Pushing Rigor:

Why should students see a weekly mini-version of the end-of-course standardized exam?

Again, the purpose and benefit of having weekly standardized exams is to raise the level of classroom rigor. These exams should all be topic-focused, smaller versions of the future standardized exam. That means using the same vocabulary, questioning format, and level of difficulty. When students sit down to take a standardized exam, this exam in both content and format, should be familiar to them; but the degree of difficulty should also be something for which they are familiar.

A principal cautionary note here: This approach will put a great deal of "pressure" on report card grades, and there may be some pushback from parents who are accustomed to seeing their "little geniuses" score 90% on every classroom exam and then go on to underperform or fail the standardized exam in elementary through middle. Prepare the parents at the ninth through tenth grade orientation "that because of our approach to teaching and learning in this school, students (depending on the sending school) may need to work a lot harder to receive the high grades for which they are accustomed." That will soften it, but it will not solve it, so stay in continued communication with the parents on this topic; they may want "academic rigor," but they possibly will not know what that really looks and feels like. You can't just have the academic rigor" conversation one time at orientation, for you will with some parents receive a lot of "false positive" (who is not for higher academic standards?). But how that plays out in day-to-day teaching and learning, in behavioral expectation, is a more complex and therefore long-term discussion. The good news is that the students will almost always successfully adjust to the change!

The great failing of public education is this gap between what students receive on their report cards, and how they then go on to perform on standardized exams. This is the great disconnect and shame of our profession, and any school that hopes to be academically effective must attack and fix this problem. For a school's students to be successful on standardized exams, there must be a grade-earning consistency-equivalency between how students perform in school on a daily, weekly, semester basis, and how they perform on the end-of-course/grade standardized exams. In that sense, student performance (outside of a few predictable factors) on standardized exams, should not be a surprise.

Creating a standardized testing school culture that is academically advantageous builds teacher and student confidence and positively positions students for the best post-high school outcomes.

The principal should work to create a school culture that is both test-friendly and test-fearless. This is particularly true of Title I schools where additional student academic support funding is linked to family income; we should be able to transform that additional funding into better test results outcomes. However, additional compensatory funding will not help, if it is not joined to a strategically comprehensive and well thought out real test-prep plan.

Be careful to not encourage and whip up a collective "anti-standardized testing" mentality in the minds of parents, students, and staff. That "dog may come back to bite you" when you want students to perform well on exams that directly affect their future education, career, and life options. As a superintendent I have known principals who were in search of an unprincipled anti-testing alliance with teachers and/or parents. But I called them into my office to remind them that sometimes the painful reality of leadership is that you must often lead in some difficult terrain. "Your school can jump on this anti-standardized testing-boycott bandwagon if they so choose, but remember, at the end of the day, how your students show up and perform on standardized exams is vitally important for them individually, the school's access to academic support funding, and you."

Leading a shift in a school's culture is not easy. It is very often a slow and difficult process, and the school family members may not be able to turn a comfortable organizational cultural belief off and on quickly. The principal must plant his or her flag decisively in one philosophical place or another; that means a consistency of language and behavior, and no "saying and winking" in two different directions. The principal must also take an account of their particular student body and the life options they have available to them. A lot of U.S. citizens can make decisions about their children because those children have multi-resourced, multi-dimensional, and multi-entitled paths to adult success. My approach in both of my schools was that we deal with the immediate and concrete challenges to our students and the school's success, which is in front of us, not the many educational policy debates that always surround schools. As a principal you are the leader-practitioner of the present and the practical; in large part because unlike the casual "drive-by" pseudo educational theoreticians, you are dealing with real students and real parents who are facing a real world. At this present moment, standardized testing is a reality, and therefore our feelings about them is, in a sense, irrelevant. I pushed the idea that standardized exams aren't good or bad, they simply are. We all must recognize how performance on these exams affects the long-term well-being of our students. So, I actively sought strategies, initiatives, and campaigns that encouraged students to study hard and do well on standardized exams. In that way, performing well on standardized exams makes these exams our "temporary" friend; performing badly on them means that they represent harm. It is important that the principal understands the concept that all assessments, including external standardized exams, are ways in which we can improve teaching and learning. And for those traditionally disenfranchised students in our society, a way to empower themselves. Flip the script. Turn standardized testing into an exercise of empowerment, rather than a prelude for mourning, and the annual urge for schools to "beat up on themselves!" Schools should not surrender, nor should they surrender their right to define schooling and themselves in their own terms. A school constantly being told that, because of standardized exam scores, that they are part of an achievement gap, teachers that their craft-work is ineffective, or entire school families (and their communities) being told or telling themselves that they are a failing school is not a healthy approach to education. The challenge is to be standardized test-taking thoughtful, aggressive, and audacious; however, at the same time, the goal is not to be obsessive and engaged in wasted and nonproductive test-preparation practices or particular practices that remove students from a rich and exciting curriculum experience to a boring, "turned off to school" drudgery exercise.

In line with making the school a test-friendly environment, I always encouraged the taking of the PSAT/Pre-ACT starting in ninth grade. Here again is another role for the entrepreneurial principal. Funds must be raised to publicize, provide the space, the proctors, the testing instruments, gifts and rewards, and the celebratory food and party activities as a way to reward students for taking these exams. This is just one of many ways to make the school a "standardized-test safety zone." The emphasis in this promotion is on the benefits of taking these exams. It does not hurt that students are able, sometimes for the first time in their educational lives, to have in their hands the comparison of their ability with other students in the nation. This comparing and contrasting themselves with their national and international peers is particularly helpful for students (and their parents) who have attended middle schools where they were the top performing honor roll students. Because most public education systems don't really have a strategic plan to address the needs of students of color who are on or above their academic achievement grade levels. These students' sense of where they stand in terms of skills, knowledge, and information with their city, state, national, and international peers can be distorted. Teaching students to see themselves in the context of national percentiles can be a difficult conversation, but it can motivate them to ramp up their study-work habits if they hope to make themselves a viable competitive force in the world.

In sports we have no problem motivating students by informing them as to the skill level of their competition. There are two types of people who don't want a standardized testing system of a common core of academic standards: Those whose children, or their privileged cohort of family, neighbors and friends, already enjoy the advantage of having an instructionally effective, rich, and rigorous curriculum complete with and exceeding the very same core curriculum standards that are tested on national exams (SAT, ACT, GRE, LSAT, NTE, MCAT, etc.) The second group is made up of those for whom the testing of all students utilizing a common core of learning standards will reveal [publicly] that they are doing a really terrible and inadequate job with our most poor and politically disenfranchised students.

Teachers should teach the "talking mind" techniques of good test-takers.

Teachers should also employ a "talk-walk" through exam questions and answers. In this situation it is the teacher who is actually taking the exam out loud as the students follow and take notes on the exam in front of them. This linguistic-learning method of real test-prep allows students to hear out loud the thinking of a good test-taker. This aligns perfectly with teaching students the skills of metacognition and how good test-takers are having a reflective mental conversation as they take the exam.

Math journals as a pre-standardized test diagnostic tool

In mathematics, I have found that the use of math journals is extremely helpful in assisting both students and teachers in pinpointing the exact step when they misunderstand either the question, the steps to solve the question, or the proper algorithm that is required to solve the problem. An amazing thing happens when students are asked to utilize words rather than numbers and to place those numbers in steps—they (and us) can actually see at which step they went wrong. This method can also help teachers to identify those concepts that the student does not fully understand. And as the student moves up in the math course, this project will assist us in stopping the unproductive practice of trying to overlay new mathematical concepts on top of poorly understood prerequisite math concepts.

The role of Cultural Linguistics and Standardized Test Scores' achievement levels

A type of "linguistic-cognitive creativity" is sometimes dangerously utilized by some students who end up getting a question wrong on a standardized exam, even as their analytical reasoning was correct. For example, I wrote back in 1990, a journal article where I hypothesize that students of color may need to utilize a "bicultural" approach to standardized test-taking:

"Preparing students to take the (NYS) Regents examination forced the Center's staff to think a great deal about the art of taking tests—a separate issue from learning biology. Perhaps, many of the low scores earned by minority students in the public school system might be more of a reflection of not understanding key elements in taking tests than of their ability to assimilate the subject matter. One of the important points was learning to answer the questions posed by the examiner. This may sound simple, but even so-called 'high achievers' took great liberties in restructuring questions. For example, this question was asked. 'A school is planning a trip to the zoo. Each bus seats forty students. There are 100 students. How many buses will be needed for the trip?' The possible answers were: 2, 2 ½, 3, and 4. Many students circled the answer 2. When asked why, they replied, 'In order to save money, the extra ten kids could be divided between the two buses and the smaller ones could sit three to a seat.' This, of course, was a good answer and relevant to the economic environment of the students. However, it was explained to them that the examiner wanted the answer 3. Those students who circled 2 ½ were told that, although the calculation was correct, it was not the answer the examiner wanted because there is no such thing as half a bus. In this, and other lessons, students were advised that they must take a bicultural approach in order to understand the language of the test-maker. Although the students felt that this was basically unfair to African-American and Hispanic students, it was explained that this is the world in which they live and, therefore, they must accommodate to it for the present..."

— *Johnson, Michael A., "Science Assessment in the Service of Reform," AAAS, 1991*

A school that serves any number of racially and ethnically diverse students, must confront the cultural-linguistic challenges students may face when taking standardized tests. Students must be taught to linguistically "code-switch" when it is appropriate; one of those appropriate events is when they are taking a standardized exam. We want students to feel confident and in control, but we also want them to understand that they can't choose to rewrite the questions. We also know that exams are put together by people, not machines, and these people, as in every situation, bring their cultural linguistic view of the world into the making of the exam. A critical standardized test-taking skill is for students to learn to answer the question being asked of them. Understanding what they are being required to do, versus what they want to do, is the first and most important tool any good test-taker must use. Getting that first critical question asked and answered is perhaps one of the biggest stumbling blocks to high student performance on standardized exams. Which is why the question of, "What am I being asked to do?" is the center of the "talk-walk" technique utilized in the test-prep process, which consists of these critical questions:

- What am I being asked to do?

- Have I seen this, or a similar question, before?

- What answer is the test creator and/or evaluator seeking?

- What information, skill, technique, or algorithm do I need to success-fully answer this question?

- How do I know that my answer is complete?

- How am I able to check and verify my answer?

All of the above questions can only be taught through the standards and rubrics method; and it comes easier to students when standards and rubrics are utilized on a daily classroom basis, such that the students perform these techniques naturally. Students must understand (prior to taking the exam), the type of test format they will be facing. As well as what behaviors and actions will either lower or raise their final score. Part of this strategy can be taught in the anatomy of a question. Good test-takers know that particularly in a multiple choice format, each answer choice is performing a role. The wrong answers are there to distract the test-taker, and to determine if they really understand and can successfully answer the question. With questions involving passages, there is always some structure and sensible format as to where the answers

404

are placed in that passage. Students must be taught how to deconstruct these passages during the test-prep sessions, utilizing highlighters and underlining the answers that are already present in the passage. They must also be taught to highlight the turnkey words and phrases in the wording of the question.

Again, we return to the importance of a strong ELA program, starting in the ninth grade. The more students engage, become familiar, and feel comfortable with the written word, the better they will perform on standardized exams, regardless of the subject area.

Effective post-standardized exams analysis

The effective school must use strategic analysis to determine whether the students have mastered a particular content area. One of the primary purposes of "grading" exams is not just to give a student a failing or passing grade; an electronic scanning grading machine can do that! Rather, test results provide the diagnostic opportunity to personalize and focus that student's tutorial session's needs. It is also a way to identify those students who scored just below or above a cut-off point for performance/grade point level. Schools must pay important attention to these "just below and above" the minimum passing standard, for in many ways these two cohorts of students are statistically the same student. Both are in serious danger of failing the exam. The difference between these two students could boil down to the format of the exam that year, or having one or two questions that a particular student will get right or wrong. Or, as I learned as a superintendent, prior to the test results being released to the public, the test-making company discovers 'technical difficulties' in the exam that lead to changes in how the exam is scored. For those students just barely above or below the passing threshold, these changes are significant. Which is why, as mentioned above, it is important to give weekly exams that mirror the end-of-course/year standardized exams. This approach, if followed throughout the school year, will allow for a strategic instructional-tutorial plan for:

- students who are seriously struggling to fully understand the skills and concepts being tested;

- students who are hovering just above or below passing status as well as those who have an "incomplete" or "weak" understanding of a concept;

405

- students for whom we need to improve their non-content test-taking techniques/mechanics. In other words, they know the concepts but get tripped up in the applications (answering) phase, or are too easily confused by how the question is being asked;

- grading results that reveal those very specific skills and concepts for which any student could be struggling to master. The school can then set up a comprehensive topic-issue specific tutorial program that can address these deficiencies directly; even accommodating those students may cross over into two or more of the above testing-evaluations revelations groups.

Finally, the strategic test preparation process should also help students to be confident, stay calm, and make better test-taking decisions even when struggling with a question.

Despite its effectiveness, this approach is "labor-efficacy intensive" for your teaching staff. Much more time and energy is being asked of them, and so you, the principal, must support, reward, and recognize them in every possible way. And you can start by making their classrooms more teaching- and learning-friendly. Creating a rigorous instruction and school-based testing system that mirrors the external standardized exams is a schoolwide team effort. The truth is that like "smartness," student performance on standardized exams can be raised, continually and permanently. I further affirm that achievement levels can be raised with the involvement of effective parental support. But "no parental help" should not be an educational deal-breaker for a child's ability to do well on a standardized exam. Not having perfect, or even good, parental support cannot be our excuse for not creating an environment where all students can be academically successful.

A final note on standardized exam and testing security

I added this section because "testing security" is a cause of anxiety for many principals and APs; and, unfortunately, the cause of many career-ending events and even law enforcement legal penalties for some teachers and administrators. Several critically important points to establish:

- Don't do anything stupid, illegal, or professionally unethical. The test results are what they are. You can only really help children by making them smart. If you help them to cheat, or you and your staff cheats for them, then you are educationally hurting and intellectually crippling your students. Do the hard work of pushing high academic standards and expectations on the front end, and then live with the results.

- Keep in mind that the principal is always responsible, not necessarily for anything that goes right in the school, but absolutely for anything that goes wrong. Test security is no different; you must work with a committee to make it work well, but know that you are the ultimate sole owner of the outcome. You need to invest serious time and attention to this area from the point of receiving and securing the exams, to distribution for testing, the testing environment and proctoring, to exams being administered to students who have a right to mandated test accommodations, the collection and grading of the exam, and the packaging and returning of the exams.

- The principal and SBL team must design a comprehensive Test-Security Plan (TSP) if the district does not provide one and/or where the district's plan is lacking in parts or whole. The school's plan must fill the gaps, particularly in the area of monitoring, verification of the adherence to rules and regulations, and insisting on having an overlapping and redundant supervision system.

- If particular staff persons, parents, or students don't understand (or agree) with the high level of security, integrity, and monitoring procedures you have assigned to this effort, they will have to get over it, or perhaps they won't.

- The selection of a test coordinator is critical. My choice was to always assign an Assistant Principal to the task. If a teacher is the assigned person in your school, remember that technically they can't supervise or exercise authority over another teacher. You really need the best person suited for the job here, or you are asking for disastrous trouble to descend upon the school if the wrong person is charged with this important responsibility.

- The job requirements of the test-coordinator must be totally clear in your head. First, they must have a detail driven, well organized, commitment to planning, systemic view of the world, be analytical, non-people-pleasing, a problem-solver, an outcome focused form of thinking. One other quality is fearlessness.

- If a parent, student, or staff person "incorrectly" and/or in the wrong way challenges a procedure or policy in a way that compromises the integrity of the testing process, the test coordinator's response must be swift, decisive, clear, and uncompromising. Hence, the reason for that important totally clarifying test proctor's professional development session for all teachers.

- The test coordinator should come up with, as part of the school TSP, an after-school professional development (PD) session(s) for all test proctors (feed them a nice meal!). If you can, don't let first-year teachers proctor a major standardized exam; instead, let them proctor with your best veteran teacher proctors for their first year of teaching. If you must use first-year teachers for proctoring duties, provide them with a lot of school administrator "shadow" support. The regular week-ly classroom exams can also give the SBL team and those first-year teachers and their teacher-mentors the opportunity to provide "mini-test proctoring PD" in a space safer than a major standardized exam. Prior to the standardized exam I would also give first-year teachers an additional after-school test proctoring PD session where they are allowed to ask as many questions as they want (again, feed them a nice meal!). With these types of after-school PD sessions, you are going to need to get your building union representative on your side. One motivation (beyond the catered food) is your assertion that these PD efforts, although voluntary after-school sessions, are designed to help everybody keep their jobs! I always had 100% attendance at these voluntary test proctoring PD sessions. If you can't get that level of af-ter-school volunteerism from your teachers, then you must figure out how to do these test proctor PD sessions during the school day (small groups during prep periods?); but do them you must. Also, written test proctor instructions and directions are crucial for every teacher and administrator involved in testing because they must all be on the same page. Quality Q & A sessions are essential. Clearly, teacher commit-ment is critical here, and for that reason I say,

- One of the best foundational supporters of an effective and successful test security program is a strong and rigorous academic and testing (prep) program throughout the year, and the entire school. Teachers and school administrators who have done their best to prepare their students to succeed on exams see cheating or the falsification of test results as an insult to their professionalism and efficacious efforts. These schools want to win based on the teaching and learning abilities of the school family members because the pride they feel in successful student testing results can only be truly realized and enjoyed if those high achieving scores are obtained honestly.

And finally, on standardized testing, as principal you will absolutely take the "heat" for poor student performance. And so (I always thought), why not take the heat early for pushing high and rigorous teaching and learning standards; besides your students will be academically better off and their lives will greatly benefit from your head and heartwarming sacrifice!

Chapter 26:
Coordination of Student Out-of-Classroom, After-School, and Out-of-School Learning Activities

Our SuperVision requires that we see education beyond the end of the school day, outside of the school's walls. This concept may take on a greater sense of urgency dependent upon the amount of real-world knowledge children have acquired from their parents. These projects can take on an ethical importance because you don't want children to be at a disadvantage when they are facing the informational and behavioral standards of the USA and world society. As principal, you are, of course, free to disagree on your own time with the values and structure of the American economic business system. But as ethical educational leaders, we cannot allow these political-philosophical discussions to distract us from our responsibility to make students competitive in the present political-economic structure in which we now live as well as into the future world to which the students will graduate.

A principal's SuperVision compels them to give equal attention to the learning importance of both formal and informal education. Unfortunately, many who have policy and budgetary control of your school district may not see it that way; programs like the Summer Bridge Program, an after-school chess or art club, a dance and theater company, or debate team, may not be seen as critical to what is usually associated with schooling; thus, the misnomer title "extracurricular." And to be fair, even those professional educators who have read Dewey's exposition on out-of-classroom learning still may not fully appreciate the importance of this learning experience to the shame of our profession.

In the matter of outside learning activities for Title I schools and students, the entrepreneurial principal's role is critically essential here. In order for these programs to be effective, funding beyond the basic school allocation budget must be identified and cultivated. I would add that this funding includes the identification and recruitment of human expertise outside of the school. This principle of cultivating outside resources is a critical and essential task for the principal to continually engage in. Even if it does not appear anywhere in your job description, just know it is a part of your job. Particularly in Title I schools, where extending the learning day/week/semester programs should not be seen as an "extra" educational experience. In fact, it can be essential, and in some cases, lifesaving to a child. If a school admits a sizable number of students who are unprepared to do high school work, then weekends, semester breaks, and summer vacation are necessary, not optional, teaching and learning periods. This is very important in a school that takes a pro-active approach to after-school tutorials where students can be placed at the start of ninth grade based on middle school standardized test scores and academic performance.

The school must also find the funds to provide students with reduced, or free, access to commercial test preparation courses (e.g., Princeton Review), software, and books. Let's stop pretending that students can produce their personal best on these exams without the assistance of these courses and study resources. The school should also find a way to cover the cost of taking the ACT and SAT exams. In addition to this, an effective school should support a diverse menu of after-school clubs, organizations, and activities. These programs should seek to appeal to the interests, gifts, and talent of a broad spectrum of the student body.

Another characteristic of good schools is a rich offering of AP courses, the completion of which will often be scheduled as "double periods" and extend beyond the school day. I can tell you from past experience that both AP Biology (labs/textbooks) and AP Studio Art (supplies and materials) are very expensive courses; and in a school where parents are poor, or even working class, the school will need to find the money to pay for them. The key point is that a school's budget cannot, particularly in the case of Title I schools, adequately meet the educational, social, and emotional needs beyond regular school resources.

The effective principal must establish the principles that define an out of classroom experience as a critical (not supplementary) form of education. (Again: see John Dewey's *Experience and Education*.) It follows then that every experience outside of the classroom, or outside of the school, is essentially a teachable moment in the child's life. This is not an abstract concept. In fact, there are some practical purposes involved here. For example:

- Building the student's post-high school portfolio. Starting the first day that a student enters high school, they are, in many ways, building a college and career portfolio. It should be made clear to students and parents that students cannot live by grades alone, even if those grades are high. A high school student seeking a scholarship, applying to college or a career opportunity, must be able to make the case when grades are equal, why they are the best candidate. Further activities like internships provide students with wonderful experiences that can be translated into intellectual resources and gain them access to professional contacts and excellent sources for letters of recommendation. Particularly, for those students who may not have access to professionals in various fields, there must be an instructional plan to teach the power of networking and contacts. The school should strategically plan to take students out of their comfort zones and place them (in a safe way) into environments that will open up avenues of information, knowledge, and opportunity. Students should be made aware of the fact that there is a world outside of their own communities; and every place has its own rules, standards, language, and behavioral expectations. Therefore, any out-of-school activities are excellent places for students to learn the "soft skills" needed to survive and thrive after leaving high school.

- Students don't know what they don't know; which also means that they don't know that they don't know (or even might like) something. And, so, a primary learning objective of the out-of-classroom/out-of-school learning experience (OCOSLE), is to make it clear to students that after high school, what they don't know can, and will, hurt them. The OCOSLE program must seek to expand the world knowledge of the students; to expose them to a challenging environment and give them the tools to be comfortable in different social and cultural surroundings. This makes the OCOSLE a foundation for building lifelong learning and leadership skills. It is extremely helpful to allow students to interact with other students and faculty members on a college campus, a STEM research lab, a professional workspace, a military setting and/or other types of high reliability organizations, the corporate business world, or any institution that maintains a different culture than the one that exists in public education. The OCOSLE program can also effectively redefine a young person's definition of fun. Very often students can have a limited perception of enjoyment and fun, framed to a large extent by their exposure and resources; and too often this limited concept of fun can be unsafe or unproductive. Many times, schools are culturally, racially, or stereotypically limiting students to

413

those things for which the student is already familiar and comfortable. Or, that staff may fall into that patronizing trap of trying to "keep it real" with students of color, as opposed to keeping it educational and mind-expanding. The OCOSLE program can also serve as a type of talent search project; the school's diverse activities should reveal students' talents, gifts, and interests of which they were not aware of previously. The beginning of this process is for the school to hold a week-long School Activities Fair Expo with faculty advisors and students setting up recruitment tables during lunch periods in the cafeteria and in the lobby at the beginning and end of the school day. The guidance department is important here. As they meet with individual students over the first couple of months of the school year, they should make an effort to encourage everyone to be involved in some type of school activity, club, and/or team or organization. This is a healthy and positive way for students to build productive friendships around common interests. It also allows the school to connect every student with an adult mentor since all activities in the school must be supervised by an adult staff person. A critical marketing pitch for this recruitment campaign is the importance of building a post-high school portfolio.

- The principal should conduct a "skills and interests" survey among the staff, using the interview notes collected when hiring them. The best leaders and most successful mentors for student clubs and activities can be found when you tap into the talents, skills, and interests of the adult staff members. This would include generating suggestions for clubs and activities from the staff. If there's a way to make teachers and students happy at the same time, go for it!

- OCOSLE programs serve as a safe place for students to support each other. This is particularly true of organizations whose students are: Muslim, Christian, Asian, African-American, Latino, LGBT, science-fiction fans, or "STEM nerds." In Title I schools, a primary task of the OCOSLE program is to create a bank of student activities and clubs that will help the student find an environment where they feel safe and empowered to be themselves!

A Coordinator of Out-of-Classroom Student Activities (COSA)

Having established the critical contribution your OCOSLE programs can make, there is a need for an extraordinary and especially skilled staff person to lead that effort. I know in many school districts in this nation that such an out-of-classroom position would be filled by way of some "seniority" process mandated through a labor bargaining agreement. But that would be a terrible mistake in the same way it would be a mistake to randomly assign content area teachers to teach any class in the school. The principal must be given the freedom to match the individual staff person with the unique requirements of the position.

A high school-based Informal Education Director or the Coordinator of Student Activities (COSA), and why this position is important

Let us start with the profile of the position. A staff person assuming the position of COSA should possess a unique set of people skills. They'll need to work well with students, school administrators, and other members of the faculty and staff. An effective COSA must have cultural-linguistic skills that allow them to serve as translators between teenagers and adults. The COSA must be able to also balance a sensitivity and understanding of the emotional profiles of young people, while at the same time being a strong advocate for the school's academic and behavioral standards. They need to be likable to the extent that they are capable of enrolling the students into the greater school's mission, but also making this enrollment process enjoyable. The COSA must also serve as a bridge between student aspirations and desires, and the expectations and requests of the adult members of the school's faculty. A good COSA is a good mediator, a person who can help students to frame a concern in a positive and productive way. Part of that skill emerges in the COSA's responsibility of forming and managing the student government. As with every school activity, there are always learning objectives involved. The purpose of the student government is to practice the process of participatory and legislative democracy; how to draft position/opinion papers, lobby, and effectively change an organization (the school in this case); how to lead, and how to be led by the interests and concerns of a constituency. The COSA is a master recruiter, as they are constantly on the lookout for students who are not connected to a team, club, or school activity. In that way, they are very much a part of the guidance team.

As the COSA continuously recruits students into various activities through and beyond the recruitment fairs, they are also ensuring these clubs are committed to the school's learning standards and objectives. The principal must ensure that all out-of-classroom and out-of-school activities have an educational purpose or objective, even if they are fun. These OCOSLE activities should also have learning and behavioral standards linked to the school's mission. As I stated in the section on school culture, there are no philosophical vacuums with any school effort or activity; the principal can choose to lead in this area, or choose to be led. In almost every case, the latter choice will certainly lead students away from high academic and behavioral standards achievement mission of the school. The COSA and the principal must be co-leaders in inviting students to become involved with one of the school's many out of classroom programs. But this effort is also an invitation for students to discover and make new friends, grow their knowledge and information capacity, learn a new skill, discover a gift or talent, build their senior college-scholarships portfolios, and make a positive connection to an advocate-faculty member.

Chapter 27:
Profile of a Good and Effective Teacher

Too often in public education we try to solve problems by avoiding them or we engage in wasteful, misguided theories. Academic achievement is ultimately linked to the quality and quantity of good instructional practices that exist in the student's class and school. It is hard to have an honest discussion about the quality of teacher instructional practices when so many people who are making policy decisions are deficient themselves in theoretical and practical pedagogy. I vividly remember being summoned to the Chancellor's office to answer for a complaint from the teacher's union (UFT) about an Instructional Best-Practices Fair I was holding as an NYC superintendent. This professional development idea was based on the fact that while visiting schools daily, I saw examples of wonderful and effective teaching methodology in both "academically struggling" as well as "higher academically performing" schools. I often imagined the powerful effect of having those great practitioners present their effective techniques in one place, on a single day, as a professional development event. I anticipated that there would be some degree of pushback; I was challenging that powerful institutional cultural belief that all teachers are the same and that the difference in academic outcomes was based solely on the financial and "other" capabilities of the parents and students. But I believe that great instructional practices and efficacious behavior, matched with a theoretically smart and focused principal can counteract and overcome any societal challenges a child will bring to school. Therefore, there is a great benefit to identifying and codifying and sharing mastery teaching techniques. This was proven when the fair took place, despite opposition. Many of our teachers immediately began applying the knowledge and techniques learned at these sessions to their daily teaching methods. I also received a great deal of positive feedback from many teachers who attended.

As an NYC superintendent, I proved that we could identify these expert teachers from every school in the district, regardless of the school's position on the overall academic performance scale. Further, my experience suggested that teachers in any school, despite the political position taken by the union, know who the "best practitioners" or best teachers are within that school. Very often they will steer their own or friends' children into these expert teachers' classrooms. And, further, those "professional courtesy class assignment requests" also often came directly to the principal (or superintendent) from some "colleague" working in another school or district in the system. It is not uncommon practice in public education to placate powerful, active, or politically connected parents by allowing them to maneuver their children through a school (particularly in the elementary grades) by placing that child into the classrooms of the school's best instructional practitioners. As a school system, we sensibly select instructional coaches and staff developers from the ranks of mastery-expert teachers, so it is hard to make the case that we don't know what "good teaching" really is. But for financial and political reasons, we simply choose to act like we don't know.

We don't effectively talk about teacher effectiveness, and/or the wide spectrum of instructional quality between school districts, across school districts, and across classrooms inside of schools. Because those realties would perhaps reveal that specific populations in our nation's public schools are not underperforming because of some inherited brain-intelligence deficiency, or because they are poor, but because of the level of expertise and experience of their teachers.

This book sets out to examine and explain the principal's role in building a high academically achieving school. The principal as Chief Instructional Coach (CIC) is a critical part of that examination and explanation. If as a principal you are nervous, uneasy, or unwilling to explore the question of quality instruction, then perhaps the principalship is not the best job for you. But to avoid this discussion is to do the children and the society that pays you a salary, a terrible disservice. The quality of the school's instructional program, and the quantity of that quality, is the CIC's rubric for self-evaluation. And, so, an objective of that CIC's work is to create a school environment where the largest number of effective teachers' work practice reflect "good teaching techniques." We are then led to define and explain the *Profile of an Effective Teacher.* Perhaps, the first step in this examination is to explore where that effective teacher stands ethically.

The primary ethical concerns for effective teachers are:

- "To do no harm." Meaning that your experience with your students should be life-enhancing and a process through which they discover their best selves. They should come out of the teacher-student learning relationship in a better situation than when they met you; and by no means should they be in worse condition after having encountered you. Therefore, one definition of a progressive education is that the student must make substantial grade and/or subject (qualitative and quantitative) progress under the teacher's care.

- The teacher should take full responsibility for the safety, physical, and psychological well-being of all of students in their charge.

- The teacher must vow to engage in an efficacious professional approach to education, in thinking and practice. In other words, the teacher firmly believes that their knowledge, actions, and behaviors are the most significant factors that will impact the academic success or failure of the student.

- A teacher must treat all children equally; in other words, the teacher should not use race, financial capability, ethnicity, language proficiency, disability, gender, political beliefs, political connections, religious beliefs, or the level of parent involvement to determine the quality or quantity of education a student should receive. Every student should be educated to the maximum of their abilities.

- A teacher should not promote or impose their own religious and political beliefs on students.

- A teacher is charged to discover the singular and individual gifts and talents that each student brings to the class; to effectively guide each student to their unique calling in life.

- A teacher, at all times, must employ "Best practices," sound and innovative instructional approaches, and utilize a pedagogy of resistance to societal, economic, political, and cultural discrimination, depersonalization, and dehumanization. This is to make sure that students receive the best possible opportunity to succeed academically. Negative tracking, or engaging in, or utilizing low-expectations strategies for any reason is unethical.

- As a professional, a teacher must continuously improve their professional practice—always seeking new and better methods to teach students. Every teacher should design a personal professional development plan, which spans multiple years of practice. Each year, the teacher should become better at the art of teaching.

- A teacher must always by way of dress, language, work habits, personal hygiene, appearance, punctuality, attendance, and attitude, project the best attributes of the profession.

- A teacher cannot ever engage in, or support, any type of negative, disparaging, dismissive, or degrading conversations about the students, the students' families, or the communities in which they live.

- A teacher can never take advantage of the trust of a child; nor can they fail to report any and all forms of abuse or neglect, regardless of who is the perpetrator.

- A teacher must never evaluate (test) students on content and skills that they have not been taught. Further, teachers must use a fair, objective, and transparent grading policy. A teacher should use both in-class and external standardized testing for student diagnostic/academic improvement purposes. A teacher can never falsify the results of any assessment or test result.

- The teacher should be a model of the social behavioral objectives given to every student. That is, to be tolerant of others, sensitive to the differences and challenges that represent the human family spectrum, and be kind, compassionate, considerate, and attentive to the feelings and humanity of others.

- A teacher should maintain confidentiality of student academic, disability, family, and health records.

- Even in the face of a real or perceived disrespectful behavior on the part of a parent or guardian, the teacher can never inflict a payback, or a policy of unfairness, ill-treatment on a child, in response to a parent's behavior.

- Effective and experienced teachers should make themselves available to serve as mentors and coaches of teachers.

- Teachers are not required to "like" every student, but you are called to love the humanity and potential greatness presented in every child you encounter.

- A teacher should want for his/her students, what they want and wish for their own child. That means helping parents to learn the standards, practices, and procedures involved with the informal educational system.

- The teacher must enroll themselves into a belief system and practice that is centered in empathy and solidarity with the challenges the students and their parents face on a daily basis, and always bring to school.

- The teacher must not, by way of behaviors both inside and outside of the school, cause the school, district, or profession to be discredited, subject to ridicule and embarrassment, and/or be penalized and forced to pay punitive damages.

- **If a teacher is incapable of adhering to the above ethical principles, then the right thing to do is pursue another career option.**

The positive, proactive, professional considerations for effective teachers

- To remember that everything a teacher does teaches a lesson to students; how the teacher behaves and acts; how the teacher talks and treats students; how a teacher consciously and overtly, or unconsciously and subtly regards the student's community, living conditions, family structure, and history is a primary lesson for the students.

- Teachers should know that even when students don't want to be challenged academically, they will still resent a classroom environment of low expectations. Students are always learning from the teacher before, during, and after the lesson. Along with the content and skills learning objectives, they are learning objectives of caring, empowering, and insisting that students develop their best gifts and talents. Inside of those relational learning objectives are the values of tolerance, patience, concern, level of commitment, and the appreciation for the presence of the students. Messages are being continually sent by the teacher (and continually being received by the students). *Do you really, I mean really care about us (me)? Are you here because of a job, or is this a calling?*

- The teacher must professionally prepare for each lesson. (By the way, in high schools the students know when the teacher has not prepared for the lesson!) An effective lesson is always grounded in an effective lesson plan. Failing to properly prepare a well-thought-out lesson plan is a statement about how the teacher feels about the profession, the students, and sadly, themselves. Presentation and performance skills can vary from teacher to teacher, but there is no substitute for the great intellectual investment, creative and thoughtful effort, and finally, determination and commitment in the art of creating a great lesson.

- Each classroom and teacher should be an elemental part as well as an example of the larger school's academic mission. High school students in particular can detect the slightest sliver of philosophical difference that exists between the teacher and school administration; as well as the teacher's efforts and the school's academic and behavioral standards. In too many school situations, the students will exploit those philosophical differences to the detriment of themselves, the teachers, and to the school's institutional objectives. And just as a principal should never display disagreement, annoyance, or conflict with a teacher in front of students, a teacher should also not enroll students into discussions concerning their disagreements with the school administration or policies. The adults in the building (that includes teacher to teacher disagreements) should clear up any misunderstandings away from the students. Of course, it is always helpful to model the type of conflict resolution we want to see the students practice when they have conflicts with each other.

- The teachers in a school can have a positive culture of friendly academic achievement competition. But all teachers, both inside and outside of the diverse departments in a school, are in fact one single professional team, focused and committed to a single professional objective of student success in every aspect of the school's endeavors. In that sense, no teacher should ever disparage, dismiss, or denigrate the work of any teacher in the school; and absolutely never in front of students. The teachers in an effective school are more likely to offer support, resources, and when necessary, constructive criticism and advice in order to help their colleagues to be successful. Just as it is important for principals and school administrators to be focused on helping school staff members to realize success, it is also important for staff members to desire and help their peers to be professionally successful. For too long and in too many schools, teachers have been content to simply close their classroom door and say, "The other person in the other classroom is not doing an effective job; I am going to just stay in my room and engage in good and effective practices," but that approach not only hurts large numbers of children, it severely damages the standing perception and quality of the work of the profession. Schools work best when they are a community of teacher-learners and learning-teachers who support each other. Sports teams get this concept that an underperforming teammate endangers the success of the entire team. The principal must inspire a teaching team that is willing to self-motivate, correct, and raise the level of standards amongst themselves. A principal will do herself a disservice if she thinks that she alone can raise the level and quality of teaching methodology without the teaching staff taking on this responsibility for, and amongst (within), themselves.

- The teacher must constantly be in a dynamic and innovative mindset as to ideas that can help students to achieve academically, a major component of an efficacious practice. The world outside of the school is constantly changing and the students arriving from that world into the school are also changing. The teachers must be aware of all the elements and conditions that make up the students' lives outside of school. This knowledge acquisition is not for the purpose of creating an attitude of pity or condescension. Rather, the effective efficacious teacher is seeking to discover every possible pathway to helping students to realize success. But they are also actively seeking to discover and dismantle every hurdle and obstacle that a student can face on that path to success. A student's family history and biography are instructive to the point of framing a support plan, but that family history information does not necessarily speak to destiny; and, so, it is knowing about a student that informs the teacher as to the best methods, tools, and strategies, that would be of the most beneficial student support strategy. Finally, the effective efficacious teacher will find and utilize those positive attributes and strengths that are present in both their own and the student's biographical story, family, community, and cultural background, to maximize the teaching and learning experience.

- The effective teacher believes that all parents want to see their children succeed, even as those parents might be deficient and unaware of the techniques, strategies, and methods for doing their part to make that success happen. The teacher is fully aware of the many socio-economic struggles that families face in our nation. The teacher must be committed to doing everything in his/her power to neutralize and close that life-determining entitlement gap between students. Public schools are the best and most naturally-situated institutions in our nation to create "level playing fields" where with every student regardless of the level of "parent push-power" in their lives, can grow into their full inherent greatness. This teacher is committed to not only educating a child, but also their family. Seeing every parent, no matter where they exist on the parent effectiveness spectrum, when given the right information can perform their parenting roles more effectively. But even if that improvement and parent effectiveness does not emerge despite the best efforts of the school and teachers, that teacher must still be committed to filling in as many parental awareness gaps as possible in order to make that student successful.

- The teacher must be well versed on instructional/curriculum matters, meaning:

    o The content area/grade level standards.

    o The rubrics by which those standards are measured.

    o The official syllabus and pacing calendar.

    o The content and behavioral skills that appear on particular standardized exams.

    o The "language of the standardized exam," meaning the vocabulary, phraseology, format, and grading structure for the related standardized exam should be familiar to the students.

    o The effective teacher must, if the profile of the class calls for it, teach the students to be bi-culturally fluent and have the ability to code-switch when the situation (e.g., standardized exam, job interview) requires the student to do so. "Keeping it real" in the wrong place and time can cause things to go really wrong!

    o How to use in-class and external assessment in a diagnostic process that informs teachers and students of the complete, incomplete, or total absence of understanding a concept.

o   How to use those same internal and external assessment tools to guide, reassess/redirect a particular teaching approach; and to assist the teacher in reaching the mastery level in the profession.

o   Knowledge of the current discussions about instructional practices in education generally as well as in their specific content or grade level. Being thoughtful and fully aware of the relational dynamics that exist between teaching and learning that they are inseparable, such that the commonly used phrase, "Well, I taught it, they just didn't learn it!" is in fact a contradiction.

o   A strong theoretical foundation in developmental psychology: that is, understanding the behaviors, physiological, and psychological dynamics in play with various child age groups, the perceptions and pressures they face, including those we adults incorrectly feel are not serious. The ability to self-analyze and to engage in metacognitive self-reflection.

o   Classroom questioning, in-lesson, and post-lesson assessment techniques to determine the level of student learning. The ability to assess individual student learning when students are engaged in group work. (Having a mental and written "shorthand" system for taking student assessment notes during a lesson.)

o   Curriculum/lesson development skills and knowledge that embraces the learning objectives of cultural diversity, the enhancement of problem-posing and problem-solving skills, group work, independent work; the ELA communication skills of reading, writing and speaking, career-connection, technology, investigation-research methodology, and the creating of relationship analysis skills.

o   A teaching methodology that combines best practices, strong content/subject area knowledge, investigative and strategic in lesson questioning techniques, awareness of the classroom's internal architecture and the social dynamics and learning implications of where and with whom students sit; an effective teaching style that maximizes the teacher's personal strengths and talents, standards/rubrics rich, seeing the entire class as well as the individual students in the class, redefining "at-risk," and being an at-risk champion, which means taking smart, brave and thoughtful risks to defeat at-risk.

- o (Theoretically speaking) a good teacher should be able to observe a lesson and determine if that lesson is effective. That same teacher is able to decenter and observe their own lesson (in real time), and determine if they are being effective with all or some of the students.

- o Practically speaking, a high school principal must be able to observe a lesson in any content area and determine if that lesson is effective!

- A teacher must see supervisory observations as a critical component of professional development. They must also engage in the continuous practice of decentering, self-reflection, and meta-cognition that allows them to observe and analyze their own teaching methodology in real teaching time. This means that the principal and the rest of the SBL team must be thoroughly and sincerely immersed in matters relating to curriculum and instruction. The teachers won't believe you to be an instructional coach if you don't display knowledge, an expertise, and interest in theories of teaching and learning. It is particularly critical for the high school principal to study and make themselves credible in the content knowledge and teaching methodologies of the various subject area departments. But the important key is to bring a strong knowledge of instruction such that you can translate that knowledge when observing a class. It is also important that the pre- and post-observation process should be narrative rather than a check-off list. *Critical note to principal: unless the teacher perceives that the formal lesson observation process is designed for professional development purposes, the process has lost a considerable amount, if not all, of its credibility and effectiveness.*

- No school, no matter how effective, and having the most effective school-based leadership team, can make every teacher happy all of the time. As a principal that is a worthy, but humanly unattainable goal. A good teacher will avoid getting totally enrolled (and get mission distracted) in negativity coming from any of their peers. A poisonous working environment can be draining; and since teaching itself is extremely taxing, taking on additional emotional burdens can help lead teachers to a place of cynical disconnection or physical-psychological burnout.

- A teacher should look, dress, and carry themselves as models for young people at all times. As a principal I always followed the model that my work was a life calling, and, therefore, I was never in public "off-duty." On weekends, holidays, and school breaks, I always gave some thought as to how I was presenting myself just in case I ran into one of my students. I know that the topic of dress codes and appropriate professional attire in schools is a controversial issue. My position is that the school is a special and important place in a society, therefore I dress in such a way that brings honor to the field of professional education, the school building where that education takes place, the students, parents, and other educational professionals that work in the building. We know from our study of developmental psychology that the sending and receiving of messages to/from adolescents and teenagers can be a tricky affair. They will often send us conflicting requests to be loose, less-strict, dress, talk and act like them; when in reality, they want structure and standards, so that they can understand the rules, predictability, and order they will encounter in the adult world. They really want us to act like adults by shepherding and mentoring them into the adulthood that is rapidly moving toward them.

- If you want friendships, find people your own age! Having a productive line of communication with students is immensely important; and, of course, raising the level of student comfort with the adults in the building can lead to some effective prevention-support actions. But teachers should never be confused concerning their roles in the school; your job is always to offer good and sound practical advice as well as to remind students of their personal and schoolwide academic goals and responsibilities. The teacher must always remain above the fray and be a voice of reason and inspiration that will help students to find the most peaceful, positive, and productive (for all involved), ways to handle challenges in life and in the school. Unfortunately, a large number of teachers end up in a very bad place, including suspension, termination, and sometimes jail, because they are confused about the rules and regulations concerning the protocols for proper teacher-student relationships.

- Never step out of your professional role. For example, if a parent curses at you or engages in any other type of disrespectful behavior, simply say in a calm voice, "I am sorry, but we cannot continue this conversation until you provide me with the respect that I am showing you." It is important here that the principal establish clear guidelines as to how parents can speak with, to, and about, teachers. At the same time, strict guidelines as to how parents are spoken to and treated should also be made clear. The customer may not always be right, but they should always be treated right! Meanwhile, the teacher must keep in mind the standards and expectations for public professionals must be higher than the public we serve. This also covers the actionable areas of revenge/retaliation as well as the inability to let something go and move on. The best and most effective teachers I have met in my career maintain a thick skin and a thin memory for insults. Besides, if a teacher has a career objective to become a school administrator, then they need to get into the practice of not responding to every negative comment that comes their way!

- Don't ever look down on the students, their families, or the communities where they live. All communities, regardless of their socio-economic status, have cultural strengths, many positive attributes, and harbor great hopes and expectations for their children, even if that hope and expectation is not always presented in the most effective way. Teachers can't get lost in the look and sound of the "messenger." Instead, they should focus on the core message that all parents want their children to be successful; and for many parents we may need to offer assistance in helping them to successfully operationalize that desire. We don't want to romanticize poverty, neither do we want to empower it as a final determiner of the child's potential. These teachers must work hard to support those students for whom education represented their only hope as a way out of poverty. Despite all of the roadblocks, barriers, disappointments, and all that was lacking or not provided, we still want them to soldier on to academic success.

- That you are changing the world for the better; for each child is a world unto themselves, and how they perform and act in the world can make a huge difference. Education is the great determiner of the quality and quantity of every person's contribution to the well-being of our civilization. And great teachers see themselves as the critical guides who are called to draw out the unique gifts and contributions of the young people who enter their classrooms. I read once that "you don't get a second chance to make a good first impression." The children that enter our classrooms, our sphere of influence, don't get a chance to do that semester or year over. We must approach every day, every lesson, and every child with a sense of sacred urgency, knowing that what we do or don't do will have a rippling effect on the students as they travel through this life. And, so, what lasting effect do we want to plant and nurture?

The exceptional and effective teacher teaches on the EDGE.

The ethical where, why, and how of teaching is a political decision. Political, meaning, what segment of the access-to-power spectrum of society do you champion? Each teacher must decide where he or she stands in this work. Teaching is a risky emotional business, as it asks the practitioners of this art to be fully open, committed, and sacrificing to children with whom they have no family ties. In many ways, being a teacher is that profession which challenges one to want for their students what one would want for their own biological children. And just like in any parenting situation, one is called upon to sometimes struggle through feelings of being underappreciated by a society of stakeholders external to the school, and sometimes parents and even students. Teaching in a career-safe, "it's just a job," non-confrontational space surely has its benefits; you can hide, earn a decent salary with good benefits and a reasonable retirement program in a system that has designated favorite and favored students. But that state of pedagogical inauthenticity is something other than what I would call teaching. Teaching on the EDGE means teaching with a persistent courage that does not allow the teacher to sell out students or their parents, even when those same parents and students get upset with your refusal to do so. A teacher teaching on the EDGE will always speak truth to the powerless; clearly and honestly explain the challenges that must be overcome; they will not pretend that there is an easy and simple path to academic success. EDGE teaching means that you as a teacher give your best, as you persistently request the best from every student in your class. This kind of teaching is a dangerous enterprise because it seeks to upset the political status quo that exists in public education. The EDGE approach rejects a pedagogy of submission, cultural domination, and second-class citizenship. Rather, an EDGY teaching approach means that you affirm, strengthen, and empower the best attributes and talents of those who are most ignored and dismissed in our society. Teaching on the EDGE is in every way a political act!

- *Engage* their minds to effectively engage the world: Intelligence, inquisitiveness, and good reasoning/thinking methods can be taught and grown. If as a teacher you are wedded to all of the terrible indicators, predictors, and prognosticators that say that students from certain groups or zip codes suffer from organic, genetically-inherited, or socially-determined achievement ceilings, then the game is already lost. Create in students the ability to be the tenders of their own intellectual garden. Push their vocabulary beyond their peer social circle; don't "dumb things down" in an attempt to "keep it real." All racial, cultural, ethnic groups in this nation live rich and diverse cultural lifestyles. Don't restrict and confine students to an "intellectual ghetto" in the false attempt to make them comfortable with school and learning. A brief historical study of the many cultures who make up this nation, one would quickly find that there is a rich STEM, art, literary and creative, intellectual tradition that is richly distributed before and after arriving to the shores of America. This leads me to one of my primary concerns of teachers serving as guardians of the right of children of color to be smart. How a school or a classroom informs students as to who owns smartness, learning, intellectual curiosity and academic achievement will determine whether wings or limiting balls and chains are placed on the minds and aspirations of those children.

- *Demand* their best: Draw out the best and except nothing less from every student in your charge. Like many things in life, in education, you get what you ask for! At the core of the teaching experience, I would even go so far as to say the rudder that directs the classroom's learning ship, is the quality level of teacher expectations. My experience is that young people have this strange natural instinct and ability to rise to the expectations demanded by those who educate them (and this goes for you also, parents!) Even as they may push back against rigor and high expectations, particularly in middle and high school, especially for boys of color, the teacher must also audaciously push them by maintaining and insisting on the establishment of high academic and behavioral standards. Bravery is properly preparing students who are

430

not expected to succeed in a political and economic system that generates a large amount of jobs and money to service their failure. A teacher engaging in this type of courageous pedagogy of affirmation should not expect to be recognized for this effort. Unfortunately, the culture of public education is to reward the many who don't shake things up. Staying below the radar and not crossing the line that divides average and exceptional is too often the safe career choice for many teachers. Some teachers become ineffective or disinterested because of a truth that our society does not properly pay teachers for the important and essential work they perform. One of the tragic shames of this great nation is our unwillingness to pay teachers enough money in some cases to adequately live in the communities in which they teach. But the effective teacher will be able to expand their definition and understanding of payment to include the positive transformation of the students in their care. My advice is that if appreciation and thanking arrives, by all means accept it; but don't expect it, and don't make it a condition for being an excellent and effective practitioner. Perhaps students and parents will thank you later, or perhaps never, but it does not matter, your job is to maintain your personal standards of high expectations.

- *Give* the children in your class a chance to demonstrate their giftedness: the possibilities of the human brain and the capacity of the human spirit to create beauty are two vastly underexplored regions of our humanity. Teachers first have to be strong, particularly with student populations who have been told for many years that they are the "anti-talented and gifted" (except for the social service/criminal justice systems) to American society. Those same powerful skills of persistence that we have identified as essential qualities and academic success, must also be applied and thoughtfully practiced by teachers. The first step is for the teacher to not allow any separation between student academic success and teacher professional success. This approach must be culturally embedded both in the generally accepted peer professional standards as well as the individual personality of each teacher. The bond between effective teaching and effective learning cannot be broken if that classroom or that school hopes to be successful with students. The effective teacher will actively seek out the unrealized and undiscovered talents of the students in his class. And that will require thoughtful patience and an affirmative discovery process. An important starting place for this process is that teach-

431

er's questioning technique. Principals, you could learn a great deal about the quality of your school's instructional program by spending time in classrooms just focusing only on the questioning technique of teachers. This technique, if used effectively, will draw all students into a better understanding of the lesson's learning objectives; and at the same time, draw out the creativity, quality thinking capacity, and brilliance of individual students. Even as the theory of "multiple intelligences" has been challenge by many educational theorists recently, the effective teacher must still discover and develop each child's unique modality talents and utilize that child's natural gifts as a path to greater student learning. All professional educators are by purpose and practice society's intellectual talent scouts. We have an efficient and predictive process for the early identification and the feeding of the NCAA, NFL, MLB, and NBA systems. Somehow, we are able to discover and prepare young people whose talents are required by these organizations. And, so, it is not a question of capacity when it comes to identifying and developing talents and gifts in young people in the areas of STEM, invention-innovation, research and design, the performing, graphics, musical arts. I'm talking about all of the many creative and talented young people who are eliminated because they lack early access to training and exposure; therefore, never gaining admission to excellent arts high schools. The effective teacher is always on the lookout for talents and gifts; and most importantly, they do something about that knowledge once they acquire it.

- *Expect* the unexpected, the amazing, and the great to happen, and it will! The effective teacher who is teaching on the edge does not waste a great deal of physical or mental time and energy being slowed down by school system complaints that too often dominate the conversations in teacher's lounges and cafeterias. I have said for many years that the persistent and public proclamation of "woe is me" does great harm to the public image and perception of the profession. For sure our schools are tragically underfunded, but that societal error can't be translated into a rationale for our inability to adequately educate so many children who spend a great deal of time (years) with us.

Despite the obstacles, if we chose to enter the profession, then we also chose to serve the children in our care in whatever state they arrive to school, and to make them academically successful even as we work to change the conditions of the society that places certain students at a great disadvantage.

In a world that is not perfect, it is perhaps naïve to think that any professional would expect to labor in perfect working conditions. I have heard professional educators exclaim on many occasions after a bad encounter with a healthcare professional, postal worker, transit worker, sanitation department employee, or any other member of a profession that "they should leave their personal problems at home and just act professional!" Well, guess what? Citizens are also observing (and listening) to us. And part of the reasons the public and policymakers can't hear our legitimate complaints and concerns are for the following reasons:

- We have not effectively, in the minds of external stakeholders, established the link between more money and better educational outcomes. There are districts that have high average per pupil expenditures and perform poorly academically. It is also not always clear that we are the best financial custodians of the money we presently receive.

- Often there is no sense-making and consistency of our complaints and concerns. It is not always clear that our primary concern are the students. The presence of too many non-professional educators' "voices" leading the discussions and claiming to speak on behalf of the students and their parents is also not helpful.

- The complaints and concerns often lack an ethical or professional foundation and focus. These gripes also emerge unaccompanied by a thoughtful and strategic alternative.

- We have not made a decision that is clearly understood by the public, whether or not we want to be seen and treated like an assembly line of workers manufacturing things; or as professionals who are charged with the sacred duty of educating human beings who represent the hopes, dreams, and aspirations of a present and future society. I may be wrong here, but I suspect that the public is not going to let us have it both ways. We won't be able to say we are professionals and deserving of professional respect, recognition, and pay, and then take no professional responsibility for our work. In fact, we continue to insist on having the "Lake Wobegon" effect in our schools, which says we can only be successful with perfect children, born of perfect parents, who live in perfect communities.

Professions and those who call themselves professionals all have similar attributes. A system of professional ethical standards, theoretical and operational standards, and a process that identifies, recognizes, and codifies mastery. (See medicine, law, engineering, etc.) Further, professions establish a thoughtful internship where a new professional is not put in a position to harm the public. There is oversight, theoretical and practical training, real mentoring, standards and rubrics that determine competency and, eventually, certification. There are also professional standards developed by the professionals themselves, which would seek to bar and terminate any individual who does not meet those professional standards. Professions do this, in part, so as to maintain control over the standards that are used to evaluate, and if necessary, restrict a member of their profession from practicing. This approach to self-monitoring also gives these professionals a great deal of leverage in determining their compensation as members of this profession. Professional organizations are really the folks in this nation who want to see the government out of their business. If professional educators want the many unproductive external stakeholders "out of our business," then we need to adopt a professional, no-excuses approach to our work. If we insist (openly or in secret) that we can't educate children who are poor, or if their parents don't have a college degree and a great deal of financial and informational resources to fund informal education activities, then the public is not going to fully grant us professional status. And to earn the public's respect, principals must lead on the EDGE and classroom teachers must teach on the EDGE!

Principals, how do you recognize an exceptional and effective teacher?

Selecting excellent, efficacious, and methodologically effective teachers, is one of the most important responsibilities of the principalship; and, unfortunately, rarely covered in graduate school administration and supervision certification programs.

Principals are under tremendous time restraints, so the necessary skill of the initial quick and focused recognition is essential. You use it daily as a way of identifying potential organizational practices, conditions, or situations that could lead to a negative or dangerous outcome. But this SuperVision recogni-

434

tion skill is also a critical tool in practicing instructional leadership. Each principal must design a theoretically rich shorthand that allows you to recognize the possibilities and potentiality of an interviewing teacher you are meeting at a time-challenged event like a hiring fair. You must perfect this SuperVision skill because hiring a teacher is like marriage—easy to get into but potentially ugly when it does not work out! More importantly, the quality of your hiring practices will bring either harm or help to the children and school you serve. Here are some traits you should look for:

- **Ethical Exemplar**: the teacher will follow an uncompromising and overarching list of ethical standards. That essentially places the educational well-being of the child at the front and center of a practice, rejecting all excuses, rationales, and conditions that suggests that a student is incapable of learning at the height of their best ability. And that the teacher will defend his students from all external acts of cultural aggression, depersonalization, and the denial of the promise of a positive future.

- **Efficacious Ethos**: that the teacher sees himself/herself as the primary catalyst, scaffold, motivator, healer, and bridge that the student can cross to realize academic success. These teachers truly believe that they are the single, most important variable in determining academic success. They are not doubtful, discouraged, or deterred by the high-volume of socio-political economic noise outside of the classroom. The teacher who practices efficacy is fully aware and accepting of their unique and significant power to influence a positive outcome in the lives of children. They are true believers of the idea that if there is any hope for it to be well, then their will and actions are a critical part of the process.

- **Experienced Expertise**: Whether a first-year or fifteen-year teacher, the effective teacher is in a constant state of learning. Not just continually learning, but a professional yearning to move closer and closer to a place of excellence. Taking in as much positive pedagogy as possible and avoiding the negative conversations about the ability and capability of the students. As a principal, I have had some really wonderful first-year teachers. The key is to provide a tremendous amount of school-based support and multiple mentoring opportunities from strong veteran teachers. But I also know as a superintendent some of our most academically struggling schools find themselves overburdened with first to third-year teachers. On the other hand, schools that are housed in more favorable zip codes are able to staff those schools with teachers who combine expertise and experience. This is why we need teachers who want to invest long-term in the profession and with their schools. Experience matters because a large part of teaching, as in any profession, are those subtle, unwritten, and only revealed in actual practice things you don't learn in a college class, or that are not measured on a certification or licensing exam. When you ask high school students to describe a good teacher, they usually mean a teacher who is rich with content knowledge, exhibits an excellent awareness of what students know and don't know, possesses an inspiring and engaging teaching style, and it is clear that the teacher is in love with the subject matter. More importantly, they want to transfer that love to the students in their classes. Effective teachers with rich reservoirs of expertise will always inspire students to appreciate and fall in love with the subject area, even if that is not the student's future career choice. And that, in many ways, is the purpose of education—to have the student fall in love with the subject area.

- ***Excitement and Enjoyment***: the effective teacher's class is always a center of intellectual enthusiasm; these teachers bring an excitement and energy that is centered in their passion and commitment to create a dynamic learning space. There are the small things like a wonderful sense of humor, storytelling abilities, and being able to pull groups and individual students inside of the lesson through some connective narrative. We don't like to talk too much about personal style because in many ways it is personal and individual. I always advise new teachers to be themselves. Every teacher, regardless of time in the classroom, should rely on their own personal strengths when employing a teaching approach. But what should be present in every class presentation is an interest and anticipation on the part of students before class and a thoughtful and inspiring excitement at the end of that class. We have mentioned pedagogical knowledge, content mastery, and lesson planning, but we must also include delivery as an important factor in effective teaching and learning. Now, this interesting and exciting delivery should not be confused with a dramatic entertainment presentation. The idea that teaching can duplicate or emulate TV, movies, electronic media, or comedy skits is silly and diminishes the profession. However, there is nothing wrong with students actually enjoying a class, and that should include even the most challenging and rigorous courses we offer. A core part of our professional development strategy and plan should be how to make teachers and teaching more interesting. Our teaching methodology should focus on engaging and enrolling students into the subject/content area, as opposed to a policy of exclusion and elimination.

- ***Elevating and Ennobling***: one possible fundamental definition of the school-learning process is that having entered a classroom, you exit in a higher state of knowing. The effective teacher seeks to effectively change the student's present state and place of knowledge. That means that the act of teaching is visionary and is accompanied by a plan to move students to their best possible classroom experience. This could also mean that the teacher must present an academic achievement outcome that may appear to be impossible. This skill of convincing students to believe in their own power and greatness, even as the students themselves may not recognize these internal attributes, is a primary tool of the effective teacher. This is particularly critical in the middle and high school years of a student's life. For it is then that critical independent and peer-driven life decisions are made. The effective teacher must simultaneously lead the students down a good decision/academic achievement path, while at the same time, enrich them with the habits, skills, and knowledge to serve as authors, agents, and activists of their own life success story.

- ***Endurance and Earnest***: make no mistake about it, teaching is hard, very hard; and it is extremely draining of both physical and emotional energy, particularly when you are effective in the craft. The smart effective teacher will seek to balance hard work and hard rest. Teaching is not a sprint, and although the rewards are many and far outweigh the negatives, there are also setbacks and disappointments, most of which are outside of your control. Over the years, I have noticed that the teachers who don't bailout early are the ones who enter the profession with a sense of humility and respect for its serious awesomeness! Sadly, I have also seen bright and enthusiastic individuals who underestimated the difficulties of teaching; their arrogance and underestimation often lead to an early exit that harmed the children. As a superintendent, it was not uncommon to receive a call from a principal giving me a heads up for parent calls because a teacher quit the first day, week, or month of school. "Teaching is easy" says civilians who live and work outside of schools; they often get confused by the posted length of the workday, school holiday/semester breaks, and summers off. My first full-time job in college was with the post office. I can honestly say that there is a major qualitative difference between working with "things" and human beings whose entire futures, hopes, and aspirations are in your hands. The effective teacher works before school, during their designated breaks, after school, evenings, and weekends. There is just no way to do this work properly without that level of time and energy investment; at least I have never seen a serious and dedicated teacher who did not invest a huge amount of unpaid work hours into their students. And this does not include the large number of teachers who spend their personal money on their students and classrooms. Teachers must also work under terrible societal conditions and perceptions that don't recognize, reward, or respect the education profession. Even though I confessed the reason for that lack of recognition earlier in the book, is in part due to our failure as a profession to adopt a code of ethical principles that place the education of children, above adult employment. Still, the teaching profession itself deserves universal respect and honor from the citizenry, and that respect and honor should be "operationalized" into better pay!

Finally, a few remaining characteristics to look for in the hiring process

- The prospective teacher must have high levels of self-confidence and self-esteem, or they can't lift the confidence and self-esteem levels of the students; and they probably are not very good at teaching.

- (If applicable) Carefully read the teacher's past observations.

- Carefully read the undergraduate and graduate transcripts.

- Check with the former principal(s); try to figure out if the principal is competent, then, based on that, listen to their comments through that filter.

- Never hire on the spot; set up a second interview with the departmental staff and other (non-departmental) teachers who personify the school's mission and culture. Trust their input and advice!

- If during the course of the conversation they speak badly about the last principal, rest assured you are the next principal that they will be talking badly about. Further, they are unprofessional and will not provide good advice to the students.

- Have the prospective teacher come in to teach a demonstration lesson. Observe the lesson with teachers and APs. Debrief with the students (out of the presence of the presenting teacher); don't underestimate the instinctual knowledge and information that can be gathered from that student debriefing. Talk to them as you give them their promised pizza party and the ideas will flow!

- Make nice with the folks in Human Resources (HR). The HR department is one of a principal's best friends. If they like you, your school is in great shape, and if they don't, well…

- Establish and invest your time in the bench-building program of having a strong undergraduate student teachers program at your school (a notable quality of many high-performing schools). This allows you, the SBL team, and teachers to take a good look at a possible teacher to recruit. Is the person coachable? Is that student teacher strong in content, and possess the appropriate amount of methodological skills. The staff can see and talk to the student teacher to ascertain if they are a good philosophical fit for the school, which means meshing with the school's culture, mission, and values. (To my college student teachers, know that a placement with a thoughtfully strategic principal is essentially a "job interview," or if they don't have a position for you, at least a referral to a colleague-friend's school!)

- Build a school where good teachers and other school personnel will want to work; while at the same time incompetent and less than effective individuals will avoid your school. A good place to be as a principal is when your own teachers serve as a referral and/or screening process for those inquiring about working at your school. Even if your school does not have a strong recruitment profile, it does not mean that you should lower your recruitment standards. In fact, if your school has a lot of academically unprepared and struggling students, it is all the more reason to double your efforts and recruit good teachers. You can help yourself and the students by strategically and effectively addressing two of the primary concerns of teachers who are seeking a position: safety and support. But you also want to make sure that you recruit teachers who, in their heart of hearts, want to work with the children in your school building; not some students who are well resourced by their parents, rich with informal educational experiences, and politically entitled by the larger society to receive a quality education. You want the teacher who is enthusiastic about teaching those children who are ignored, who have the least, and are left out of the American promise. That attitude and commitment, matched with excellent content knowledge and teaching skills, are the effective champions of public education. And if I could, I would double their salaries!

Chapter 28:
Practices of a Successful High School Student

Every year for eleven years, I stood as principal before a large gathering of eager young people and their anxious parents at the incoming student/parent orientation. Every one of those years, I have tried to hammer home the same list of themed warnings and recommendations. Here are some examples from my speech:

- "I will first get out the saddest and most difficult part of my message today. And that is, as I look out at this lovely audience, think and ask myself, which parent is an enabler of academic poor performance and negative non-productive behavior? And, which parent is fully supportive of what we are trying to achieve in this school and supportive of their child being an academic success? Who in this gathering of parents and students, is *really* listening to me? Which student is wrongly and tragically planning, at this very moment in their minds, to bring their old school to this new school; bringing their old selves when a new self is required? Which way will this or that person go, based on hearing or not hearing my words?"

- "Don't surrender to the illusionary promised glory of the ninth grade failing-comeback narrative! In a few years you will be competing with students for internships, jobs, college seats and scholarships, not just in this school, but from schools all over the world, many of your competitors will have an advantage because of their outstanding ninth grade academic performance."

- "One of the first and most important decisions you will make as a freshman is your choice of friends. There is no truer saying then "birds of a feather flock together!" Eagles don't associate with pigeons or chickens unless its mealtime, and that means the other two birds are on the menu! As you move through life, your priorities will change, and with that change there may need to be a change in social relationships; don't stress, it's a natural evolutionary part of life. Pick friends who are moving in a positive direction. Pick friends who are as, or more focused and disciplined than you are!'"

- "Your guidance counselor will help you to complete the required assignment of designing a Graduation Critical Plan/Path Chart. This plan starts with your graduation objective; flows backwards, taking notice and care of every decision until it reaches your present moment. It will map and guide you through the difficult first day, week, month, and year of high school. Your ninth grade's schedule and your attitude in response to that schedule determines your true intentions for achieving your graduation objective. This plan will measure your level of commitment by your academic performance in your ninth grade classes; it will expand to include critical actions to be taken, and the many important decisions that must be made during that same time period. The quality of your study and schoolwork production. Your plans, goals, and objectives for after-school, weekends, school breaks, and holidays, seasonal and summer vacations, from the first ninth grade semester, through to the last semester of your senior year. You should change the plan/path for improvement and enhancement purposes only! Too many students are forced on lowering their personal career goals and life expectations because somewhere between the ninth and twelfth grades they lowered their commitment to work hard for their dreams. *Enter* high school with a good plan. *Evolve* throughout your high school experience guided by a good plan. *End* your high school journey with a good senior post-high school plan!'"

- "The first grade of the year in English will be determined by your work on the written assignment from your before-school book reading project[10]. Not only will this be your first recorded grade in high school, it will also (based on the work you put in) give us, the staff, a first look at your readiness and serious profile!'"

- "In this school, ninth graders will be required to take the Pre-Act and PSAT 10.'"

- "Failing Classes makes high school life less fun and challenges a student's ability to pursue a desired career objective. Failing classes can knock you out of exciting electives that enhance your transcript and are enjoyable to take. Failing classes lowers your GPA! And how many students have I seen scrambling in the tenth, eleventh, and twelfth grades, struggling to raise their GPAs to meet internship criteria, a college program, or scholarship GPA requirement they are pursuing; blocks you from great and wonderful after-school programs, activities, and trips. If you are in a course-grade aligned specialized major or CTE program, a failed class can take you out of sequence, thus disabling you from finishing the program in the scheduled time period. No matter what anybody tells you, summer school or any other type of credit-recovery program, will more often than not, offer a less rigorous/demanding level of academic work than the course you failed in regular school."

Note to principal: A sure sign of a district or school's academic-supervision ineffectiveness is a huge and wasteful amount of money being spent on students who fail classes, too often for reasons totally unrelated to ability. The principal should meet early in a term to discuss with the APs and teachers, those students who are simply "choosing" to fail a class; and then, with an academic intervention/counseling strategy, support and encourage those students to move into the "pass" column side of the ledger. Now, understandably, the school and district are obligated by regulation to make credit recovery expenditures; but we should not kid ourselves, it costs the individual students, districts, and schools dearly when high school students fail classes. It is a huge, and for the most part, unnecessary cost for either establishing a credit-recovery program, or when a failing student occupies a seat in the same course the next semester or year. In any event, the money being spent in the credit-recovery area could be utilized in more positive and productive ways. Finally, students should seek to protect the good image and integrity of their transcripts at all times! C's, D's, and F's are like those lights on a well-lit Christmas tree that don't work—dark spaces on their transcripts!

- "If your middle school experience was less than exemplary, you should think of the moving to a new school experience, where people are going to meet you for the first time, as an opportunity to redefine yourself into a new and better student self-image."

- "Hard work and perseverance can match and overtake natural skill. But when you match hard work, perseverance, and natural skill and talent, what we have is an academic power agent!"

- "You don't get a second chance to make a first impression. Impress teachers and administrators early and in all of your classes. Teachers, like all professionals, talk passionately about their work. When your name comes up, let it be in the context of admiration and praise! (Plus, you will need many of these teachers to provide both verbal and written recommendations over the next four years!)"

- "You will start out in all of your classes with an "A." You will then, through your actions (or inactions), maintain or lower that "A" designation. Teachers here don't give grades; they simply match an A-F grade with your effort and performance, and record the result."

- Then it is that painful recognition moment when I explain the difference between the K-8 "Age-Seat time" promotional system; and the precise, credit-earning driven high school "Carnegie" system for promotion to the next grade. Further, explain (again I apologize to my wonderful elementary-middle school friends and colleagues), "That for the first time in your public school education life, you are about to embark upon a journey to earn a legally determined, regulated, and monitored graduation diploma. The only power the staff has in this process is to add up your credits, confirm that you have taken and passed the required courses, and that you have sat for and passed the required standardized exams, including labs if required. We then submit your name as a candidate for graduation to the superintendent's office. Welcome to the high school world!"

- "One of the greatest threats to ninth grade success is planning and organization. Each of you will receive an academic year planner/calendar. Your student handbook as well as individual teachers' syllabi will advise you as to how to plan long-term assignments and projects. Your academic boat will sink early if you don't effectively plan and organize your schoolwork, study schedule, and personal life…"

- "There is a qualitative and quantitative difference between homework and study. And the differences are connected to the variations of external (teacher assigned) and internal (self-organized by student) motivational and actionable approaches to learning and mastering the academic work. You must understand the difference in the time you devote to homework, class projects, assigned daily readings, and self-organized study periods. We will help you in this school by teaching you how to study; you would be wise to pay attention to those instructions!"

- "You must adjust and manage the different personalities and teaching styles of individual teachers. They (having 150-200 students/day) will not adjust to you!"

- "I have never known a high school friendship that was so strong, that an on-time graduating senior told their best friend, 'You know, we are such good friends that I am going to delay my participation in all of the graduating senior activities, including the prom, senior trip, and the graduation ceremony itself; and stick with you for a summer or January graduation date!'"

- "The audience in the classroom that you entertained with your sit-down comedy routine will not be there to applaud you when you are facing the consequences of your actions in the dean or principal's office; and they definitely won't be with you as they get internships, jobs, and pull in college acceptance letters and scholarships!"

- "If you know more than your teachers then you are in the wrong place and position. You should be applying to the school for a teaching position, not a student position!"

- "In this school, you will be asked to produce your personal best in every aspect of school life. It will, at times, feel uncomfortable, and perhaps even a little painful; but you can, and will, survive it. Others have done so before you, and you will also be successful."

- "You may feel at some point during the next four years that you are falling in love. I can assure you that this terribly distracting ailment, like a head-cold, is temporary and will go away if treated with intense academic study and a focus on a successful graduation."

For high school orientations, it is always good to include student ambassadors/tour guides. In this way, I am trying to present students who could serve as models for what the high school represents. I am also informally setting up and encouraging a new set of friends and mentors for incoming students. A common question a parent will ask after the tour and orientation is who the students were who presented poised, presentable, professional and well-spoken guides to the attendees? And, so, I now discuss the attributes of these collective successful profiles. Keep in mind that I am presenting here a composite of attributes of the best student practices of many (thousands) students that I have worked with over the years. We should also keep in mind that there is no such thing as a perfect student or human being for that matter. But I do believe that there is a way to at least make one's life more positive, productive, emotionally satisfying, physically comfortable, meaningful, and educationally and professionally successful!

Who are the most successful high school students, and what is it that they do to make themselves successful?

- It always increases the students' chances for success if the parent and school are "tag-team" members. That teamwork is enhanced when the parent and school share and enforce the same learning and behavioral values and standards.

- Having a parent or guardian who sees and understands public education as the only real and important path for the child to realize generational improvement. (These parents are not playing NBA/NFL lottery with their child's future, rather the type of letters they are focused on are CTE, BA, MS, MBA, M.D., JD, DDS, P.E., RN, and PhD, etc.!)

- Parents are aware of the purpose, role, and meaning of informal (out of school) educational activities such as dance/music/art lessons, martial arts, tennis, chess, scouting, and visits to museums, cultural institutions and public learning activities.

- Even though the student is a teenager, the parent still exercises a great deal of effective supervision and advisory oversight over the critical successful transition into adult aspects of the child's life.

- The student has the advantage of not being forced to make critical life-determining decisions without the wise experience of a parent or guardian who does not believe that the start of high school signals the end of their parenting responsibilities. These students are not unnecessarily thrust into the dangerous position of learning by their own mistakes. (Oddly, some parents of not-so-successful students have even verbalized that wish to me!) However, the parents of successful students help that success by providing them with lessons of their own life mistakes as well as the lessons of the mistakes made by other adults they have encountered during the course of their lifetime. These parents understand that good parenting is nature's way of minimizing the number of harmful, and sometimes deadly, events that could prevent an offspring from reaching a successful adult life.

- (Not advocating for religion here, just stating an observation.) Students who are regular attendees and actively involved with a faith-based institution.

- (For Black and Latino students) Did not attend a middle school where they were forced to hide or suppress their smartness. It helps to have a high standards, high expectations, and rigorous middle school academic program, particularly those students who have taken algebra or some other rigorous high school course in eighth grade.

- "Emotionally-Situationally intelligent": Able to pick up human-interaction social cues, aware of unwritten rules, pick their battles, knows there is a time to play, a time to work, a time to laugh, and a time to be serious. These students tended to respect adult authority figures, even if they are lodging a protest, they always protest smartly, seeking not to seriously damage or sever the relationship with the staff person against whom they are lodging the complaint. Often it is in reference to a grade a teacher awarded that they thought should be higher. These students are well mannered, well spoken, polite and generally likable. As in all social, political, organizational interactions, likability is an advantage providing strength.

- Students who are either first or second-generation U.S. citizens; e.g., the children of emigrants. (Just saying, don't shoot the messenger!)

- Those students who are more interested in pleasing their parents as opposed to pleasing their peers. The upholding of some family tradition or expectation for educational academic success.

- Hard work, academic success, and a positive attitude gives these students an advantage. Now, I don't have quantifiable data to prove this. But based on my observations and conversations with teachers over the years, I believe that these students are able to gain (based on their past performance; and usually positive attitude) an advantage in the gray area grading phenomena. That is, when a grade of a student's work product (as often happens) falls between a B+ and an A-, or an

A- and an A, these students will always be given a higher grade (or if appropriate, the benefit of the doubt!) Perhaps, unconsciously or not, on the part of their teachers. I have always warned students of two realities outside of the control of the principal: (1) Teachers are human (have feelings). (2) Teachers talk.

- These students will automatically seek to connect with other high-performing students in their grade. Often, this is because of the constant contact of being in the same clubs, programs, activities, projects, elective classes, advance and AP classes. Also, the transition to high school will be used by some high achieving ninth grade students to make friendship and social association changes. Some students who attended high-powered middle schools or programs will, once they reach high school, lock in with other high achievers and stay connected with that group for four years.

- Starting in the ninth grade (and definitely by the tenth grade), these students, with or without adult encouragement, will quietly, in almost a natural and unconscious way, seek out and begin to model themselves after the high-performing eleventh and twelfth graders. In another related and interesting phenomenon, the junior and senior high academic performers will somehow recognize this, and, seeing them as kindred spirits, begin to "adopt" these ninth and tenth graders. This is why it's important for the principal to establish a School-Based Honor Society, complete with identifiable clothing, recognition ceremonies, fun activities, trips and rewards, so that high-performing students can meet and establish friendships, mentorships, and a mutual support society. Further, you should ignore and reject any criticisms that you will receive if you work in a majority Black and Latino school saying that all you care about are the smart kids. The effective principal seeks to serve and protect all of the different cohorts of students in the school. High academic performers deserve as much of your attention as any other group of students in the school; students should not be ignored or penalized because they do well academically. Plus, that positive attention you give to high-performing students will actually serve to empower and strengthen the resolve of underperforming students, and at the same time, also grow their ranks!

- Sometimes these high-performing students will reveal themselves early. They did not come to high school to play! You can even see it in their eyes during the Summer Bridge Program, the high school fair, orientation, a school tour, or even when you make a presentation at their middle school. That look that says, "I am serious about my education!" And important in Title I schools, those focused students of color, who by some means have built up a natural immunity to negative peer pressure about appearing, acting and being smart.

- High-performing students are equal opportunity course attackers. This means that even though their career objective might be in a particular area, they will proceed to systematically and aggressively try to earn an "A" in all of their classes, regardless of the academic course/department. The best ones have the ability to make every teacher feel that the class they are teaching is the most important class in the school. These students are constantly checking their GPA's and the status of their class ranking.

- They possess the ability to understand that the course syllabus is finite. And, yet, they know that their infinite minds, combined with their discipline and mastery of their own time and effort, can successfully overtake and conquer any course in the school because it has already been done many times before. As mentioned earlier, I always made sure to have multiple copies of textbooks on the same subjects, but from different publishers in the library. These are the students who take advantage of that technique, and will read three different chemistry textbooks on a single topic until they understand and absolutely nail that concept!

- Students who read independently for fun and enjoyment.

- They are prepared to take full advantage of the most unexpected arriving opportunity. A special trip, a networking-empowerment event, greeting a guest to the school, a print, radio or television interview, scholarship opportunities, internship and jobs. These are the students who have followed instructions and have their resumes updated and ready; they can prepare a speech immediately with the help of an ELA teacher who they have enrolled by virtue of that student's work; and they are fully prepared (the next day) to "dress for success" (having been taught by the staff) for any type of setting.

Note to principal: The school must prepare students not only for the linguistic code switching demands of society, but also the behavioral and presentation code switching requirements. Skills like "networking" or the "3-minute elevator pitch", are not naturally acquired by any teenager regardless of socio-economic status. What also must be taught is a working knowledge of situationally appropriate attire; what is "formal wear", "interview attire", business professional, business casual, professional, etc. All of this under the standard of "Dress for Success"; which you may want to dedicate one day a week to this effort (and buy the dresses, skirts, suits, ties, shoes, blouses, shirts, etc., for students who can't afford them, and distribute them confidentially). A lot of clothiers and department stores, fraternal-sorority originations and corporations, will be more than happy to help you with acquiring these items for your students. Invite prominent professional men of color for a "How to tie a tie breakfast" (Professionals are more likely to help you with this and similar efforts if you don't take up their whole day!) This event may sound simple, but for many male students this wonderful experience maybe the first and few positive experiences they have had like this with a male figure. Don't have the quantifiable data or explanatory line/bar chart, but I can assert with the utmost "memory-confidence" a guarantee that on "Dress for Success" days, your student to student, student to staff conflicts, disciplinary issues will drop dramatically!

- Strongly self-reflective and meaningfully metacognitive: These students continually think about their own thoughts, behaviors, the effectiveness of the strategies and techniques they utilize, and how to rid themselves of unproductive and unrewarding practices. The ability to both see and change an approach that is not yielding the results they desire.

- These students have a four-year plan of action! They will seek to avoid any and all engagements, involvements, and actions that would threaten the success of their four-year plan.

- They are fiercely, though not necessarily viciously, competitive.

- The top students always appear to have great time management and organizational skills. They have the ability to prioritize assignments and projects weekly, monthly, and across an entire semester or year, including avoiding that common ninth grade curse of disorganization. They start and finish high school in the same effective way. Again, they have their eyes on that GPA race from the start of ninth grade!

- They have figured the principal out! They best understand the role and power of the principal, and they utilize that understanding to their advantage. Just as they have successfully done in all of their classes, they have also analyzed and processed the standards and expectations of the principal. They will come and speak to the principal if they feel that they are not being adequately prepared to be their best academically competitive selves. For a high school principal, this is one of the most difficult (and fulfilling) conversations to navigate, as you try to balance professionalism and professional ethics. The students will never come to you prematurely, which means they are almost always correct. In order to maintain your moral authority and credibility, you must take some kind of affirmative problem-solving action. The good news is that these are more likely the types of students who won't show their teachers up because of the actions you have taken to correct the situation.

- High-performing students seem (with some exceptions) to avoid intense high school romantic relationships that can distract them from their academic work.

- The awareness to maximize their gifts and talents, and at the same time, successfully minimize and manage their weaknesses.

- They know how to effectively utilize the text book, review book, and class notes.

- These students will be the first to sign up for the six-week Saturday, three-hour ACT or SAT review study class (e.g., Kaplan or Princeton Review). They will also make sure to attend every session and invest all of their energy into the course assignments.

- For the academically successful student, school is a fun-filled, fulfilling, reaffirming, and enjoyable place. For some of these students, the school also serves as a safe and peaceful academic achievement sanctuary.

- There is a certain maturity about them that allows them to rise above the typical teenage fray and drama. They see high school as just another area of challenge for which they must conquer and move on to the next level of challenge. And, so, there is a certain emotional efficiency skill to the way they deal with institutions, people, and situations.

- The high-powered students are critically aware that their competition is not just the students in their school or the classmates sitting at the desk next to them. Rather, their competition exists in other schools in the city, state, nation, and the world.

- (Important for educators) They see group work, study groups where they don't choose the members, or team/group projects as unsatisfying, frustrating, and non-productive; as these formations tend to slow them down and undermine their style and approach to work; and often compromises their quest for excellence and high grades if the other members of the group don't match their work effort and commitment.

  Note to principals: They will come to you to complain about a group project that they feel threatens their GPA. Use this as a teachable moment for the student to learn empathy and compassion. But meet with the teacher privately to come up with a plan to not let the student's GPA suffer. Have the teacher talk to and encourage the student as they work with their less than ambitious classmates.

- They don't feel the need to necessarily like the assignment, they only feel that they need to get the highest grade allowable for that assignment. Teachers: For all students, be very certain as to why you gave a particular grade (have evidence). A clear set of grading rubrics are always essential. These students in particular are going to involve the principal into their "grade appeal" process if not satisfied with your explanation-decision, when she would rather be doing something else!

- The highest performing students spend quality time doing homework and even more time studying; they clearly understand the difference between homework and studying.

- For Black and Latino high-achieving students, being in the right school (where high academic achievement is honored, recognized, and praised) will give them the confirmation and self-authority permission and protection to act and be smart. Not being forced to hide their smartness allows these students to produce academically at an amazingly high level.

- If there is extra credit or bonus points to be earned for an assignment, project, or on an exam, they will take advantage of it. Given the option of taking a hard or easy assignment or project, they will opt for the most challenging, knowing (or not knowing) that they are positively influencing the teacher's attitude toward them! (Again, teachers are human, too!)

- These students are first in line (having the academics and behavioral qualifications) for: paid and unpaid internships, service projects, special in- and out-of-school projects, programs, activities, and educational trips. All of these are opportunities for informal education, capacity building, and experience to enhance the student's resume and biographies for scholarships and college admissions.

- High-performing students don't waste their time on violating even the smallest school rules, such as the dress code. They seem to have little interest in the average act of teenage rebellion to adult rules. They weigh all of their actions against their primary principle and goal of high academic achievement. These students will, however, often voice their concerns about a particular rule to the principal, even as they follow that rule.

- Their style of notetaking and notebooks (well organized by subjects and topics) are themselves, essentially course study guides!

- These students are totally not invested (or interested) in the personalities or stylistic traits of individual teachers or administrators; they are absolutely focused on their own personal educational mission. They will not confront or publicly challenge a teacher, but will not hesitate to come to the principal privately if they feel they have not been treated fairly or in the "adult definition" of a respectful way. They will avoid if at all possible involving themselves in any situation that will hurt their final grade.

- The students seem to get from day one that they are on the last leg of their K-12 public school experience. These students see every class, grade on a report card, any and all exam scores, term-semester success, and the significance of each of the four high school years as extremely important to their future life objectives.

- These students have their own personal high standards and expectations. These personal high standards and expectations are displayed in
  their work product in every class, regardless of the level of the standards and expectations of a particular teacher. For example, once they
  master the correct research paper and essay style/format they learned
  in their English class, they will utilize that correct style and format in
  every other subject area where a written response to an assignment or
  exam is required. In other words, they will write as if every teacher
  reading their response is their English teacher.

- These students have considerable control of their school image, which
  is important when over a four-year period something can go wrong.
  I keep reminding students that the teacher you annoy today, is that
  same teacher you will need to write a letter of recommendation (LOR)
  for some important thing you want; and that writing a LOR is not a
  mandatory part of their job description! A good image in a school is
  like a gift that never stops giving a reward. Once at Phelps, a high-performing honor roll student was mistakenly (due to a teacher's error)
  referred to the in-school suspension room (ISS). The Dean, sensing
  that something was very wrong, had security track down the principal.
  I spoke to the teacher and the situation was immediately corrected and
  she was removed from the room with an apology from the teacher.
  It is important to note that even though she knew she was innocent,
  she still reported to ISS quietly. This is pretty astounding since some
  of the guiltiest referees to ISS dramatically claim that the teacher is
  wrong or has it out for them. What was also so amazing is that even
  the legitimate residents of ISS asked her, "What are you doing here?"
  Or, as one student remarked, "This must be the end of the world if she
  is in ISS!"

- There is no shame in their game when it comes to earning high grades.
  When these students have a research project or presentation, they will
  have no problem asking any and every adult in the building including
  custodians, cafeteria supervisor, nurse, APs, art or technology teacher, and yes even the principal for help. On more occasions then I can
  remember, I had to dip into my own pocket when these students approached me for something they needed for a school assignment or
  project; how could I say no!

- Despite the amount of time these students must have spent studying in order to maintain their honor roll status, I often found it interesting that they were also very "school activities" busy. They were multitaskers in many different (three to six) extracurricular activities such as the track team, dance company, band, debate team, volleyball team, art club, etc.; along with this extracurricular involvement, these students also often served in student government as ambassadors and presenters for special tours, events held at the school as well as serving as representatives and spokespersons for the school at community, city, state, and national events. It is important to note that the regular academic course load for these students was often made heavier, starting in their junior year as they began to take multiple advance and AP courses.

- Near or perfect punctuality and attendance records. Not ever late to class and don't go to the bathroom during class, less they miss something being taught.

- For Girls: They are the chief recognizers and protectors of the respect that is properly due to them by virtue of their existence. A high sense of self-worth and self-esteem are the greatest attributes, motivators, and guarantees of a young lady's success in graduating from high school, regardless of the level of academic achievement potential. These ladies (in the best meaning of the word) don't allow themselves to be physically or emotionally devalued, and see their personhood as worthy and entitled to proper attention that is appropriately due to a woman who is seen by males as meeting the standard of an honored friend or potential wife and mother of the young man's children. These ladies of distinction are not practice crash dummies; their very presence demands, and is associated with, the highest expressions of honor. These young ladies are also singularly focused on developing and enhancing what they believe to be the most attractive part of their anatomy, their brains.

- For Boys: These gentlemen (in the best meaning of the word), seem to have a powerfully high definition of manhood. This affirmation of what it means to be a man is tied to their powerful sense of self-worth which is connected to a commitment to be high academic achievers. But this emotionally intelligent position also allows them to recognize and respect the self-worth in others. They are not driven by the lowest and most primitive definitions of maleness which is characterized by the objectification and exploitation of their fellow female students. Further, those Black and Latino male students who dare to be and act smart openly are already comfortable practitioners of how they should behave with women in our society.

- Those students in the top 25 of their cohort who are clearly aware of the college scholarship acquiring/admissions value that is attached to their ranking. With all of the new media and the public's attention being focused on the problem of student college tuition debt, they are conscious of placing themselves in the most advantageous and best scholarship acquisition position. And, in a Title I high school, parental money for college is far from a given.

- They are departmental-guidance-college career office bulletin board watchers! They are constantly searching for opportunities such as internships, scholarships, college tours, speakers visiting the school, etc.

- They make sure that critical assignment deadlines are trip-wired (an early warning system) in their planner/calendar. For example, if a research paper is due on October 25, they will put two dates in their planner; the date they wish to start the project and the date it is actually due to be turned into the teacher. This approach increases the possibility that they will receive a high grade on long-term projects and assignments since they are not trying to complete these tasks "two days before it is due!"

- They establish good connections early on with the school guidance/career office staff (guidance counselors want to also work and advise high academically-performing/well-behaving students in the school). These students have a great appreciation and respect for the guidance/career office staff persons, but they realize that they are ultimately responsible for reviewing their own transcripts and making sure they are in the right classes, and on track to graduate. I always tell students—no disrespect to the guidance counselors—but in a high school where there is a large number of students, with a huge part of the administrative work being done by computer systems, there is always the possibility of errors. Every student must take ownership of their transcript review process to make sure that they are in the right classes and on the right path to that graduation outcome they are seeking.

- They are definitely good test-takers, along with the ability to discern the individual teacher's standards and requirements; they then come up with a strategy to effectively meet those standards and requirements.

- The students who are able to effectively realize their interest in a STEM major/career, start the process in the ninth grade. Planning for a STEM future means planting prerequisite seeds early. "What are the college programs I am applying to looking for in the profiles and transcripts of prospective students?"

Note to principals: It is always easier to opt out of a STEM career goal than it is to opt-in as a high school junior or senior (difficulty in enrolling in the necessary courses). This is why I advocate that every high school student should take four years of mathematics and four years of a laboratory science. In this way, the student can still pursue a STEM major in college. In any event, having a strong STEM course profile on your transcript won't hurt a student, regardless of their intended college major. Those students planning to pursue a Pre-law, English Literature, or an Ethno-musicology major in college are helped, not harmed, by having taken and passed pre-calculus and physics. Meeting the goal of graduating from high school is best facilitated when the student designs and follows a four-year pacing successes chart (the GCPC); a student is always aware (or made aware) of where they stand academically at the end of every semester they are in school. I also think of this plan as an antidote and guide through the hectic last year of high school. This is a time when a great deal of things are going on in the school and personal lives of seniors; like all of the "senior activities" and preparing for that next major step into the adult world. There are many tasks that need the student's attention and time. And, of course, these students still have a full year of full-time classes, some of which might be advance or AP courses. To successfully navigate the end of their K-12 experience and positively start off in a good place for their new post-high school life, they will need a good (GCPC) plan!

Summarizing the list of best qualities and values that lead to a student's success in high school

- Good organization and time management skills.

- Pursuing excellence starting in the ninth grade: Don't fail classes!

- Good and consistent study skills.

- Utilize the planner, don't wait until the last minute to start a project, paper or assignment.

- Knowing the difference between homework and study; and investing quality time in both.

- Defer "fun": Invest in study and hard work in the present to enjoy a greater "fun" future.

- Practice real teenage independence; don't let your life depend on pleasing other teenagers.

- Set a goal to master the ACT/SAT turnkey test vocabulary words and phrases by the tenth grade.

- Pick friends who are moving in the right direction.

- For the college admissions application essay, work toward a "consistently rising since the ninth-grade" story line rather than the "I fell down in the ninth grade and then I got up" narrative.

- Designing and working a four-year academic achievement strategy, across all academic departments. The Graduation Critical Path Chart (GCPC)

- Make summer jobs, summer internships, volunteer and service projects match the post-high school objectives in your GCPC.

- Understanding that high school years will move amazingly fast; there is really not a lot of time for corrective actions.

- Think early and act accordingly for acquiring internships, jobs, and college admissions and scholarships recommendations.

458

- Approaching every class with the same powerful passion!

- Turning any situation into an opportunity by being prepared.

- A well-rounded portfolio of classes, clubs, athletics and participation in school activities.

- Establish and protect a "good name" (profile) in the school.

- Seek balance in study, spiritual, social, and personal life.

- The ability to be:
    - Self-reflective
    - Self-inspired
    - Self-disciplined
    - Self-evaluating
    - Self-correcting
    - Self-aware
    - Self-determined
    - Self-confident
    - Self-controlled
    - Self-motivated
    - Self-preserving
    - Self-reliant

The key things all students need to be aware of before embarking upon a high school journey

- Does my state, Local School District (LSD), or school offer different types of diplomas?

- What are the requirements for graduation for the LSD and the school?

- How is the GPA ranking calculated in my LSD/school; how are AP/honors classes counted?

- Does my school have different academic tracks and/or majors? What are they?

- Do I know how to read and interpret a high school transcript?

- Have I fully read and understood the student handbook?

- What are the specific disciplinary rules and regulations for this partic- ular school?

- Where do I go when I have a question? Who is in charge of what?

- I have my program/schedule, am I signed up for the right classes?

- Setting a positive tone early with teachers in preparation for letters of recommendations down the line.

Principal, tell them to stay focused!

- Pass every class you take!

- Adults in the school building talk to each other about students: What are they saying about you?

- Act as if your life depends on education, because it does!

- Some of your friends are secretly hitting the books but they are not telling you.

- Depending on the "deliverer" of the information, peer advice can be either very hurtful or helpful.

- Read each course syllabus carefully. It is you that must make the nec- essary adjustments to each individual teacher's work, teaching expec- tations, and evaluation style.

- Start building a powerful transcript, resume, and senior portfolio from day one!

- Physical or mental abuse is never a sign of love; and, yes, they are go- ing to do it again and again and again, after each time they apologize.

- Some friendly, but fierce, competitiveness is acceptable like getting on the honor roll, pushing for a high GPA class ranking, acquiring internships, receiving academic awards and recognition, earning a lot of college scholarship funding, etc.

- Learn something new (sport, hobby, skill, craft, art form, etc.) every school year!

- The high school success formula in its simplest form:

  Graduation = # of Credits Earned + Required Classes taken and passed + Required Standardized Exams Taken and Passed.

- Take responsibility for the monitoring of your own transcript.

- Don't do or engage in anything for which you will need a "cleanup-explanation" letter later.

- Make sure you are in the right (required) courses, and the right sequence of courses.

- I know your teenage brain is telling you that it is *love*; it is not!

- Your high school four years move quickly; next stop, adult world!

- Practice "Distance Learning." Learn from the mistakes and bad decisions of other people.

- If you are a student of color, be smart and intelligent brave! (Not afraid to be smart!)

- Just try to be nice, it's a very appealing and rewarding quality!

- Life is absolutely not fair, so adjust your attitude and behavior to address and defeat that unfairness.

- There is a world outside of your block and neighborhood that you need to know.

- The vast overwhelming majority of teachers actually want you to pass their class!

- Resist the teenage belief that you know everything; you will realize later as an adult, that you don't even know half of everything!

- Another expression for hard study and scholarships: starting off after college debt free!

- Be kind and compassionate and the universe will reward your acts one hundredfold!

- Teachers and school administrators are human.

- "After" should be your watch word for success or failure: "After I do or say this, what can happen?"

- Don't say or post anything on social media that you can't be proud of when you are asked about it at your senate confirmation hearings. Or any other important future governmental or non-governmental job or appointment interview.

- If you go into military service, you need a plan (including a post military plan); or I guarantee the military branch you choose will have a plan for you.

- Not knowing the standards, rules, hard or soft skills required for any given situation will not exempt you from their negative consequences (punishments)!

- The concepts of grown and dependent don't go together. You need a post-high school plan; where you are earning and/or learning.

- Your post-high school plan for success must be connected to your high school success plan.

- Try a little tenderness with those who might lack your academic gifts and talents!

- Honesty and integrity are priceless qualities; speak and live in truth!

- Believe it or not, principals hate disciplinary issues; they consider it a waste of their time.

- Show appreciation to your teachers, they are providing you with life-long gifts!

- Your parents are smarter than you think, and they will get smarter as you get older!

- Don't follow economic or societal employment trends, pursue your calling and passion!

- Study excellence when you see it in the world, no matter how humble the job classification! Strive to be excellent in every school and personal activity, no matter how humble the task.

- Laws of Life Attraction: Create your own opportunities, good people will notice, and bigger and better opportunities will come to you. Create problems for yourself, bad people will notice, and bring bigger and worse problems to your situation!

- Every student is responsible for bringing a unique gift and talent to the world that only they alone can bring. Pain and suffering is the inability and failure to express those gifts and talents. The individual feels the pain and the world suffers.

- Your gifts and talents are wrapped inside of your calling in life.

- Find your passionate calling in life, what you love to do, and then find a way to get paid to pursue that passionate calling.

Chapter 29:
How Principals Can Inspire Real and Meaningful Parent Involvement and Empowerment!

Parents are critical educational partners in effectively raising students' academic achievement scores. How, then, can principals inspire real, meaningful parent involvement and empowerment? A common modern mistake in Public Education, and one of the primary challenges to building an effective school, is the over-the-top, obsessed attention payed to collaborative decision-making. This concept of collaboration promises (falsely) to give everyone and anyone a voice in the school's educational policies and administrative practices, even if they lack the professional expertise or critical information to make such decisions. Still, it is a great and effective throwaway line for politicians. After all, who could be against parents having a voice in public education? The question (rarely asked) is whether all of these "collaborative efforts" actually result in raising students' academic achievement. When we say, "parent engagement," we should ask the questions: What exactly do we want them to engage in? And, does this engagement truly help them with their primary mission and responsibility, the educational success of their child?

The day I was forced to rethink my thinking on parent involvement and engagement!

I must admit that as a principal I made a concession, which resulted in a major change in my thinking during one of my presentations at a ninth grade parent orientation. After the list of parent workshops, activities, and committees had been distributed, one of my Asian-American parents came up to me and said, "Mr. Johnson, I respect your rules and want to follow them. However, I work day and night for six days a week; I don't know how I can participate in any of the activities you have required. I believe that you are an expert and I trust your judgment, so whatever you tell my child to do, she will do. She will not break any of the school's rules, I promise this."

465

I thought for a long moment, then said, "Don't worry about attending any of these workshops (I will send you the information), meetings, or serving on any committees; if you can keep your promise, I will work with you and we will make this work." We shook hands and that was that; well, not quite. You see that student was, for the next four years, a model student, never late to school or class, and probably could not describe the inside of the dean's office or the ISS room; never failed a subject, got on the honor roll in the ninth grade and never left, always came to class prepared to work, attended every Saturday SAT/ACT/AP tutorial, met all deadlines for college-related programs; never came to school inappropriately dressed, was ever polite and respectful of all staff and other students. She predictably graduated and went on to a rewarding college (and scholarships) education and professional STEM career. So, the questions I had to ask myself again was, "What is it that I really want to accomplish (via the parents) here, with this student and how should I define 'good parent involvement?'" I could have been persistent in discussing my views of parent engagement with this child's parent and their inability to engage in the parental activities that I felt were important, but I am glad I did not allow my ego to get in the way. Bureaucracies and the people who work and run them (bureaucrats) can sometimes get so caught up in the process, procedures, and regulations, that we lose sight of the original and true objective. I think on that day a parent showed me the true aim of parent involvement: An academic, social, moral, ethical, and successful student!

A composite profile of the most effective parents I have met

Parenting, like most things in life, is not a perfect science. Most of the parents I have met over the years are much better at parenting then they think. I have taken careful note, both as a theorist and practitioner of public education, the patterns employed by the parents of successful students. Every year, I encountered some unbelievably resilient, genius children who against all the tremendous resistance of parent negativity and home/family life dysfunction, were able to not just succeed but to soar academically. And for sure, these students are the true heroes of public education. But for those high-performing and highly successful students who do have a considerable amount of positive parent support, there seems to be a "playbook."

Let's not mince words here. There are many factors that go into making a child successful when it comes to their parents. The parents' upbringing, education level, mastery of the English language, financial resources (wealth) and economic stability, worldviews, career choices, etc., can influence the type of support system they offer their child. Indeed, many of my most successful students over the years grew up in families where English was not the primary language spoken at home. Then there were the high-performing students whose families were far from being middle class, let alone wealthy. I have also worked with students who were tremendously successful graduates, who went on to college and professional careers, despite their parents never having possessed a college education themselves. Over the years, I have seen some wonderful and powerful parenting qualities, which were able to encourage and empower students to become academically successful. Now, these exemplary criteria do not represent any single parent; rather, I have pulled together a list of the most influential factors that I have found employed by parents whose children demonstrated the highest level of consistent academic and behavioral success:

- These parents provide no extra rewards for academic achievement; high academic achievement is the expectation, not an exceptional act that warranted a reward.

- These parents reject the concept of allowing their children to find their own way in life without adult guidance.

- Dedication not Abdication: A common mistake made by parents of children transitioning from middle to high school is that they interpret this move as a signal for them to check-out of their child's social and educational life. Effective parents don't see the start of high school as the beginning of their retirement from parental duties and responsibilities. In fact, they discover that there is an even larger need for their parental involvement. The best practices I have observed began with a good balance between protection and providing the space for independent growth. This means giving a teenager choices within the perimeter of adult decisions, which encourages the growth of the young person's independent decision-making capability in a safe and productive way.

- If the parent has a complaint or concern about a teacher, the parent will figure out how to have a productive and positive dialogue with the teacher in order to resolve the matter. If that approach fails, they will not become confrontational with the teacher; but will bring their concern to the principal. If the problem is a class wide issues (even if it affects their child), they will quietly bring the issue first to the principal to solve in order to keep their child's name out of the conversation. This allows the principal to address the problem as a class and not individual student/parent concern. Like it or not, dealing with complaints is basically a daily activity of the principalship, and so deal with it!

Note to principals: Just as you tell students, remind yourself that teachers are human, and with some exceptions, don't always take student/parent complaints well. Therefore, unless it is absolutely necessary, you should strive to resolve legitimate parent (and student) complaints by keeping the name of the complainants anonymous. But as professional development for your APs, at some point you should be able to mention the name of the student/parent who is complaining about them. If the AP gets extremely petty, retributive and loses focus of the mission, then they are probably not yet ready for the principalship since parent complaints about you to the superintendent will always have a parent and student's name attached to it. As a principal you are expected (by the superintendent) to handle that information with the highest form of professional leadership decorum. You can't be small and overly sensitive, even if the complaint about you is without merit, or as is often the case in these situations, missing key facts, pieces of information and context. Ultimately, you need to reestablish a positive parent-school relationship; you must treat the parent and child as if the complaint was never made. I knew I was in trouble when I became a superintendent for the first time, that unlike my former superintendency, I had to hide the names of parents who in most cases made a legitimate complaint, because some principals could not properly and professionally handle and resolve a parent complaint; which then led to my having to professional development them in a not so enjoyable way.

◊   Parents who push their children in conjunction with the school's objectives.

◊   The parent who is supportive of establishing a quiet, productive, and resourceful place for children to study and do homework at home.

◊   Parents who do not project any of their own past negative school experiences onto their child (or the school).

◊ Parents who have determined that their primary role is not to manage the school, but to manage and monitor their child's academic performance and progress.

◊ They don't see themselves as friends or social, emotional equals with their children; even as they can be friendly, funny, and loving!

◊ They encourage their child to take a great deal of personal responsibility for their own success (and failure) in school.

◊ These parents can project their power and authority from a distance. Their children are keenly aware of the passion and commitment these types of parents bring to the school; if a child of one of these parents slips slightly, a teacher or administrator will only need to threaten that a call will be made to the parent, and the slip up is always immediately corrected.

◊ These parents offer some kind of punishment/sanction for bad behavior or low grades, i.e. loss of some enjoyable privilege, benching a student athlete, or suspending their own child from the team, even before the coach or I could act.

◊ There is usually a strong, consistent religious or spiritual foundation in the family.

◊ Parents who want to be in the know of their child's progress. They want to be alerted at the first sign of underperformance or misbehavior in any area of their child's schooling.

◊ These parents have a profound and insightful understanding of the principalship, and how it can, and is supposed to work, for them and their child.

◊ They will invest whatever time necessary, in whatever way necessary, to ensure their child's success.

◊ Any educationally beneficial program, including ACT-SAT prep classes, cultural/educational trips, college tours, additional books and educational materials and supplies, etc. The parents will insist that the child attends, and if there is a cost, they will find a way to get the money.

◊ Note to principals who lead Title I schools: You need in your entrepreneurial principal's role to seek ways to take money off the table as a factor for a student participating in any school-sponsored out-of-school, cultural, informal educational activity.

◊ All in for their kids! These parents will essentially sacrifice their personal (social) happiness in order to ensure their child's academic success.

◊ These parents see obstacles and challenges as opportunities to grow stronger. They encourage their children to work hard and never give up.

◊ These parents reject the idea of depending on professional sports as a primary career plan.

◊ These parents establish parameters and monitor very closely, or restrict completely, school love affairs. They make an effort to be acquainted with all of their child's friends.

◊ These parents insist on daily punctuality and attendance every day.

◊ Parent does not have the luxury or flexibility to take off from work for "child foolishness." The pressure is placed on the child to figure out how to keep the parent from having to lose a day's work because of an unnecessary parent conference/disciplinary meeting.

◊ Insist on respectful behavior. Students should not take it upon themselves to confront or disrespect any adult in the building.

◊ They leave no educational experience (formal or informal) to chance. They will research and find that school, program, class and organize a K-12 plan for their child. They will even send the school information on an educational opportunity.

◊ The children of these parents live in a less stressful home environment. There is a great deal of order and predictability to their lives.

◊ Active members of the Parent Association and volunteer for school events; a byproduct of these efforts is direct contact and communication with teachers, guidance counselors and administrators, the opportunity to read and review the various school informational bulletin boards; check out their child's friends and close associates, and they can also just see what's going on in the school! A direct line of communication between a parent and a school staff member will give any student a slight cause for concern because that communication link can be utilized at any time.

◊ These parents are sensitive to even the slightest diminution of their child's academic work effort; they are interested in classroom and weekly grade results; and absolutely review the child's report card. In many cases will request their own copies of the child's transcript. There is some type of home-based accountability system for any drop in grades. Very likely to attend open school days and evenings, parent workshops such as "How to read your child's transcript."

◊ For high school students, it helps a great deal if the parent(s) have gone through a college experience. "Legacy" status is helpful in the college admissions and scholarship process.

◊ Parents who know how the system is organized. They understand that public education rules are, in many cases, flexible and based on the discretion of the individual responsible for making the decision (e.g., disciplinary suspensions).

◊ They don't rely on their child (especially boys) to find out about the different programs and activities in the school; which means they strategically develop an alternative source for gaining school information.

◊ They have computer access and may be aware of certain critical and important websites like: DOE, the school's website, FASFA, https://fafsa.ed.gov; Brainspace: http://www.brainspacemagazine.com/; National Geographic's for Kids: http://kids.nationalgeographic.com/; FIRST Robotics scholarships: http://www.firstinspires.org/scholarships).

◊ A clear understanding of the role of the informal education system. They understand that public (or any) school is only half of the child's learning process. They set aside time in their personal schedules to do things like take trips to museums, film festivals, technology fairs and exhibitions, nature experiences, special exhibits and classes. They will either go themselves or provide the resources and opportunity for the child to go alone.

◊   Resource sharing capacity: They have information access to similar parents in their neighborhood, ethnicity, education/economic class; these parents collectively acquire and share information concerning informal educational events and art, music, and dance classes, educational toys and games, magazines, books, science-hobby kits and software.

◊   These parents know how to accurately evaluate the quality of a school, its teachers, and the principal. They know that what happens outside of the classroom areas of a school is just as important as what happens inside of the classroom. They seek out schools that invest resources into intellectual, creative, and imagination-building programs.

◊   Parent participation and/or involvement means balancing general schoolwide support activities (volunteering, fundraising, committee service, etc.); while at the same time monitoring their child's academic progress.

◊   The home is a rich learning environment that includes a designated study area, technology and reference materials. The vocabulary and conversations are about current events, news, politics, art, culture, books, and topical issues. There is a deep inquiry into the quantity/quality of the child's school. The home is an extension of the school; the school is an extension of the home.

A word of caution for parents of color who, despite their wealth and level of education attainment, may not be aware that access to wealth and formal education does not automatically remove your child of color from the at-risk pool. The public educational system does not have the differential mechanism you may think it has to address uniqueness and individuality of children from particular U.S. racial, ethnic, and cultural groups. Your child can still be stereotyped, go unrecognized, subjected to low expectations, overlooked for gifted and talented/special academic programs, over-recruited for special education services; and face higher documented disciplinary penalties for normal correctable childhood mistakes. For girls, some cultural verbal and body linguistic styles that are appropriate in certain communities, and in fact may be a sign of endearment and comfort with the person they are speaking to, could be misinterpreted as sassy, aggressive, and disrespectful. The parents of boys must take special care that normal boy behaviors are not misclassified and officially treated as pre-criminal justice system behaviors.

Good and effective parenting skills can be taught by the school.

We can't give parents jobs or better housing, but we can give them the tools to do the best that they can with what they have; and then we should co-parent with them by providing informal educational experiences for their children. I point out the advantages of having a well-resourced parent, not as a way of suggesting that these parents have a higher level of caring and concern for their children, but their ability to turn that concern into a concrete advantage plan for their children. Poor parents, parents of color, newly-arrived Americans, the politically disenfranchised and disempowered members of our society, also are concerned and want the best for their children; they simply don't often have the information and resources to exercise that concern. But the non-monetary aspects of effective parenting can be utilized by any parent, regardless of their level of education and financial resources. And that is the place where the school can play a critical role of developing effective parent equity. Finally, it is important to note that effective parenting skills and techniques can be grown. But that would call for the principal and the school to challenge and redefine the present public conceptions; and, yes, even the school system's definitions of parent involvement, an approach that presently is only successful at giving parents a lot of busy work. This busy work ultimately distracts them from their first and most important job of being the homebased director of the academic achievement educational team!

A question for principals (and the question I had to ask myself): If we accept that the effective parenting standards I have laid out are indeed critical to a student's success in school, then how does that knowledge inform the kind of parent-engagement education programs we should design for our schools? And what would be the best application of parent time and energy in seeking the objective of raising academic achievement? Lastly, do we need to review and rethink the present definition of parent involvement? Is it applicable, or even possibly harmful, for particular parents with children in particular schools?

The good news is that in thirty years, I have never been told by a parent that they wish their child would become an academic failure, drop out, and/

or become a permanent client of the criminal justice/social service systems. I suspect that educational leaders working in even the most economically depressed communities will also not hear a parent's request for a child's failure. Parents, no matter their financial status or level of formal education, want their children to be successful in school, and ultimately graduate from high school. This is important and may warrant a sign in the principal's office as a constant encouragement reminder as parents engage in less than helpful behavior during the course of your career. Despite wanting the best for their children, some parents just don't know the ways in which they can effectively support and help their child to be academically successful.

As the school's principal, you can provide the necessary information to parents that will allow them to act effectively as academic achievement advocates for their child. You can create a school cultural practice of providing students with experiences that are commonly provided outside of school by well-resourced, information-rich parents. The effective principal must work two strategic plans simultaneously. First, support a type of parental education that informs parents how to effectively serve as home educators, and also how to engage in the area of informal educational activities. Put an end to the myth that all learning takes place inside of the school. A student missing the lessons that are being taught in the informal educational system is the equivalent of not taking required courses in the formal school system. Second, where essential parent informal educational activities are missing or come up short, the school must then assume that responsibility without criticism of the parent; don't wait, don't complain, just do it, principal!

For principals leading Title I schools, you should know that your parents may not have access to the information and resources that would help them to improve the chances for their child's academic success. Conduct an informal education workshop and fair of all of the Community Based Organizations (CBO's) that sponsor educational, sports, performing and creative arts programs, museums, cultural, science, historical institutions; private dance, music, drama teachers (offer scholarships for students). Provide information to parents on a regular basis on educational events on the weekend, school breaks, and the summer. Design programs like a weekend family trip to the museum or botanical gardens. Reach out to public cultural institutions to obtain free passes for families.

The principal who hopes to be effective must clearly understand that children arrive to school and will return daily to their families. What must be determined, honestly and quickly, is to what extent that family is able to hold up their end of the informal education program; and then do whatever is necessary to support those parents with information and/or the resources to participate in these activities.

Finally, because you have put in place a strong fundraising and resources acquisition program, discuss with your parents the fact that you are relieving them from endless school fundraising efforts. You can still have fundraising events such as a student faculty basketball game, the school foundation luncheon, friends and supporters of the school donates items for an auction, a dance or dramatic performance, a parent "oldies but goodies" dance at a venue outside of the school (no kids!), etc. But you should make it clear that the kind of extra money you need can't be raised through small fundraising efforts. In fact, the greatest contribution that any group of parents can make to a school is to help us help their children to study hard, pass their classes and graduate on time. The best investments a parent can make is (1) a monitored quiet and equipped study/homework area at home; (2) making sure the child comes to school every day on time, prepared to work, having done the assigned pre-class study work; (3) holding their child accountable for their decisions as they help the child make the right decisions; (4) make sure their child is following the school's rules, mission, and objectives; (5) provide their child with the educational equipment, supplies, books and other supplemental materials to support and expand their educational possibilities; (6) be their parent and not their friend, stand for standards and mean it; (7) give their children the opportunity to engage in positive and productive out-of-school informal educational activities, programs, and classes; (8) continually monitor your child's progress in school; (9) as your child enters high school, don't reduce your interest and involvement, a lot can (and does) go wrong in four years, be unashamedly nosey; (10) and the personal best principle: holding their child to the highest academic, behavioral, and moral standards.

Like many things in public education, it all boils down to determining what outcome we truly want; and in the case of the parent-school partnership, that outcome is an academically successful graduate.

Chapter 30:
The End and the Beginning of the School Leadership Story

The Knowledge and Practice of the Principalship: Think like a philosopher, pray like a priest, create like an artist, strategize like a corporate executive, and fight like a samurai!

I strongly believe that a great deal of what is presently wrong with our nation can be traced to an uninspired, inadequate, incomplete, limited, or ineffective school educational experience. Yes, I know there are well-educated people who do bad things. But I truly believe that the odds of a whole and good person emerging from childhood increases with that person's exposure to books and learning.

Over the course of my career as a principal and superintendent, I learned how important it is for a school district to have its complete focus on the educational well-being of the children. For this reason, I have dedicated my time, energy, and resources in working with those children and families for whom society has given up on and failed. I wanted to make sure they got as good of an education as those in favored and better resourced communities. Those thoughts are what always bring me back to the work I must do.

Education is power in the present and the future.

For most young people, their hopes and dreams are predicated and dependent upon a positive experience in public education.

The high school principal as samurai is a perfect metaphor for the position, for it speaks to our undying loyalty to the children we serve, our conscious disregard for our own safety and happiness, and our rejection of careerism as a

477

motivating philosophy for our work. And like those Japanese warriors of old, there are things that are far worse than the job's day to day discomfort, disappointment, and discouragement. After all:

- Every year there is the nervous excitement and expectant joy on the faces of that incoming class as you admire their great potential promise. Why after so many years can't I sleep the week before the start of school?

- The confidence and trust of thousands of parents who have invested their most treasured resource, their children, into the care of your professional and personal wisdom and judgement.

- Standing at the front entrance door each morning to sincerely thank students for coming to school that day because you know what it took for many of them to get there.

- The faith of your fellow school-based colleagues in every job category, who year after year, put up with and sincerely support your many interesting (dare I say crazy?) ideas!

- The community who claims your school as part of their portfolio of pride!

- Those who support you when you want to do something special and wonderful for the students and steps up out of nowhere and writes a check.

- You get a visit from the top educators in the city, nation, and world because they want to see your most advanced in the city applied technology labs and teleconferencing center.

- The many gracious volunteers that prompted both the head of a U.S. governmental agency and a CEO of a fortune 500 company to remark, "I have just never seen my folks so excited, dedicated, and willing to help out a school."

- Calls, e-mails, and letters you receive from the public saying something like, "I saw some of your students on the bus/train today, and I was amazed at how well-mannered, intelligent, and studious they were!"

- The FIRST Robotics (first majority-minority) team that shocks everybody and makes it out of the east coast regionals and into the finals in Florida, but you need to pull together approximately $30,000 in a week and then the "universe" responds to save you!

- When the NYC Senior Superintendent of High Schools says, "Your school reminds me of why I went into education!"

- Members of the NYC technical college staff and audience are in agreement after a dance concert. "You should charge more money for tickets; this is not a high school performance, this is a professional dance company!"

- That moment when a student gets it, turns a corner, gathers control of their life and then chooses to seek the true greatness of their personality.

- The joy of seeing students return safe to school the next day after a weekend or a school break.

- You are a STEM-CTE school and a student wins first place in the Congressional Art Competition.

- The parent who thanks you in tears for saving their child, and you thank them because there is something about that moment that saves you from any doubt you might have had about the importance of your calling.

- That e-mail you received from a former student who is now a parent of a teenager saying, "Oh my goodness, I can't believe it, I was talking to my son, and I sound just like you!"

- Watching students' faces as you take them to their first Broadway play, cultural institution, museum, college tour, corporation headquarters, conference, dress up dinner and luncheon.

- Students' joyful faces when they ace a standardized exam.

- The loud cheer in the courtroom and the stunned faces of the losing mock trial finals competitors from that "exclusive and elite" school who were just defeated by who? Wait, what school?

- The CTE director and I notice, but we don't tell the members of the team so as not to distract them, the other high schools who have entered the Cyber Forensics national competition. I am thinking, *these Phelps ACE kids don't know that they are probably the only majority Black student school competitors.* At that moment I am also thinking of my 1990's SSCHS FIRST Robotics team and how both of these teams are the student Jackie Robinsons of STEM!

- Sending our students who are learning Chinese as a foreign language off to do summer language immersion study in The People's Republic of China [PRC]. Or watching them have confident fun as they answer questions from the news reporters from the PRC in Chinese!

- The frenzied and happy excitement of the college/career going activities.

- Seeing nervous first-year (and sometimes crying in my office at the end of a rough school day) teachers grow into confident, experienced, and expert teacher mentors.

- A student who faces the most difficult and challenging home situation, and against all possible human and rational odds, they make it and are successful graduates!

- The many teachers who became APs and staff developers, the APs and departmental chairpersons who became principals!

- And then there is the graduation ceremony itself, the best and most fulfilling moment of the principalship; and the only event that did not allow me to hide my tears!

So many memories, so many victories

I always take care to remember that in my many school leadership experiences, the good will always outweigh and outlast the bad. Successful graduates can't become ungraduated. Smart and knowledgeable students can't become unknowing. Generational curses and chains have been broken. The many predicted bad destinies have been redirected toward the good and beautiful. A good education is the most powerful weapon in the battle to attain a meaningful, positive, and productive life, and I have effectively armed a lot of young folks, forever. I know that despite the many challenges and hardships I faced throughout my school leadership career, I would not change my choice to become a principal. Every one of my former student graduates is a reminder and testimony to my finding and living out my true calling in life. Forever will the stories remain of the many brave and wonderful young people I have been honored to serve in the most honorable of professions, the Principalship!

End Notes

1   Creative and Performing Arts Programs that are comprehensive and intense in preparation, practice, skills development; and producing one or more major high quality public events a year.

2   An exam given to Summer Bridge Academy students and/or entering ninth graders the first week of school. This exam covers third through eighth grade math concepts. The objective is to see where the students "fall-off," specifically which mathematical concepts (e.g., decimals, place value, arithmetic rules, translating word problems). Based on how a student performs, they would be recommended for a small (fifteen students) double period algebra course, along with an end-of-day additional period for tutorials placed on their schedule. The ELA exam also given in the Summer Bridge Program, and/or the first week of school, will inform the staff whether the student is able to read and write effectively on a high school level. Those students are also provided an additional ELA support class, essentially focusing on reading comprehension and expository writing.

3   Readers to Leaders is a yearlong independent reading project that encourages students to read 100 books in a calendar year. This amounts to about an average of fifty to sixty minutes of reading a day (approximately 4,358,000 words a year!). During the summer, spring, and winter breaks, the students demonstrate and record their reading achievements by way of a single page response sheet. In-class reading is monitored by the ELA teacher, and each book read is recorded on a star achievement board (yes, high school students like to get gold publicly acknowledged achievement recognition!). The word number and time standards are important because it allows for a wide spectrum of literary genres such as poetry, reference books, short stories, essays, speeches, biographies, narrative nonfiction, articles in magazines and newspapers, drama, etc. At the end of the year, the winners, all of whom reach 100 and the top performers over 100 in each class, all receive an award ceremony, certificates, trophies, gift cards, iPods, special trips, laptops, and other prizes. The overall objective here is to first grow intellectual capacity, strengthen reading ability by the daily exercise of reading skills, expand vocabulary, and finally, have young people to develop the habit of reading for learning as well as pleasure.

4   SAT/ACT flashcards can be reasonably purchased commercially; there are also online versions of these flashcards provided by free websites. The electronic versions of the flashcards are wonderful additions to any ELA classroom that is fortunate to have computers. The upside to the students creating their own boxed vocabulary flashcards is the fun and learning reinforcement of doing the project themselves. Further, it gives teachers and students the ability to add important words and phrases that may be missing from the commercial flashcards products. Finally, if students design, build, and take ownership of their own flashcards, not only will they have a project-product they're proud of, but this path also allows them and their teacher to insert an additional field/sentence of interest on their cards, for example, etymological origin of the word. And yes, give all students who complete this project a grade equivalent to a quiz score!

5   I have already stated my preference for the core subjects in that four-year sequence to be biology, environmental or earth science, chemistry and physics. I'm also fully aware that many inner-city Title I schools and rural schools regardless of their Title I status, can face a great deal of difficulty in finding certified teachers in these specific science content areas. Washington politicians are always talking about bipartisan political engagement. Well, this is actually a perfect situation where it could be practiced. There should be a national effort to expand the number of 8-12 certified science teachers. This could be done in cooperation with the sciences and science education departments at

most of our colleges and universities. This would involve a worthwhile investment in recruitment, training, tuition forgiveness, master's degree fellowships, a local supplemental housing allowance, and/or real estate tax exemption. With these incentives, we could expand the science teacher pipeline quickly. The investment in creating these teachers will more than pay for itself as the students will be better prepared to enter the job market that is rapidly establishing science skills as an essential competency.

6   As with all teacher-individual student-parent communication, clear, strict, and written schoolwide guidelines must be established and presented to teachers in a staff meeting. Don't assume, especially with new teachers, that they will automatically know the rubrics of establishing proper, appropriate legal barriers and restrictions when it comes to communication with students and/or parents. Teachers should also be aware of the legal implications connected to students living under "special circumstances," (e.g., students who may live in a group home).

7   Standards and rubrics for class website behavior as outlined in a "good and proper use" manual/agreement must be taught, monitored, and enforced by the teacher and TC. Even when an infraction occurs after school hours, weekends, and/or on holidays, the school should enforce the penalties as set out in the "proper and good use" document. The class website should be linked to the school's main website. Teachers should be given guidelines and professional development for setting up class websites. The principal, a school administrator/AP) should review the class websites weekly.

8   Although the posting may state "confidential" (and in many ways the information is confidential), students will take this to mean a "secret" between them and the professional they are speaking to. School administrators, the nurse, guidance counselors, school-based psychologist and social workers, must inform the student, that based on the nature of the disclosure being made, or the information being sought, that the law prevents them from keeping certain types of information a "secret," e.g., sexual abuse. However, the staff service provider should also explain the school's plan and procedures that are in place to protect the student for any type of retribution for a disclosure.

9   As superintendent, I needed to learn a great deal quickly about the quality of a school's leadership team. One of the first things I did was visit during school lunch periods. The quality of a school cafeteria's atmosphere is a good indicator of how much strategic planning is invested into the upkeep of that space, and speaks to the amount of thought invested in the academic upside of the equation. Effective schools see no distinction between operational excellence and academic excellence. In fact, both areas of excellence support each other!

10   Before the start of a school year, distribute (via open-house, orientation, post mail or even send to middle school administrators/counselors) three books; include an explanatory standards and rubrics response sheet. This will establish in the students and parents' minds the level of academic expectations the student will face for the next four years. Books: one nonfiction work required. I recommend The 7 Habits of Highly Effective Teens by Sean Covey. Student choice: Pick one book from the list of biographies. Student choice: Pick one book of listed works of fiction. Note to principals: make sure the ninth grade English teachers give you a list of those students who read several, all, or none of the books! This first school project will tell you a great deal about students and their parents. For example, you know because you have seen their K-8 standardized reading test scores and their academic records that for some students the reading assignment will be challenging; how do they and their parents respond to the assignments?

89530025R00268

Made in the USA
Lexington, KY
31 May 2018